LONDON CIVIC THEATRE

Civic theatre – drama and pageantry sponsored by city and town governing bodies – is prominent in histories of early English provincial drama, but has been largely ignored for pre-Elizabethan London. Anne Lancashire explodes the widely held notion that significant London theatre arose only in the age of Shakespeare, when the first commercial playhouses were built. She outlines the extent and types of early civic theatrical performance, specifically in London, from Roman times to Elizabeth I's accession to the throne in 1558, focusing on Roman amphitheatre shows, medieval and early Tudor plays, mummings, royal entries, and other kinds of street pageantry. With evidence from a multitude of primary sources and extensive use of early chronicle histories, the book raises new questions about this urban, largely political theatre which provided an important foundation for the work of Shakespeare and his contemporaries.

ANNE LANCASHIRE is Professor of English at the University of Toronto. She has edited the texts of John Lyly's *Gallathea* and *Midas*, of Thomas Middleton's *The Second Maiden's Tragedy*, and of Clifford Leech's *Christopher Marlowe: Poet for the Stage*, and has published numerous articles and essays, and given many conference papers and public lectures, on medieval and early modern theatre and drama.

View of London, late fifteenth century. Duke of Orleans in the Tower of London. BL Royal MS 16, Fii, f. 73 (by permission of the British Library).

LONDON CIVIC THEATRE

City Drama and Pageantry from Roman Times to 1558

ANNE LANCASHIRE

CAMBRIDGE
UNIVERSITY PRESS

PUBLISHED BY THE PRESS SYNDICATE OF THE UNIVERSITY OF CAMBRIDGE
The Pitt Building, Trumpington Street, Cambridge, United Kingdom

CAMBRIDGE UNIVERSITY PRESS
The Edinburgh Building, Cambridge CB2 2RU, UK
40 West 20th Street, New York NY 10011-4211, USA
477 Williamstown Road, Port Melbourne, VIC 3207, Australia
Ruiz de Alarcón 13, 28014 Madrid, Spain
Dock House, The Waterfront, Cape Town 8001, South Africa

http://www.cambridge.org

First published 2002

Printed in the United Kingdom at the University Press, Cambridge

Typeface Baskerville MT 11/12.5 pt   *System* QuarkXPress® [TB]

A catalogue record for this book is available from the British Library

Library of Congress Cataloguing in Publication data

Lancashire, Anne Begor.
London civic theatre : city drama and pageantry from Roman times to 1558 / Anne Lancashire.
p.   cm.
Includes bibliographical references and index.
ISBN 0 521 63278 1
1. Theater – England – London – History.   2. Pageants – England – London – History.
3. Festivals – England – London – History.   I. Title.
PN2596.L6 L35 2002   792'.09421 – dc21   2002023378

ISBN 0 521 63278 1 hardback

For Ian

Contents

Acknowledgments

My debts to the various institutions and individuals who have aided me in the writing of this book are numerous and extensive. First, my most appreciative thanks, for generous provision of access to their records both at Guildhall Library (Corporation of London) and in their halls, and for citation and quotation permissions, to all the London livery companies whose manuscripts are cited here (in alphabetical order, the Worshipful Companies of Armourers and Brasiers, Bakers, Blacksmiths, Brewers, Butchers, Carpenters, Coopers, Curriers, Cutlers, Drapers, Founders, Goldsmiths, Grocers, Ironmongers, Leathersellers, Mercers, Merchant Taylors, Parish Clerks, Pewterers, Scriveners, Skinners, Stationers, Tallow Chandlers, Vintners, Wax Chandlers, and Weavers. (The Pinners/Wiresellers no longer exist.) My sincere thanks also to all the other companies whose archives, by their kind permission, I consulted as well but whose manuscripts are not cited here. I owe special thanks (in alphabetical order of company) to Mr. Claude Blair (Armourers and Brasiers' Company), Mr. D. E. Wickham (Archivist and Librarian, Clothworkers' Company), the late Mr. R. T. Brown (Education Officer, Drapers' Company), Ms Penelope Fussell (Archivist, Drapers' Company), Ms Raya McGeorge (Archivist/Librarian, Fishmongers' Company), Miss Susan M. Hare and Mr. David Beasley (former and current Librarians, Goldsmiths' Company), the late Mr. R. Cother and the late Mr. J. B. Hadlow (Leathersellers' Company), Mr. Negley Harte (Historian, Leathersellers' Company), Ms Ursula Carlyle (Archivist, Mercers' Company), Dr. Anne Sutton (Archivist/Historian, Mercers' Company), and Mr. E. J. Hall (Skinners' Company).

At the Corporation of London Records Office, the former Deputy Keeper of the Records, Ms Betty R. Masters, and the present City Archivist, Mr. James R. Sewell, with all of their staff members, have been of enormous help, as have also the former and current Keepers of Manuscripts at the Guildhall Library, Mr. C. R. H. Cooper and Mr. Stephen

Freeth, and the Guildhall Library staff members also (both in Manuscripts and in Printed Books). I have been privileged to have worked also at the British Library, the Institutes of Historical Research and of Classical Studies (University of London), the Bodleian Library, Cambridge University Library, and the Public Record Office; all have been generous with access and with help. (Other libraries both at Oxford and at Cambridge have yielded material not for this book but for the next, and will be acknowledged there.) In Toronto I have been fortunate in having the resources of the University of Toronto Library available to me. Funding support has been gratefully received from the Social Sciences and Humanities Research Council of Canada, from the Travel Fund of the Dean of Arts and Science, University of Toronto, and from the conference travel funds of the Department of English, University of Toronto.

For kind permission to publish in this volume the more extensive transcriptions from various company and city manuscripts, I am grateful to the companies concerned – the Worshipful Companies of Blacksmiths, Brewers, Drapers, and Mercers, largely in relation to the transcriptions in Appendix B – and to the Corporation of London. For permission to publish revised versions of previous articles, as cited in detail at the relevant points in this volume, I am grateful to Editions Rodopi BV (for "Continuing Civic Ceremonies of 1530s London" – see chapter 10), to the Board of the Medieval Institute, Kalamazoo, Michigan (for "Medieval to Renaissance: Plays and the London Drapers' Company to 1558" – see chapter 4), and to the Records of Early English Drama project (for two items from the *REED Newsletter* – see chapter 4). For image reproduction permissions, I owe thanks to the Society of Antiquaries of London and to the British Library.

For continuing encouragement, support, and useful queries and suggestions, I am much indebted to Drs. Caroline Barron and Vanessa Harding and their colleagues and students in the annual medieval and Tudor London history seminar at the University of London, to Dr. Alexandra Johnston of REED, to the REED staff and especially Dr. Abigail Young, and to my patient and ever-helpful colleagues in the annual theatre history seminar at the meetings of the Shakespeare Association of America. Dr. David Parkinson (University of Saskatchewan) has provided considerable aid with the early Goldsmiths' and Merchant Taylors' records; Dr. Stephen R. Reimer (University of Alberta) has expertly answered my queries about Lydgate; Dr. Nicholas Bateman (Museum of London Archaeology Service) has generously answered my questions on London's Roman amphitheatre. Dr. Brian Merrilees (University of Toronto) provided aid with Anglo-Norman problems; Dr. Marion O'Connor (University of Kent, Canterbury) responded nobly to a request for a last-minute manuscript check. Mr. Peter Snowden and Mr. Mark Loman (Corporation of London: Guildhall Art Gallery, Technical Services) kindly enabled me in summer 2000 to view the not-yet-exhibited amphitheatre. And, as always, I have relied on the knowledge, support, and unfailing encouragement of my colleague and husband, Dr. Ian Lancashire.

This book also would not have been completed without the support and interest of Richard and Elisabeth Hoskyns and, in its embryonic stages, of the late Isa Morley, and of Helen Burrows, former Accommodations Officer at William Goodenough House, London.

Despite so much information, help, and encouragement from others, I will inevitably have made errors, omissions, over-generalizations and too-wild speculations, the blame for which is mine alone.

Abbreviations

A Chronicle	*A Chronicle of London, from 1089 to 1483* [, ed. Nicholas Nicolas and Edward Tyrrell]. London: Longman *et al.*, 1827
A-ND	*Anglo-Norman Dictionary*, ed. Louise W. Stone and William Rothwell, 7 fascicles. London: Modern Humanities Research Association, 1977–88
Anglo, *Spectacle*	Sydney Anglo, *Spectacle, Pageantry and Early Tudor Policy*. Oxford: Clarendon Press, 1969; 2nd edn. 1997
Annals	Alfred Harbage, ed., *Annals of English Drama 975–1700*, rev. S. Schoenbaum. Philadelphia: University of Pennsylvania Press, 1964
Anon. Cant.	*Chronicon Anonymi Cantuariensis*, in *Chronica Johannis de Reading et Anonymi Cantuariensis 1346–1367*, ed. James Tait. Manchester: Manchester University Press, 1914, pp. 187–227
Anon. Chronicle	*The Anonimalle Chronicle 1333 to 1381*, ed. V. H. Galbraith. Manchester: Manchester University Press, 1927
Arber, *Garner*	Edward Arber, *An English Garner*, vol. 2. London: E. Arber, 1879
Atlas	Mary D. Lobel, gen. ed., *The British Atlas of Historic Towns*, vol. 3: *The City of London: From Prehistoric Times to c. 1520*. Oxford: Oxford University Press in conjunction with The Historic Towns Trust, 1989
Axton, *European Drama*	Richard Axton, *European Drama of the Early Middle Ages*. London: Hutchinson, 1974

Bale	Robert Bale, *Chronicle*, in Flenley, see below, pp. 114–153
Barron, *Atlas*	Caroline Barron, "The Later Middle Ages: 1270–1520," in *Atlas*, see above, pp. 42–56
Beadle	Richard Beadle, ed. *The Cambridge Companion to Medieval English Theatre.* Cambridge: Cambridge University Press, 1994; rpt. 1995
Beaven	Alfred B. Beaven, *The Aldermen of the City of London*, 2 vols. London: Corporation of London, 1908–13
Bernardo Andrea	Bernardus Andreas, *Historia Regis Henrici Septimi, a Bernardo Andrea Tholosate Conscripta*, ed. James Gairdner. RS 10. London: HMSO, 1858; rpt. Lessing-Druckerei, Wiesbaden: Kraus Reprint, 1966
BH	Bridge House (MSS at CLRO)
Biddle, *Atlas*	Martin Biddle, "A City in Transition: 400–800," in *Atlas*, see above, pp. 20–29
BL	British Library
Brief Latin Chronicle	*A Brief Latin Chronicle*, in James Gairdner, ed., *Three Fifteenth-Century Chronicles.* Camden Society, NS 28, 1880, pp. 164–185
Brooke, *Atlas*	Christopher Brooke, "The Central Middle Ages: 800–1270," in *Atlas*, see above, pp. 30–41
Brut	*The Brut*, ed. Friedrich W. D. Brie, vol. 2. Early English Text Society, OS 136, 1908
Cal. LB	Reginald R. Sharpe, ed., *Calendar of Letter-Books Preserved Among the Archives of the Corporation of the City of London at the Guildhall*, 11 vols. London: Corporation of London, 1899–1912. Volumes run A through L (without a J); each specific volume reference in this book therefore includes the alphabetical letter (e.g., *Cal. LB K*)
CBA	Council for British Archaeology
Chronicle of Queen Jane	*The Chronicle of Queen Jane, and of Two Years*

	of Queen Mary, ed. John Gough Nichols. Camden Society, os 48, 1850
CLRO	Corporation of London Records Office
Collections III	Jean Robertson and D. J. Gordon, eds., "A Calendar of Dramatic Records in the Books of the Livery Companies of London." *Collections III*. Malone Society, 1954
Collectanea	John Leland, ed., *Antiquarii de Rebus Britannicis Collectanea*, ed. Thomas Hearne, vol. 4. London: Benjamin White, 1774
CSPV	*Calendar of State Papers and Manuscripts . . . Existing in the Archives and Collections of Venice*, vols. 3 (1520–1526) and 6.1 (1555–1556), ed. Rawdon Brown. London: HMSO, 1869 and 1877
DTR	Ian Lancashire, ed., *Dramatic Texts and Records of Britain: A Chronological Topography to 1558*. Studies in Early English Drama 1. Toronto/Cambridge: University of Toronto Press/Cambridge University Press, 1984
EES	Glynne Wickham, *Early English Stages 1300–1660*, 3 vols. London/New York: Routledge and Kegan Paul/Columbia University Press, 1959–81
EETS	Early English Text Society
EP	Robert Withington, *English Pageantry: An Historical Outline*, 2 vols. Cambridge, MA: Harvard University Press, 1918–26; rpt. New York: Arno Press, 1980
Fabyan	Robert Fabyan, *The New Chronicles of England and France*, ed. Henry Ellis. London: F. C. and J. Rivington *et al.*, 1811
Flenley	Ralph Flenley, ed. *Six Town Chronicles of England*. Oxford: Clarendon Press, 1911
GL	Guildhall Library, Corporation of London
Gesta	*Gesta Henrici Quinti*, ed. and tr. Frank Taylor and John S. Roskell. Oxford: Clarendon Press, 1975

Grafton	Richard Grafton, *Grafton's Chronicle* [, ed. Henry Ellis], 2 vols. London: J. Johnston *et al.*, 1809
Great Chronicle	*The Great Chronicle of London*, ed. A. H. Thomas and I. D. Thornley. London: Corporation of London, 1938
Gregory	William Gregory, *Chronicle*, in James Gairdner, ed., *The Historical Collections of a Citizen of London in the Fifteenth Century.* Camden Society, NS 17, 1876
Grey Friars	*Chronicle of the Grey Friars of London*, ed. John Gough Nichols. Camden Society, OS 53, 1852
Grose	Francis Grose, ed., *The Antiquarian Repertory*, 4 vols. London: Edward Jeffery, 1807–09
Hall	Edward Hall, *Hall's Chronicle* [, ed. Henry Ellis]. London: J. Johnston *et al.*, 1809
Historical Charters	Walter de Gray Birch, ed., *The Historical Charters and Constitutional Documents of the City of London.* London: Whiting, 1887
HMSO	His/Her Majesty's Stationery Office
Holinshed	Raphael Holinshed, *Chronicles of England, Scotland, and Ireland* [, ed. Henry Ellis], 6 vols. London: J. Johnston *et al.*, 1807–08
Jor.	Journal (MSS at CLRO)
Kingsford, *Chronicles*	Charles Lethbridge Kingsford, ed., *Chronicles of London.* Oxford: Clarendon Press, 1905
Kingsford, *EHL*	Charles Lethbridge Kingsford, *English Historical Literature in the Fifteenth Century.* Oxford: Clarendon Press, 1913; rpt. New York: Burt Franklin, Burt Franklin Bibliographical and Reference Series 37, n.d.
Kipling, *King*	Gordon Kipling, *Enter the King: Theatre, Liturgy, and Ritual in the Medieval Civic Triumph.* Oxford: Clarendon Press, 1998
Kipling, *Receyt*	Gordon Kipling, ed., *The Receyt of the Ladie Kateryne.* EETS, OS 296, 1990

L&PH7	James Gairdner, ed., *Letters and Papers . . . of Richard III. and Henry VII.*, 2 vols. RS 24. London: HMSO, 1861–63
LB	Letter Book (MSS at CLRO)
Legg	Leopold G. Wickham Legg, *English Coronation Records*. Westminster: Archibald Constable, 1901
LMAS	London and Middlesex Archaeological Society
Liber Albus	*Liber Albus: The White Book of The City of London*, ed. and tr. Henry Thomas Riley. London: Richard Griffin, 1861
Liber Regalis	In Legg, see above, pp. 81–130
Lyell-Watney	Laetitia Lyell, assisted by Frank D. Watney, eds., *Acts of Court of the Mercers' Company 1453–1527*. Cambridge: Cambridge University Press, 1936
Machyn	Henry Machyn, *The Diary of Henry Machyn, Citizen and Merchant-Taylor of London, from A.D. 1550 to A.D.* 1563, ed. John Gough Nichols. Camden Society, os 42, 1848
Malverne	John Malverne's continuation of Higden's *Polychronicon*, in Ranulf Higden, *Polychronicon Ranulphi Higden Monachi Cestrensis*, ed. Joseph Rawson Lumby, vol. 9. RS 41. London: HMSO, 1886, pp. 1 283
Manley, *Culture*	Lawrence Manley, *Literature and Culture in Early Modern London*. Cambridge: Cambridge University Press, 1995
McGee-Meagher	C. E. McGee and John C. Meagher, "Preliminary Checklist of Tudor and Stuart Entertainments: 1485–1558," *Research Opportunities in Renaissance Drama* 25 (1982), 31–114
MG	Henry Thomas Riley, ed., *Munimenta Gildhallae Londoniensis*, 3 vols. (2nd in 2 parts). RS 12. London: HMSO, 1859–62
New History	John D. Cox and David Scott Kastan, eds., *A New History of Early English Drama*. New York: Columbia University Press, 1997

Nightingale	Pamela Nightingale, *A Medieval Mercantile Community: The Grocers' Company & the Politics & Trade of London 1000–1485*. New Haven and London: Yale University Press, 1995
NS	New Series
OED	*Oxford English Dictionary.* Compact edn., complete text reproduced micrographically, 2 vols. Oxford: Clarendon Press, 1971
OS	Old/Original Series
PRO	Public Record Office
REED	Records of Early English Drama
Rep.	Repertory (MSS at CLRO)
RS	Rolls Series
RSTC	A. W. Pollard and G. R. Redgrave, *A Short-Title Catalogue of Books Printed in England, Scotland & Ireland . . . 1475–1640*, rev. W. A. Jackson, F. S. Ferguson, and Katharine F. Pantzer, 3 vols. London: The Bibliographical Society, 1976–91
Stow, *Annales*	John Stow, *The Annales of England.* 1592. *RSTC* 23334
Stow, *Survey*	John Stow, *A Survey of London*, ed. Charles Lethbridge Kingsford, 2 vols. Oxford: Clarendon Press, 1908
Streitberger	W. R. Streitberger, *Court Revels, 1485–1559.* Studies in Early English Drama 3. Toronto: University of Toronto Press, 1994
Thrupp, *London*	Sylvia L. Thrupp, *The Merchant Class of Medieval London [1300–1500].* Chicago: University of Chicago Press, 1948
TLMAS	*Transactions of the London and Middlesex Archaeological Society*
Two London Chronicles	Charles Lethbridge Kingsford, ed., "Two London Chronicles from the Collections of John Stow," in *Camden Miscellany* 12. Camden Society, 1910, pp. iii–x, 1–57
Usk	Adam Usk, *Chronicle of Adam Usk*, ed. and tr. C. Given-Wilson. Oxford: Clarendon Press, 1997

Vita & Gesta	*Vita & Gesta Henrici Quinti*, ed. Thomas Hearne. Oxford, 1727
Westminster Chronicle	*The Westminster Chronicle 1381–1394*, ed. and tr. L. C. Hector and Barbara F. Harvey. Oxford: Clarendon Press, 1982
Wickham, *History*	Glynne Wickham, *A History of the Theatre*. New York: Cambridge University Press, 1985
William of Worcester	William of Worcester, *Annales*, in Joseph Stevenson, ed., *Letters and Papers Illustrative of . . . the Reign of Henry the Sixth*, vol. 2.2. RS 22. London: HSMO, 1864; rpt. Wiesbaden: Kraus Reprint, 1968, pp. 743–793
Williams	Gwyn A. Williams, *Medieval London: From Commune to Capital*. University of London Historical Studies 11. London: University of London, Athlone Press, 1963
Wriothesley	Charles Wriothesley, *A Chronicle of England during the Reigns of the Tudors*, ed. William Douglas Hamilton, 2 vols. Camden Society, NS 11, 1875, and NS 20, 1877
Wylie, *Reign*	James Hamilton Wylie, *The Reign of Henry the Fifth*, 3 vols. Cambridge: Cambridge University Press, 1914–29 (vol. 3 with William Templeton Waugh)

COMPANY DESIGNATIONS

In a few cases the names of the London livery companies discussed in this book changed during the period between their founding and 1558 or have changed since that date. In all such instances, for the sake of continuity and consistency, the current name has been used throughout: thus Grocers for Pepperers, Merchant Taylors for Tailors, Armourers and Brasiers (the combined company) for Armourers and Brasiers as separate companies, Fishmongers (the combined company) for Fishmongers and Stockfishmongers as separate companies.

A large number of London livery company manuscripts are cited throughout. The locations of these manuscripts are noted in the List of Works Cited, at the end of the volume, and my thanks for access are included in the Acknowledgments.

LONDON MAYORS AND SHERIFFS

The only list of London mayors and sheriffs, to 1558, which includes their livery company memberships and the exact day/month dates (where known) of replacements for mayors and sheriffs dying in office or removed from office is this author's "The Mayors and Sheriffs of London 1190–1558," forthcoming as an appendix in Caroline Barron's *The Government of London 1200–1500* (Oxford University Press). A typescript copy of this list is also available at the CLRO, and will eventually also be available on the Web. For all references to mayors and sheriffs by company, see this list, which is also used for the spellings of the names of mayors and sheriffs.

TRANSCRIPTION PRACTICES

MS abbreviations have been expanded in italic; MS letters raised above the line have been silently lowered except where misreadings might result; and MS deletions have been placed within square brackets. Interlineations have been indicated by half brackets (upper for above the line, lower for below the line) or are specified in footnotes. Original MS lineation has not been preserved unless so noted. In quotations from older printed works, long s is reproduced as short s, and thorn is reproduced as th.

Introduction

The history of the pre-Elizabethan theatre in England, from about the twelfth century to 1558, has traditionally been a history of provincial – i.e., non-London – theatre: above all because of the survival of the manuscripts of the great Corpus Christi cycles from York, Chester, Wakefield, and N-Town, because of corresponding interest in the performances of these cycles and therefore in the surviving theatrical records associated with them, because of the provincial origins of other plays surviving from the medieval period in manuscript (such as the Digby *Mary Magdalene* and the Macro plays' *Castle of Perseverance*), and because of the apparent touring nature of a linguistically and physically exuberant play such as *Mankind*, which in part inspired the seminal work done on travelling professional companies *c.* 1475–1590 by David Bevington in the early 1960s.[1] These rich resources of both texts and records have served as magnets, from the nineteenth century to the present day, for scholars interested in the medieval English theatre: in text and performance analysis, in theatre history, and in theatre as a part of social history. Most recently, in the late twentieth century, the Records of Early English Drama (REED) project, established in the 1970s and dedicated to the finding, editing, and publishing of the records of drama, theatrical pageantry, and minstrelsy of the various cities and shires of Great Britain, from the beginnings of such records to 1642, has focused, to date, on provincial theatrical records and on great households outside London. Although REED will eventually be publishing several London records volumes, its nineteen collections currently in print (to the end of the year 2000), dealing with cities such as Coventry, Chester, and York and with areas such as Lancashire, Shropshire, Dorset, and Cornwall, have given renewed impetus to research into early English provincial theatre.

No play texts have survived, for pre-Elizabethan London, similar to those which exist for the provincial centres; and early London theatre records – both in manuscript and in print – largely cannot be matched with dramatic texts and also are considerably more scattered and harder to find than theatre records for provincial cities such as Coventry and York. Recent general histories of the early English theatre reflect the lack of attention which – despite the work of a few individuals – has accordingly been paid, overall, by theatre scholars to pre-1559 London, even though the city was increasingly, from the twelfth century, the economic, social, and political capital of the nation. The 1994 *Cambridge Companion to Medieval English Theatre*,[2] for example, is divided largely into sections defined geographically by the four English provincial cycles, Cornwall, and East Anglia; it virtually ignores London also in its chapters on other types of drama (morality plays, saint plays); and there are only a few brief references (only four of them indexed) to London, overall, in the book's 372 pages. The medieval volume of the *Revels History of Drama in English*,[3] eleven years earlier, also managed indexed references to London – although more extensive ones – on only four pages. (A 1974 exception to the norm is Alan Nelson's *The Medieval English Stage*, which includes an eight-page section on London.[4]) The situation in relation to early sixteenth-century London theatre has been little better: even though, for the sixteenth century overall, English theatre historians have traditionally made a 180-degree turn at *c.* 1558–76 and have begun to deal from that point on with almost nothing but London-based theatre (and the court). The 1990 *Cambridge Companion to English Renaissance Drama*[5] essentially begins with the reign of Elizabeth I;[6] and although there is a *Revels History* volume entirely devoted to the period 1500–76,[7] it has no focus on London as a theatrical milieu. The 1997 *New History of Early English Drama*, however, following the marked shift in late twentieth-century scholarship from authors and texts to contexts, includes a section on London's 1377–1559 royal entries: formal processions through the city's streets, with elaborate, constructed visual displays, speeches, and music, on occasions such as the coronation of a new monarch, the arrival home of a monarch victorious in war, or a state visit by a foreign ruler.[8] Other sections of the *New History* also include some useful references to the pre-Elizabethan city.

The very size and complexity of London, and its close relations – geographically and politically – with the royal court, from the medieval period on, have worked against it in terms of any development of a city-focused theatre history for the period before the initial construction of London purpose-built playhouses in the 1560s and 1570s. Extant early Tudor play texts, for example, by Londoners such as Henry Medwall and John Heywood have been routinely discussed by scholars mainly in

terms of courtly performances, interests, and politics: which have traditionally been privileged in academic study above "street-level" performances and concerns, and which have not yet been displaced from this
position by a growing number of scholars more attuned to popular culture.[9] City medieval and early Tudor theatre records have been sparsely
used by scholars: in significant part because largely having to be hunted
down in thick manuscripts dealing also with a multitude of non-theatrical
matters (orphans, night watches, rebellions, loans to the king, trade regulations and disputes, legal cases, etc.), with the size of the city having
resulted in an overwhelming amount of such kinds of manuscript
material having survived, located in a very large number and variety of
archival collections, both public and private. Comparatively few theatre
records from such sources have been published (and then with varying
degrees of accuracy), and in a variety of venues some of which have not
been well known to literary/theatre scholars.[10] (Social and political historians have made more use of them.) The misperception also of many
Renaissance theatre scholars that the London authorities at all times
were implacably opposed to the theatre – a misperception generated
by narrowly focused studies of sixteenth and seventeenth-century city
play prohibitions and regulations – has led as well to a general failure in
early English theatre scholarship to consider London itself (except in
medieval and early Tudor royal entries, as noted above and below) as a
positive theatrical force;[11] and the general prejudice, until very recently,
of theatre scholars against pageantry and in favour of play texts has also
thus been a major factor in the traditional disregard of London by literary and theatre historians. London's medieval and early Tudor theatre is, to an important extent, a pageant theatre of the streets. Such
theatre – to which largely belong the few pre-1559 wholly "theatrical"
manuscripts to be found in London archives – "cannot be treated as
'literature'," states the 1994 *Companion* (p. 38), on the omission of pageant
theatre from the volume; and the civic theatrical form of the royal entry –
although a provincial as well as a London theatrical form – accordingly
receives in the *Companion*, like London itself, only a few brief references.
Only within the last four years has the Cox-Kastan *New History*, with its
individual sections on a wide variety of topics such as household
drama, printed plays, and popular culture rather than on authors,
texts, or periods, notably demonstrated in a history of the English
drama the late twentieth-century shift in "literary" studies to a very
broad view indeed of the province of early English theatrical criticism
and history.

Since 1984, however, there has existed a published, comprehensive listing of all the in-print records of pre-1559 London theatrical performances (both of pageantry and of the drama proper): Ian Lancashire's *Dramatic Texts and Records of Britain: A Chronological Topography.*[12] *DTR* puts London together with Westminster and lists for those locations, as part of one chronological grouping, the in-print records of all of court performances, private performances in the houses of the nobility and the higher clergy, school drama, civic street theatre, parish drama, and livery company plays. The volume thus gives a broad picture of the extensive theatrical activity (including prohibitions against theatre) ongoing in this one geographical area, over a period of some 400 years, c. 1170–1558, with one earlier listing even noting Roman archaeological remains, and with the picture widening further when the listings are also examined for areas such as Clerkenwell and Shoreditch, now parts of London but formerly separate from it.[13] Records dealing specifically with the original city of London only, as separate from Westminster, can also easily now be extracted from the grouping; and these records point to what we should expect, given the prevalence of theatre elsewhere in England in the early period and the size and importance of the early city of London compared to other major centres such as York, Chester, and Coventry: an active and extensive theatrical life in London itself, without Westminster, from at least the twelfth century on and perhaps from Roman times. Roman activity has since been confirmed by the 1987–88 archaeological discovery of Roman London's amphitheatre; and a London theatre history for Roman and Saxon times can also now begin to be written. The records listed in *DTR* as now in print are not numerous when one considers London's size (even though a few more records publications have joined the group since 1984); and they are scattered, and in many cases consist of merely illustrative excerpts from manuscripts. They also largely cannot be linked, as already noted, with extant play texts; and much of London's recorded theatrical activity from the thirteenth century on, as also already noted, is seen to be in the form of the elaborate street pageantry not only of royal entries but also of occasions such as the annual Watch at midsummer and the annual inauguration procession of the city's new mayor to Westminster and back. But the grouping of these records together in a reference work has been a major step forward in the study of pre-1559 London theatre as a comprehensive whole, even while the listing together of London and Westminster material also points to one of the factors, already touched on, which has held back such study: the tendency of scholars to think of

London's theatrical significance, in the medieval and early Tudor periods, largely in terms of the court, or as overshadowed by the court. (It is no accident that royal entries – involving the city focused on the court – are currently receiving much more academic attention than are wholly-civic pageant events such as midsummer watches.) The court, however, was not a London phenomenon but was, rather, peripatetic throughout this period, moving with the king or queen from one royal seat to another; and Westminster palace itself was located up the river from the city. Given that a number of medieval and early Tudor royal palaces were in the vicinity of London, and given the political and economic interdependence of the city and the Crown, the court and its theatrical tastes were clearly important influences on London theatre: but London, as a city, was not a satellite of the court. Indeed, politically, the London authorities spent a good deal of their time demonstrating the city's independence from the court.

What, then, can be said about the theatre, originating in the city itself, that the citizens of London experienced and participated in from earliest times to 1558? This, after all, was the theatre that eventually gave rise, in the late sixteenth century, to Shakespeare and his contemporaries, in what has long been considered to have been the golden age of English drama. Shakespeare was not a product of the court theatre; and commercial professional theatre did not suddenly spring up in London in the mid sixteenth century, with the construction of the first known purpose-built playhouses there, without a strong base in ongoing city theatrical traditions. Examination of the records, moreover, specifically of London *civic* theatre – of *city-sponsored* plays and pageants – from material records, such as archaeological remains in the Roman period, through written records such as early church prohibitions and chronicle histories, to surviving city and London craft-guild/livery-company manuscript records series from *c.* 1275–76 (when the city's series of official Letter Books begins) to 1558, both gives a new perspective on post-1558 London developments and above all begins to provide for London a pre-1559 theatrical history somewhat parallel to those we already have for cities such as York, Chester, and Coventry: for the theatrical histories of these other English cities have been, to date, largely histories of city-sponsored theatre. The study of early London, including its theatre, as itself an urban cultural phenomenon has also recently been gaining interdisciplinary scholarly attention (as sociohistorical criticism has become increasingly popular), and has recently been given special prominence by Lawrence Manley's sweeping 1995 *Literature and Culture in Early*

Modern London,[14] covering a 200-year period from *c.* 1475 and including important work on London's pre- (and post-) 1559 street pageantry as a major element in what Manley argues to be the city's increasing self-awareness as an urban political/cultural centre. Narrowing the focus taken by Manley (who broadly covers many forms of literature and culture), and extending the time period, this present book is intended to begin a study specifically of London's theatrical culture as developed by the city itself, from earliest times to the beginning of the so-called Shakespearean period: which is here taken, in its broadest definition, as starting with the 1558 accession of Elizabeth I. Because the subject of London's specifically civic theatre has been so little treated to date, I have not broadened the book's scope so as to deal also, except in a few passing references, with London's medieval and early Tudor parish drama or school drama, or with the city's longstanding theatrical folk culture (for example, of May games). I have also not treated court theatrical activities (such as Cheapside tournaments) taking place in London itself. The focus is entirely on civic theatre (as defined briefly above and in more detail below), though with attention also given to court-city theatrical interrelationships. Although these other theatrical forms should eventually also be examined in detail, in a broader work on the city's pre-1559 theatre, London's civic theatrical culture would seem first to deserve and to require some focused attention.

This book is, then, an examination of various aspects of specifically civic theatre in London over a period of some 1500 years: from the city's founding *c.* 60 AD to the accession of Elizabeth I in 1558. Within the term "theatre" I include not only plays (drama, or "theatre proper") but also, as clearly indicated by this point, other kinds of performances involving constructed set pieces and/or costumed and choreographed/designed role-playing: such as Roman amphitheatre shows, and the medieval to early Tudor street pageantry – stationary and portable – of constructed towers, castles, arches, Assumptions of the Virgin, giants, Jesse trees, and the like, and of the recitation of speeches or the singing of songs involving reciters/performers playing parts (of figures such as apostles, angels, and virgins). Such theatrical displays/performances were a major part of the social and political life of London over these 1500 years, and also were a significant part of the foundations upon which the theatre of Shakespeare and his contemporaries was built. For the period before 1200 I also include role-playing activity more generally, given the major uncertainties of theatrical terms then, and the scarcity of records. Simply ceremonial decoration/display, such as streets decorated with banners and tapestries hanging from the windows of houses, and processions of elaborately dressed dignitaries through the streets, has been included only where it would seem to be necessary background to the development of actual theatrical display/performance; and purely religious ritual or display, even where involving civic officials and institutions, has been excluded. "Theatre" is thus defined more or less as are the drama and pageantry covered by the published records volumes of the Records of Early English Drama project, but without REED's close attention to folk practices. The term "pageant" itself is here used to refer to formal visual displays (with or without spoken text) involving costumed role-players and/or constructed set pieces (stationary or portable). This is not what the term "pageant" often means in the pre-1558 civic records themselves; and I deal with this issue specifically in chapters 3 and 10. Nor is it the broader use of the term as increasingly found today in sociohistorical approaches to theatre.

By "civic" theatre I mean theatre sponsored, wholly or in part, by the city of London itself or by the London craft guilds or livery companies: organizations which, originally formed by particular occupational groups (brewers, goldsmiths, ironmongers, etc.) for purposes of trade regulation, religious worship, and/or mutual social support, from early times began to function in London as political groups of businessmen through which much of the city's governing was carried out.[15] (This book is thus in part "middle class" – as opposed to courtly or popular – theatre history,[16] although the city's governors provided theatre for all social and economic classes, from entertainments sent as gifts to the court, to street theatre which could be watched by all, whatever their status or economic level.) From the early fourteenth century, virtually no one could be a free citizen of London, with all the rights and responsibilities of such citizenship (including participation in city government), without belonging to a London craft guild:[17] and the companies therefore indirectly controlled the city's governing operations, as well as its economy.[18] Inevitably some of the companies, wealthier and more influential than the rest, came to play a larger part than the others in the civic government, and therefore also in the public street theatre – of royal entries, of mayoral shows, of the celebrations known as the Midsummer Watch – sponsored by that government: a theatre of political, religious, and civic obligations and rituals, and of public relations, as well as of entertainment.[19] What are today called the twelve Great Companies of London – in order of processional precedence, the Mercers, Grocers, Drapers, Fishmongers, Goldsmiths,

Skinners, Merchant Taylors, Haberdashers, Salters, Ironmongers, Vintners, and Clothworkers[20] – came to control the mayor's office (by custom, from the fifteenth century, virtually no citizen could be an alderman or mayor of London if he did not belong to, or agree to be transferred to, one of the Great Companies[21]); many sheriffs also belonged to the Great Companies;[22] and these companies therefore also became largely responsible for the civic theatre of the streets in which the mayor and sheriffs played such a significant role.[23] The mayor, with other prominent London officials and citizens, escorted English and foreign royalty and other dignitaries, formally entering the city, along streets decorated not only with rich hangings and banners – and with the companies lining the route – but also often with set-piece pageant stages constructed in traditional locations. The mayor and sheriffs were the civic leaders of the Midsummer Watch each June (to the early 1540s), in which portable constructed pageants (from at least the late fifteenth century) were carried in procession through the streets. The procession of the newly elected mayor each year to take his oath of office at the royal Exchequer at Westminster had also become, apparently by the late fifteenth century, an occasion for the carrying of portable pageants. All such events normally also involved music. The company each year to which the mayor belonged had special responsibility for street (and, by at least the late fifteenth century, river) pageants: especially (on land) at midsummer, when the sheriffs' companies also had to provide pageants, and for the mayoral oath-taking. Meanwhile many of the companies also seem, from the fifteenth century on, to have sponsored play performances at their major feast times (times of company celebration involving both religious services and secular activities such as the election of company officers), by performance companies which, by the early to mid sixteenth century, were the forerunners of the late sixteenth-century companies which acted the plays of Shakespeare and his contemporaries.[24]

The scholarly work available to date on early London theatre overall is sparse but slowly growing. As we have seen, London has been largely missing from the theatre-history picture of England generally constructed by scholars until, in the second half of the sixteenth century, permanent theatres were first built there, both for public professional companies and for the so-called private-theatre boys' companies (the latter focused on court performances as their raison d'etre), and secular plays for these theatres, by dramatists such as Marlowe and Shakespeare, began to survive in significant numbers. The early fifteenth-century mummings of

poet and dramatist John Lydgate, for example, although including the
only extant theatrical texts we can definitely assign to performance in a
pre-1559 London civic hall, have been pretty well ignored as London
drama.[25] A few late fifteenth and early sixteenth-century play texts – such
as Henry Medwall's *Fulgens and Lucres* – can be attached to performance
in the London area; but to date, as already noted, these texts have
largely been of interest to scholars for their associations with private patrons and above all with the court. Early sixteenth-century London
printings of plays have been studied by bibliographers, and by scholars
interested in what such printings might indicate about theatrical performance, but not with relation specifically to performances in London
itself;[26] and theatre historians have been largely discouraged by the early
London play-performance records available to date, which have tended
to be tantalizingly meagre (as in the case of London's late fourteenth-
century Clerkenwell/Skinners' Well play, discussed in chapter 3) and scattered. The Malone Society, however, in 1931 and in 1954 published what
late fifteenth and early sixteenth-century London civic play-performance
records it could find: twenty items (fifteen of them involving play suppression and control), between 1522 and 1558, from the city's official
manuscript records series of Letter Books, Journals, and Repertories,
and play performance records 1485–1558 from the manuscripts of the
London Great Companies, though these latter records were so few as to
seem to indicate very little company interest in the drama.[27]

Growing throughout the twentieth century, however, has been scholarly interest in pre-Elizabethan London pageantry: in part because a
good deal of it has survived (at least in terms of extant descriptions), in
part because of the mid-century rise in scholarly interest in performance studies and because of the development in the 1970s and 1980s of the
New Historicism, with its emphasis on contexts and on the politics of
theatre. The major work has been focused past 1558, in Shakespearean
times; but the medieval and early Tudor period has also received some significant attention. E. K. Chambers in 1903, in his two-volume anthropo-
logically focused *Mediaeval Stage*, provided only eight pages on London
pageantry (largely on royal entries) to 1559,[28] but Robert Withington in
1918–26 published a two-volume history entirely of English pageantry,
from early times to the nineteenth century, with a good amount of his
material coming from pre-1559 London.[29] Withington also, unlike
Chambers, was interested in the actual early theatrical displays themselves, rather than in the religious and folk beliefs in which they might
have originated; and he provided descriptions, records transcriptions

and paraphrases, and numerous citations of sources (including of a significant number of early manuscripts as well as of printed dramatic histories, livery company histories, and London histories) for material on London (and other) entries 1298–1558, and also on London's annual pageant-filled Midsummer Watch and annual mayoral inauguration show (though on the latter largely after 1558). His wealth of detail is still useful today.[30] Moreover, in 1954's *Collections III* and in 1960's *Collections V* the Malone Society published a part-calendar, part-edition, with a substantial amount of material, of the pre-1559 (and later) records of the London Midsummer Watch and Lord Mayor's Show found in the extant manuscripts of London's twelve Great Companies.[31]

In 1966 Glynne Wickham began the publication of the eventual three volumes of his monumental *Early English Stages*:[32] examining early English theatre above all in terms of its visual stagecraft and hence paying a great deal of attention to London's royal entries, its "pageant theatres of the streets" (the heading of volume 1's third chapter) from 1377 to 1603.[33] Such pageant theatre was for Wickham central to the evolution of English stagecraft; and his extensive use of manuscript records of London theatre can be seen at its height in his transcription and translation of a lengthy Latin record, from London's Bridge House manuscripts, of the pageants constructed for the 1465 processional entry across the Bridge of Elizabeth Woodville, queen to Edward IV, coming to London and Westminster for her coronation.[34] (Wickham also unusually spent part of a chapter, in volume 1, examining Lydgate's mummings.) While Wickham was approaching London royal entries from the direction of stagecraft, Sydney Anglo was examining them – like Wickham, along with courtly theatrical forms such as tournaments and disguisings – in terms of their importance as tools of political policy. His influential *Spectacle, Pageantry, and Early Tudor Policy*,[35] published in 1969 (with a new edition in 1997), examined the political aspects (from a court perspective) of the various theatrical displays of the reigns of Henry VII through Mary, to the 1559 coronation of Elizabeth I, such displays including seven major and several minor London entries.

From the later twentieth century to the present, pageantry studies in general have been expanding significantly for both English/London and continental theatre, but largely, for London, past 1558.[36] Until very recently, London pageantry before 1559 has been part of the consistent, long-term working field of (besides Anglo) only one scholar, Gordon Kipling, whose focus on European court culture and festivals has included important historical and interpretative work, over some twenty

years, on London royal entries.[37] David Bergeron since the 1960s and
1970s has been publishing books and articles calling attention to London
civic pageantry in general, and not only to royal entries, as a major theatrical force;[38] but Bergeron's work is entirely past 1558 (except for one article, by Kipling, in Bergeron's 1985 collection of papers on pageantry [39]),
as are other recent developments such as Arthur Kinney's new anthology of English Renaissance drama, which includes the texts of two
post-1558 London royal entries and one post-1558 London mayoral
show.[40]

Recently, however, attention to the field of pre-1559 London theatre
in general has begun to widen. The discovery in 1987–88 of a Roman
amphitheatre in London has given the city at last a definite Roman theatrical past; and not only has the Cox-Kastan *New History* included a
chapter (by Kipling) on pre-1560 London royal entries in a volume devoted to a non-periodized approach to the early theatre, thus calling the
attention of Renaissance scholars to these earlier pageants, but – as previously noted – Lawrence Manley has reached back to 1475 in his *Literature
and Culture in Early Modern London*, which includes important work on
London's street pageantry in general (not only on royal entries) to 1558
(and beyond).[41] *DTR* as a reference work is also now available to point
theatre historians to all pre-1559 theatrical areas of potential importance
and to earlier work on them; and Greg Walker's work on early sixteenth-
century political drama has begun to move into consideration of civic
audiences.[42] Finally the REED project early in this century will be publishing volumes of London theatre records, from the beginnings of their
survival to 1642, divided by record origin and in some cases by period:
for example, parish records, Inns of Court records, civic records to 1558.
Westminster records will be separated from those of London proper.
Meanwhile London archaeologists continue to examine Roman and
Saxon London; and social and political historians continue to be extremely active in the medieval and early Tudor fields, so that, for example, the 1485 entry of Richard III through London to his Westminster
coronation is now available in Anne Sutton's and P. W. Hammond's edition of the extant coronation documents.[43] (Unfortunately Richard's
procession does not seem to have involved constructed theatrical pageants.) New editions of livery company manuscripts – some of which
will include theatrical records – are also beginning to appear; and a limited
number of articles on London pageantry by both theatre historians and
social and political historians (such as Malcolm Smuts[44]) continue to be
published, a number of them cited in the various chapters of this book.

London as a major centre for professional, public-oriented (as well as court-oriented) theatre – plays and pageants – was not a sudden, new development *c.* 1567, with the building of the Red Lion theatre just outside the city walls and with the gradual elaboration (from the 1550s to the Jacobean period) of the pageantry of the mayor's oath-taking procession to and from Westminster every 29 September. The immediate predecessors of Shakespeare in London, who inspired the young Stratford-upon-Avon actor/writer to undertake a career in the theatre there, did not emerge from a civic and professional theatre vacuum. A major (amphi) theatrical city during the Roman period in Britain, providing civic-sponsored theatrical entertainments for all, London emerged again, after the departure of the Romans and a long period of time about which we know little, as a major performance centre apparently by the end of the twelfth century; and, as more and more civic manu-script records and written chronicles begin to survive, from 1200 to 1558, we can recognize how extensive may have been the earlier activ-ity upon which the later recorded activity is apparently based. Civic theatrical activity in medieval and early Tudor London, of course, was closely related (as in royal entries) to the activities of the court: espe-cially as the court gradually became more and more administratively based next door, as it were, at Westminster; but a study focusing on the specifically civic aspects of London drama and pageantry seems long overdue, righting a balance previously tilted in the extreme not only towards provincial theatre but also towards early court theatre and spectacle.

This book does not attempt to be an all-inclusive historical and inter-pretative account of London civic theatre from its beginnings to 1558. It is intended, rather, to begin the construction of such a history, and of a broader history of early London theatre in general: by providing a historical outline of what can now be ascertained about civic theatre in London before 1559, relying above all, for the medieval and early Tudor period, on civic records manuscripts and on chronicle histories, and by suggesting new ways of approaching the subject and new questions to be asked about it. The focus is historical and speculative, rather than theoretical or interpretative: hence the absence of much of the kind of general theoretical work on civic and royal ceremonial, carnival, and the like, cited by more theoretically oriented scholars. Establishing the historical facts of early London civic theatre, insofar as this is possible, has been the priority.[45] The book is divided into two parts. Part 1 pro-vides a chronological survey of London civic theatre from Roman times to 1410, in three chapters: the first two providing overviews of the civic theatre, as a whole, of the Roman period and (tentatively) of the centuries from 410 to 1200, the third – as we move forward in time and more information becomes available – summarizing what is known, and what can reasonably be guessed, to date, about the various kinds of civic theatre (mummings, pageants for the formal entries of dignitaries into the city, plays, the beginnings of the Midsummer Watch and of the Lord Mayor's Show) in existence between 1200 and 1410. Part 2 is divided into seven chapters (numbered 4 to 10) on different types of London civic theatre, each chapter covering the period 1410–1558 and approaching its subject matter from a new perspective: making use of a fresh examination of civic manuscript records to provide new information and to question old assumptions. Chapter 4 attempts to establish, through examination of the major surviving records of the London livery companies, the extent of the performance of hall plays for the companies, 1410–1558, by both amateur and professional groups of performers available for hire in London throughout this period. Chapter 5 speculates on the kinds of plays such acting troupes might have performed, and on relationships between the performers and the livery companies; and chapter 6 comments specifically on the theatrical work of the author of the only surviving texts (from the early fifteenth century) that we can know, with certainty, were performed in London civic halls before 1559: several mummings by court and civic writer John Lydgate. Chapter 7 turns to the civic pageantry of the formal land entries into London – on occasions such as coronations, marriages, military victory celebrations, and state visits – by English and foreign royalty and other such dignitaries, and, given the existence already of a good deal of excellent interpretative scholarship on the overall religious and political meanings of royal entries, focuses on some of its practical civic details that would seem to be worth further investigation. Chapter 8 considers the civic water pageantry, for royal and equivalent entries and for civic officials themselves, which appears to have become important from at least the mid fifteenth century, and which has not to date received the attention that has been given to the land pageantry. Chapter 9 looks at the extensive spectacle – by at least the late fifteenth or early sixteenth century – of the London Midsummer Watch, and at the debate over when and why it came to an end. Finally chapter 10 takes up the London Lord Mayor's Show as a pageant spectacle, discussing the pre-1559 beginnings of what had by the seventeenth century become London's major annual civic processional display.

Two appendices are also provided. Appendix A provides additional information related to chapter 7: a listing of all major royal entries into London, 1400–1558, and of some selected minor entries, with details such as specific dates (about which chronicle histories and other such sources so often disagree), routes, and the locations in each entry (insofar as this can be ascertained) of the mayor. Appendix B provides transcriptions of eleven selected records and groupings of records, from civic manuscripts, which throw new light – as discussed at various points throughout the book – onto several aspects of London civic theatre.

A wide variety of sources has been consulted for the various chapters, and individual manuscripts and printed works are cited for each; but most important has been my reading through of all of the extant manuscripts in the City of London series of official Letter Books, from *c.* 1275 through 1558 (18 volumes), Journals, from 1416 through 1558 (17 volumes), Repertories, from 1495 through 1558 (14 volumes), and Bridge House accounts, from 1381 through 1558 (17 rolls and 16 volumes), and also of all of the likely-relevant manuscripts of the London livery companies with such pre-1559 manuscripts extant: account books, court minutes (i.e., minutes of company meetings and decisions), books of ordinances (bylaws), memorandum books, and charters. This work has been undertaken for an early twenty-first-century edition of the London civic records, to 1558, for the REED project; and so I have been able to work also from my own transcriptions of much of the material. (My thanks for the access granted me to this material, by the Corporation of London and by the livery companies, are expressed in the Acknowledgments.) My most important sources, other than such civic manuscripts, have been early London and national chronicle histories; and I have also relied extensively on modern printed editions of some London civic manuscripts (such as custumals), and on modern livery company histories. My debts to such sources are specifically acknowledged in the footnotes to each chapter; and I am also greatly indebted to the published scholarly work, similarly acknowledged, of London historians past and present, and of early-theatre historians and literary scholars, both those cited and others whose work I have also consulted. In chapters 1 and 2 my debt is largely to London archaeologists, and to historians of Roman London and of pre-twelfth-century English theatre in general. Printed scholarship has in general been consulted to the end of 2000.

Other sources which I have not used would doubtless also have yielded important information about early civic theatre in London: such as the wills of London livery company members, and company property deeds, the sheer surviving quantity of which, however, has precluded my use of them other than where I have been pointed to a specific item by some other source. Legal and ecclesiastical manuscripts not yet combed by other scholars would certainly also have provided, in some cases, additional significant material: but, again, because of the quantities of manuscripts involved, I have limited my examination of such sources to specific documents already noted by others. This book is the beginning, not the end, of the building of a new theatre history for early civic London and for early London more broadly as well: an enterprise which will eventually require the contributions of many scholars, working in a variety of fields and over a lengthy period of time.

PART I

From Roman times to 1410

CHAPTER I

Roman London

The earliest records of civic theatre in London are not written but
material: the earth, timber, and stone remains of an amphitheatre, built
in Roman London (Londinium) in the late first and early second centuries AD, and abandoned by some time during the fourth century.[1]
Major Roman towns throughout the Roman Empire in the early centuries AD almost invariably had a theatre, amphitheatre, or both;[2] and
archaeologists working on Roman London, who for many years had
been expecting to find a theatre and amphitheatre in the course of their
excavations,[3] at last found the amphitheatre in 1987–88, though in a
location they had not expected: beneath the Yard of London's Guildhall,
the latter of which in its first form originated in the twelfth century.[4]

Londinium – a city created by the Romans shortly before 60–61 AD,
destroyed in an uprising against the Romans led by Boudica, queen of
the Iceni, in 60–61, and then almost immediately rebuilt – had reached
its peak of population size and imperial importance by *c.* 100 AD, and
continued to be an important Roman centre, though with a gradually
declining population and diminishing administrative and political significance, over the next 300 years.[5] By *c.* 100 AD Londinium, thanks to its
geographical location on the major waterway of the Thames, and as a
point through which all Roman roads in Britain passed, was a major
Roman administrative centre: a flourishing city of up to perhaps 60,000
inhabitants, "one of the largest cities in the Roman west," with urban
features such as a planned road system, piped water, and public buildings such as a forum, baths, and temples.[6] Such a Roman city would be
expected normally to have had both a theatre and an amphitheatre; and
both kinds of buildings, largely from the first to fourth centuries, have
been found in numerous other locations in Britain, though together, as
separate buildings, only perhaps in Cirencester (the Roman Corinium
Dobunnorum) and St. Albans (the Roman Verulamium) – which, however, as Roman towns were (arguably) not as significant as Londinium.[7]

Both structures would have been part of the operations of civic government in Londinium: not simply as public buildings but also because it was customary throughout the Roman Empire for city magistrates to arrange for shows, funded by civic grants and often also in part by additional monies from the magistrates themselves, for the general population at festival times honouring the gods and/or in celebration of major political figures and events and even of their own civic office-holding and major domestic occasions.[8] These shows would have included both plays in theatres and other kinds of entertainments – for example, blood sports such as wild animal fights and hunts, gladiatorial combats, and some athletic contests – in amphitheatres.[9] The inhabitants of Londinium would perhaps have watched, in the amphitheatre, travelling troupes of gladiators (and perhaps locally trained ones);[10] the animals involved would probably have been bears, wild boars, and bulls (a bear bone from the site has been identified; and the skull of possibly a bull has been found in a perimeter drain[11]); and there might also have been exhibitions of acrobatics, wrestling, boxing, and racing (unless a separate stadium and/or circus had also been built for racing and some athletic contests; see below).[12] In the as-yet-unfound theatre – unless the amphitheatre doubled as a theatre[13] – professional actors would have performed, by the first century AD, largely mime (variety entertainment) and pantomime (dance-drama); regular tragedy and comedy, though still performed, were no longer popular on the Roman public stage by the first century, and even farce had declined in audience appeal.[14] Both amphitheatre and theatre (if both existed in Londinium) were, then, public performance centres with religious, social and political functions. When the Emperor Hadrian, for example, toured Britain in 122, and presumably visited Londinium, large-scale and lavish entertainments were doubtless laid on in the amphitheatre and, if it existed, in the theatre, in honour of both the gods and the emperor;[15] the theatrical sites would have served as centres not only of entertainment but also of community religious celebration, political affirmation, and civic pride.

The Roman amphitheatre discovered in London in 1987–88 has undergone several different size estimates; the most recent being a capacity of *c.* 6,000 spectators.[16] This was a respectable size for a city with a population *c.* 100 AD of perhaps up to 60,000, and growing in prosperity from the early to mid second century.[17] Initially built in 70–71 AD, of earth and timber, by *c.* 125 AD it had been rebuilt as part of a major public works program,[18] with an enlarged arena and eastern entrance way,[19] and had been provided with a curved brick and ragstone wall enclosing the arena and retaining the earth banks which would have supported tiers of wooden seats.[20] There was also an extensive drainage system. The amphitheatre was a major public structure where large numbers of the inhabitants of Londinium would have come together on communal festive occasions; and perhaps, like most Roman amphitheatres, for reasons above all of size it was built not in the central part of the city (for example, near Londinium's forum, on what is now Cornhill) but to the northwest of Cornhill, across the now-infilled valley of the Walbrook stream (now the location of, for example, the Bank of England and the street named Walbrook) and at the southeast corner of the Roman fort located in the area.[21] It has also been suggested, however, that a possible military presence by 70 AD in the area of what had become by the early second century the Roman military fort may have dictated the amphitheatre's location: the structure then serving – and continuing to serve – both a military and a civilian spectatorship.[22] As Londinium went through a lengthy period of general contraction *c.* 150 to 300 – though with a burst of urban renewal again *c.* 200, when a city wall was built – and other buildings both private and public were gradually levelled (for example, the forum in *c.* 300), the amphitheatre survived: despite Londinium's turn, by *c.* 200, to a focus more on private than on public structures, as the city became wealthier but less populated.[23] At last, however, as Londinium declined further, the amphitheatre was abandoned and then largely destroyed. Still apparently in use in the late third century, and at least still open (for whatever purposes) in the mid fourth century, in the late fourth century (or perhaps later) it was clearly no longer in use as its walls were robbed of stone.[24] If it had indeed been in use, for any purpose, until the mid fourth century, "it had outlived most of the other public buildings of Roman London," including the military fort; and if its use had continued to be even in part for civic shows, such entertainments clearly had more continuing power and appeal for the inhabitants of Londinium than had many other facets of public life in the city.[25] It has also been suggested, however, that in its later years the amphitheatre might have served largely as a market,[26] and recently a slaughterhouse or a municipal dump have also been proposed.[27] It certainly seems to have had no continuing life, as a performance space, into the medieval city which from the late ninth century grew up within the area of the Roman walls; by the late fifth century, if not before, Londinium itself – for reasons geographical, social, and political – no longer existed.[28] The Romans themselves had abandoned Britain in 410; and the original Roman city appears to have vanished well before 500, with a new Saxon town (Lundenwic) growing up in the sixth or seventh century just to the west of the still-surviving walls of Londinium.[29] As described in the following chapter, the amphitheatre site itself has been argued by some to have continued in some way as a public centre into the resettling of the original Roman city in the late ninth century; but the archaeological evidence is against such a theory. Whatever the site situation, however, a living theatrical continuity would have existed, via local troupes of travelling professional performers: acrobats, jugglers, tightrope walkers, singers, dancers, who would previously have performed in Londinium's amphitheatre and perhaps theatre, as well as elsewhere in Britain, and at least some of whom would have continued to perform in the London area, and to travel elsewhere in Britain, after Londinium's disappearance, trying to make a living out of the provision of entertainment wherever they could find individuals or a community willing to pay for it.[30] People's thirst for entertainment (and for performance generally) does not die when cities do; and performers pass their expertise and performance traditions – from all sources – on from one generation to the next.

Was there likely to have been a theatre, separate from the amphitheatre, in Londinium? – a characteristically Roman structure (or variant on the norm) with a raised stage, decorated stage wall, semi-circular orchestra area in front of the stage, and tiered seats for the audience around the orchestra?[31] As previously noted, Roman theatres existed, largely between the first and fourth centuries, in other British centres, but only perhaps Cirencester and St. Albans had both a theatre and an amphitheatre as separate structures. Given the size and importance of Londinium, a separate theatre might well have existed;[32] but there is no consensus among archaeologists as to where such a theatre might have been located, except that it was likely west of the Walbrook,[33] and as yet no firm sign of a theatre structure in any excavations made.[34] Fragments have been found of three first to fourth-century masks, two in excavations at the Walbrook and one from a Roman waterfront site; and it has been suggested that these masks, possibly imports depicting "grotesque old men," were likely "worn in semi-religious performances and processions;"[35] but such performances and processions need not have involved an actual theatre structure; and the masks, if theatrical, could in any case – for example, as votive offerings cast into the Walbrook, or simply as rubbish dumped there – have been found elsewhere than an actual theatre site.[36]

Might London also have had a (civic) circus or a stadium, along with its amphitheatre and perhaps theatre? The question is relevant, given the lack of firm demarcation lines during the Roman period as to what kinds of entertainment events might take place in what kinds of structures. No sign of a stadium – a smaller venue than a circus but similar in plan, involving an arena divided into racing lanes, and used largely for athletic contests such as foot races, wrestling, and boxing – has yet been found in London, or its possible existence suggested;[37] and John Humphrey in his monumental *Roman Circuses* has noted that, in the Roman period, although the very largest cities seem to have had both a stadium and a circus, otherwise stadiums were generally built in the eastern Roman Empire and circuses in the west.[38] A stadium in Londinium would thus seem unlikely, especially given the existence of the amphitheatre, which could easily have been used for athletic contests. Circuses, larger and longer than stadiums and with a track running around a central spine, were intended primarily for chariot-racing although they could also be used – generally when other types of entertainment buildings did not exist – for events such as wild animal hunts, gladiatorial combats, and athletic contests (and even, rarely, some kinds of theatrical performances);[39] but though chariot-racing was the most popular and extensive mass spectator sport in the Roman Empire,[40] it could be carried out simply in the fields, or with makeshift arrangements such as temporary wooden structures; and there is also no firm evidence either of the sport having been popular in Britain or of any circuses having been built there.[41] Humphrey has suggested that if a circus had been constructed anywhere in Britain, it likely would have been in Londinium, and has also suggested a possible location in the area of the modern Knightrider St.[42] He is careful, however, to point out that the archaeological evidence for a circus in Londinium is inconclusive so far; and archaeological analyses since 1986 do not support the circus theory, though it has not been ruled out as impossible.[43] In Londinium the amphitheatre and perhaps theatre could have served the population for all types of festival entertainment except chariot-races, which could have been carried out (if at all) without a major constructed location for them.

Londinium, then, a Roman creation in the first century AD, was home definitely to a public amphitheatre in which entertainments would have been provided by the city's magistrates on public festive occasions; and it may also have had a public open-air theatre for civic-sponsored performances of above all mime and pantomime, although the amphitheatre could have doubled as a theatre. (No public open-air theatrical building existed again in London until Shakespeare's time, in the mid sixteenth century.) A separate stadium for athletic contests has not been suggested so far (and would have been unusual for the Roman west); and a circus primarily for chariot-racing might also have been built, but as yet there is no firm archaeological evidence for one either in Londinium or anywhere else in Britain. All such entertainment locations as did exist in Londinium, however, would have been dedicated to civic performances of religious, political, and social significance – binding the city together. Also possible would have been, as in Rome in the early centuries AD, private entertainments for the ruling class: entertainments paid for by the rulers, for their own consumption only; and perhaps there were even also some commercial public performances by travelling entertainers;[44] but theatrical shows and related entertainments in Londinium would above all have been civic, for the population at large, and related to religion and political order: just like much of the theatre (significantly including street pageantry) of medieval and early modern Christian London, to which we will turn shortly. Like much of this medieval and early modern theatre, the Roman civic shows would also have involved spectacle, sometimes violence, comedy, and music – mass performance/ entertainment, and aimed in large part at the religious, social, and political ends of the ruling classes.

CHAPTER 2

London c. 410–1200

Old assumptions that all Roman theatrical traditions in Britain would have died during the so-called Dark Ages after the Roman withdrawal from Britain in 410, with a revival of theatre only in the tenth to twelfth centuries under the auspices of the Christian church, have taken too long to disappear entirely but may finally now be extinct. Increasingly during the twentieth century it became recognized that humankind has always loved and engaged itself in storytelling and role-playing; that theatrical activities, whether associated with religious ceremonies or purely secular in nature, have been from early times a part of human cultures worldwide; that folk culture, which includes theatrical performance, tends to persist, unrecorded, through the centuries, both continuing old traditions and assimilating new influences; and that theatrical traditions, both folk and non-folk, tend to survive over long periods of time in continuing performance. Moreover scholars such as Allardyce Nicoll (early to mid century) and Glynne Wickham (mid to late century) have cogently argued for the persistence of Roman theatrical traditions, throughout Europe, both on a general popular entertainment level and in terms of specific performance developments (such as the Italian *commedia dell'arte*, the special effects of medieval religious drama, and the tournament).[1]

Amateur (folk) and professional entertainers, both individually and in small groups, would certainly have continued to perform in England – despite Saxon raids – after 410, with songs, dances, juggling, acrobatics, farce, and miming; and they would naturally have continued to make use of any theatrical/entertainment traditions which had become established in England during the Roman period and had become assimilated into the local cultures.[2] And even though local cultures then gave way to the Saxon invaders, some continuities would have existed; and some aspects of Roman theatrical performance, and of Roman entertainment generally, would therefore have survived in Britain, regardless of political and economic changes, along with pre-Roman religious and folk theatrical forms and events.

Wherever in Europe, including Britain, actual Roman theatrical – including amphitheatrical – structures survived, they too likely influenced subsequent theatrical/entertainment development.[3] In London, however, quite apart from the problem of the decay of the amphitheatre site from the fourth century on, a definite break between the Roman Londinium and the later Saxon town of Lundenwic makes more than normally speculative the suggestion that the Londinium amphitheatre remains (and the remains of a theatre, if any) might have exerted an influence on theatrical performances, civic or otherwise, in the London area after *c.* 410. After the decline and disappearance of Londinium sometime during the fifth century, as previously noted, the new Saxon town, Lundenwic, by the seventh century had grown up to the west of the previous walled city. Londinium's major public buildings such as the forum, baths, and amphitheatre had been demolished or abandoned between the third and late fourth centuries; and by the late fifth century the old city area within the walls may have become largely farmland or unused space,[4] around the remaining ruins.[5] But also, although from the fifth to the late ninth century we know very little about the walled area, the London bishopric first known in 314, re-established in 604, and continuous from the later seventh century, is thought to have been located there, where the first St. Paul's cathedral church was also founded *c.* 604;[6] and a royal palace has been suggested for the walled area as well.[7] The former Londinium, still a meeting point for roads (as established by the Romans) in and out of the area,[8] might thus have become in part an episcopal and royal locale;[9] and it has been suggested – although the most recent archaeological evidence is against this (see below) – that the area of the old amphitheatre, its arena suitably clear of previous building, might have been used for public assemblies.[10] Archaeologists discovered, in excavating the amphitheatre, that London's first Guildhall – the city's major early medieval civic building – was in the twelfth century constructed in the area of the former civic amphitheatre and even over the original location, on the amphitheatre's north side, of the seating for Roman and local community leaders.[11] A continuity of the amphitheatre location, from Roman times, as some form of civic assembly space was therefore originally suggested;[12] and if such a continuity of assembly space had existed, so might also a continuity of some kind of civic theatrical performances, ceremonial and/or in association with religious celebrations, although Christian religious celebrations would more logically have been associated with the nearby St. Paul's. Even if the amphitheatre location had not remained public space but had become part of a Saxon royal enclosure,[13] as has also been suggested, and the later civic Guildhall had then been built on a site of earlier royal rather than public authority,[14] some continuity of civic assembly, and perhaps of theatrical activity, could still have existed there – in significant geographical symbolism – though under royal auspices. Martin Biddle has noted, for example, general European use in the early Middle Ages of Roman amphitheatres, theatres, and circuses as "a backdrop for royal and imperial ceremonial."[15]

Continuous assembly and/or performance use of the amphitheatre arena, however, would seem recently to have been demonstrated, by archaeological analysis, to have been physically impossible, given not only the original lack of archaeological on-site evidence for any such use but also now the findings that drainage problems from perhaps as early as some time in the fourth century had left the arena "waterlogged and silted up."[16] By at least the end of the tenth century the area had apparently become "a boggy hollow."[17] Might the amphitheatre area initially have retained, nevertheless, some symbolic communal value for public assemblies and civic theatrical performances nearby? – perhaps at first, for example, in the vicinity of St. Paul's? The walled area of the old Londinium was then resettled as a town – Lundenburh – in the late ninth century, under Alfred the Great, at a time when Viking raids made the unwalled Lundenwic a dangerous place to inhabit;[18] and although the waterlogged amphitheatre location remained clear of buildings for some time (the town developing at first to the south of the modern Cheapside and therefore also of the amphitheatre location[19]), it only remained so for about a hundred years. In the eleventh century the waterlogged amphitheatre space was filled and levelled, and used both for a burial ground (in the south-west corner) and (further north and east) possibly at first for a cattle market. By the later eleventh century, Saxon housing was constructed here, on both sides of a lane running north-south through what had been the centre of the old amphitheatre.[20] This had to be cleared away in the twelfth century for the building of the Guildhall and of additional buildings down to the former amphitheatre's south side.[21] A clear space to the east of the Saxon housing area, however, of *c.* 300 square meters, appears to have persisted – possibly as a market and/or assembly space – throughout the Saxon settlement period;[22] and it should also be noted that by the mid eleventh or early twelfth century (or possibly earlier) Cheapside – a wide market area suitable for public assembly and display – had come into existence,[23] just to the south of the amphitheatre area and leading west to St. Paul's. During the Middle Ages, as London's widest street, Cheapside was used for processions, other major civic ceremonial displays, and even tournaments. Whether or not any historical continuities involving the amphitheatre had initially affected such developments, the amphitheatre had in effect been replaced, in the same general vicinity. Roman amphitheatre performance had become medieval English street performance.

In short, we can safely assume some general continuing theatrical activity, from *c.* 410 to the late ninth century, in the London area; but whether the Londinium amphitheatre remains exerted any influence on performance activities at any time during this period, perhaps initially, for example, as background to another civic assembly and/or performance location, or merely as a symbol of a civic past, we cannot know. We can only be comparatively sure – through general knowledge of theatrical practices and traditions – of local and travelling entertainers associated, after the first hundred years or so past Roman withdrawal from England, with the new, upstream settlement of Lundenwic, which archaeological evidence shows to have been in existence by perhaps the sixth and certainly the seventh century,[24] which fluctuated at first between paganism and Christianity,[25] and which was a thriving centre of international trade by sometime in the seventh century.[26] Lundenwic's theatrical life would certainly have involved performances (we do not know where), by local and travelling individuals or small groups,[27] in part simply as ordinary entertainment (including juggling, acrobatics, and the like) but probably also in part as performances, perhaps sometimes civic, linked to times of religious festivities, pagan or Christian. It is highly likely, for example, that communal celebrations involving some broadly theatrical non-Christian activities (farces, costumed dances, other costumed role-playing perhaps related to festive inversions of social order) would have taken place annually in Saxon Britain on occasions such as May Day and Midsummer – important community dates from a non-Christian past and not even entirely Christianized by the sixteenth century: despite the early Church's determined efforts to take over older community festivals such as midsummer (as in, for example, the festivals of St. John Baptist and of Sts. Peter and Paul, around midsummer, on 24 and 29 June).[28] Whether, for civic (or royal) ceremonial purposes, any of this broadly theatrical activity might have taken place for some period of time in the general area near the former Roman amphitheatre, within the walls of old Londinium, we cannot know without further historical/archaeological discoveries and analyses.

Then, during the ninth century, as has previously been noted, Viking raids apparently forced the abandonment of Lundenwic and the establishment of Lundenburh within the area of the former Roman Londinium. Presumably the more secure Lundenburh, within its city walls, would have followed generally along the performance paths already set in Lundenwic (despite the severe distractions of Viking invasions again from the late tenth to early eleventh centuries).[29] As far as civic outdoor theatrical/performance locations are concerned, however, the old Roman amphitheatre, with the decline and disappearance of Londinium, had become waterlogged; and in the eleventh century it was filled and levelled: for a cemetery, perhaps a cattle market, and by the later eleventh century for Saxon housing, although with a limited market/assembly/performance space. And, of course, we have no evidence of any other performance locations in Londonium, surviving or not past Roman times: although, given the common associations of Roman theatres with temples, we might speculate that if a Roman theatre had indeed existed in early London it might have been deliberately replaced (in terms of general geographical area) by St. Paul's, which from at least the thirteenth century was also associated with a folkmoot, i.e., a civic assembly and court.[30] In later medieval times St. Paul's was to become a focus of civic street pageantry, associated with royalty and other dignitaries, as discussed below in chapter 3. Above all, by at least 1104 and perhaps much earlier the broad market area of Cheapside had come into existence, and was to function in part as civic theatrical space throughout the Middle Ages and beyond.

Do we have any documentary indications of civic theatrical performance, in whatever location(s), for whatever purposes, in seventh to ninth-century Lundenwic or in the succeeding Lundenburh? We do have a few surviving records of apparent theatrical knowledge and activity in Britain in general, although not specifically related to London or to civic theatre, between 679 and the rise of Christian religious drama in the tenth and eleventh centuries.[31] Several Christian ecclesiastical records involving Britain, and expressing hostility towards "ludos" (games and/or plays), "spectaculi," and the like, are extant for the period 679–1100; and linguistic evidence of theatrical knowledge and activity in Britain during this time has also survived, although we cannot be sure of how the various terms are being applied. The records involve Christian attacks on or prohibitions of what appear to be, at least in part, role-playing

entertainments (though the terminology is very general);[32] and Old
English glosses on Latin, from the tenth and eleventh centuries, include
Old English terms for Latin words such as amphitheatrum, spectaculi,
histriones (actors/entertainers), and theatri.[33] We cannot of course be
sure of just what is being attacked or prohibited by the Church; terms
such as "ludi," for example, can include a wide variety of activities
(athletic contests, dancing, juggling, and so forth, as well as plays); but
role-playing of some sort seems contextually likely (rather than simply
activities such as animal-baiting, acrobatics, and the like) in at least
some instances. The glosses also suggest some Old English recogni-
tion of ongoing types of theatrical performance – not just of general
entertainment – and perhaps of habitual performance locations. Performance activity attacked by the Church, however, is unlikely to have
been civic: at least in any formal way.

The Church, however, would have been largely or wholly responsible
for the non-popular survival of Roman theatrical forms and traditions
in Britain, or for their reintroduction there by the seventh century.
Church-educated men and women throughout Europe – not all of
whom would have been opposed to the theatre despite the attitude of
the Church authorities towards it – would have acquired or maintained
knowledge of Roman drama as part of their learning of Latin writings
and language generally, throughout these centuries; so, for example, the
plays of Plautus and those of Terence, along with Horace's *Art of Poetry*,
would not have been forgotten in Britain – beyond the level of popular
entertainment continuities – as long as the Christian church persisted
there.[34] And Christian churches and other institutions such as abbeys
were re-established in Britain from the seventh century on: with
London, as we have seen, being provided again (after a long gap of time –
perhaps two hundred years) with a Christian bishopric in 604, which
was continuous from the later seventh century. St. Paul's was founded
also in the early seventh century, and Westminster Abbey – upstream
from the city – in the seventh to tenth centuries.[35] Other Christian religious establishments also began early in the London area: abbeys, for
example, at both Chertsey and Barking in the late seventh century.[36]
And at last, in the late twelfth century, we have a theatrical record – of
Christian performances – specific to London itself, and possibly though
not necessarily civic.

During the tenth to twelfth centuries, of course, Christian drama was
significantly coming into existence, both in Europe generally and in
Britain specifically. Probably built upon both the Christian liturgy and

existing non-Christian (including Roman) role-playing traditions, and in part intended to displace non-Christian entertainments (though more importantly to celebrate God, to educate the people, and to direct clerical histrionic impulses into religiously appropriate channels), it begins to be found in Winchester in the tenth century and throughout Britain by the twelfth century,[37] but most significantly in the twelfth century in London, which in the eleventh century went through a major period of the founding of churches,[38] and from 1066 to 1200 saw the establishment as well of numerous other religious centres, such as priories and hospitals.[39] In the late twelfth century London, which had been growing and flourishing in what has been called an urban Renaissance throughout Europe at this time,[40] was a thriving political, economic, and international trading centre, with close ties to the Crown.[41] Its population has been estimated as probably 10,000–20,000 in the late eleventh century,[42] and presumably growing into the twelfth; a number of guilds had formed for purposes of trade, religious celebration, and mutual social help;[43] over one hundred churches (monastic and parish) had been built;[44] prelates and the nobility had begun by 1200 to establish luxurious town houses in or just outside the city for the times of their stays on court, ecclesiastical or personal business.[45] The old wooden London Bridge was rebuilt in stone *c.* 1176–1209.[46] Records of Christian drama from elsewhere in Britain before 1200 are of performances seemingly limited in scope (for example, an Easter resurrection play at the abbey at Eynsham, Oxfordshire[47]); but the first written record of Christian theatrical activity in London, from the end of the twelfth century, would seem to indicate a flourishing religious theatre not in its infancy, matching the flourishing political and economic state of London itself, and its record number – for western Europe at the time[48] – of churches within its walls. William Fitz Stephen's *Description of London*, written probably *c.* 1170–82,[49] during the reign of Henry II, and a major source for our knowledge of the twelfth-century city, includes some brief comments on the city's religious performances, which the London-born and Church-educated Fitz Stephen (secretary to Thomas Becket before Becket's 1170 murder) compares to theatrical shows and stage plays in (seemingly ancient) Rome. Compared to Rome, writes Fitz Stephen, London has "holier plays, wherin are shown forth the miracles wrought by Holy Confessors or the sufferings which glorified the constancy of Martyrs."[50] There is no sense in Fitz Stephen's text that he is describing a rudimentary kind of performance activity, although his main point of course is to praise London's performances for their religious subject matter. He is pointing out one of the city's noteworthy attractions, in a work overall devoted to London's praise and which at first may seem overly glowing but the basic information in which has been largely accepted by modern historians.[51] The "holier plays" would seem, from his reference, to have been either numerous enough or large-scale enough to merit attention,[52] and to have been something very different from itinerant entertainment. We cannot, of course, assume that they were civic; they may have been entirely a Church matter; but they need not have been partly or wholly non-civic, either, given the civic auspices of the later "holy" Corpus Christi plays in cities such as York and Coventry. John Schofield has pointed out a strong tradition, by the late twelfth century, of wealthy Londoners demonstrating a "combination of civic works and conspicuous piety" in building works;[53] and such a tradition could also have fostered the sponsorship by civic leaders, working independently or together, via guilds or the Church, of civic religious performances.

A second, late twelfth-century possible reference to theatre in London also should be placed beside Fitz Stephen's text: a narrative reference to an apparently secular "theatrum" and to "histriones" (actors/entertainers) and "mimi" (mimes). A story told in a chronicle by Winchester monk Richard of Devizes involves a young man being warned about the iniquities of London: with the "theatrum" in London being equated with the tavern and with gambling, and with "histriones" and mimes listed as urban "evildoers" along with jesters, dancers, pimps, sorceresses, extortioners, magicians, and the like.[54] This is certainly not the territory of Fitz Stephen's "holier plays." In Devizes' narrative, a smooth-talking villain is thus describing London; he is not necessarily to be believed; but the story nevertheless may indirectly indicate to us the narrative credibility of twelfth century London as a site of non-religious (or irreligious) types of theatrical entertainment, and may encourage us to speculate as well about the term "theatrum" here as a possible indication of one or more habitual London performance locations (though performances other than the theatrical, including the obscene, could be meant). If the chronicle should indeed be referring to secular role-playing performances, as opposed to merely entertainments such as tumbling, juggling, animal-baiting, prostitution, and the like, Richard of Devizes and Fitz Stephen together would indicate a flourishing London theatre both religious and secular in the late twelfth century: although we cannot know from these references how extensive this theatre might have been, or whether any of it was civic theatre wholly or in part.[55]

Do any dramatic texts survive from this period, to enhance the credibility and likelihood of Fitz Stephen and Devizes as commentators on both religious and secular theatre in London shortly before 1200? We have no extant texts of any kind from pre-1200 London (or even from pre-1300 or pre-1400 London). We do, however, in relation to Fitz Stephen's noting of "holier plays," have one to two major surviving texts, of twelfth century non-liturgical religious drama, which may have originated in England. These texts, although not identifiable with London specifically or with civic theatre in general, are useful as examples of the high intellectual and performance level of at least some possibly English drama at this date. The Anglo-Norman *Service Representing Adam* and *Holy Resurrection* are not about miracles by Holy Confessors or about the sufferings of martyrs, at least as far as we have them (both texts are incomplete); they deal with Adam and Eve, Cain and Abel, and Old Testament prophets (*Adam*), and with Christ's crucifixion and resurrection (*Holy Resurrection*); but they are sophisticated and lengthy "holy" plays written for perhaps outdoor performance, either in England or in France, and involve carefully crafted verse dialogue (a mix of the formal and the colloquial), integrated use of chants and (in *Holy Resurrection*) possibly narration, choreographed action, significant interweaving of religious formality and everyday realism, and special effects (such as, in *Adam*, a mechanical ["*artfully constructed*"] snake in the temptation of Eve, a flaming sword in the expulsion from Eden, and "*a great smoke*" emanating from hell).[56] Anglo-Norman was the language of the English court at this time; it was used in the upper levels of civic London as well, for example in city record-keeping (where it only gradually fell out of use during the fifteenth century);[57] and although a manuscript of *Adam* is now located in the Bibliothèque Municipal de Tours, in France, the play is believed as likely to have originated in England as in France, while of the two extant manuscripts of *The Holy Resurrection* (both incomplete), one (now in the British Library) is a mid-thirteenth-century revision (of the original play) probably originating in Canterbury.[58]

Where these plays were originally performed, however, or their manuscripts written, does not really matter.[59] Given the extensive cultural, political, and religious interchanges between England and France in the twelfth century, they illustrate the sophisticated state of vernacular religious drama at the time in both countries: for there is no reason to believe that England – and especially London, with its extensive European trading connections and its close associations with the Anglo-Norman court – would have been any less sophisticated than France in matters theatrical.[60] The surviving Latin music-drama of *Daniel*, though definitely from Beauvais (France), thus may be taken as demonstrating, as well, the sophistication of twelfth-century Latin religious drama – though indoor and Church-performed, not civic – doubtless on the west as well as the east side of the Channel. With its elaborate processions, paralleled and contrasting characters, thematic use of performance areas and actor movement, and (now reconstructed) musical text, *Daniel* has even been successfully recreated, in twentieth-century performance, as a moving and impressive musical, visual, and verbal display.[61] And *Daniel* is also an example – though not a civic one – of twelfth-century "holy" plays celebrating miracles (although Old Testament miracles in this case, most notably Daniel's escape from the lions' den, and not the Christian miracles indicated by Fitz Stephen); examples of others, also in Latin but dealing with the New Testament, are *The Raising of Lazarus* by the possibly English Hilarius (the manuscript is now in the Bibliothèque Nationale), *The Conversion of the Blessed Apostle Paul*, and *How St. Nicholas Freed the Son of Getron*, the last two being from a playbook associated with the monastery of St.-Benoit-sur-Loire at Fleury, France.[62] Thus, given Fitz Stephen's description of London, what we know about the overall sophistication and wealth of late twelfth-century London, the number and wealth of London-area churches, abbeys, and monasteries, and the surviving texts of major twelfth-century religious plays, both in the vernacular and in Latin, from France and probably in some cases from England, we can indeed have a fairly detailed sense of at least some of the kinds of religious performances – some of them perhaps with some kind of civic involvement – which could have been taking place in London in the late twelfth century. Also possible in performance in the city would have been short vernacular plays on individual biblical and hagiographic subjects and more or less of the length and complexity of the single plays, and groupings of plays, which together make up the extant but much later provincial cycles.[63]

As for secular drama: we have only one secular text in England surviving from the twelfth century, although one more from the thirteenth century and one from the early fourteenth century. None of them are from London; but all three at least illustrate some kinds of secular drama – other than folk plays – available elsewhere in England, and so surely also in London, from the late twelfth century on.[64] A Latin comedy, *Babio* (*c.* 1160–85), dealing with an attempted seduction and an accomplished castration (and being perhaps a satiric commentary on the notorious real-life seduction of Heloïse by the subsequently castrated

Abelard), was possibly written for the court – to be read or to be performed – by author/scholar Walter Map, whose patron was Henry II.[65] There is no need to assume that this kind of text would have been limited to the court, given the wealth and sophistication of London's mercantile elite in this period;[66] and we know that, in a later period, this civic elite sponsored indoor play performances for its entertainment (see below, chapters 4 and 5).[67] The East Midland vernacular dialogue *Dame Sirith* (from before *c.* 1272–83) – about a man who bribes an old woman to trick a virtuous wife into accepting him as a lover – is an example of literary work which may have been mimed by a minstrel,[68] or even sometimes have involved a small performance group (of three or four); any performance could have been private or public, non-civic or under community auspices, given the wide appeal of the subject matter and the lack of any special physical performance requirements. Finally, from the early fourteenth century we have, from the north of England, the in-complete *Interludium de Clerico et Puella*,[69] a work in English (despite the title) in which a cleric attempts to get the help of an old woman to se-duce a maiden. The story, as far as we have it, is close to that of *Dame Sirith*, with the same (or increased) performance possibilities (there is no narrated material, only dialogue).[70] Moreover we have surviving French secular dramatic texts, of the twelfth to thirteenth century, dealing with subjects such as wooing, financial trickery, and satire of everyday life;[71] such texts' existence surely indicates (non-surviving) English equiv-alents. Secular drama (other than folk drama), both written and per-formed, certainly was part of both English and French society of the pe-riod, though whether any such drama would have been performed with civic sponsorship in late twelfth-century London – indoors or outdoors, be-fore a civic elite or before a wider public audience[72] – cannot be known.

Certainly London's civic leaders at this period would have been capa-ble of sponsoring theatrical performances, private or public. London's merchants, as noted above, were rich through trade;[73] a number of guilds existed; and Fitz Stephen describes a city with an organized administra-tion, including a system of wards, sheriffs, and other civic leaders.[74] Espe-cially if working with the Church (religious institutions and parishes), London's leaders would have been financially and administratively able to organize theatrical performances, on festive religious or secular occasions, outdoors for a wide community, and certainly also fully capable of inde-pendently sponsoring indoor performances for a civic elite. As the twelfth century changes into the thirteenth and then the fourteenth, we begin to learn more about London's civic theatre: both actual and possible.

CHAPTER 3

London 1200–1410

For the period between 410 and 1200, as we have seen, we are dependent, for our speculations about London civic theatrical performances, on a small number of sources, most of which are general rather than London-focused. We now indeed – since the discovery of Londinium's amphitheatre – can be sure of less about Saxon and Norman London to 1200, in civic theatrical performance terms, than we can be about Roman London; and the situation is not much different for the thirteenth century, especially in relation to plays rather than pageantry. Across Britain as a whole, we have a variety of theatrical and potentially theatrical records for the thirteenth century: a good number of ecclesiastical documents concerned about "inhonesti ludi" on consecrated ground and about members of the clergy going to "spectaculi" (defined in one case as "miracles"); plays/players before royalty; in one case, clerical foolery; Christmas games at Oxford; Robin Hood plays in Scotland; Easter and Christmas plays; a St. Nicholas play.[1] There is, however, no way of determining whether some of these events (especially the ludi) were truly theatrical, or whether any of them were under civic auspices.[2] London, as a major national and international centre in the thirteenth century, increasing its wealth, population, and political influence,[3] must have had games, entertainments, and plays of various kinds, taking place within and without its walls, whether some were under civic auspices or not; but the only two records potentially of plays, disguisings or mummings in London (the latter two entertainment forms involving costume, dancing or mime, and music) are two non-specific prohibitions from the diocese of London, typical of what is found elsewhere in Britain at this time, of "ludi" in consecrated places, especially churchyards and church porches.[4] Were these "ludi" theatrical? – or merely horseplay, physical contests, or other foolery of some sort? They seem certain, in any event, to have not been civic, since the London authorities would hardly have sponsored activities in locations unacceptable to the Church.

Thirteenth-century London clearly would have provided at least growing private employment opportunities for entertainers (fulltimers, or part-timers with other trades as well), who would also have been available for civic purposes. Prelates and nobles, who were increasingly acquiring London town houses for business purposes, would presumably from time to time have hired entertainers, although their own household entourages would doubtless often have included at least musicians.[5] Fitz Stephen in the late twelfth century commented on the lavish spending in London of such visitors;[6] and entertaining would have been a necessary part of their political and business dealings as well as an element of their personal enjoyment of their time in the city. The city's economy continued to grow, as did its population, which has been variously estimated as either *c.* 45,000 or 80,000 or more by 1300: if the latter, London had reached a size it was not to attain again, after the Black Death of 1348, until 1550.[7] Royal administrative offices and courts – including the Exchequer in the late twelfth century – gradually became settled by the mid fourteenth century at Westminster, just up the river from the city, and where the Parliament also regularly met by that time;[8] and also by the mid fourteenth century the Great Wardrobe, a major provisions department for the court, was settled in London, at first in Lombard St. and then near the Blackfriars monastery.[9] Organized and/or recognized craft guilds (largely including religious/social fraternities as part of their structures) multiplied.[10] It would be most surprising if London between 1200 and 1400 had not had extensive theatrical activity, at the civic level as well as at other (religious, commercial, folk) levels.

London's own regular extant series of manuscript records of civic government – preserving some of the city's decisions and acts, and sometimes also the documents upon which these decisions and acts were based – begin in the late thirteenth century, with the first of London's Letter Books: Letter Book A, running 1276–1298,[11] and also Letter Books B and C, running 1276–1312 and 1291–1309 respectively. One of the city's manuscript custumals (books of customs and precedents), the *Liber de Antiquis Legibus*, also dates from this time; and other custumals, compiled later, contain some early material.[12] We might therefore expect, from the late thirteenth century on, to learn from London's own civic records something about civic theatrical performances. Before 1300, however, although the custumals provide some slight information, the Letter Books mainly include debt recognizances and deeds (although C's contents are broader than A's or B's – including, for example, civic ordinances); and they are kept neither consistently nor regularly. And although a number of religious and craft guilds were operative in London by this century,[13] and in later centuries craft guilds' (livery companies') records become key sources of information on London civic drama (as later chapters will demonstrate), no craft guild accounts or meeting minutes – the kinds of guild records most likely to include information on pageantry and entertainments – are extant before the Goldsmiths' in the early fourteenth century.[14] Chronicle histories are the major information sources specifically for London theatrical entertainment history before 1300: providing information, though minimal, on thirteenth-century London civic street pageantry. Unlike England's other cities, London, given its location on the Thames and its proximity to Westminster, where a major royal palace had been located since the time of Edward the Confessor and in whose abbey English kings were regularly crowned from the thirteenth century on,[15] was constantly finding itself, as a civic entity, having to celebrate royal occasions, and to welcome visiting dignitaries from abroad, with ceremonial processions, music, banners, and sometimes also with pageantry of more elaborate visual display. We know an increasing amount about such civic street pageantry from the fourteenth century; but for the thirteenth century we must largely speculate from chroniclers' generalities. An exception to our lack of detailed knowledge of thirteenth-century London civic street pageantry is a 1298 procession by the London Fishmongers, for which we have a description (discussed below) involving portable images of fish and of St. Magnus. A second exception involves records of the London puy, tangentially related to civic theatre (and also discussed below).

From 1300 to 1400, the extant major civic records themselves become greater in number and more detailed, and so begin to be of real use to the theatre historian, although still surpassed as information sources by the chronicles. The city's Letter Books A to I cover the fourteenth century; the city's administrators of London Bridge – across which moved into London many processions welcoming royalty and other dignitaries, and which was often the site therefore of major visual display – kept their own Bridge House series of payment and receipt records which survive from 1381 (although these are overwhelmingly concerned with receipts of rent for Bridge premises and with supplies and labour for Bridge maintenance);[16] and four important London craft guilds/livery companies – the Goldsmiths, Grocers, Mercers, and Merchant Taylors – have fourteenth-century accounts and/or minutes extant.[17] Not all of these civic sources are helpful for telling us about fourteenth-century London theatre; but by examining them and putting the relevant information together with that from other sources such as chronicle histories, ecclesiastical prohibitions, and literary references, we can build an increasingly detailed picture of London civic theatre between 1300 and 1400: a time when flourishing civic theatre in the provinces included the late-fourteenth century beginnings of the great provincial cycle dramas of York and of Coventry.

London itself in the fourteenth century was considerably larger and wealthier than any other English city,[18] although its economy did not advance steadily[19] (the Black Death of 1348, for example, reduced its population probably by about forty per cent[20]). And from the extant records and references we can gather that either the city in general was becoming more theatrically oriented than previously (410–1300), in terms of civic shows, or that the records of and references to civic shows were simply beginning more often to survive, and to provide more detail.

I THE LONDON PUY

The London puy is related only tangentially to London civic theatre but provides a useful thirteenth to fourteenth-century starting point. Puys – urban social/religious societies devoted to the Virgin Mary and to musical composition and performance in her honour, and drawing their membership from royalty, nobility, clerics, prominent civic leaders, and others – were found in a number of French cities in the early Middle Ages, especially in the north; and the statutes of a puy in London, *c.* 1300, have been preserved in a fourteenth-century London custumal, the *Liber Custumarum*.[21] Thanks to a detailed study by Anne Sutton, we now know a great deal about the London puy's likely nature and proceedings.[22] Puys in general arose as part of the eleventh to thirteenth-century cult of the Virgin Mary, throughout Europe, especially flourishing in the thirteenth century; and love of the Virgin became mixed with secular love and social conviviality. A puy would hold an annual song competition involving its members, and also to which minstrels throughout Europe might travel; and play performances (sometimes highly political) could also take place, as in Arras, France, whose puy Sutton argues was most probably the direct inspiration for London's.[23] Wealthy London merchants accustomed to travelling on the Continent would have been familiar with puys; and Edward I himself, before he became king of England (in 1272), had been a judge at an Arras puy competition. London's wealthy and powerful mercantile elite would have had every reason to want to follow European models and to try to establish a puy themselves, in the best elitist, continental, musical and intellectual mode. (The London puy's articles indeed even refer to one purpose of the puy as being to bring renown to London.) The king himself, Sutton suggests, might even have been personally involved.

Puys were, of course, private, not public, groups, although in some cases, Sutton notes, they became closely identified with civic governments; and the London puy also does not seem, from the limited information we have, to have involved itself in theatrical activities, though its founders would certainly have known about such activities on the Continent. Moreover, although having been established only, it seems, in the 1270s, the London puy did not survive long into the fourteenth century. Sutton suggests that the economic and political downturns of the early 1300s made its survival impossible.[24] Nevertheless, although it was not an institution of civic government, nor apparently even a semi-theatrical organization, and did not last for long, its brief existence indicates not only a desire among London's civic elite *c.* 1300 for engagement in social performance but also three aspects of civic London that we will find to be ongoing in the city's genuinely theatrical activities from *c.* 1300 to 1558: a closeness, if not identity, of civic and courtly tastes in types of performance entertainment (not surprisingly, since the great merchants of London were as cosmopolitan as the court itself, and both used and served it in relation to their business purposes); an easy mixing of court and city for social and entertainment purposes (even if only potentially so, with London's puy, since we do not know whether the king or any great lords were actually members); and a tendency of London's civic leaders to see "entertainment" and cultural interests as to be met in part by private institutions, or by civic institutions (such as craft guilds/livery companies), rather than directly by the city itself. This third aspect of London entertainment/culture may be related to civic London's perception also of performance entertainment as potentially (dangerously) political and therefore to be separated from direct civic government presentation where possible. Certainly by the fifteenth century, Caroline Barron has argued, London's leaders were trying to maintain, for the preservation of civic liberties, as distanced as possible a stance from royal politics.[25]

It is always possible, of course, that the London puy – a creation of and for London's civic leaders – might have had, as London's livery companies later did, some general civic responsibilities. Public and private concerns in medieval and early Tudor London, in relation to civic leaders, can almost never be wholly disentangled. The puy, for example, became involved with the late thirteenth-century establishment of a chapel at the Guildhall – the seat of London's civic government.[26] Even without civic responsibilities, however, the London puy is at least a significant case of a civic elite turning to performance – though in this case of music only, apparently not of theatre – for reasons having to do not only with religion and with entertainment but presumably also with politics: its members thus enhancing their prestige and influence both within the city itself and at court, and apparently (from the puy's articles) also hoping to increase the cultural renown of London more generally.

2 MUMMINGS AND DISGUISINGS[27]

From the mid fourteenth century (in both 1334 and 1352[28]), and especially from 1370 on,[29] we find in the city's Letter Books prohibitions against going about at night, in the Christmas season, wearing "faux visage" (a false face) or visors (masks) and entering people's houses to play at dice. In the Christmas season of 1380 citizens are also forbidden to receive such masked individuals in their houses.[30] Such prohibitions are apparently aimed at itinerant Christmas mummings (mumming is specified in 1387[31]): ordinary London inhabitants and/or professional entertainers putting on masks and costumes and going from door to door, performing dances, songs, and mime, and playing at dice for money. The city's concern must have been with nuisance, or with mumming used as a cover for criminal (or other anti-government) activities. Cheating at dice and at other games of chance was a problem in early London (the Letter Books record punishment of such cheaters[32]); and mumming disguise obviously provided excellent opportunities for other crime as well.[33] Such mummings were of course not civic: indeed, given the government's attitude, they might be considered anti-civic, although they were at least communal insofar as they were entertainment for Londoners in general during a festive period.

More formal mummings were, however, a popular form of secular city-sponsored entertainment: at least from the later fourteenth century, when Londoners several times are recorded as having offered them as civic entertainment gifts to please the king. These would have been fairly elaborate displays of costume, probably dance, and music; and the first of which we have a lengthy record also included dice playing. This mumming, described in detail in one chronicle source, was given to the young prince Richard in January 1377, before he became king (on 22 June), at the palace of Kennington in Surrey.[34] London's leaders were clearly trying favourably to impress their future monarch. One hundred and thirty mummers rode at night from Newgate through Cheapside, with music and torches, costumed as forty-eight esquires, forty-eight knights, an emperor, a pope, twenty-four cardinals, and eight or ten legates with "visers nayrs come deblers" (black masks like devils[35]). Providing thus a civic street spectacle as well as being mummers for the prince, they rode through the major London streets to London Bridge and across it to Kennington,[36] where they played at dice with the young Richard so that he would win three gifts ("une pelit," "une cupe," "une anel," i.e., a ball, a cup, a ring, all of gold), and with gifts to be won also by the queen his mother and by the Duke of Lancaster and others.[37] Mummings apparently remained popular with Richard (who may even have had his own mumming troupe[38]) after he became king: for the Mercers' Company records payment of costs for five of their members in relation to a mumming for him in the Christmas season of 1392–93 at the royal palace of Eltham (Kent);[39] at Christmas time 1393–94 Londoners again presented a mumming to him, at Westminster;[40] and the Mercers' accounts record another royal mumming clearly paid for by Londoners (given the Mercers' involvement) in 1395–96, although the Christmas season is not specified.[41] In 1400–01, under Richard's successor Henry IV, Londoners performed a mumming (of twelve aldermen and their sons) at Eltham at Christmas, when the Emperor Manuel II was visiting the court.[42] Given the similar tastes and types of entertainment already noted, of the court and of the city elite, possibly the Christmas 1400 mumming referred to in the records of the Merchant Taylors' Company, in association with the Guildhall, was a civic mumming for the mayor and aldermen and their guests (who might have included some members of the court);[43] but more likely the record concerns a contribution to the Eltham mumming. Performers in these mummings could have been the mumming-givers themselves, and/or professional entertainers if elaborate music and choreography were involved. For every record of a formal mumming that has survived to come down to us, there were doubtless many more unrecorded mummings that took place; and mummings indeed during the reign of Richard II and then again in the early years of Henry VI appear to have become the secular entertainments of choice for special occasions, as discussed below in chapter 6. Clearly they had significant political purpose. Not only could they be given as politically motivated gifts (to royalty, to nobility, to ecclesiastical authorities, to civic leaders), but their subject matter could carry direct or indirect political significance. The apparently loaded dice rolled by the young prince Richard in the early 1377 mumming at Kennington, for example, served not only as a means to provide gifts to the future monarch but also, through the consistent royal winnings they yielded, as a diplomatic suggestion of Richard's rights, skill, and good fortune. The sinister potential of the disguise aspect of mummings, however, as seen at a lower level in the civic prohibitions already noted, existed at the courtly level as well; at Christmas time 1399–1400 a mumming is said to have been planned as a means to the assassination of Henry IV at Windsor.[44] Ian Lancashire has suggested that the mumming dangers made apparent by this plot, and by another against Henry V in 1415, were responsible for what seems to be an absence of mummings – presented by London or by anyone else – at the courts of Henry IV (except for the one already noted, for Manuel II at Christmas 1400–01) and of Henry V.[45]

The popularity of disguisings (i.e., elite mummings) at court preceded the reign of Richard II, just as did the popularity of mummings within the streets and households of London itself. We have records, for example, of court tournament disguisings in London in 1331 and in 1343, and of a play or game of King Arthur at a 1299 London court tournament; and the captive King John of France was treated to a type of Robin Hood disguising (supposed outlaws in green appearing as he passed a forest) as he was led by the Black Prince to London in 1357.[46] Civic presentation of mummings at court (or elsewhere), however, is so far undocumented before 1377, although lack of records is no evidence of the non-existence of such mummings.

3 ROYAL AND OTHER ENTRIES

Thanks largely to writers of chronicles, we have a number of references to and descriptions of street pageantry in London in the thirteenth and especially fourteenth centuries, some of the later descriptions being of considerable length. It appears to have been standard practice in the thirteenth century, on special occasions such as coronations and the welcoming of foreign monarchs, for the city to have decorated a processional route through the streets, with rich cloths hanging from the windows of buildings and, certainly by the mid fourteenth century if not earlier, also with street stages erected to display symbolic figures and scenes. Mechanical devices were also used.

Brief references to entries in all of 1255 (Prince Edward from Gascony on 29 Nov.;[47] Eleanor of Castile, wife of Prince Edward, on 17 Oct.[48]), 1256 (the king and queen of Scotland on 27 August;[49]), and 1258 (the king of Germany on 1 Feb.[50]) mention only very generally that the city was decorated and/or hung with cloths;[51] but two early thirteenth-century chronicle accounts, of the entry of Otto, the visiting Holy Roman Emperor, in 1207 and of Eleanor of Provence, coming to be crowned at Westminster after her marriage to Henry III, in 1236, speak of the city as adorned with amazing devices (1207 – "prodigialibus adinventionibus;"[52] 1236 – "prodigiosis ingeniis et portentis"[53]). Historian John Stow, in his great historical-topographical work, *A Survey of London*, first written in 1598 and using many older manuscript sources, cites and loosely paraphrases Matthew Paris on the 1236 entry, referring to "many Pageants and straunge deuises;"[54] and although the term "pageant" could be used at this time to refer simply to elaborate decorations (for example, banners and images),[55] and "strange devices" is equally broad in possible meanings, something more than hangings does seem to be indicated in Paris's account, especially since hangings are also noted separately. In 1299 we find that for the coronation entry of Margaret of France (married to Edward I on 10 September 1299) two wooden towers were constructed in Cheapside, from which eight outlets discharged wine, and the road was covered with cloths of gold;[56] were these towers the kinds of devices referred to in 1207 and 1236, or were they a new kind of device specially designed to utilize Cheapside's Great (water) Conduit once it had been built *c.* 1245[57]? To celebrate the August 1274 coronation of Edward I and Queen Eleanor, the conduit in Cheapside had itself run with red and white wine;[58] and again it flowed with wine in November 1312 to celebrate the birth of Prince Edward (later to become Edward III).[59] Wine running from water conduits had become a routine element of London entries and other such celebrations, it seems, from the late thirteenth century on.

By the fourteenth century, accounts of civic entries have in all but one early case become more specific and detailed: leaving us to speculate as to whether some of these specifics were also operative in the thirteenth century, when (different) chronicles refer only briefly to entries.[60] London for the entry of Edward II with his new queen Isabel from France, in early 1308, is recorded only as looking like a New Jerusalem, with golden hangings;[61] but for the 24 May 1357 entry of Edward the Black Prince in victory from France, with his prisoners including the French King John, an elaborate constructed device and action in Cheapside is described in some detail in different sources; and we have even more details of entry display by the time of the 1377 coronation entry of Richard II and then his second major entry in 1392, with some information also on the 1382 entry of Anne of Bohemia coming to marry Richard. The 1357 entry included a display in Cheapside, arranged by the Goldsmiths, of two maidens marvellously suspended by cords "in quadam catasta" (in/on a certain cage or scaffold/platform, probably the latter[62]), who scattered gold and silver leaves onto those riding by in the entry procession;[63] and for Richard II's entry there was provided a Cheapside wood-and-canvas tower/castle with maidens (this time four, one in each turret of the tower/castle) blowing gold leaves and scattering imitation gold coins, and a golden angel, on a higher tower in the centre, which leaned down to the king with a gold crown.[64] In 1377 the Cheapside conduit is also specified as painted in various colours and as running with red and white wine. The symbolic meaning of the 1377 display has been much discussed by scholars, without reference to preceding entries such as in 1299 and 1357.[65] A device specified as a "summer-castle" (an elevated structure or movable tower;[66] compare the towers of 1299 and 1377) was provided by the Goldsmiths' Company in Cheapside for the entry of Anne of Bohemia in January 1382; again maidens (this time three), apparently suspended (as in 1357), scattered leaves.[67] And in 1392, after Richard had quarrelled and then reconciled with the city, a second major entry (much discussed in pageantry scholarship today) was provided by London for the king (with his queen), in which, after he had been censed processing (after crossing London Bridge) up Fish St. (in a separate ceremonial display usually ignored in modern analyses of the entry),[68] the Cheapside conduit again ran with wine, a Cheapside tower/castle was again utilized (suspended on cords), gold leaves/coins were again scattered by maidens, an angel and another maiden descended to the king in clouds (a variant of the 1377 angel), and other religious pageants were provided as well at St. Paul's Cathedral (God and angels) and at Temple Bar (a wilderness, St. John the Baptist, wild beasts, another descending angel) as the procession moved out of the city and on towards Westminster.[69] When for other entering dignitaries of the period, as for the child-queen Isabella (age six to seven) coming to her coronation in January 1397 after her 1396 marriage in France to Richard II, we do not have records or accounts of elaborate pageant display, we cannot know whether there was none or whether we simply do not have or have not yet found records.[70] Chroniclers describe what interests them or what fits their writing agenda;[71]

they do not record everything; and we are largely dependent on them for entry information before 1410. They do not provide, for example, any specifics about the 1382 entry of Anne of Bohemia;[72] we know some details about it only because the Goldsmiths' Company, one of only two London craft guilds with extant accounts and/or minutes from before 1390, recorded payments for the Cheapside summer-castle. Nor do they usually interpret the pageantry for us; and Richard Maidstone's account of the king and queen speculating about the meaning of the 1392 Cheapside pageant suggests that interpretation was a major source of interest for the audience.[73]

There is also the disquieting possibility, of course, that when a chronicler makes a brief, formulaic reference to pageants, with no detail, he is simply assuming a pageant norm, without having any actual source for the information; or in some cases he may be reproducing – deliberately or unwittingly – political propaganda.[74] John Hayward's 1599 *Life* of Henry IV, for example, refers to Bolingbroke upon his return to England – which eventually led to the defeat and deposition of Richard II – as having come to London and been entertained by Londoners "with processions and pageants, and diuers other triumphant deuises & shews": most unlikely under the political circumstances. Hayward may have been thinking of Henry's eventual coronation entry.[75] Elaborate pageantry may have been provided for some entries without ever having been recorded; brief references to pageantry on other occasions, in some chronicles, may be formulaic only, without pageants necessarily having been provided. We can, however, at least be sure that musicians would normally have been a part of formal entries: processing and/or located on stationary stages along the entry route; and only musicians – along with the processing civic leaders and their entourages – appear to have been provided at this time for welcomes not of the top level of political importance, such as the return of Richard II from Ireland in 1395, when the Mercers paid for minstrels.[76] Often we have no records except of citizens riding out of the city to meet some notable personage (such as the king himself, a great lord, or a major foreign visitor).[77]

The general routes for major entries were established early. Cheapside appears to have been an essential component of the processional route from early times; and Bolingbroke is said to have deliberately entered London in 1399 through Aldgate, after capturing Richard II and before that monarch's formal deposition, in order to pass through Cheapside.[78] By at least 1357 a monarch or other such important dignitary formally entering the city, except for a coronation, would normally have been met by the mayor and other civic leaders outside the city to the south, have entered in procession with them across London Bridge, and then moved up Bridge St. and (New) Fish St. to Gracechurch St. and to Cornhill, and along Cornhill and Poultry to Cheapside and then to St. Paul's, eventually exiting the city at Ludgate, and moving along Fleet St. and past Temple Bar to proceed to Westminster.[79] For a coronation, the king or queen would spend the night before the entry at the Tower of London (territory of the Crown), and the next day, accompanied by the mayor, would process from the Tower along Tower St., up Mark Lane, and along Fenchurch St. to join the other standard route in Gracechurch St., and on to Cornhill and Cheapside, and eventually Westminster.[80] Certain points along the routes provided special opportunities for pageant display: London Bridge itself, with its gates and drawbridge; the conduit in Cornhill at Gracechurch St. (from the late fourteenth century);[81] the Great Conduit in Cheapside (first built *c.* 1245 and castellated); the conduit at the Standard in Cheapside (by 1395–96, and perhaps much earlier[82]); the Cross (erected *c.* 1296[83]) in Cheapside nearer St. Paul's. By the late fifteenth century new points potentially useful for display had come into existence, with the overhauling and extension of the city's water supply[84] and the building of new conduits, therefore, in Cheapside by Paul's gate, in Cornhill (one conduit half-way between Gracechurch St. and Poultry, and another at Poultry), and in Gracechurch St. itself.[85] Lawrence Manley has written at length of the religious and political symbolic importance of the processional routes;[86] but practical considerations were doubtless also important: for example, establishing the route along the city's widest streets (especially Cheapside), and placing special displays where special street structures were located.[87] Practicality and symbolism, however, could go together. Derek Keene has noted the early (and continuing) importance of Cheapside as the city's most important open space for public display, not only for its width but also for its religious associations specific to London.[88] Early in the thirteenth century a church and a religious house were established on the site of Thomas Becket's *c.* 1118 Cheapside birthplace; and processions between this church and St. Paul's "became an important feature of civic ceremonial."[89] Becket, featured on the city's official seal until the Reformation, had become London's major saint: and, moreover, one who had died opposing the authority of the Crown, thus furnishing a continuing reminder of London's desired and expressed independence – even at times, as in royal entries along Cheapside, of deference to royalty.

From at least 1207 (and perhaps earlier) to 1400, therefore, civic London had developed elaborate forms of street pageantry for important official occasions involving processional entry into the city by native or foreign dignitaries: the decoration (through rich hanging materials, by at least 1207) of the buildings along fixed processional routes, distinctive livery (special ceremonial, identifying garb) for the civic officials riding in the procession, musicians also processing and/or stationary, and, for major entries, constructed stages (the first we definitely know of, two towers, being in 1299), with special displays, at convenient fixed points along the city streets. Much of this display, moreover, had complex symbolic religious and/or political import – probably from the start – beyond its nature simply as lavish spectacle and sound indicating the city's acknowledgment of the importance of the entrant being thus honoured. A water conduit running with wine, for example, had obvious Christian suggestiveness as well as providing celebratory drink for the crowds; a castle would have a variety of potential associations: for example, with the Heavenly City, with the state or political city, with defensive human virtue, with medieval romance, and with the tournament.[90]

Another kind of civic street pageantry, however, was also used on some occasions in London: processions by citizens carrying portable displays. On 19 August 1298 the guild of Fishmongers in procession, according to Stow's *Survey of London*, "passed through the Citie, hauing amongest other Pageants and shews, foure Sturgeons guilt, caried on four horses: then foure Salmons of silver on foure horses, and after them six & fortie armed knights riding on horses, made like Luces of the sea, and then one representing Saint *Magnes*, because it was vpon S. *Magnes* day, with a thousand horsemen, &c."[91] *The Chronicle of Dunmow*, Stow's source, adds that the Fishmongers' procession was to Leadenhall,[92] although where it began is not specified; it may have begun in Cheapside, and have moved along Cheapside to Poultry, along Poultry to Cornhill, and along Cornhill to Leadenhall at the intersection of Cornhill and Gracechurch St., or it may have begun at St. Magnus Martyr church, at London Bridge, and have moved up Bridge St. and Gracechurch St. to Leadenhall.[93] The occasion was the celebration of a military victory by Edward I over the Scots; and the Fishmongers in celebration of Edward also celebrated themselves – their importance achieved through their trade – by processing and by carrying emblems which both had religious significance and were associated with their craft. (Luces became a part of the company's later coat of arms.) Stow tells us that other Londoners also made shows according to their various trades, but provides no further details; presumably the Fishmongers' display was the most extensive. Just over fourteen years later a similar celebration marked the birth of Prince Edward, the Fishmongers, this time with a portable ship pageant (i.e., with a pageant again both with religious meaning and related to their trade; their patron saint was St. Peter), again processing through the city, along Cheapside, to meet the queen at Westminster, and then accompanying her back through the city to see her off on her way to Canterbury via the royal palace at Eltham.[94] The celebratory pattern would appear to have been that a major formal entry into the city, with the honoured dignitary riding in a procession also featuring major religious and other political figures – such as invariably the mayor – would involve stationary decorations and pageant displays; and a major celebration which did not involve the formal entry of a non-city dignitary in procession, or which accompanied a dignitary simply travelling through the city, would involve portable pageants and/or other in-motion display – if any such display – only. Such portable display by the late fifteenth century appears to have become limited to specific kinds of civic celebrations: the Lord Mayor's Show, the Midsummer Watch, and formal city entries by water.

As has routinely been noted by researchers, the kinds of displays involved in early London civic street pageantry, both stationary and moving, are significantly like the displays we find in the provincial religious drama of the fifteenth century.[95] Towers, suspension devices, angels, pageant ships, castles: all are to be found, with symbolic religious and sometimes trade meaning as well as entertainment value, in plays such as the York cycle (begun in the late fourteenth century but the extant manuscript of which is fifteenth century), *The Castle of Perseverance* (1397–1440), and the Digby *Mary Magdalene* (1480–1520).[96] London clearly had considerable scenic theatrical expertise, certainly by the mid fourteenth century and probably well before then, to be linked both to the needs of the court (with its lavish displays) when in the vicinity of London and potentially to London's own large-scale religious drama of the late fourteenth and early fifteenth centuries (and perhaps of the twelfth and thirteenth centuries as well), the Clerkenwell/Skinners' Well play, which is discussed below. Moreover, with its emphasis on civic entry display, London had differentiated itself from the provincial cities, which did not have London's geographical closeness to Westminster and the court. On an ongoing basis the streets of medieval London had

become in part the equivalent of the amphitheatre of Roman times –
the major venue for civic religious and political display.[97]

4 THE MIDSUMMER WATCH: BEGINNINGS

At the beginning of the sixteenth century in London, until the 1540s, a
major annual civic theatrical occasion was the Midsummer Watch: a
procession provided by the city and its livery companies along a defined
route through the city (Cheapside, Poultry, Cornhill, Aldgate St.,
Fenchurch St., Gracechurch St., and back along Cornhill, Poultry, and
Cheapside[98]) of armed men, light-bearers, mechanical giants, musicians,
devils, and wood and canvas pageants carried by porters, on the eves
through to the early mornings of the religious feasts of St. John Baptist
(24 June) and Sts. Peter and Paul (29 June). The Watch is best known
today from historian John Stow's 1598 nostalgic description of it, in his
Survey of London, as he remembered it from his boyhood years,[99] and –
as a largely sixteenth-century theatrical phenomenon – is the subject of
a later chapter. When, however, did the Watch begin to be a major occasion in London civic theatre?

The Midsummer Watch originated in part as an ordinary security
measure and in part, it seems, as a military muster.[100] In 1181 the Assize
of Arms had set out requirements, according to rank and wealth, for
free men to own arms for use, if necessary, in national defence;[101] and in
1252 and 1253 Henry III, for the preservation of civic peace, had ordered summer season watches to be kept in cities (and watches in
London probably much pre-dated this order[102]) and had linked them in
his orders with the Assize of Arms.[103] Midsummer – given its traditions
of folk celebration – would have been a time, in any case, especially requiring attention to civic security[104] (though early London civic records
suggest the Christmas season to have had more potential in the way of
disorder than midsummer[105]). Then, in 1285, came the Statute of
Winchester, which confirmed watch provisions and also required towns
throughout England to view citizens' arms twice a year, to ensure ongoing ability to provide soldiers in time of war.[106] (The statute continued
to be reconfirmed, into the sixteenth century.[107]) In London the requirements seem at some point(s) to have become combined at midsummer, along with midsummer folk celebrations: for in the 1540s
London could not on its own cancel all elements – even when providing regular watchmen – of what had by then become a major, two-
night show of both military strength and celebratory theatrical

display. Cancellation required the permission of the king.[108] As early as 1379 the Watch is said to be for "lonur mes*sieur* le Roi" as well as for the honour of the city: although the reference could be simply to display which would cause respect for the king, as well as for the city, among any (especially foreign) dignitaries watching it or hearing about it.[109]

In London, civic records of ordinary security watches, at the gates above all but also often involving the streets and walls, exist from as early as the late thirteenth century when the Letter Books begin.[110] Such watches became especially necessary at times of political unrest, of holiday (above all in the Christmas season), and when Parliament was in session at Westminster; but the earliest extant record of a London watch at midsummer that indicates any kind of special decorative display is from 1378.[111] City Letter Book H contains a bill sent to each alderman on 16 June, in that year, commanding that each city ward provide for the eves of St. John Baptist and Sts. Peter and Paul armed men dressed in red and white; and the marchers who assembled in Smithfield on midsummer eve and moved through the city included light-bearers carrying cresset lights (fires burning in iron pans mounted on poles) and men carrying lances decorated in various ways: white with red stars, white with red wreaths, black with white stars, all red only, all white only.[112] Clearly the Watch in or by 1378 involved decorative visual display, i.e., was more than a security/military matter.[113] Other pre-1400 Watch records, however, from the city's Letter Books in 1379, 1384, 1385, 1386, and 1387, seem to indicate nothing visually special beyond, in some instances (1379, 1385, 1386), a stipulation as to red and white dress, with cresset lights also specified again in 1379, 1384, and 1386.[114] By at least 1384 there are two groups of watchmen: those who watch within the wards and those who accompany the mayor and aldermen as they march through the city, although in 1378 and 1379 only the marchers appear to be discussed, and in 1387, only the ward watchmen.[115] Watch records then cease, to 1400. Presumably there is still a Watch, but it is no longer being recorded in the Letter Books (perhaps because it has become routine? – or because it is being recorded elsewhere?). A Grocers' Company payment of 13s 4d for "port*ou*rs" may or may not be related to the 1386 Watch; it is listed in the Grocers' accounts between a Watch expense (for lights) and a non-Watch expense,[116] and in the sixteenth century Midsummer Watch porters carried sometimes special banners, sometimes large portable wood and canvas pageants, through the streets. Given the early date, however, of this record, and apparently no further Watch records of porters until the later fifteenth century,[117] a

Watch porters expense here is unlikely. The 1384 and 1387 records (the least specific of the group) say that the Watch directives are according to "launciene custume" (the quotation is from 1384) of the city; but we do not know what was considered traditional about the Watch by this time, or from what date. The records also refer not only to the honour and profit of the city (1384, 1385, 1386) and to its security (1378, 1386, 1387), but also, as noted above, to the honour of the king (1379) and, in 1406, to his pleasure.[118]

According to the available evidence, therefore, an originally functional civic watch at midsummer had become also decorative and processional in or by 1378, and red and white dress and cresset lights may have become standard then or earlier. We do not know, however, whether the 1378 decorative lances were unique in the late fourteenth century, for one special occasion only (1378, for example, provided the first normal midsummer of Richard II's reign, given the unusually heavy military security at his accession in summer 1377), or whether they may have indicated a standard customarily followed for special occasions earlier or even regularly at midsummer thereafter.[119] They at least are unlikely to have been customary in 1378, since they had to be described in detail in the bill; but, once described, possibly they were thereafter expected. It may be significant that 22 June – the day before Midsummer Eve – was Richard's accession date, and the beginning therefore of the new regnal year from 1377 to 1399.[120] As for the Grocers' 1386 porters: it is impossible to say whether they did belong to the Watch or, if they did, what they might have been carrying in 1386.

5 THE LORD MAYOR'S SHOW: BEGINNINGS

Traditionally the term Lord Mayor's Show has been used for the London ceremonies surrounding the oath-taking of the annually-elected new mayor before the monarch, or before the representatives of the monarch, the Barons of the Exchequer, at Westminster, only from *c.* 1535: when records, it was believed, first showed the use of canvas-and-wood portable pageants in the processions from the Guildhall to the waterside, where the mayor took a barge to go up the river to Westminster, and/or in the processions from the waterside back to the Guildhall, when the mayor returned by water to the city from the Westminster presentation. The fifteenth or sixteenth-century beginnings of the Show are the topic of chapter 10; but it is important to recognize here that the mayor's oath-taking journey to Westminster had been a civic ceremony – though without theatrical accompaniments – from very early times, involving elaborate dress, formal processing, and (though perhaps not at the start) musicians. The 1215 charter given to London by King John required London's newly chosen mayor to be sworn, after his selection, to the king or his representative; and the location of Westminster was specified in 1253.[121] Given his and his city's economic and political status, the mayor (whose office developed in the late twelfth and early thirteenth centuries[122]) would doubtless never have gone informally to Westminster to take his oath, although the costs of the occasion, and therefore presumably the extent of the ceremonial, appear to have developed gradually in the late thirteenth and early fourteenth centuries;[123] and although the earliest civic records provide no information on elaboration of processing, once in the fourteenth century the livery companies' extant records begin – since the companies provided much of the mayor's inauguration ceremonial, especially for their own member mayors – in 1369 the Goldsmiths' records show a payment for minstrels at the installation "riding" (as it was called) of a Goldsmith mayor, and again in 1377 (a Grocer mayor) and in 1388 (another Goldsmith).[124] In earlier times (late thirteenth and early fourteenth centuries) the mayor appears to have gone to Westminster either on foot by land or on a boat by water,[125] but by the late fourteenth century the event appears to have routinely taken place on land and on horseback. In 1378 Letter Book H provides an order for every alderman to ride with the mayor from the Guildhall to Westminster, dressed in scarlet and white, on the usual presentation day (29 October, the day after the feast of Sts. Simon and Jude).[126] In the 1390s the records of all of the Grocers, Mercers, and Merchant Taylors – the latter two companies with significant accounts and/or minutes not surviving from before that decade – show payments for minstrels on the mayor's riding to Westminster,[127] and without regard to the specific company membership of the mayor. The route was from the Guildhall through Cheapside to Newgate and along Fleet St.[128] Before the late fifteenth century, however, there appears to have been no special display involved beyond banners and livery dress, with music; and the mayor's inauguration ceremonial is therefore noted here only to provide the starting point for discussion in chapter 10 of its fifteenth-century theatrical elaboration. The processional inauguration journey to Westminster becoming regularly made by water, from the mid fifteenth century, is also discussed below, in chapter 8.[129]

Similarly the sheriffs, elected each 21 September (from the early fourteenth century to the early sixteenth century)[130] and sworn into office at the Guildhall on 28 September, were presented normally at Westminster every 30 September; and music and some elaborate display, at least of clothing, appears to have been the norm for their procession as well: which, like the mayor's, had apparently become regularly a horseback procession by the late fourteenth century. In the 1380s the Grocers pay for minstrels to accompany a Grocer sheriff;[131] and the Goldsmiths perhaps do so as well.[132] In 1389 the city decided that the sheriffs should no longer ride to Westminster but, as a cost-cutting measure, should always go by water or on foot;[133] the order may not have been finally established, however, or else it was ignored intermittently or entirely, as in 1422 the records of the Brewers' Company clearly refer to the sheriffs as though they were intending, at least in that year, to ride to their Westminster presentation on horseback.[134] Minstrels were not a cut cost; the Mercers' records show payments for minstrels to accompany Mercer sheriffs in all of 1391, 1393, and 1396, and the Grocers', for minstrels for a Grocer sheriff in 1402.[135] The sheriffs' procession to Westminster does not appear, however, ever to have become a theatrical show.[136]

Although, as already noted, there are no pre-1400 records of a mayor's or sheriffs' Westminster procession involving any display beyond special livery dress, banners, and minstrels, the records do show – given the 1389 order – that even before 1400 there was significant expenditure for the display involved in each riding: to the extent that the 1389 attempt was made to cut down on the expenditures involved in the sheriffs' presentations.[137] This uneasy alternation between spending money on display, and trying to save money, is a continuing alternation in the ceremonial surrounding the inaugurations of London mayors and sheriffs right up to 1558 (see below, chapter 10) and prevents any assumption of a gradual and regular increase in mayoral inauguration ceremonial from the thirteenth century to the accession of Elizabeth I.

6 THE CLERKENWELL/SKINNERS' WELL PLAY

Perhaps most significantly of all, for fourteenth-century London civic theatre, in both the early and the late fourteenth century – and perhaps therefore throughout – London appears to have had outdoor religious plays being performed just beyond its walls, to the northwest, in Clerkenwell.[138] Fitz Stephen in the late twelfth century comments on this area as highly popular with students and young men of the city "who go out on summer evenings to take the air;"[139] it was just to the north of Smithfield (with its cattle market) and of the priory of

St. Bartholomew (with its annual three-day late-August fair). Legal records have survived dealing with a complaint by the prioress of St. Mary Clerkenwell (a nunnery established in the twelfth century) *c.* 1300–01 that audiences for "miracles et lutes" there were trampling on priory crops, hedges, and ditches.[140] (The "lutes" were wrestling matches: a popular, continuing activity in the area right through to 1558.[141]) These "miracles" in another document are apparently called "ludos," and so may have been miracle plays of some kind.[142] Were they even perhaps the descendants of the late twelfth-century holy plays of London, praised by Fitz Stephen, of miracles and the sufferings of martyrs?

By the late fourteenth century, a religious play at Clerkenwell/ Skinners' Well (the two wells were close together and the two names, at least by this time, appear to have been used interchangeably to indicate the same location[143]) seems to have been a major, perhaps annual or at least periodically recurring spectacle, taking place over several days and before audiences including royalty and nobility.[144] In 1384, 1390, and 1391 (the late fourteenth-century years for which we have references to or records of performance), the performance by London's parish and other clerks (the "other" providing a wide range indeed of possible per- formers and supporters) was apparently of a "play *of the Passion of our Lord and the Creation of the World*" (as it is called in a record of a royal re- ward paid for the 1390 performance), thus combining Old and New Testament material, and was presented over three to five days in sum- mer.[145] Richard II and his queen apparently attended at least the 1390 performance. In 1409 it was also a multi-day summer event (four or eight days, but probably four), dealing with the history of the world from Creation to Judgment, and watched by the "most part of the no- bles and gentles of England," including Henry IV.[146] This would seem to have been a major biblical drama or cycle, in line with the continen- tal practice (as might be expected in London) of multi-day performance of large-scale religious plays, rather than in line with the apparent English provincial norm (despite Chester in the sixteenth century) of single-day cycle performance.[147] In 1385 it was apparently also scheduled to be per- formed; but on 12 August the city prohibited it, along with wrestlings and any other play, pending receipt of news of the king's (military) do- ings (in Scotland).[148] The city was in fear of a military invasion by the French.[149] The performances in 1385 (intended) following 1384, and 1391 following 1390, suggest that the play was an annual event; but no record or reference seems to refer to it as such until Stow's *Survey* two hundred years later.[150]

There are no records of or references to any Clerkenwell/Skinners' Well plays between 1300-01 (the recording of the prioress's complaint about "miracles et lutes") and 1384 (when a Clerkenwell/Skinners' Well play is noted in two chronicles); had the late fourteenth-century play developed or continued from the miracles that so annoyed the prioress, and thus been a sporadic or more-or-less continuing event over the eighty-three intervening years? Might it too thus even be linked to Fitz Stephen's late twelfth-century "holy" plays?[151] Some kind of tradition of performance at Clerkenwell/Skinners' Well, at the least, seems likely. We might have expected at least one chronicler to have noted a performance of a major biblical play, if any had existed, during 1300–83; but, as we have seen in relation to London's street pageantry, the chroniclers were neither consistent nor methodical in what they recorded; and other large dramatic spectacles – the Corpus Christi cycles – in some provincial towns continued over a period of some two hundred years (late fourteenth century to late sixteenth century, for example, in York and in Coventry[152]), so that such a continuing play, though not necessarily annual or even regularly recurring throughout the period, would not have been unusual in itself, although beginning in London – an urban centre much larger and wealthier than the provincial towns – some seventy-five years earlier than in the provinces. Chroniclers, normally interested in the unusual rather than in the routine, might have recorded only performances out of the ordinary in some way: perhaps when especially elaborated, and/or when attended by royalty, in the late fourteenth and early fifteenth centuries. If such a play had indeed begun in some form(s) *c.* 1300, or even earlier, it would not have been in part inspired – as has sometimes been suggested for the provincial cycles – by the Church's establishment in the early fourteenth century of the Feast of Corpus Christi,[153] although Corpus Christi could still have influenced its development.[154] If this early, it could itself have influenced the development of the provincial cycles.[155] On the other hand, the play noted in the 1380s may have begun only in the late fourteenth century, like the cycle plays of York and of Coventry, and have been either sporadic (and recorded when it took place) or regular (and recorded only at times of special elaboration); or it may have begun earlier in some form but have become elaborated – and recorded – only in the late fourteenth century.[156]

Although there are several Clerkenwell/Skinners' Well play performances recorded in the late fourteenth century, only the 1409 performance is recorded in the early fifteenth; and the chronicles seem to imply that it is then an unusual event. After 1409, references to it cease, even though the number of surviving chronicles in which one might expect to find such references increases, as do the number of surviving London civic manuscripts and the extent of London civic record-keeping in general. Presumably the play no longer existed, at least in any major form.[157] It thus ended some one hundred and fifty years before similarly large-scale biblical plays in York and in Coventry ended. Why? And why have no other records or any texts of the Clerkenwell play survived?

The answer may lie in part in the play's auspices, for it has not been recorded as organized, even in part, by the city government itself (unlike cycles in cities such as York). London-area parish and other clerks performed it just outside London, presumably with the support of at least some of London's many parishes;[158] and given its high profile by at least the 1390s, the clerks seem unlikely (at least then) to have operated alone, and perhaps had ecclesiastical – rather than civic – sponsorship beyond the parish level. Besides the priory of St. Mary Clerkenwell (a nunnery possibly including also a group of resident brothers), Clerkenwell was the site from the early twelfth century of the priory of St. John, headquarters of the Knights Hospitaller in England: a wealthy religious house with considerable financial and political power in England.[159] Also, as already noted, just to the south, from the early twelfth century, lay the priory of St. Bartholomew, which held a three-day fair every August (from St. Bartholomew's eve, the 23rd).[160] Did St. John's decide to make its mark in England in part by sponsoring, from some point in time, summer performances of major religious plays for London's and Westminster's politically and commercially important audiences? Was it perhaps competing or cooperating with St. Bartholomew's? Or might St. Bartholomew's itself have taken a play sponsorship initiative, for ongoing or intermittent biblical performances in conjunction with (though not always at the same time as), or as a religious equivalent to, its commercial fair?[161] London may thus not have needed, unlike provincial towns such as York, to become involved in major religious drama itself. Not only did it have more parishes (both wealthy and otherwise) than any provincial town, but also major religious institutions established in and around London, because of its unique position in England in terms of wealth, population size, and relationship with the Crown, might have eliminated, through their own initiatives, the need for any direct involvement in religious theatre by the city government. The play might then have ended when the religious institution(s) involved became uninterested, for whatever reasons, in further sponsorship, and London already had its theatrical hands full with the handling – unlike provincial cities – of frequent royal entries and of other ridings and entertainments involving the court. The priory of St. John, for example, was decreasing in membership by the later fourteenth century,[162] and in 1381 was burned down in the Peasants' Revolt, although it remained a strong force in English political life. Its treasures lost in the Revolt were returned to it by Richard II in 1393,[163] and it had been rebuilt at least in part by 1399, when Bolingbroke stayed there briefly after his taking of Richard at Flint Castle and before the deposition of Richard and his own accession to the throne.[164] (He was perhaps there again in 1409 for the Clerkenwell play.[165]) The priory of St. Bartholomew was in financial trouble in 1409 and following years.[166] Or perhaps the play's supporters – whoever they were – dropped their involvement because the city itself became nervous over the gatherings of large audiences in one place (royal entries, for example, spread audiences out, and the livery companies lined the streets partly as a form of crowd control): since London was so much larger than cities such as York and Coventry,[167] and so much more appealing an object of attack, because of its wealth, power, and proximity to Westminster, to mobs moving – as in the 1381 Peasants' Revolt – against the Crown or other authorities.[168] Perhaps the city and/or the play's sponsors – because of London's ever-increasing wealth and size – simply no longer needed (unlike provincial towns such as York) the religious, political, or commercial "draw" of a major play/cycle performance.[169] Perhaps the craft guilds, increasing in numbers and in strength, were causing a refocusing of performance interests in the city.[170] Lollard sentiment in London has also been suggested as a cause of the play's demise.[171]

Perhaps no text(s) and few records of the Clerkenwell/Skinners' Well play have survived, then, because, held in the hands of parish clerks or of a priory, the text(s) and most records eventually became victims of Lollardry or, eventually, of the destructive anti-Catholicism of the English Reformation.[172] Or perhaps, for other reasons, they simply became unwanted and discarded. But also the Clerkenwell/Skinners' Well play may have begun well before the four provincial cycles whose texts have survived; and in any case, whenever it began, it apparently ended before any one of the surviving manuscripts of the provincial cycles was written. Being both early, and probably not developed (at least directly) by the city itself, it would thus have been much less likely than the provincial cycles to have had any of its details included in the city's own records manuscripts (which also had not become extensive by the early fifteenth century); and any play text(s) would have had to survive from about forty to fifty years before the date from which we have any surviving text of a provincial cycle.[173]

But civic London might also, of course, have had, after all, a cooperative or indirect hand in the Clerkenwell/Skinners' Well play to 1409. A close association existed between St. John's Priory, for example, dedicated to St. John Baptist, and the powerful London guild of Merchant Taylors (then simply the Tailors) with its religious fraternity devoted to St. John Baptist. In the fourteenth century the fraternity was admitted to confraternity with the Priory, eligible to hold and to participate in religious services at St. John's;[174] and the Merchant Taylors were also closely associated with the court, at this time having kings – for example, both Henry IV and Henry V – as members.[175] Meanwhile the guild's yeomanry – of Merchant Taylor members not (yet) advanced to the company's senior ranks – held at St. John's Priory their own annual religious service on 29 August, the day commemorating the beheading of St. John Baptist.[176] It may be significant that the Clerkenwell play in the late fourteenth and early fifteenth centuries appears normally to have been held between the two days in the year – 24 June and 29 August – commemorating St. John Baptist: on 29 August in 1384 and after 24 August (St. Bartholomew's Day) in 1390, intended for some time after 12 August in 1385, and apparently in mid to late July in 1391 and 1409.[177] Through its fraternity, the Merchant Taylors' guild secured both prestige and eventually wealth,[178] along with a connection with Clerkenwell through St. John's Priory.[179] The company would have been ideally positioned for involvement in the Clerkenwell/Skinners' Well play. Meanwhile the Parish Clerks' Company, probably in existence at this time though not yet incorporated by charter,[180] was closely associated with London's civic government at Guildhall at least by the mid fifteenth century: holding its religious services in the chapel there.[181] How far might the London civic government have been indirectly involved in the Clerkenwell/Skinners' Well play through the Merchant Taylors and/or the Parish Clerks? A link with the Skinners' Company is also possible, given Stow's statement that Skinners' Well was so named for the London Skinners who at one time yearly performed scriptural plays there.[182] Stow is usually assumed by modern theatre historians to have been wrong or confused in citing the Skinners; but perhaps the Skinners were, after all, originally involved in Clerkenwell/Skinners' Well drama, but with their contributions turning at some point before the 1390s into their annual Corpus Christi procession through London: a procession which is noted in chapter 6.[183] (This procession continued into the six-teenth century but was suppressed at the Reformation.[184]) The early Skinners' Company, with its religious fraternity of Corpus Christi, also had court ties through royal and noble members.[185]

Different scenarios can be posited to link the Clerkenwell/Skinners' Well play with St. John's, with St. Bartholomew's, with the Parish Clerks only (in conjunction with their parishes), with the city indirectly via the Merchant Taylors, Parish Clerks and/or Skinners, or with some combi-nation of these elements. Lack of information leaves us with a number of different possibilities. Most significantly, however, the city does not appear – from the references and records we have – to have exerted any kind of direct authority in the running of what was apparently, at least in the late fourteenth century and either on a recurring basis or on sev-eral special occasions, a major performance event held at London; and when the city prohibited the play for 1385, it seems from the wording of the prohibition that the performers would have been capable of pro-ceeding without any city government support. It should be noted that the prohibition also perhaps refers to (an)other major play(s) also being performed in London in the 1380s, in that it covers not only the Clerkenwell/Skinners' Well event but also any other such play:[186] al-though perhaps the city was simply making sure that the Clerkenwell/ Skinners' Well play was not performed, despite the prohibition, in the guise of some other dramatic activity or in some other location. A play of St. Katherine, for example, which a chronicle tells us was performed in London in 1392–93,[187] could have been – though need not have been – a recurring rather than a one-time-only event: presented, for example, by a church or by a religious or civic guild with St. Katherine as its pa-tron saint, perhaps on her day (25 November).[188] And Old Testament plays may have been performed on a recurring basis – though not un-der civic auspices – at Christmas time at St. Paul's or in its vicinity; in 1378 "the Scholars of *Paul's* School" are said to have petitioned the king to prohibit other, "unexpert People" from competing with them in this respect. Indeed, if the Clerkenwell/Skinners' Well play began only shortly before our first 1380s records of it, it could itself have been the initially "unexpert" competition objected to by the Paul's scholars: although the different time of year involved makes this possibility less likely than it otherwise would be.[189] The 1378 petition may, however, be fictitious; Robert Dodsley mentions it in his 1744 *Select Collection of Old English Plays*, but gives no source, and to date it has not been found elsewhere.[190]

London, then, in the Clerkenwell/Skinners' Well play, regularly or occasionally, over a period of some twenty-five years (1384–1409) did have an equivalent to the provincial cycle dramas: beginning perhaps earlier (possibly even originating in some form[s] in the twelfth century, and changing over the years) and certainly, at least as a major event, ending much earlier (over one hundred and fifty years before the ending of all of the Chester, Coventry, Wakefield, and York cycles). The play's auspices may have been ecclesiastical and/or guild (religious guild and/or craft guild), with or without some city involvement as well; the city may have been able to rely wholly or partly on other institutions for what elsewhere of necessity was civic drama.[191] The Clerkenwell/Skinners' Well play may have begun as separate plays by one or more groups, or as a long biblical drama or cycle from the start (whenever its start); and it may have had different relationships with the city – and with royal audiences – over its performance period, however long or short that period may have been.

Who acted in the Clerkenwell/Skinners' Well play? The London-area parish and other clerks appear to have been the actors; did they manage the acting alone, and perhaps with other volunteers,[192] or with professional performers also hired for major roles? Whichever was the case, and at whatever time periods, perhaps significantly it is immediately after the end of records of the Clerkenwell play, in the early fifteenth century, that London livery company records begin to indicate the regular hiring of performers to present plays in company halls at company feasts: such feast-time plays being the subject of the next chapter. Did small groups of clerks decide to continue their performances in new ways? Or had they – or others – always been available for such kinds of performance, and were they now being hired – or was their hiring simply now at last being recorded – as companies (also gradually now becoming incorporated by royal charters) began to acquire halls in which to hold their communal celebrations and to keep their records?[193] A reference has survived to the actors of London playing before the abbot and convent at Westminster on the feasts of St. Peter and St. Edward in 1374–75;[194] were these clerks? Small groups of clerks may have begun to spend a considerable amount of their time performing in London, both before the ending of the major Clerkenwell play and especially after its demise. London, after all, given its size, wealth, and political influence, was fertile ground for those seeking to profit from entertainments both for a small elite and for a broad popular audience.

Outdoor civic or civic-like drama in London – the Clerkenwell/Skinners' Well play – appears in any event to have changed to private indoor civic drama in the early fifteenth century: the latter involving mixed private/civic institutions – the livery companies – entertaining their own members and guests, including royalty and nobility, at company feasts. London's civic leaders from *c.* 1410 appear to have focused on street pageantry as civic theatre for the public at large, while plays were relegated to the internal festivities of the livery companies, to which all London freemen – citizens – perforce by this time belonged, and whose indoor play performances were therefore civic theatre of a different sort.

7 COURT INFLUENCES

The English court, despite the cautious and sometimes tense relations between itself and the city, was obviously a major influence upon London's civic theatre: for although from Anglo-Saxon times through to 1558 (and beyond) the court was a peripatetic enterprise, the Crown having a number of palaces, in different geographical locations in England, among which it moved around as the immediate circumstances dictated, the palace at Westminster was just a short journey by land or by water up the Thames from London and had a special status with the Crown from its beginnings. As has already been noted, by the fourteenth century many of the administrative and legal functions of the Crown had become based at Westminster; and otherwise London's size and economic power also exerted a magnetic force on royalty and nobility. Other royal palaces were also near London: for example, Eltham, Kennington, and Windsor. London, unlike other English cities, thus continually experienced the court: a major reason for the development of its civic theatre in somewhat different directions from those taken in the provinces. The street pageantry of royal entries – financially demanding and occurring at unpredictable intervals – was major civic theatre in London as nowhere else in England; and lower-level ridings into and through the city by lesser dignitaries, or by the king, queen, or great nobles on lesser occasions, also often required citizen attention and participation. The London's Lord Mayor's Show grew out of the requirement that the mayor take his oath of office before the king at Westminster, and by the seventeenth century was to have developed theatrically, beyond mayoral inauguration shows elsewhere, in part as a competitive response to royal entry display of necessity focused on the Crown. The Midsummer Watch, as discussed in chapter 9, by the late fifteenth century was to have developed in part as a diplomatic tool of the Crown, while London fought in the early sixteenth century to maintain the Watch as an expression of civic power and independence. Mummings under both Richard II and Henry VI appear to have become civic theatrical art in response to special monarchical interest. Part of the impetus behind the founding of the London puy was a desire to emulate continental models of such societies, which included royal members. Finally the great Clerkenwell/Skinners' Well play may have had its start, or an important push along the way, in its sponsors' desire, at least in part, to attract and to make an impression on a courtly and even royal audience: an audience it certainly found, at the least, in 1390 and in 1409.

Courtly theatrical forms thus also must have been a major influence themselves on London civic theatre. Courtly tournaments, numerously recorded in the chronicles in the fourteenth century and frequently involving costumed role-playing, sometimes took place in Smithfield (as in 1343 when knights dressed as the pope and twelve cardinals[195]) and in Cheapside (as in 1362 when challengers represented the Seven Deadly Sins[196]), as well as in the near-vicinity of the city (as at Stepney in 1309[197]). Edward III built a special location in Cheapside *c.* 1331 from which royalty and nobility could watch jousts and shows; and in the 1390s two lords jousted on London Bridge.[198] The costumed role-playing and general spectacle must have directly influenced London's civic theatrical display.[199] Important Londoners were regularly invited to court banquets and other events where they would experience court entertainments, musical and theatrical. When London in turn – the civic government itself or its most influential livery companies – held civic banquets at which it feasted royalty, nobility, visiting dignitaries from abroad, and important Crown administrators, it must have provided similar entertainments. Use by the city and by the court often of the same entertainers (as Part II, chapters 4 to 6, will demonstrate for the fifteenth and sixteenth centuries), would have furthered the influence of court tastes upon civic (and vice versa): tastes inevitably already in part similar through the international sophistication of the London merchants whose travels abroad brought them into contact with the same continental entertainment practices affecting the court.

Court and city, in short, were inevitably as intertwined in theatrical interests as they were in political and economic interests: sometimes cooperating, sometimes competing, always affected by one another. Royal and other entries provide perhaps the clearest example: sometimes or usually mandated by the Crown, devised and paid for largely by the city, and creating formal, theatrical, highly political occasions visibly uniting city and court in processional display, with the city offering courteous welcome (homage in the case of the monarch and his family) to the entering dignitary and "inviting" him/her within its walls. The mayor, sheriffs, and aldermen would ride (or sometimes go by boat or barge) out of the city to meet the approaching dignitary, to formally accompany him/her in procession; s/he thus did not enter without visual city acceptance.[200] Royal status and civic status were diplomatically balanced; each side could see itself, as it wished, as the principal in the process. Such diplomatic manoeuvres are also significantly suggested in a three-day 1359 tournament in London in which Edward III with four sons and nineteen noblemen held the field dressed as London's mayor and aldermen.[201]

Also important is a 23 September 1390 civic order for a special city watch to be kept during upcoming (court) revels and jousts:[202] certainly a preview of the city's concern with public order, in relation to theatre, in the early sixteenth century and beyond, and its concern as well with the court's interest in theatrical entertainment not only at the court itself but also within the city.

SUMMARY

By the start of the fifteenth century, London was a city full of theatrical and potentially theatrical activity, a significant amount of which was definitely or possibly civic. Although the London puy had both risen and fallen quietly *c.* 1300, mummings and disguisings as city gifts to royalty (and perhaps also on civic occasions) were being recorded by the second half of the fourteenth century; elaborate civic street pageantry, both stationary and portable, was being used on various kinds of formal celebratory occasions such as coronations, visits by foreign monarchs, and the birth of an heir to the throne; the Watch at midsummer, an event by now apparently combining security needs, perhaps muster requirements (these appear to have been involved at least by the sixteenth century), and civic celebration, had taken on an element of decorative visual display, on either a special-occasion basis or a more regular basis; the new mayor and sheriffs rode annually to Westminster, for presentation to the Crown, with livery display and music which, for the mayor, by the end of the next century would develop into a theatrical show; and a regular or occasional religious play at Clerkenwell/Skinners' Well, performed over several days by London-area clerks, perhaps with indirect civic government involvement, drew audiences including royalty and nobility. Court tournaments and jousts took place sometimes in the London streets or just outside the walls at Smithfield; important Londoners attended entertainments at the court itself. A few records also provide brief, tantalizing glimpses of other (non-civic) theatre, such as a play of St. Katherine, besides the general entertainments (tumbling, juggling, street plays, May games, and the like) always available to a broad urban population though seldom recorded.

Civic London in the fourteenth century was no mere administrative and economic unit; it was theatrically oriented, valuing public and private civic display, apparently above all for its political uses although surely also for entertainment's sake.[203] As we move past 1400, civic theatricality increases: street pageantry expands; water pageantry becomes significant as well; the Midsummer Watch comes to include portable wood-and-canvas "pageants" (scenic and figural displays), as eventually does also the Lord Mayor's Show; and hall plays – together, at least at first, with elaborate mummings – become of importance to (or begin to become recorded by) the livery companies, to which every London freeman/citizen belonged. For civic theatre from 1400 to 1558, therefore, it seems useful to look at the records not chronologically, across all types of theatrical performance, as I have done to this point, but in terms of different kinds of performances, beginning with plays and mummings, and then proceeding to examine the varieties of street and water pageantry: land entries, water shows, the Midsummer Watch, the Lord Mayor's Show. In each chapter I will focus on what more we can now learn about these theatrical forms, and what new questions we might ask about them, from a new examination of the extant civic records.

PART II

From 1410 to 1558

CHAPTER 4

Company hall plays: performance records

In the early fifteenth century, as indicated in section 6 of the previous chapter, a major change appears to have taken place in the way in which Londoners experienced plays, on the civic level.[1] The intermittent (over a period of more than two hundred years) references to and records of performances/plays of some kind at Clerkenwell/Skinners' Well – London's version, at least by the 1380s, of the civic biblical cycle dramas beginning in the late fourteenth and early fifteenth centuries in English provincial towns – disappear, as we have seen, after 1409; and although absence of records of an event does not necessarily mean the cessation of the event itself, in this case the former would seem almost certainly to indicate the latter, given the high profile 1384–1409 of the Clerkenwell play, with its multi-day performances and attendances of royalty and nobility. 1409 may not have been the final year; but surely if the play had continued for much longer, at least in its elaborate 1409 form, by the 1420s or so we would have at least one more extant reference or record: especially given the survival into our own time both of a number of sixteenth-century national chronicles using earlier manuscript sources and of an increasing amount of London chronicle material after *c.* 1400.[2]

Some time in the early part of the fifteenth century the Clerkenwell play – as a regular or as a sporadic major performance occasion – thus appears to have ended: for reasons about which we know nothing. Had the size of London's population begun to make a single-location dramatic spectacle difficult? – logistically, or in terms of real or perceived political danger? Did ecclesiastical sponsors (if they existed), for whatever reasons (some have been suggested in chapter 3), pull out? Did Lollard hostility end clerks' performances in London although it could not stop guild/lay performances in the provinces? Did a royal and noble audience lose interest or otherwise disappear? The play survived the 1399 deposition transition from Richard II to Henry IV, but we do not know how many times from 1399 to 1409 it was performed again: perhaps only once (in 1409); and Henry IV's successor, Henry V, spent much of his reign at war in France. Finances may also have been a major issue. If the city had been an indirect supporter of the play, perhaps its expenses associated with Henry V's wars, after his 1413 accession, made the indirect costs of this large spectacle impossible. Or perhaps, given the necessity for London frequently to pay for royal entries, for the meeting of and gifts to foreign ambassadors, and for other such events dictated by the combination of its location near Westminster and its economic importance and size, a time finally arrived when a choice had to be made between a civic focus (financially and otherwise) on such events and support for a major biblical play. Perhaps a religious play had lost its political and/or economic attractiveness. Or perhaps leading Londoners' interests in private performances (since at least the *c.*1300 puy) finally made a division seem desirable between the public spectacle of royal entries and the private possibilities of the performed play: indoor performances of the latter, for individually paying civic groups, becoming privileged as the London livery companies became wealthier and in many cases acquired halls in the fifteenth century to serve as their permanent political and social headquarters.[3] Perhaps the rise of cycle drama in provincial towns even influenced Londoners to establish a different pattern. Any one or, more likely, a combination of some of these factors may have led to the change.

What we do know is that, shortly after records of the Clerkenwell play cease, records begin, in the extant manuscript books of a few individual London craft guilds, of payments for plays and/or players (the latter differentiated from minstrels) in these guilds' owned or rented halls, normally at the annual (or biennial or triennial) feasts at which new guild officers were chosen and inducted into office but also at other celebratory times of the year such as Christmas and Candlemas.[4] These records are not plentiful – but they are significant in relation to the kinds and total number of surviving craft guild records for the period (within which I include records pertaining to the craft guilds' internal religious fraternities).[5] They give us, in the fifteenth century, two companies (Drapers, Blacksmiths) with early ordinances specifying or assuming play performance as part of the company's feast-time celebrations, records for at least two other companies (Cutlers, Brewers) of annual feast-time plays and players over a good number of years from the early century on, records of yet another company (Grocers) with at least a decade of mid-century play/player performances, and records also of at least occasional feast-time plays and players in the latter half of the century for one other company (Carpenters). One company (Merchant Taylors) provides a solitary, very early record of players at a feast in 1411.[6] At least six London companies during the fifteenth century, with at least three of them in the early part of the century, were thus regularly or occasionally offering plays/players to their own members at hall feasts to which non-company guests – prominent civic figures, court officials, sometimes royalty itself in the case of the Great Companies – would also normally have been invited; and the single Merchant Taylors' players record extends matters slightly further. The fact that payments were being made for the plays and players indicates that professional performers were being hired, although these were not necessarily fulltime entertainers.[7] Such plays may, of course, have been offered even before our earliest record of them; what we have, however, is records evidence of company hall players and plays (several of the plays being identified as performed by clerks) once records of the Clerkenwell play cease. Given the number of companies for which no early major manuscript records books are extant, along with the varying accounting and minuting practices both among companies and, over time, within companies, the companies with surviving records of fifteenth-century plays and players are probably indicative of a number of other companies in the century also sponsoring performances, regularly or occasionally, the records of which have not survived.[8]

The term "play," of course, especially in the earlier fifteenth century, could be used with great elasticity: covering a full range of entertainment activity from dicing games to theatrical performances, and including satirical sketches, juggling, acrobatics, sports, and the like; and the term "players" had a similarly extensive range of meanings, including players upon musical instruments. In London livery company feast-time records of both the fifteenth and the sixteenth centuries, however, normally a distinction is made between "minstrels," who seem, from various company records contexts in which the term is used (such as formal processions through the city streets), to be principally musicians, and "players," both groups often being regularly and separately paid for services on the same occasions, or hired for different occasions (for example, one group for the election time, one group for Candlemas celebrations) during a company's year. The "players" are also often associated in the records with "plays" (the noun, unlike the verb, being rarely used in the period for primarily musical performances). Early minstrels (for whom we have London company records both in Latin and in English) could act, storytell, and juggle, as well as play musical instruments and sing. Players doing "plays" (and the English terms only, not Latin ones, occur in these records[9]) could sing and doubtless play one or more musical instruments, as well as act, juggle, recite, and the like. But at the fifteenth and sixteenth-century dinners held by companies employing both kinds of groups, the functions of the two groups would appear to have been different, and in the records of companies with continuities of plays and/or players over time, the "players" by the sixteenth century are sometimes identified as a specific group, such as the King's Players, we know to have consisted of actors (who, of course, could also dance, sing, juggle, etc., as occasion demanded), while in the fifteenth century some of the players are specified to be clerks. In the early fifteenth century, therefore, although we cannot be sure that a "player" is always an actor, at least the likelihood is that some of the time and perhaps much of the time he acts (as well as sings, dances, etc.); and by the sixteenth century "players" would seem normally to be actors. Minstrels, in company records, are associated especially with music, although before the sixteenth century they too may have been more general performers, especially when a company did not employ players as well. It would thus seem logical to assume that the players hired by companies were likely to have performed, at least in significant part and certainly by the sixteenth century, primarily non-music, and the minstrels, primarily music, especially when both groups were included at the same festivities. And although, especially in the fifteenth century, the "play" performances might sometimes have been an eclectic mix of recitations, jesting, juggling, and the like, with some music included, by the sixteenth century the terminology would appear to have become fairly stable, while regular and substantial payments to players would also seem to indicate a substantial kind or amount of performance fare.[10]

The great London Clerkenwell/Skinners' Well play, then, which was possibly civic or semi-civic, and certainly was a major outdoor theatrical event in late fourteenth-century London, appears to have experienced changing circumstances and to have disappeared, at least as a major event, after 1409; and by the 1420s we have records of civic "play" performances which are entirely hall events, paid for by individual London guilds for the entertainment and/or edification of their own members and guests: who included in some cases, as for the Clerkenwell play, members of royalty and of the nobility. This change in the circumstances of public play performance in London, if indeed it was a change (rather than simply reflecting a move to fuller record-keeping then, by the companies, and a greater survival, to our day, of company manuscripts from that time on), would have been transformative for audiences and entertainers alike: plays in effect becoming significantly a hall experience for London citizen audiences, and a multiple-performance, direct-income business for London-area performers, a steady source of income with a reliable base in the annual election feasts of guilds (feasts which spanned the whole year's calendar) as well as in guild celebrations at general festive times such as the Christmas through Shrovetide season. The richer and more prestigious of these guilds, moreover, had close connections with the court; and in the early sixteenth century a major performing troupe for the London companies had become the King's Players. Once again we see city and court performance interests as closely intertwined.

GREAT COMPANY HALL PLAYS

Of the twelve London Great Companies, the Drapers' Company uniquely from its records can be seen to have been highly active in hiring players for hall performances from the early fifteenth century on. The company, existing from well before its 1438 charter of incorporation and continuing into the present,[11] possesses today large numbers of major early manuscripts; and these manuscript records demonstrate a continuous company tradition of play performances at its annual election feasts, for a period of over a hundred years, from the early fifteenth century to almost 1558. Such plays would have functioned both as entertainment and as a demonstration, both to company members themselves and to invited guests, of the company's wealth, status, and taste; and indeed from at least 1516 the company regularly hired actors to perform not just one but *two* plays, at its annual election feast-time *c.* 15 August, the Feast of the Assumption of Our Lady.

References to plays/players in the records of the Drapers' Company are found in the earliest Drapers' manuscript ordinance book.[12] An ordinance near the start of this "Book of Ordinances 1405" – a manuscript volume containing company bylaws ranging in date from 1405 to the latter half of the sixteenth century – indirectly specifies players as a required component of the regular entertainment provided at the annual election feast, or dinner, which was given by the wardens for the brotherhood *c.* 15 August each year. That the feast concerned is the Drapers' annual August election feast is clear from the manuscript context in which the ordinance occurs. The date of the ordinance could be any time between *c.* 1418 and, at the latest, 1462.[13]

For The ffeeste What Euery Brother shal Paye[14]

Also that euery Brothir Whet. [h]er[15] that he be In Towne or noon shall Paye hys aferant for the Dynner or feeste that ys to seye that ŷer þat they haue Clothyng ij s. And that ŷer no Clothyng ys iij s. And euery Brother shall Paye for his Quarterage xij d a ŷer [And þouŷ he be Wedyd he schall Paye for him and for hys Wyfe but xij d/[16] And also the Wardeyns as for þe ŷer beyng shal haue to þer alouans As for Rysches Mynstrals Pleyers and oþer Pety Costys xx s. And no more Also yf yt so be yat ther be a Mayr at þe Dynner And he be of the seyd felyschypp the Wardens to be alouyd for his Mes xl s. And yf yt lyke the War- dens to haue at the Dynner. [a meir] of anoþer Crafte withouten the assent of þe felyshypp þan they to haue noon Alowans As for the Meyrs Messe][17]

The wardens of the Drapers thus received, by ordinance, from some time in the first part of the fifteenth century, an allowance from com- pany funds to cover the costs of rushes, minstrels, *players*, and "other petty costs" of the annual election dinner, which the wardens arranged and paid for; and in years when a Draper was mayor, or when a mayor of another company was invited by general assent to the dinner, the al- lowance included additional funds for the "mayor's mess": that is, for the mayor and his party dining together.[18] The specifying of players as part of the regular costs of the feast, to be met by a standing allowance, shows that players were a regular, expected part of the proceedings. And that these players were indeed non-musical performers, and not musicians, would seem to be indicated by the specifying of minstrels and players as two different groups, and by an ordinance slightly later in the manuscript, to be dated between 1436 and 1462,[19] which refers specifically to plays to be seen at the feast time.

The ordinans Made to Exchewe pres off Menis Men In þe Halle þe day off þe ffeeste.

Also Ordeynd ys By All The hooll ffelischipp off This ffraternite that for As Moche as here to fore This tyme At The ffeste or Dynner off This forseyd fra- ternite hath ben Greet Pres And Multitud of ŷonge Men In Greet Dyshonour of All the Bretheryn And Prynspally to the Mayster And Wardens for the tyme Beynge for They myght have no Rome nor space to serve nor to do her Besynes In savyng of þer Worshipp And of alle the Bretheryn And Prynspaly That þe statys ne þe Brethryn myght not se ne be holde Pleyes & oþer dyuers sportys ffor that Tyme Ordeynd Ther fore ordeynd ys be the Avyce of all the Brethryn That Noman of þe ffraternyte Exccpt Aldermen And they That haue borne states In the Cyttee schal brynge noman Wyth hym ne Chyld to þe feeste or Dynner Wheþir yt be saffe only They that haue ben Mayster or Wardens to fore . . .[20]

The two above ordinances together indicate plays to have been regularly performed, by bylaw, at the Drapers' annual election feasts, from some date in the first sixty-two years of the fifteenth century. And the first extant set of Drapers' wardens' accounts (Drapers' MS +140), beginning more or less in the early 1420s (with one complete and one partial earlier account year) and running, though with numerous gaps, to 1440–41, records regular payments to players (along with minstrels) at the Drapers' election-time feasts from 1430 on.[21] There are no payments to players before 1430 (though the manuscript is incomplete); but from 1430 to 1441, feast-time players are paid in all years for which accounts are extant.[22] Tom Girtin has suggested that the Drapers, who built a new hall for themselves in the late 1420s, first occupied this hall in 1430.[23] If so, perhaps the company began more elaborate feast-time practices, including the regular appearance of players, in this year.

The first set of extant Drapers' wardens' accounts (Drapers' MS +140) ends in 1440–41; the next set (Drapers' MS +403) does not begin until 1475–76. That feast-time players continued through the mid fifteenth century to be a norm for the Drapers' Company, however, is indicated by another ordinance from the Drapers' early Book of Ordinances, this one specifically dated in August 1474. The ordinance concerns a change in (presumably ongoing) funding arrangements for the annual feast – i.e., it implies a continuation to August 1474 of the conditions it is now changing.

Also by the said assent aggrement and consent It is ordeyned the day & yere aforsaid that the wardeyns of the said ffraternite for the tyme beyng shall haue none allowaunce vpon the dyner for the Meyres Messe though*e* he be there Nor for none of those Straungers Which by my maisters the Aldremen and by the Wardeyns for the tyme beyng With the Counseill of the Craft shall be appoynted and boden to the dyner for garnysshyng of the high Table nor for rysshes mynstrell*es* nor players[24]

Again, players are cited as a normal part of the annual election dinner costs – though within the context now of withdrawal of the company's standing allowance covering them. The company was probably not, however, financially mistreating its wardens, in this ordinance, in withdrawing the whole funding allowance for these specified dinner costs and leaving all these expenses to be paid by the wardens themselves, out of their own pockets. In August 1473, one year earlier, another bylaw had been passed, providing the wardens with other sources of income (fines and apprentice-enrolment fees) from which dinner expenses in general could be met;[25] and these sources were further augmented in

August 1474.[26] But that the company itself, or the wardens, were going through financial changes and/or problems is suggested by the fact that the second manuscript volume of extant wardens' accounts (Drapers' MS +403), which begins in 1475–76, does not record any feast-time payments for players, minstrels, etc., until 1481 (f. 20r): after another bylaw had been passed in August 1478 restoring the above company funding allowance to the wardens for the annual feast. This bylaw again mentions players as a part of the expected feast expenses.

> . . . that the wardeins that shall be frohensforth shall haue for theire Allowaunce yerely for the Meyres messe and for suche as shall be Appointed by my maisters the Aldermen and by the Wardeins for þe tyme being for þe Garnisshing of the high table Also for players mynstrelles and Russhis the somme of vj li xiij s iiij d sterling . . .[27]

(The ordinance continues, naming other income sources also for the wardens.)

Once this new funding bylaw of 1478 had been passed, the extant wardens' accounts running 1475–76 to 1508–09 indicate players performing every year but three, from 1481 to 1507, at the Drapers' annual election feast. The accounting formula used, however, unfortunately provides no details of who is performing, or what, nor of what the specific performance costs are. The usual formula runs: "Item for the Meyrys Messe mynstrelles pleyers and Russhis vj li xiij s iiij d."[28]

In the three years between 1481 and 1507 in which players are not mentioned in the formula, the formula once (in 1488) omits the players only, once (in 1489) cites only the mayor's mess, and once (in 1493) refers only to the mayor's mess and rushes.[29] The total allowance claimed by the wardens is always, however, the full £6 13s 4d set in the company's 1478 ordinance quoted above. It is impossible to tell whether the words are being varied deliberately, to provide an accurate record of what usual expenses were and were not involved in those three years, or are simply being arbitrarily abbreviated by the scribe since the amount of allowance to be paid by the company to the wardens is the same in each year. Players thus may or may not have performed in the three years in question: and also in the years 1479 and 1480, immediately after the passing of the 1478 ordinance, when the full allowance is also claimed (at once) by the wardens in the account payment records but only the mayor's mess is mentioned.[30]

The two latest feast years, however, covered by this second extant volume of wardens' accounts, that is, the years 1508 and 1509, also contain no record of players at the annual feast, and no formula or allowance otherwise, either. And the next set of wardens' accounts (Drapers' MS +143), running on to 1546–47, similarly contains no players expenses, no allowance, no mayor's mess, until 1512: when the players, minstrels, rushes, and mayor's mess formula occurs once again (f. 22v), and then not for the next three years, though for 1515 the formula is found once more in its abbreviated form (f. 45v), citing only the mayor's mess. (Significantly, in both August 1512 and August 1515 a Draper mayor was in office.) As in the 1470s, the fact that few feast-time players records – or mayor's mess records – are to be found over this eight-year period may be associated with financial rearrangements or problems, in that the period coincides with a time when, as seen in the early Book of Ordinances, the company seems to have been making a number of (limiting) changes in the kinds and terms of company income available to the wardens for payment of their recurring expenses of office. In 1505, for example, the company further regulated the wardens' income from apprenticeship fees;[31] in 1512 it made a major reduction in the wardens' income overall;[32] in 1515 it limited the years in which the feast-time funding formula would be paid – though this 1515 act was then annulled 4 August 1519.[33] (Also the company's court minutes record, for 8 August 1519, some new funding arrangements for the wardens.[34]) And, after 1515, no record of payment to players, and very few references to the mayor's mess, occur again in the wardens' accounts, to 1558.

This does not mean, however, that players ceased performing at the Drapers' annual election feast; for the Drapers' regular court minutes are extant from 1515–16,[35] and the court minutes, which include some accounting records, show that from 1516 to 1541 players were paid by the wardens to perform plays at the annual August feast-time, normally one play on each of two separate days during the celebrations, for all years in which Draper feast dinners were held and records are extant: though the performance in 1519, the year of the annulment in August of the 1515 funding bylaw, was minimal – simply one performer (status unknown) at a supper held by the bachelors (company members just below the livery).[36] And, much of the time, the court minutes provide detail about payment amounts (usually 6s 8d per play, 13s 4d for two plays, and often dinner for the actors) and – unlike the earlier wardens' accounts – about the playing companies involved, who seem usually to have been professional acting companies with royal or aristocratic patronage. There are performances by the King's Players in at least seven years from 1517 to 1541.[37] Individual King's players named include John

English, [William] Rutter, and [Robert] Hinstock.[38] A (John) Sly and his company perform in at least four years from 1516 to 1530;[39] a John Sly was player to Queen Jane Seymour before her death in 1537, and another or the same was interluder to Henry VIII,[40] and this is probably the same actor as one or both of them. In 1521 payment is made, for two performances, to English, Sly, and their fellows;[41] were they performing together, in one company, or in two separate companies (perhaps the King's and the Queen's, performing one each day for two days)? By 1529 other companies are being employed, in different years, as well: the Prince's Players (1529, 1540), the Duke of Norfolk's Players (1529), the Duke of Suffolk's Players (1531, 1532). The Queen's Players are specifically recorded in 1539. In 1540 we also find the only perhaps amateur play performance recorded over this period: a performance by "our paryshe clerck and his compeny pleyers".[42] Finally, after 1541, feast-time play performance records cease, and in the Drapers' revised 1543 ordinances (MS +795, from p. 55) no ordinances involving feast-time plays/players are to be found.[43] If any plays continued to 1558, we have no records of them.

A new look at the manuscript records, then, shows that the London Drapers' Company included play performances as a regular, expected part of its annual election feast celebrations over a period of about one hundred and twelve years: from at least 1430 to 1541. Occasional interruptions or gaps in the regular pattern of recorded performances – in the 1470s and in the early sixteenth century, in the extant records – are perhaps to be associated with funding rearrangements between the company itself and its wardens; and – given the silence in the wardens' accounts on payments to players after 1516, when we know from the court minutes that performances were indeed taking place – perhaps the performances themselves were not interrupted after all, but simply the records. The fifteenth-century records unfortunately do not tell us what kinds of performers were involved; but from 1516 the details provided in the court minutes show that the players at that time, at least, were almost invariably well-known professionals with royal or aristocratic patronage, and at least sometimes (perhaps usually?) numbering about four, since part of their payment sometimes is specified to involve a dinner "mess" (food for four persons).[44] Finally, two plays per feast time, at *c.* 6s 8d per play, seems to have been the norm from at least 1516 until 1540. The comparatively large sum of 8s paid to players in 1430 might suggest a norm of two plays from the start;[45] but between 1430 and 1516 the payment to players is not recorded by itself, so we cannot know the amount paid; and 1430, as already noted, may have been the special inaugural year of the Drapers' hall and perhaps of feast-time plays as well, thus calling for special elaboration. Also fees paid to players at the time could vary. The Brewers (see below), for example, in 1421 paid 7s for apparently a single play, and in 1432, 3s 4d.[46] Varying costs could presumably be due to any one of a number of factors other than varying numbers of plays: for example, different acting troupes employed, simpler or more elaborate plays being performed, players doing extras (as specified for the Brewers at least in 1439),[47] some of the player costs being handled by the wardens personally, or a separate play collection also being taken up and not recorded in the main accounts.[48]

We also have one sixteenth-century record indicating that the Drapers might sometimes make use of plays on special occasions other than their feast times. In 1557 they paid the fashionable Children of Paul's – probably the boy choristers of the cathedral rather than the St. Paul's grammar school boys – to perform an interlude at a company dinner for the Russian ambassador.[49]

What about the eleven other London Great Companies, from the early fifteenth century to 1558? The Drapers' Company is the only London Great Company to show in its extant records books a regular, ordained involvement with feast-time players from the early fifteenth century to the 1540s; but for three other Great Companies – the Fishmongers, Haberdashers, and Salters – there are almost no surviving manuscripts of the types most likely to yield play records (no manuscript books of accounts or of court minutes, and few ordinances) for this period; and although other Great Companies' potentially-useful records manuscripts *have* in part survived, the vagaries of what has survived, and the varying accounting and minuting practices of the London companies in general, do not permit us generally to infer from manuscript silence that feast-time plays were not performed. Payments for plays at a company feast might normally be expected, for example, to be recorded in a company's manuscript books of wardens' accounts; but as the example of the Drapers after 1515 shows, a company might choose to enter its play arrangements instead in its court minutes; so that where only a company's wardens' accounts or its court minutes have survived, and not both, we cannot be sure that we have the "right" set of records for finding (or not finding) references to plays. (For the sixteenth-century Mercers, for example, we have court minutes, and renter wardens' accounts, but no regular wardens' accounts.) Also, in some companies, at least some feast expenses might be the personal responsibility of a company's wardens rather than of the company itself – as, for example, with the Goldsmiths and their annual feast on St. Dunstan's Day;[50] and the wardens' personal arrangements or costs might or might not be entered and/or itemized in the company records, depending on the particular company's arrangements and accounting system. (Only, for example, because the Drapers provided a fixed and broadly itemized feast allowance to their wardens – which was recorded in company accounts – do we know about the Drapers' players 1475–76 to 1508–09.) In some companies, feast accounting details might have been kept in separate (perhaps even only rough) manuscripts, which have not survived, rather than in the main accounts; the Skinners, for example, from at least 1491–92 kept in a separate manuscript book, not now extant, the details of their major annual procession and other expenses at Corpus Christi,[51] and the Merchant Taylors in the mid-sixteenth century recorded their Lord Mayor's Day pageantry expenses in a separate, roughly-kept manuscript book (which in this case *has* survived).[52] The more extensive a company's arrangements for any given kind of occasion, indeed, the more likely it is that a separate accounting might have been made.[53] Finally, one standard company method of paying for feast-time expenses generally, including plays, seems to have been through taking up a special collection from members:[54] a collection which in some instances might not ever make its way, wholly or in part, into the formal, ongoing accounts – for example, if paid directly to a warden otherwise personally responsible for feast costs. Individual players might even conceivably sometimes have been paid not in cash but in food (though food seems normally to have been a part of a company's payment only);[55] or some players might themselves have been company members, with an annual or occasional no-cost obligation of performance (as discussed below in chapter 5). It cannot be assumed that where we have no records of payments for plays at company feasts, no such plays took place.[56] Moreover, in the fifteenth century (especially early on), where some companies record only minstrels at their feasts, and not separate groups of minstrels and of players, the minstrels might also have been involved in some types of non-musical entertainment/performances.

Clearly, however, we cannot assume either, from manuscript silence, that plays normally did take place at a number of Great Company annual feasts; and it is notable that no regular or even occasional plays are recorded in the extensive early extant manuscripts of the Goldsmiths: a Great Company whose early extant manuscripts, uniquely among those of the London companies, routinely combine wardens' accounts and court minutes in the same volumes, beginning in 1334 and running through to 1558 (and beyond): though inevitably a few years are missing. The accounts, however, are often partial only, expenses are frequently not itemized, and from 1531 the manuscripts consist largely of court minutes: although when feast costs *are* itemized, most notably for nine years between 1516 and 1527, no play is to be found.[57] We should also remember, as noted above, that some of the Goldsmiths' feast costs were, at least at some periods, the personal responsibility of the wardens; and the Goldsmiths' extant manuscripts also significantly contain no references to costs such as the company's 1430 Candlemas presentation to mayor William Estfeld (a Mercer) of a mumming by John Lydgate. We know about the mumming only because its text has survived, with an unusual explanatory rubric.[58] The Mercers' Company, first in precedence among all London companies, placing significantly more of its members as mayor or as sheriff, between 1400 and 1558, than any other company, and with pre-1558 wardens' accounts surviving for 1347 and 1391–1464, and court minutes from 1453 (and renter wardens' accounts from 1442), also has no manuscript evidence of play performances at its major feasts or at any other time. Its accounts, however, also include no reference to a Lydgate mumming this company, too, commissioned for presentation to Estfeld in early 1430;[59] and the Mercers are also notable for the non-inclusion in their sixteenth-century court minutes (during a period for which their wardens' accounts are not extant) of any significant detail of the extensive midsummer street pageantry that we know from non-Mercer sources that the company provided in at least the 1530s.[60] The Merchant Taylors, whose accounts have survived for most of the years 1398–1484, 1489–1503, and then 1545–57, but with extant pre-1558 court minutes only for most of 1486–93, have only one recorded payment to players (named separately from minstrels) for the entire period: in 1411 (i.e., just after the time of the final known record of the Clerkenwell play).[61] The company, however, as noted above, has extant a separate manuscript record book for the pageants it provided on Merchant Taylor mayors' inauguration days in all three of 1556, 1561, and 1568; perhaps it had earlier separate record books as well, which have not survived, for the details of other regular kinds of entertainment costs. The company did record in its wardens' accounts, however, from 1399 on, the regular costs of minstrels at its major annual feast, so that one might expect any separate player costs to have been recorded as well, unless these were a personal expense for the wardens, or an expense met through a separate money collection from company members. The Merchant Taylors interestingly do record in the mid fifteenth century a payment of £6 13s 4d "toward" the costs of the mummers of "my lord of Glouce*ter*" riding "thurgh london" to Tailors' hall in the Christmas season of 1440–41;[62] did Humphrey Duke of Gloucester, who was an honorary member of the company (and apparently attended its annual election feast in 1423[63]), perhaps otherwise "give" the mumming to his fellow Merchant Taylors, or were the mummers celebrating the season by visiting a number of London companies all of which would provide rewards? Might Gloucester's own sponsored troupe of players sometimes have provided feast-time plays for the Merchant Taylors, through special arrangements not included in the regular accounts?[64] Most importantly, the £6 13s 4d was in part specially collected from company members for the mummers; it was not all from general company coffers, and may have made its way into the accounts only because on this particular occasion the collection itself did not cover the entire sum required, so that the company had to add money of its own. Might plays/players for the Merchant Taylors have been routinely covered by special collections? The Merchant Taylors had strong ties with the court throughout this period (with even kings as members, as noted in chapter 3[65]); and their feasts surely would have included some of the same kinds of entertainments, including plays, that were provided at court and in aristocratic households. Their extant accounts for 1545–57, for example, show the company then paying the fashionable boy choristers of St. Paul's for feast-day entertainment (certainly musical only, in some years, and so probably musical throughout) in all of 1550 to 1557 (inclusive).[66]

Two other Great Companies with major surviving pre-1558 records – the Ironmongers (with wardens' accounts from 1455–58 although court minutes only from 1555) and Clothworkers (accounts from 1528–29, court minutes from 1537) – provide no evidence of plays or players at company feasts in the fifteenth and sixteenth centuries; and in the sixteenth century the Vintners (wardens' accounts from 1507, no court minutes for this period) record only two definite plays, in 1539 and in 1542 (with payment made on both occasions to one Golder).[67] The Skinners (wardens' accounts from 1491–92, court minutes only from 1551), have records of payment only towards the costs of a Christmas season interlude at the house of a Skinner sheriff in 1511–12 and for a disguising in their hall in January 1519 (when a Skinner was mayor).[68] The Grocers, however, provide some records support – though on a limited basis – for regular or semi-regular feast-time plays as a provable phenomenon not restricted, among the London Great Companies, to the Drapers. The Grocers record payment, in their all-purpose early Black Book, surviving for the period 1345 to 1463 (but with its included accounts incomplete before 1417–18), to the players of (presumably again the Duke of) Gloucester in 1431–32 (a year in which a Grocer was mayor);[69] and subsequently payments are recorded for plays or players (along with minstrels) at the annual election feast in five years (three of them consecutive) in the 1460s, in the Grocers' first two surviving manuscript volumes of wardens' accounts, which end with the account for 1470–71. In 1461 we find "payd to William off Grescherche ffor A pley vij s" (presumably this William is a clerk), and a separate payment to minstrels and a trumpeter. In 1465 comes "Item to william of Grescherche And his felows viij s iiij d" and a separate payment to two minstrels; presumably a play is also involved here.[70] Then, for all of 1467, 1468, and 1469, we find a payment of 8s 4d to players, identity unspecified; and that these are play performers (probably even the same clerk and his fellows) is suggested not only by the continuity from 1461 and 1465 but also by the fact that minstrels again are separately paid on all three occasions.[71] A gap in the extant accounts then occurs, however, until 1511, after which we find only three records of payments to players (to 1558): all to the King's Players, between 1514 and the mid 1530s.[72] A "clerke of seynt magnus and his children" are also paid 3s 4d (separately from the minstrels and waits) at the election dinner in 1532[73] – and are paid as well (6s 8d for "The Clarke of Saynt maugnus & his Cumpany", separately from the minstrels and waits) by the Vintners at their July St. Martin's Day feast in 1533;[74] were these a group of child actors and/or of musical entertainers?[75] The Grocers also paid clerks and choristers, otherwise unidentified, 4s "for singyng Balattes and other goodly pastyme" in 1531;[76] were these also perhaps the St. Magnus group? Finally the children of the Duke of Suffolk's house (perhaps a chapel group attached to the Duke's household) were paid 4s 8d by the Grocers at their election supper in 1535, but for what is not specified, though minstrels were also paid separately.[77]

The Drapers were thus possibly unique among Great Companies in their regular employing of players during the fifteenth and early sixteenth centuries; but at least the Grocers also had some plays and players, regularly or occasionally, at some times; and it would seem unlikely for at least the Merchant Taylors (and the Mercers – see below, chapter 5) not to have been theatrically involved to some extent as well. And, as already noted, given the accounting and minuting practices of the companies and also the many early company manuscripts known not to have survived, it is never safe to assume absence of activity from absent or silent manuscript records. The demonstrable play situation is very different, however, when we turn to the non-Great companies. Seventeen of these companies have manuscript accounts surviving from before 1558; and the manuscripts show about one-third of the seventeen to have regularly or occasionally employed players at major company feasts between 1400 and 1558. Improbably, did the non-Great companies in general like plays more than did the Great Companies? Or were they less likely – because of less complicated finances – to have had additional accounting manuscripts, which were not kept as permanent records, supplying some kinds of financial detail, or less likely to have had wealthy wardens capable of personally financing company feast expenses including players? Were they also less likely to have had members of their own with the theatrical expertise and connections to have provided performances for special company occasions? – a possibility discussed below, for the Great Companies especially, in chapter 5. Whatever the reasons for the differences between Great and non-Great companies in this respect, non-Great company records show that plays and players did become a reasonably widespread form of entertainment at London guild feasts in the fifteenth and early sixteenth centuries – starting for the non-Great companies, as for the Drapers, shortly after records of the Clerkenwell play cease.

NON-GREAT COMPANY HALL PLAYS

In the year 1426 the London Blacksmiths' Company issued a set of ordinances which included the following regulation concerning the company's annual winter feast on the Monday a week after Twelfth Day (6 January).

... & þey shal haue at the saide quarter day. goode brede & goode ale & Conyes bake a goode fire & a play & euery man & woman þat commyth þerto shal pay ij d a pece & þe maister & þe wardens shalbe rewarded for þe play of þe box euery yere iij s iiij d.[78]

The ordinances assume that a necessary part of the annual quarter-day feast here being regulated, as to its provision by the master and wardens, is, along with good food, the performance of a play; and general financial resources ("the box") are to be drawn upon to reimburse the officers for play costs (at least to the extent of 3s 4d). 1426 is, of course, within the date span – *c.* 1418–1462 – of the early Drapers' ordinances also assuming a play as a necessary component of a company annual feast, and within four years of (what is otherwise, if the ordinances are post-1430) the earliest surviving record, in the Drapers' wardens' accounts for 1430, of the Drapers' feast-time play. It is also within twenty years of the last extant record of the Clerkenwell play. Note that both the Drapers' and the Blacksmiths' ordinances specify the play in the context of providing the officers in charge with funds to cover feast expenses.

Significantly, although another set of Blacksmiths' ordinances only eight years later, in 1434, does not include this feast regulation,[79] the annual play seems to have been a continuing event for the Blacksmiths from at least 1426 to at least 1555. (Play expectations obviously existed independently of what might or might not be in the ordinances.) The extant records of the Blacksmiths are not continuous from 1426 to 1558; apart from the ordinances of 1426 and of 1434, specific company records dealing with company activities begin only in 1495 with wardens' accounts; and these accounts are themselves incomplete (with a gap, before 1558, from 1499 to 1509), are jumbled in their chronological order in the two volumes covering 1495–1565, and are defective for the late 1520s and early 1530s. The extant court minutes of the company begin only in 1605. The records we do have extant, however, when sorted into chronological order, indicate a company tradition, extending over a minimum of the one hundred and thirty years from 1426 to 1555, of first an annual and then a biennial play at the company's major winter feast – called the "cony feast" from at least 1512,[80] apparently from the most important item (rabbit) on the bill of fare. The earliest extant wardens' accounts, of 1495–97,[81] include a payment of 3s 4d – the amount set in the 1426 ordinances – "toward*es* our*e* pley vpon our*e* q*uarter* day", 1496;[82] and similar entries are found for 1497, 1498, and 1499.[83] A gap then occurs in the accounts; but when they begin again in 1510, players are again, for eleven consecutive years (from 1510 up to and including 1520), paid to perform at the cony feast with the amount paid – while still officially at 3s 4d, as set in the 1426 ordinances – inconsistently increasing.[84] There is no record of a cony feast in 1521 or in 1524, but cony feast players are paid again in 1522, 1523, 1525, and 1526.[85] The accounts are defective at this point; but starting again in 1529, and up to and including 1541, a cony feast is recorded every second year (only), with players invariably involved and paid usually at the rate of 5s.[86]

Details of the Blacksmiths' major feast expenses, including those of the cony feast, then (accounts of 1541–43) begin to be recorded in another manuscript book not now known;[87] and though some details of some feasts are again included from 1543–45, no cony feast or midsummer feast details are to be found in the wardens' accounts for the next six to seven years. Cony feast details – including payments to players – then recur, however, for 1549 (the players being paid 5s 4d),[88] 1551 (8s 4d),[89] and 1555 (6s 8d).[90] Identifiable cony feast records then cease altogether; perhaps the feast, including its play, has ceased, perhaps it is being accounted for generally as simply a dinner without its play, or perhaps its expenses are being recorded elsewhere (as *c.* 1541–43) in a manuscript no longer extant.

What plays or kinds of plays did the members of the Blacksmiths' Company expect to watch at their cony feasts for a period of apparently at least 130 years, from 1426 to 1555, and who performed them? No play title or subject matter is ever given in the records; and only once are the actors themselves identified: as the "king*es* plears" in 1525.[91] That the unusually large sum for the company (for that time) of 6s 8d was paid to the players in 1525 may indicate that the Kings' Players were a special "catch" that year and not usually performers for the company; payments to players before 1525 had never exceeded 5s 4d (in 1523), and were not to reach past 6s again until 1551.

The Blacksmiths' Company was not a London Great Company which might be expected to have had especially costly and impressive annual company feasts. It was a stable, non–Great company – and hence its cony-feast plays are all the more significant, as potentially typical of what an ordinary London company might present as usual feast-time entertainment in the fifteenth and early sixteenth centuries: unless we are to believe that the Blacksmiths had a special, unusual interest in plays, which differentiated their feasts from those of the many other craft guilds operating in London during this period. Over one hundred crafts (though not all necessarily with guilds) were in operation in London in 1421–22: providing a sizeable pool, even with non-company crafts and very small or poor companies left out of consideration, of civic institutions which might have employed actors at their feast times; and *c.* 1500 there existed seventy-eight London craft guilds.[92] What other non-Great craft guilds have extant records from this period, and what do such records indicate – or not – about plays?

The Cutlers' Company – another prosperous and stable non-Great company of the time (with a hall rented by the Blacksmiths for their feast times from 1442–43 to 1464–65) – possesses a fifteenth-century incomplete series of wardens' accounts, in 36 rolls of annual accounts, for the fifty-six-year period from 1442–43 to 1497–98.[93] Only about two thirds of the rolls for the fifty-six years have thus survived; but fortunately the missing rolls do not cover large blocks of years. The largest group of missing rolls is for the years 1445–49, a space of four years, and otherwise rolls are missing for only one and two-year periods between surviving rolls.[94] The surviving rolls are thus likely to be representative of the entire original series of fifty-six, and an entry appearing consistently in all thirty-six extant rolls is very likely to have appeared regularly in the twenty non-extant rolls as well.

In all surviving thirty-six rolls occurs an entry for the payment of players at a company dinner. Moreover, as with the Blacksmiths' Company, this dinner is apparently an annual cony feast. The first three rolls (1442–45) record payment to players at the cony feast; the next sixteen (beginning 1449–50) speak of players at a dinner at Christmas,[95] the next seven (beginning 1473–74) then specify the cony feast "at" (two rolls) or "after" (five rolls) Christmas, before the final entries return again to mentioning only the cony feast.[96] The feast is doubtless a cony feast, during the Christmas season, throughout, and appears to be one of two major annual Cutlers' feasts during this period, the other being the election feast shortly before Trinity Sunday. These "players" might of course be musicians or general entertainers, rather than performers of plays; but one entry (1497–98) in the series does refer to "the play"; and the players from 1442–43 to 1444–45 are paid 3s 4d, the same amount as that set down in the Blacksmiths' 1426 ordinances for the annual play payment for that company. By 1449 the players have won an increase to 7s, and that sum remains pretty well constant through to 1497–98.[97] Beginning in 1486–87, however, the players may have received a regular bonus, for from that year with one exception (1489–90) the accounts also contain an entry for the players' dinner.[98] Perhaps the players were fed before, without entries being made; but more likely some kind of change has taken place, for earlier accounts scrupulously record the names of various other individuals for whose dinner at the cony feast the company is paying but players are never mentioned.[99]

From the dinner records we can calculate that at least from 1486–87 the company seems regularly to have had four players at the cony feast, for the cost of a dinner for one person is 4d and the players' dinners cost 16d. But as with the Blacksmiths' accounts in the fifteenth century, neither the identities of the players nor what they performed are ever mentioned. Playing company identification seems more likely to occur in sixteenth-century records than in earlier ones, as company records in general become more detailed; and no Cutlers' wardens' accounts have survived between 1497–98 and 1586 (by which date no cony feast with players is any longer recorded), and no company court minutes are extant until the early seventeenth century.

Among the non-Great companies the Blacksmiths and the Cutlers – like the Drapers among the Great Companies – are unusual in the extent of their surviving records of plays and players at major company feasts: allowing us to trace such performances over time spans of considerable length. As is not the case with the Drapers among the Great Companies, however, a number of other non-Great companies also have a respectable amount of surviving manuscript evidence of play/player activity at company feasts. Most significant is the Brewers' Company. The Brewers' earliest accounts cover the years 1418–19 to 1438–39, with four years missing (1425–26 to 1428–29).[100] During this period the company's major election feast is biennial to 1424–25 and annual from 1429–30; and for every feast recorded from 1419 to 1439, a play and/or players (the latter distinguished in the manuscript from minstrels) is recorded, except in 1430 (when costs were a special problem and also one folio has survived as a fragment only).[101] In five of the fourteen years (the first of which is only some ten years after the last record of the Clerkenwell play), the players are specified to be clerks (in three years, clerks of London);[102] and in six years the number of players is specified to be four.[103] The amount paid for a play/players varies: from 7s in the 1420s to a range between 3s 4d and 5s 4d in 1431–37; and in 1433–35 the players' dinners are also specified as included. In 1438 the players are paid together with singers (and with minstrels still separate), for a total payment of 7s 8d; in 1439 (specified as clerks of London) they are paid 10s for a play plus their "labour" at the feast.[104] (There is also a payment of 2s 8d to players at a dinner other than the election dinner, in 1423.[105]) When the Brewers' accounts become extant again, however, 1500–01 to 1546–47 (with yeomanry accounts, also, from 1555–56), there are no further plays or players recorded. Either plays/players were provided regularly at Brewers' feast times only in the fifteenth century, or play/player expenses had become paid or recorded in some other way by the sixteenth century.

Another non-Great company with probably significant play/player records is the Carpenters' Company. The Carpenters' fifteenth-century wardens' accounts (extant from 1437–38) record a play on the day after the company's regular August feast day, in 1454 (3s 4d paid), and a play at Candlemas quarter day in 1490 (4s 4d paid);[106] players are also recorded, on different occasions, in 1466–67 (an unspecified quarter day), 1480 (feast time), 1482 (Easter quarter day), 1495 and 1496 (both Candlemas), and 1497–98 (unspecified – perhaps also Candlemas, 1498).[107] Players then appear again, only at Candlemas, in 1502 and regularly from 1505 to 1513, though not in 1514 or 1516;[108] and accounts are damaged for 1515, and then missing 1516–17 to 1544–45.[109] When the accounts begin again, no more play or player records are to be found (to 1558), although feast-time minstrels, regularly recorded since 1475, continue. Players and minstrels in the Carpenters' records are normally separated by occasion (only occurring together once, in 1480 at the feast time): the minstrels at the feast time (except for a single minstrel at Candlemas in 1493) and the players, from at least 1502 and perhaps from 1490, always at Candlemas; and the players after 1500 are consistently paid between 2s and 6s 8d (i.e., a substantial sum, and in the neighbourhood of the 1454 and 1490 "play" payments), while before 1490 minstrels (usually only one) regularly are paid only *c.* 20d.[110] A real difference between players and minstrels would seem to exist.[111] The fact that twice before 1500 players are paid only the minstrel(s)' usual pre-1490 20d might raise questions about the Carpenters' use of minstrel/player terminology: but these players, in 1482 and in 1496, are not at the feast time (the minstrels' usual occasion) but at Easter quarter day and at Candlemas, and 20d, though not enough for a regular play, would have covered a short entertainment or sketch: compare the Grocers' 20d payment (see note 72) to John English and a juggler in 1526. It is also true, however, that between 1490 and 1499 minstrel payments at the feast time fluctuate wildly, from 14d (1499) to 2s 8d (1490) and perhaps even more (in some years the minstrels' payment is combined with others, so that a minstrels-only sum cannot be ascertained), and that after 1499 the feast-day minstrels almost always receive 3s 4d, with waits from 1505 being paid usually 20d for the feast time in all but one year (1507) – perhaps to do what the minstrel(s) did before 1490. (This 20d activity probably involved playing for election induction ceremonial.[112]) Do we have here an indication of lack of performance differentiation between minstrels and players? In recording the 1498 feast expenses, the scribe apparently begins to write "players", cancels the "p", and puts "Mynstrel*es*" instead;[113] this may indicate scribal and/or company care with terminology, but possibly instead it indicates simply a practice by 1498 of writing "minstrels" in the feast records and "players" in the Candlemas ones – i.e., the terminology being dictated by company occasion rather than by type of performance group.

We might finally note that in the earliest years of the sixteenth century the Carpenters, while at Candlemas paying only players, seem to have been interested in entertainment in general at their feast time: paying, for example, besides the regularly larger sum for the minstrels and now usually 20d for the waits as well, a separate 3s 4d in 1505 for singers to perform not only at the feast-time mass but also to sing ballads in the hall at dinner, and a separate 8d in 1506 for morris dancers and 4d for "barnard pleyer" (what kind of a player was he?).[114]

In the sixteenth century, apart from the Drapers' and Blacksmiths' records already dealt with, the most important records of continuous play/player performances are those of the Tallow Chandlers. The company proper has itself only one certain play performance recorded in its pre-1559 surviving accounts (extant from 1549–51 only), at the election feast in 1557–59 (5s – to "the Boyes of the hospitall"[115]), and a payment to players (separately listed from minstrels) at the election feast in 1551–53 (6s);[116] but the accounts of the Tallow Chandlers' yeomanry – the company's members just below the rank of the livery – are extant from 1518–19 and record players (who are consistently distinguished in the manuscript from minstrels), at what is probably their *c.* 2 July annual feast, in all but two years from 1521–22 to 1547–48.[117] The amount paid varies from 3s 4d to 7s; the players are never identified. The sixteenth-century records of the Pewterers are also significant. Wardens' accounts are extant from 1451–52, and include no play records until 1559; but there we find an entry that there was paid "more for the playe then was gathered of the [p<..>e] Companye" (3s 1d):[118] raising the question of whether a play paid for outside the accounts, by a separate collection, was a unique event in 1559 or had perhaps been a regular company event for some time. The accounts of the Pewterers' yeomanry, moreover, in 1559 contain an order that for the regular yeomanry dinner "every man in the company shall paye as they haue done in tymes past j d toward*es* the play".[119] Since these yeomanry accounts, extant from 1496–98 for all but two years, include no other play references, payments for plays at the dinners "in tymes past" (just when were these?) must regularly have been made outside the formal accounting system. Does the 1559 entry in the main company accounts refer to a separate (perhaps recurring) play, or to the yeomanry-dinner play? How long had one or both plays – the yeomanry's recorded in 1559 as though a continuing tradition – been taking place, and how widespread among the London companies might have been the practice of non-recorded special collections for feast-time performances?

The records of the Bakers' Company, whose accounts are extant from 1490–91 (though incomplete), also raise the latter question, although the company does have a few instances of recorded play/players payments. The Bakers had one major annual feast-time, *c.* St. Clement's Day (23 Nov.), in the fifteenth and early sixteenth centuries; in their accounts to 1547–48, feast-time dinner expenses are itemized in (only) six years, all six between 1525 and 1546; and in one of those years, 1536, we find a play payment for St. Clement's Day.[120] In two other years between 1525 and 1546 – 1528 or 1529 and 1538 or 1539 – a play is also recorded in the accounts but without its occasion being specified; it may also have been for St. Clement's Day (1529 and 1539).[121] From 1547–48 to 1558 dinner costs are not always itemized but, when they are, no play is listed, although always there are minstrels. Significantly, however, the 1538 or 1539 play record is for a payment for "the rest of A play at the hall". The main play payment (I assume the most obvious meaning of "rest") must thus have been recorded elsewhere (if at all; a general collection might simply have been made and not recorded), in accounting papers kept outside the main accounts and which have not survived.[122] Were plays at Bakers' Company feasts thus more widespread than the accounts themselves would otherwise indicate? What are the implications of this possibility for play performances at the feasts of other companies for which we have few or no play records? Twice the Bakers' players are identified: in 1528 or 1529 as the children of John Wilmot, Clerk of the Market,[123] and in 1536 as the King's Players.

Six other non-Great companies have manuscript accounts (wardens' accounts are the type of manuscript most likely to yield records of plays by paid performers) extant from various years in the fifteenth century and in some cases on into the sixteenth: the Coopers (1439–40 to 1517, but this MS is largely a quarterage book; and from 1527–28), Wiresellers/Pinners (1462–64 to 1507–10, incomplete), Leathersellers (1471–72 to 1493–94, incomplete), Weavers (from 1496, incomplete), Armourers and Brasiers (from 1497, damaged), and Founders (from 1497–98, incomplete).[124] The accounts of two of these six companies – Founders and Weavers – contain (only) one reference each to players, in the sixteenth century. The Founders record players (differentiated from minstrels) at dinner in 1529–30, and the Weavers record players at Christmas quarter day in 1552–53.[125] Non-Great companies with accounts surviving only from the early sixteenth century are the Wax Chandlers (from 1528–30? – incomplete), Butchers (from 1544–45), Stationers (from

1554–57), and Curriers (from 1556);[126] among these four, only the Wax Chandlers have a record of players: at their Jesus Day dinner (and differentiated from minstrels) in 1538.[127] Several companies also have extant court minutes from the early sixteenth century:[128] but only one set of minutes is a source of play/player records: "baldock ye playr" is listed as present at an Armourers and Brasiers' dinner in October 1541 (presumably his meal was a performance [likely part-] payment).[129]

The various play/players records which have survived, however, of both the Great and the non-Great companies, suggest that feast-time plays were a significant aspect of London company life between 1400 and 1558: regular for some guilds, though only sporadic for others, and doubtless more widespread than can be demonstrated today from extant records alone.[130] And although the recorded "players" could in some cases have been musicians, generally the companies do not seem to have used the terms minstrels and players interchangeably; and when they wrote "players," as differentiated from "minstrels," in their records, they appear normally to have meant performers of "plays" – whatever those plays may have been. What these entertainers might actually have performed for the companies is the subject of the next chapter.

Who were the performers? The records so often do not name them that only general speculation is possible. In the fifteenth century, players are wholly unidentified when employed by the Drapers, Blacksmiths, Cutlers, Carpenters, and Merchant Taylors; but the Brewers name clerks five times out of fourteen, and the Grocers twice pay a clerk's company and, once, the players of the Duke of Gloucester. Were clerks – perhaps with the ending of the major Clerkenwell play *c.* 1409 – typically hired by the London companies as performers in the fifteenth century, or were the Brewers and the Grocers unusual in their preferences? Were there also non-clerk professional or semi-professional troupes available for hire, and/or troupes with noble patrons?[131] In the sixteenth century the Drapers used a varied group of mainly professional companies with royal or aristocratic patronage (only once in nineteen occasions employing a clerk's company), plus at least once the children of Paul's; the Grocers also employed the King's Players (at least three times) and the children of the Duke of Suffolk, though also a group of clerks and choristers, at least once, to sing and make "pastyme"; and both the Grocers and the Vintners at least once hired a clerk's group (probably both times of children) from St. Magnus Church, though whether for music or for acting, or for both together, we do not know. The Merchant Taylors in the 1550s employed the children of Paul's: though perhaps for musical performances only. When the non-Great companies' records specify a performance troupe (which is seldom), twice (Blacksmiths, Bakers) it is the King's Players, once (Bakers) the children's group of John Wilmot, Clerk of the Market, and once (Tallow Chandlers) a schoolboys' group. By the sixteenth century it seems that London-area acting troupes employed by the Great Companies were in general attached to important patrons or, in the case of the children of Paul's, to St. Paul's Cathedral, moving easily back and forth between city and court; and at least the King's Players were also used by the non-Great companies. Non-specified acting companies may have been household troupes, moving in and out of the city, or professional or semi-professional performing groups operating from a London base. Any remaining clerks' drama would probably have been amateur, tied to particular parishes; and indeed sixteenth-century clerks' troupes may have become dominantly groups of children. Child singers/actors, under the tutelage of clerical masters and of schoolmasters, were of course in demand for the street pageantry of the period (see below, chapters 7 and 9) – singing on stages, reciting speeches, playing on instruments, carried in processions in tableaux vivants; and they would doubtless then have been available, in some cases, for civic hall performances, of some types, as well. A Robert Golder, for example, instructed child performers in the Drapers' midsummer pageant of 1541 (see note 67); and, as we have seen, one Golder was then paid also for play performances for the Vintners in 1539 and 1542. Might Golder even have been the clerk of St. Magnus with his company/children? Whether the clerk of St. Magnus or not, Golder might well have been a typical sixteenth-century London parish clerk, with a group of child choristers, available for hire for musical and/or theatrical performances by the companies which also made use of his services regularly in their displays of street pageantry for royal entries, for the Midsummer Watch, and, by mid-century, for the Lord Mayor's Show, all of which are discussed in chapters 7, 9, and 10.[132]

Schoolboy performers were also active on the civic level in early to mid sixteenth-century London: and not only the Boys of the Hospital hired by the Tallow Chandlers in 1551–53. The boys of St. Paul's grammar school – founded 1512, and a civic school because governed by the Mercers' Company – performed two or three times in the 1520s under their master John Rightwise for guests being entertained by Cardinal

Wolsey;[133] and although these Paul's boys may or may not have been otherwise theatrically active, by the 1550s the choir boys of St. Paul's Cathedral were being hired by the Merchant Taylors' Company as musical (though probably not theatrical) performers, and probably also (unless the other Paul's boys were involved) by the Drapers' Company for an interlude at a major company dinner.[134] Here, as in the use by the companies of acting troupes with royal or aristocratic patronage, once again London civic drama and music was interwoven with the court drama and music also of the period.[135]

CHAPTER 5

Company hall plays: types and performers

Just what kinds of plays were performed at livery company feasts from the fifteenth century on to 1558? On 14 March 1914 the master of the London Armourers and Brasiers' Company, G. Newton Pitt, gave an address at Armourers' Hall concerning his company's history: including not only the company's part in major London political events and city-wide celebrations but also its traditions of internal feasts and celebrations. Company history, always a subject of considerable interest to the London guilds, seems to have become of special interest to them around the start of the last century. 1914, for example, was the year of publication of the first volume of A. H. Johnson's five-volume history of the Drapers' Company: still today the longest single history, ever written, of a London company.[1] The preceding year, 1913, had witnessed the publication of the first of what became an ongoing series of edited volumes of Carpenters' Company manuscript records.[2] Pitt's 1914 address itself was subsequently put into print by the Armourers and Brasiers' Company, as a valuable addition to their own company's historical record.[3]

What did Armourers and Brasiers' master Pitt – whom I cite as an example, only, of early twentieth-century interest in company history – have to say at Armourers' Hall about plays and players at pre-Elizabethan company feasts, and where did he get his information? Sources available to company historians then included, as today, printed works, to date, on London history and on the London companies generally, major city records sources, and a company's own manuscript records such as accounts and court minutes; but the use then of the latter two kinds of manuscript sources by company historians often involved simply the copying down of interesting extracts to be woven into an overall historical account. Some of these extracts would be reproduced in the eventual printed company histories, others would be merely cited; and some would be dated – either from the records themselves (with the dates accurately or inaccurately read) or according to historical guesswork – while others would not. Moreover, by all but the most scholarly historians, the records extracts would often be intermingled, explicitly or without note, with general descriptive details and records from earlier printed historical works, on London generally or on the company specifically, or from other manuscript sources: without exact record citations being given. The aim was an interesting and generally accurate company history, not an academic and exact one. For the historian today, accordingly, approaching many older company histories and trying to disentangle record from historical guess or elaboration can be a frustrating process. And when some of the original manuscript records have in the meantime been lost or damaged, the historian's work becomes even more difficult.

In 1914 G. Newton Pitt described, to the assembled audience, early Armourers and Brasiers' traditions of festive celebration. On p. 23 of his printed address, supposedly drawing on the extant manuscript court minutes of the company, Pitt provides information about Armourers and Brasiers' feasting at which "The brethren and sisterne were cheered by voids of spicebrede, ypocrus and comfits to the renewed noise of the minstrels or waits or the higher merriment of the London clerks playing some holy play." The date concerned would appear, from the context, to be 1555. As an account based on the records, Pitt's description would seem to be suspect: for the details provided are very general. Early livery company court minutes are normally concerned with specific arrangements for festivities, and sometimes with costs, not with citing alternative entertainment possibilities such as minstrels or waits or a holy play. Still, this information is in Pitt's address under the heading of miscellaneous extracts from the minutes; and Pitt's description must therefore be considered seriously. Just what is Pitt's source here? Is he paraphrasing something specific from the minutes? Putting together, in his own words, several records from different places in the minutes? Or is he merely drawing on some kind of "general knowledge" of the times, and mixing this with information from the minutes, or perhaps using an older printed source? Examination of the only three earlier printed works on Armourers and Brasiers' history shows that Pitt is, at any rate, not here drawing from existing printed company sources.[4] Just how accurate and useful is his (therefore) new (in 1914) information on the kinds of entertainment provided at Armourers and Brasiers' Company feasts in the mid sixteenth century? – specifically on plays and players? Were the Armourers and Brasiers indeed entertained at one or more feasts, *c.* 1555, by London clerks playing "some holy play"? The question is important, in that the general assumption in nineteenth-century and many twentieth-century histories of other companies as well is that plays at pre-Elizabethan company feasts would have been religious in nature and performed by clerks.

The court minutes of the Armourers and Brasiers' Company have survived from 1413; but, as chapter 4 indirectly indicates, nothing resembling this specific feast entertainment description by Pitt now appears before 1559 in those minutes. Wardens' accounts from 1497 are also extant, and also yield no pre-1559 record providing a basis for Pitt's description, nor do the yeomanry court minutes extant from 1552.[5] Both accounts and court minutes, however, were considerably damaged by water during World War II, and large sections cannot be read today even under ultraviolet light. Pitt's account of holy plays *c.* 1555 cannot therefore be allowed or disallowed from consultation today of the pre-1559 manuscripts. We are forced more generally to examine the likelihood, or otherwise, of the Armourers and Brasiers' Company *c.* 1555 having enjoyed a "holy play" by the London clerks, and to make searches through other historical materials, in manuscript and in print, for a possible non-company source used by Pitt. The early records of the London Parish Clerks' Company itself are of no help; they largely have not survived, and what *has* survived includes nothing about play performances for livery companies.[6]

In fact, one does not have to go far to discover the source of Pitt's information. In 1834 William Herbert, Librarian of the Corporation of London, Guildhall, published the first volume of his two-volume *History of the Twelve Great Livery Companies of London*; and in that volume appear almost identically the words found in Pitt's address, in a section of the history dealing with the election feasts and ceremonials of London livery companies in general.[7] Herbert places within quotation marks some of the words used by Pitt ("bretheren and susterne," "voyds of spice brede ypocras and comfits," "noise," "waits," "playing some holy play"), providing himself the other words, as found in Pitt, to link the quoted ones (for which he gives no source). Pitt's feast-time entertainment information, then, first appearances to the contrary, has in fact nothing to do specifically with the Armourers and Brasiers' Company, or with its records, or with 1555. Pitt is, rather, simply taking Herbert's generalized picture of livery company festivities and applying it (perhaps inspired by some detail, now lost to damage, in the company's early manuscripts) to the Armourers and Brasiers in a 1555 context. But what, then, is Herbert's source? What lies behind Herbert's quotations, and especially his (apparently widely influential) indication that plays performed at livery company feasts in early times were (invariably or generally) "holy" ones, i.e., on religious subject matter, and acted by parish clerks?

Herbert follows his lines quoted by Pitt with a new paragraph beginning: "That the above picture is not one of mere fancy, is to be seen in all the early accounts of expenses of the companies." This suggests that, whatever the source(s), print or otherwise, for Herbert's generalizations, the records of the London companies have confirmed to him the details provided. Without further pursuit, then, of one or more possible printed sources used by Herbert,[8] the ultimate authority to be consulted is company records. Did the accounts of the London livery companies in fact allow Herbert to draw or to confirm this general picture of clerks' holy plays?

In all of the companies' extant records of pre-Elizabethan plays and players, as previously described (chapter 4), there is only once a reference to what was actually performed on a company occasion: in a record of a performance at a supper for the Drapers' bachelors (members of the company just below the ranks of the livery) in 1519.[9] A single unnamed performer played a "friar" – which sounds more like a satirical sketch than any kind of holy performance.[10] Herbert's statement about holy plays thus could not have been based upon or confirmed by company performance records of specific plays performed, unless some records were available to him that have since disappeared. Nor can Herbert have looked at the early fifteenth-century extant theatrical writings of John Lydgate (discussed below in chapter 6), since Lydgate's theatrical works associated with the London companies are largely secular. What, then, about clerks as performers for the companies? In the fifteenth century, as we have seen in chapter 4, Brewers' Company records indicate that clerks were the usual players at Brewers' feasts; and the same was possibly true for the Grocers. Perhaps clerks mainly formed the performance troupes for hire in the London area in the earlier fifteenth century, after the ending of the major Clerkenwell play (a logical suggestion): but we can only speculate, as in the extensive records of plays and players for the fifteenth-century Drapers, Blacksmiths, and Cutlers, and in the few miscellaneous fifteenth-century records of the Merchant Taylors and Carpenters, the performers are never specified. Moreover, as we have already seen, the Grocers' fifteenth-century records refer once, early on (1431–32), to the players of Humphrey Duke of Gloucester – not a clerk's troupe; and there were other non-clerical troupes also attached to members of the court, throughout the fifteenth century, and thus also potentially available to the London companies, especially to those companies with significant court connections.[11]

Then, once we reach the sixteenth century and references to playing companies by name become more frequent, named clerks' groups are outnumbered by named others and also seem generally to have changed in make-up. In the sixteenth century before 1559, as we have seen, plays were demonstrably performed very occasionally, sporadically, or regularly for all of the Bakers, Blacksmiths, Carpenters, Drapers, Founders, Skinners, Tallow Chandlers, Wax Chandlers, and Weavers, and apparently also the Pewterers; and although comparatively seldom do the records identify actors for us, when they do, the actors are seldom clerks. The only company in the sixteenth century whose records fairly consistently tell us the identity of the play performers at its annual election feast time is the Drapers, which from 1516 to 1541 names troupes with royal or aristocratic patrons eighteen times and only once, in 1540, a parish clerk's group.[12] And although the Drapers are not typical of other London companies in the sixteenth century in that they often provide acting-group names in their records, that they were not necessarily untypical in hiring largely non-clerical performers is indicated by what few other references we do have, in the sixteenth-century records of other companies, to specific acting troupes. The Bakers, as we have seen, pay for a play by the children of John Wilmot, Clerk of the Market (not a religious clerk), in 1528-29, and for the King's Players in 1536; the Tallow Chandlers have a play by the Boys of the Hospital (a school group) in 1557-59; and the Blacksmiths, with their regular cony feast performances, on the single occasion they record the identity of a performance troupe specify the King's Players (though the unusual naming of the troupe, together with a larger than usual payment, may indicate that employing the King's Players was unusual for them).[13] Only one sixteenth-century clerk's company is definitely recorded outside the Drapers' records: the company of the clerk of the church of St. Magnus Martyr, apparently a group of boy choristers, paid for one 1530s performance (perhaps musical only, perhaps not) for each of the Grocers and the Vintners.[14] The Vintners also pay a certain "Golder" for a play, in both 1539 and 1542, who would appear to be the master of a group of children;[15] possibly he was a clerk, even the clerk of St. Magnus. Clerks' plays/performances by the sixteenth century, on this admittedly slight evidence, would thus appear to have become, at least in significant part, plays/performances by children (and perhaps thus also to have significantly incorporated music); and this conclusion is reinforced by the records of performances in the 1550s, for both the Drapers (one interlude) and the Merchant Taylors (eight entertainments, at least three of them musical), by the boy choristers of St. Paul's Cathedral.[16]

Why did Herbert – who was followed by many others interested in London company history – accept or confirm clerks and holy plays as the norm for pre-Elizabethan company feasts? For the section of his *History* in which his discussion of general internal company festivities appears, Herbert seems to have used the records basically of the Brewers, Fishmongers, Grocers, Leathersellers, and Merchant Taylors. No other company's own records are referred to between the start of Herbert's general discussion of the "Ancient State of the Companies" and the end of the chapter.[17] And Herbert appears to have used, from this group of companies, above all the records of the Brewers and of the Grocers: unsurprisingly, since the Leathersellers' Company has only one account/inventory book[18] and no court minutes or other such potentially relevant (for entertainment/theatrical information) manuscripts extant for the period before 1559, and the Fishmongers also have very little of pre-1559 potential relevance. As we have seen, the Brewers' Company – although it has play performance records only for the fifteenth century – regularly specifies clerks as its performers; and the Grocers – although also naming a couple of court/aristocratic troupes – pay clerks for performances in the mid fifteenth century, and again for one or two in the sixteenth century, as well as employing on one occasion the children of the Duke of Suffolk's house (what the children did is not specified). The Duke of Suffolk's children were not a parish clerk's company, but they could have been – or could have been thought by Herbert to have been – a chapel group in the Duke's household. Furthermore, although in sixteenth-century Brewers' accounts and minutes no play or player records appear, there is a continuing association of the company with clerks. Between 1500 and 1537 Brewers' manuscripts show small payments (4d to 1521, 8d from 1527), in some twenty different years, to St. Nicholas' clerks and/or bishop on St. Nicholas' night or eve (6 or 5 December) in Brewers' Hall:[19] apparently involving the clerks' festivities surrounding the choosing of a mock "Boy Bishop," a traditional St. Nicholas Day (or Eve) activity in much of medieval Europe and continuing in England into the sixteenth century.[20] Parish clerks were especially associated with St. Nicholas (London's Parish Clerks' guild was the guild of St. Nicholas); and five of the Brewers' twenty very similar St. Nicholas payments refer specifically to a St. Nicholas Bishop. The payments are too small to involve plays; they are merely contributions to celebrating clerks; but the Brewers thus seem to have maintained a special relationship with clerk-focused entertainment, from the fifteenth through to almost the mid sixteenth century. Certainly, therefore, if generalizing largely from the Brewers' fifteenth-century play records supplemented by their sixteenth-century St. Nicholas ones, and looking also at the Grocers' manuscripts, Herbert would logically have believed that clerks normally performed plays for livery companies in "ancient" times; and the Merchant Taylors' 1550s payments to the Children of Paul's would then perhaps have reinforced Herbert in his conclusions. Herbert apparently did not consult, for this section of his work, the Drapers' court minutes, which would have given him a very different picture, at least for the sixteenth century, of the kinds of acting troupes performing at livery company feasts.[21]

Then, as for types of plays performed, Herbert seems to have assumed (or agreed), from the fact that (adult) clerks performed plays, that such plays would of necessity have been "holy." No such assumption seems safe, although London clerks did perform the Clerkenwell/Skinners' Well play, and so had religious drama in their repertories, as it were, in the early fifteenth century. Ecclesiastical concern with what the Church considered to be the unholy activities of clerks, even within Church settings, are to be found in writings and prohibitions throughout this period; and authors such as Lydgate were clerks, monks, and priests yet produced secular as well as religious writings. Moreover, even the term "holy plays" is problematic. Does it include, for example, morality plays containing – as many do – significant amounts of farcical comedy and song? Further, would troupes of boy choristers in the early sixteenth century, headed by clerks/masters, when hired by livery companies for feast time entertainment necessarily have performed "holy plays"? Not if we are to judge by what the (royal) Chapel Children performed at court, such as a disputation about Love/Cupid versus Riches/Plutus, and including the characters of Mercury, Justice, and Jupiter, in 1527,[22] or by what schoolboys performed for aristocratic audiences, such as John Rightwise's Latin *Dido*, in the 1520s, before guests of Cardinal Wolsey.[23]

Since, then, we have no records evidence – apart from the "friar" at the Drapers' bachelors' supper, and the work of Lydgate discussed in the next chapter – as to what was performed at London livery company feasts, the best we can do is to try to determine from surviving play texts of the period 1400–1558, very generally, what might have been pre-Elizabethan livery company performance fare. Moreover, especially in the early fifteenth century, as we saw in chapter 4, a hall "play" and "players" might have involved one or more of juggling, acrobatics, recitation, song, performance sketches, and so forth (although some company records specify tumblers, jugglers, and the like, separately from players[24]); and moreover, occasionally what the records call a "play" might have been what we today would call a "mumming" (as defined in chapters 3 and 6), although the records, in sometimes specifying mummings and in indicating that they were presentations/gifts to particular individuals or groups, would appear at least sometimes – perhaps normally – to differentiate between them and plays.[25] Civic mummings by the early fifteenth-century writer John Lydgate are discussed in the next chapter.

Actual plays – theatrical pieces – appropriate for livery company hall performance do exist from the fifteenth century, however, and such plays would appear (as discussed below) to have become the performance norm for paid playing troupes by at least the sixteenth century. Probably they were also the norm in the fifteenth. The surviving plays from both centuries cover a wide range of subject matter; and although none of them was ever provably performed at a London company feast, they at least demonstrate a wide variety of possibilities – both religious and secular – for feast-time performances.[26] Different livery companies may have preferred different types of performances; but there is no reason overall to suppose any narrow limitations on the types of plays that pre-Elizabethan companies watched (although religious plays might perhaps have been more likely in the early to mid fifteenth century after the ending of the major Clerkenwell play). These were largely middle-class audiences, across a wide economic spectrum, and sometimes or often – for an important and wealthy company – with guests at company dinners from the ranks of the higher clergy and the court. Since company feast times invariably included both religious and secular components, such as masses, memorials, dinners, and drinkings, almost no type of play can be ruled out as unsuitable for feast-time performance. A norm of performing company size, however, in both the fifteenth and the sixteenth centuries, as indicated by the payments records of several companies, appears to have been four adults;[27] so performances requiring more – or fewer – than four participants were apparently untypical (at least insofar as what has been recorded is concerned) of pre-Elizabethan livery company fare, unless a children's company (always larger) was involved. (Special occasions, of course, may have called for special performances.) The records we have of named children's groups – musical or theatrical – paid to perform at company feasts all come from the sixteenth century; so in what follows I will assume adult performers as typical for the companies before *c.* 1485, and both adults' and children's troupes as livery hall performers during the Tudor period, with four-adult plays as the norm, throughout the period, for recurring company occasions such as election feasts. It is certainly possible, however, that children's groups associated with London churches or with noble households were available to the companies before *c.* 1485 as well as in the sixteenth century. Chorister-children's play performances (or adult choristers', for that matter) might be hidden, for example, within some companies' payments for what appear now to be entirely religious-service expenses at company feast times.

As for play length: at an election-time dinner a play, of whatever type, would have had to share the spotlight not only with the food and drink but also with the ceremonial surrounding the selection and induction of new company officers.[28] An election-time play might have been performed, however, after a dinner or a supper, or divided between the two (in two parts), or before and on the election day, and not necessarily between dinner courses on election day or in combination with election ceremonial.[29] Also some companies, such as the Blacksmiths, did not have their plays at election times, although others did. Appropriate play length may therefore be estimated to have been anywhere from *c.* 30 to *c.* 90 minutes or even longer, depending on the specific circumstances. Musicians from outside the performance troupe itself also might sometimes have been available for use by the players, if the play required or would benefit from more music than the performers themselves could provide. Minstrels, as we have seen, were also often employed by companies at feast times – for example, at election dinners, to play for election ceremonial; so they might sometimes have been available for additional play music as well.

No company's records 1410–1558 indicate any special staging arrangements made for hired players; presumably therefore there were none, the entertainments presented being eminently portable, and perhaps simply taking place on the hall floor; or, alternatively, all staging matters (including any special arrangements and costs) may have been left to the actors themselves to work out, or staging arrangements may have been handled in ways not recorded (for example, by being assigned to a company officer as a part of his administrative duties).[30] There is no need, however, to assume consistency in this area across the companies, or from occasion to occasion, or across the whole time period from 1410 to 1558.

Finally no records exist of any plays – as opposed to mummings, such as Lydgate's in the early fifteenth century – being written to order for company performance; the performers' repertories, within which there would have been choice, presumably sufficed (as discussed below in relation to the fictional acting troupe depicted in the 1590s' *Sir Thomas More*). Nothing, however, can be ruled out, including an acting company deciding to increase its chances of livery-company employment by preparing a performance piece geared to a specific guild's interests, or individual company members commissioning (and paying for) specific pieces.

THE FIFTEENTH CENTURY

For the fifteenth century there are a number of kinds of plays extant today – probably a small fraction of the original numbers performed[31] – which suggest possibilities for London company feast-time performances: religious plays on biblical subject matter, saint/miracle plays, recitations or dialogues involving one or a few characters (e.g., classical gods or goddesses, allegorical personifications), morality plays, classically influenced plays, and folk dramas. (References to theatrical romances have also survived.) Very few of the extant texts can be linked in any way to London; largely the plays provide examples, only, of the kinds of dramatic fare that existed elsewhere and so doubtless existed in the London area as well. In what follows (and largely for the subsequent sixteenth-century section as well) I largely ignore matters of interpretative analysis, except when strong political controversy might be involved. The focus is on play availability and on practical suitability in terms of cast size, staging requirements, and overall theatrical interest.[32]

Plays on biblical subject matter

Surviving texts exist, of course, though not themselves all from the fifteenth century, for four of the great provincial cycle dramas of England (not counting the Cornish cycle), and for separate biblical plays – such as the fifteenth-century Brome *Abraham and Isaac* – which may or may not originally have been parts of a cycle. Conversely, the extant cycle manuscripts may be in part compilations of what were originally texts of single plays, or of separate groups of plays. Individual plays within cycles can be found with small casts, minimal staging requirements, and both short and long running times; and such kinds of plays, on biblical subject matter but standing independent of cycles – indeed, perhaps extracted, in early fifteenth-century London, from the materials of the Clerkenwell play/cycle – might have been performed at a company's feast times. Livery companies' election feasts, for example, were always at the time of specific religious festivals (e.g., Michaelmas, St. John Baptist's Day, the Feast of the Assumption of the Virgin); the feast time activities included one or more masses; and the companies might well have been interested – perhaps especially in the fifteenth century soon after the ending of the major Clerkenwell play – in biblical plays, especially ones appropriate to the festivals involved. The Drapers, for example, might have been particularly interested in plays about the Assumption of the Virgin, since their guild saint was the Blessed Virgin of the Assumption and their election day was *c.* 15 August (Assumption Day). Such biblical subjects were represented in the companies' street pageants in the sixteenth century London Midsummer Watch; the Drapers, for example, had an Assumption pageant in 1512 and in a number of subsequent years.[33]

Saint / miracle plays

Extant saint or miracle plays from the fifteenth century – the Croxton *Play of the Sacrament*, probably the two-day Cornish *St. Meriasek*, and perhaps the Digby *Mary Magdalene* and *The Conversion of St. Paul* (the last two being perhaps *c.* 1500)[34] – are long, involve elaborate special effects, and are connected with locales other than London; but presumably short and less spectacularly elaborate saint and miracle plays (biblical and non-biblical) also existed, and also in the London area. Chapter 3 has already noted London's 1393 lost St. Katherine play – though it may not have been short or unelaborate; and we also have records of lost saint plays from areas other than London.[35] London companies (especially considering their internal religious fraternities) might have been interested in plays about their own patron saints (such as St. Clement, for the Bakers, or St. Dunstan, for the Goldsmiths), upon or around whose days election feasts were usually held. Saints were certainly featured by the companies in sixteenth-century Midsummer Watch pageants in the London streets;[36] and a MS record well into the Elizabethan period shows a presentation, at a 1585 Armourers and Brasiers' election feast, of an armed boy (representing St. George, the company's patron saint) and a lady leading a lamb, accompanied by a recitation of some sort.[37] Early fifteenth-century writings by John Lydgate involving saints and the London companies (such as the Armourers and Brasiers) are discussed in chapter 6.

Recitations

Recitations/dialogues by one or more actors playing gods, classical worthies, allegorical figures, and the like, could have been designed around particular topics, events, or personages of special significance to a company. The 1585 Armourers and Brasiers' presentation just mentioned provides an Elizabethan example. Chapter 6 deals with the possibility of such civic recitations/dialogues in relation to the writings of Lydgate.

Morality plays

Morality plays such as the anonymous, late fifteenth-century *Mankind* (though *Mankind* itself requires six actors) would have provided serious and/or comic festive fare. Notably *Mankind* has internal references indicating that it was written as a winter-season hall play;[38] and its built-in money collection provides a model for how an acting troupe to be paid by a special company feast-time collection could have structured a text to incorporate such a means of payment. *Mankind* itself, of course, comes from Cambridgeshire and Norfolk;[39] but the model of a play incorporating not only money-collection but also – given the specific personal names, in its text, of audience members – the actors' advance knowledge of the membership of their audience, is particularly useful when we consider that company memberships were stable and well known and that major company feasts recurred annually or biennially (or sometimes triennially), always at pre-set times of the year. Incorporating word-play, song, bawdy comedy, and emotional moralizing, *Mankind* is a persuasive argument for the inclusive entertainment of this kind of drama.

Henry Medwall's two-part morality *Nature* (*c.* 1490–1500) is itself too long, and with too many actors required, for probable ordinary company entertainment circumstances;[40] but it is certainly an example of a late fifteenth-century morality specifically connected with London, containing a good number of internal London references. It was probably performed within the household of Cardinal Morton, Medwall's patron, at Lambeth or at Knole, Kent, to a courtly audience,[41] and might then have become available, from its performers, to a company for a special occasion such as entertaining royal, noble, or ambassadorial guests.[42] It did not reach print (and therefore general availability) until 1530–34.[43]

Classically influenced texts

Classically influenced secular plays would also have appealed to companies of wealthy and educated Londoners accustomed to moving in court circles. Henry Medwall's *c.* 1496–97 *Fulgens and Lucres*, also probably written for performance before Morton,[44] is another useful example, like *Nature*, of a purpose-written hall play in two parts (1432 + 921 lines), to be performed on two separate occasions in one day.[45] It requires, however, more than four actors. Of broader appeal than *Nature*, it uses a mixture of theatrical techniques (audience address, slapstick comedy, moral preaching, actor–audience interaction, and so forth) and is influenced by all of morality drama, debate tradition (philosophical, legal and literary), and bawdy farce, as well as Roman comedy (with its witty scheming servants). Medwall's play is a late fifteenth-century example; but classical influences were not a late fifteenth-century development. In the early fifteenth century classical mythology is seen, for example, in the theatrical writings of Lydgate (chapter 6).

David Bevington believes that *Fulgens and Lucres* was performed by a professional adult troupe; Suzanne Westfall agrees with Alan H. Nelson and M. E. Moeslein that Morton's household performers, including children, were the actors.[46] Either way, a livery company might have been able to hire the actors to perform the play for a special occasion; and the text became generally available in print in 1512–16.[47]

Folk-type entertainment

Folk dramas taken up by professional actors could have provided secular amusement: on topics such as courtship, marriage, and seduction, or on subjects (especially for spring-time feasts) such as Robin Hood. Robin Hood plays were performed in the late fifteenth century at the home of John Paston (at Norwich?[48]) – so were not confined to folk audiences; and there is no reason to believe that they would have been confined, either, to the provinces. The extant surviving fragment of the fifteenth-century Robin Hood play supposedly performed for the Pastons, usually known today under the modern title of *Robin Hood and the Sheriff of Nottingham*, shows how such a play could provide entertaining displays of various kinds of physical combat; and Robin Hood entertainments continued into the sixteenth century both at court and in the city.[49]

Mummings

Mummings, involving elaborate costuming display and dancing but normally without character dialogue although a presenter might recite lines, had widespread popularity in the fifteenth century, being presented at court, in the homes of civic officials at special times such as Christmas, and informally from door to door apparently largely during the Christmas season. Late fourteenth-century mumming has already been described in chapter 3. Performers could be amateur or professional, many or few; visuals could be simple or elaborate.

Might the records of plays at company feasts, especially during the winter season, refer at times in the fifteenth century to mummings? Mummings, designated as such, do appear separately from plays in company records, however, and also are normally specified as presentations to someone: to the king, to a company sheriff, to a mayor. Such records would seem to indicate that companies normally, at least, did not use the terms mumming and play interchangeably. Theatrical terminology in the fifteenth century was, however, notably elastic; and a mumming might sometimes have been included within the term play. Two or three of the surviving mummings written by John Lydgate *were* performed at London civic (though not necessarily company) feasts; but since they are not entered in the extant record books of the companies which commissioned them, we do not know what the companies themselves might have called them. They are not called plays in their surviving texts. Lydgate's civic mummings are discussed in chapter 6.

THE SIXTEENTH CENTURY

By the sixteenth century, given the known professional troupes such as the King's Players and Duke of Suffolk's Players performing at some guild feasts, the repertory of such an acting group, with its norm of four performers,[50] would seem to provide the best guess at what would have been the standard dramatic fare provided on such occasions. Court and city apparently watched at least some of the same kinds of theatrical entertainment, since they employed at least some of the same troupes.

Our sense of what would have been in such a troupe's repertory, and thus available for company feast-time entertainment, must come in part, then, from looking at extant small-cast plays by early sixteenth-century writers for the court and aristocracy, and considering also the portability, or otherwise, of these plays' staging requirements; but also we can look at other early sixteenth-century "portable" printed plays, with larger casts, some of which included directions as to how the play's multiple characters could be doubled by a limited number of actors. Such plays, however and wherever they originated, clearly had become intended, by the time they were printed, at least in part for general performances – which might have included livery company feast performances – by the acting troupes of the day. *Mundus et Infans* (*The World and the Child, c.* 1507–08), for example, has been argued to have originated as a household play in Bedfordshire for the thirteenth earl of Kent;[51] but, printed in 1522, it then became available to acting troupes in general, and as a short (979 lines), 5-character, 2-actor morality about man's progress from childhood to old age would have been ideal where a short and serious entertainment was required.[52]

We also have, however, a fictional source to give us a sense of an early sixteenth-century acting company's repertory – and one connected with acting in London itself: the *c.* 1595 *Book of Sir Thomas More*,[53] a collaborate biographical play by Anthony Munday, Thomas Dekker, Henry Chettle, perhaps Shakespeare, and perhaps others, about the noted Londoner who became Lord Chancellor of England and was executed in 1535. In *Sir Thomas More* a group of actors (four men and a boy) – called the Lord Cardinal's players – arrive at More's home and are hired to perform a play: at first before, then after, the dinner More is just about to give for the mayor and some of the aldermen and their wives; and although *Sir Thomas More* dates from some sixty years after More's death, and cannot in any case be treated as a work of historical accuracy, several of the titles recited in the play as from the repertory of the drama's fictional acting troupe are titles of actual earlier sixteenth-century plays still extant today.[54] These plays, all apparently thought by *More*'s experienced professional playwrights to be appropriately portrayed as potential dinner fare for a largely civic audience in the earlier sixteenth century, are *The Four PP* (a satirical four-character dialogue written *c.* 1520–22 by court entertainer John Heywood), *Lusty Juventus* (a morality play, *c.* 1550–53, centering on a youth who must learn to accept Good Council and Knowledge and to reject Abominable Living), *Impatient Poverty* (another morality play, *c.* 1553–58, this one about a protagonist torn between Peace and Conscience, on the one side, and Envy, Abundance, and Misrule on the other), and *The Marriage of Wit and Wisdom* (*c.* 1571–77, a morality as well).[55] The first three of the four – all pre-Elizabethan – require a cast of only four adult performers; *The Marriage of Wit and Wisdom* – chosen for the play-within-a-play performance in *More*, and past the date limits of this study – requires six.[56] All of the three remaining plays in *Sir Thomas More*'s list, all non-extant, are generally dated today as from after 1558 and so will be ignored here. (They include a morality, a piece with a title indicating biblical subject matter, and a play with a proverbial title whose subject matter is unknown.[57]) The three pre-1558 plays still extant would seem to be excellent examples of kinds of theatrical entertainment likely to have been performed at early sixteenth-century livery company feasts. *The Four PP* is a prime candidate for company hall performance: a verbal farce written by a court entertainer whose plays should certainly have been in the repertory of the King's Players or another such company. (The play was not printed until *c.* 1545.[58]) It also requires no special staging, involving simply four characters who enter, one by one, an acting area, tell one another tall tales, and sing. Moreover the jokes, largely aimed at corrupt social and religious practices and at women, can be taken "straight" or as evidence of the characters' fraudulent natures: allowing for differing points of view among audience members.[59] Both *Lusty Juventus* and *Impatient Poverty* are much later (and the latter was published only after 1558): but also require only four actors, provide considerable comedy and some uncomplicated music, and have no elaborate staging requirements.[60] The longest of these three plays, *The Four PP*, does not exceed 1236 lines, the shortest, *Impatient Poverty*, is 1100 lines; and all would seem to be hall plays, with comic audience address and/or actor–audience interaction (as portrayed in *Sir Thomas More*'s play-within-the-play) as a norm.

Other early sixteenth-century plays which would thus also seem prime candidates for livery company hall performances include Heywood's (attributed) *The Pardoner and the Friar* (*c.* 1513–21; printed 1533), a farcical comedy of *c.* 641 lines, requiring four actors, audience involvement, and no special staging, and *Johan Johan* (*c.* 1528–33; printed 1533), a three-character English version of a French farce, about a cuckolded husband, his wife, and her priest-lover, with 680 lines and also audience involvement and no special staging requirements.[61] Both plays, like *The Four PP*, would easily have crossed between court and city, in dinner-time performances. Heywood's more serious *Witty and Witless* (*c.* 1520–33; three actors, *c.* 700 lines; not printed) and *A Play of Love* (*c.* 1528–33; four actors, about twice as long as *Witty and Witless*; printed 1534), essentially philosophical disputations rather than plays, might also have worked well on some kinds of livery occasions.[62] Another playwright with both the connections and the writing and staging expertise to have had his plays performed both in royal/aristocratic settings and in company halls was Heywood's father-in-law, John Rastell. Rastell's educational play *The Four Elements* (*c.* 1517–20; 1443 lines) indeed seems a play in part designed (at least in its *c.* 1520 printing) for movement among varying performance sites and for varying theatrical requirements of length and complexity.[63] It can be acted, Rastell notes in his introduction to the printed edition, either in a short form (by five actors, as Bevington has pointed out) or in a longer, more serious form with a disguising included as well.[64] (Disguisings – involving elaborate costumes and audience participation in dancing – were extremely popular at court in the early sixteenth century, and in civic London as well.[65]) Moreover two other plays printed by Rastell, the (printed) *c.* 1523–25(?) *Calisto and Melebea* (1087 lines), based on the seduction-focused Spanish *La Celestina* but turned into a moral lesson with a happy ending,[66] and the (printed) *c.* 1519–28 *Gentleness and Nobility* (1176 lines), a disputation on social rank versus moral worth (and perhaps by Heywood),[67] also seem appropriate fare for the companies as well as for the court; and both could be performed by no more than four actors (three for *Gentleness and Nobility*).[68] Like Medwall's two 1490s plays already discussed, *Gentleness and Nobility* is in two parts, for presentation on two occasions such as dinner and supper on the same day. Both plays were also printed apparently not long after they were written, and so became generally available to acting troupes.[69]

On some occasions, of course, longer adult plays and/or ones requiring more than four actors would doubtless have been performed; and also David Bevington has demonstrated how plays in general by professional adult troupes gradually lengthened as the century moved along.[70] If we look, especially after *c.* 1550, for adult troupe pieces involving more lines and more (five to six) actors, possibilities for the companies expand further. The anonymous morality *Wealth and Health* (*c.* 1554–55), for example, probably (first) performed at court before Queen Mary,[71] though only 964 lines long requires six actors.[72] This does not mean, of course, that all plays from *c.* 1550 on were more demanding in their performance requirements. The extant fragment of a play today titled *Love Feigned and Unfeigned*, possibly as late as 1560 (*c.* 1540–60) and thought to be dated *c.* 1550, indicates perhaps a four-actor play (though we have only 243 lines and so cannot tell how long or how elaborate the full play may have been). It includes audience address and song.[73]

Probably the companies – and most certainly the well-connected Great Companies – under most circumstances would have wanted to steer clear of plays involving significant political controversy: such as the *c.* 1513 anonymous *Youth* (786 lines, five actors), which has been argued to have been a politically satirical household play, critical of Henry VIII, connected with a northern seat of the fifth earl of Northumberland.[74] Anything performed in a London company hall – especially a Great Company hall – would have become almost immediately known to the Crown; and it was in no company's interest – nor the city's generally – to cross the monarch unnecessarily. Some kinds of political drama might, however, have been desirable under some circumstances; and some noble patrons might have been eager to have their perspectives conveyed, via their players (and perhaps even sometimes without charge), to important city companies. The *c.* 1514 anonymous *Hickscorner*, for example, a four-actor hall morality (1026 lines) including specific London references, has been persuasively argued by Ian Lancashire to have been a politically-charged work originally written for presentation at Suffolk Place, the Southwark seat of Charles Brandon, Duke of Suffolk.[75] The play supported the king, and might have been available to London companies from Suffolk's players. (It was printed 1515–16.) What about John Skelton's *Magnificence* (*c.* 1519–20; 1567 lines, five actors; also containing London local references)? Paula Neuss has suggested performance at Merchant Taylors' Hall, and Alistair Fox, concurring with her, believes the play to have been written to advance Londoners' views on current affairs involving the king; but it is difficult to believe that the Merchant Taylors would have gone anywhere near the play (let alone commission it) if it were as politically flammable as both Neuss and Fox suggest.[76] In fact the play's two dialogue lines picked out by Neuss as pointing to Merchant Taylors' Hall are insufficient evidence to place the play there;[77] and only a less controversial *Magnificence* in any case, not the play as either Neuss or Fox has interpreted it, would seem plausible as a Great Company's performance piece on some special occasion. Greg Walker, in accepting Neuss's auspices suggestion, has argued for a less controversial interpretation.[78] The plays of John Bale thus also present a problem in relation to the companies: probably too ideologically strident for most, though perhaps not for all.[79] A difficulty that we have today, of course, in trying to determine politically acceptable livery company theatrical fare, is that the political nature and impact of many early Tudor plays appear to have depended on very specific political circumstances, at specific times, which today may be difficult to unearth and to interpret;[80] and the ideological make-up of a company's livery (its senior members) would be a factor to take into account when trying to determine what that company at any given time might have found to be acceptable feast-time entertainment.[81] Also some plays initially controversial, and therefore potentially risky for companies, might later have become comparatively innocuous, and vice versa.

The 1540s and 1550s were the period of greatest royal and civic concern over play performances in London, pre-1559; and when in 1542 the London civic government tried to suppress and to regulate plays in the city, it prohibited plays in company halls as well as in public places: a sure indication that company halls were not insignificant as playing places at this time. Then, in 1544 to 1546, it ruled that plays be allowed in the houses of the nobility, gentry, civic officials, and solid citizens, in open streets (i.e., in full view of civic and royal officials), *and in company halls*.[82] The companies must have provided some political reliability for the city, in terms of what kinds of performances they would permit inside their premises: and the city in the 1540s may have been not so much concerned with plays for the companies themselves as with plays in halls rented from the companies by acting troupes.[83] Hall rentals by players become significantly recorded by the London companies in the late 1530s and the 1540s.[84]

When for the sixteenth century we look at plays definitely or apparently performed by London-area children's troupes (larger than adult troupes), the variety of plays-for-hire potentially available to London companies expands further; and although some of these plays required large stage properties and musicians, company halls could have been set up in advance by the actors, and musicians could have been supplied. As we have seen, payments to a few children's companies, for music or for plays, are to be found in some London companies' sixteenth-century records. Such children's groups, when not musical only, were probably restricted to plays purpose-written for them and to classical pieces; and presumably the London companies would largely have avoided from the children, as from the adult troupes, highly political plays: such as *Godly Queen Hester*, if a children's play from *c.* 1541–42[85] (Greg Walker has recently proposed religious auspices for the play, *c.* 1529[86]), and perhaps the pro-Catholic *Respublica* (from the first Christmas of Mary's reign).[87] The

London companies might on some special occasions have enjoyed a schoolboy play such as John Redford's *Wit and Science* (*c.* 1544–47; 1101 lines), possibly written for the Paul's choristers when Redford was their master,[88] and featuring dancing, singing, music, and the giant Tediousness, or a children's piece such as *Jack Juggler* (*c.* 1553–58), an adaptation of Plautus' *Amphitruo*.[89] A classically based Latin drama such as the (non-extant) *Dido* performed by the schoolboys of St. Paul's grammar school for Wolsey and his guests in the 1520s might have been suitable for a Great Company entertaining royalty or foreign ambassadors.[90] What might a company such as the clerk of St. Magnus' have performed, if it was more than a children's company of musical performers?[91] What did the Boys of the Hospital perform for the Tallow Chandlers in 1557–59? The royal Chapel Children performed a play about Troilus, Pander, Cressida and the Greeks (not now extant) at court in January 1516,[92] and, as previously seen, a pageant and dialogue concerning Love/Cupid versus Riches/Plutus in 1527. Though they themselves appear never to have performed outside the court, this extends our knowledge of the variety of possible children's troupe offerings. Children may also have performed Heywood's satirical *Play of the Weather c.* 1519–28,[93] and did perform the classically based *Ralph Roister Doister* (*c.* 1547–48). By the 1550s the choristers of Paul's, besides doing musical performances for the Merchant Taylors, might sometimes also have been performing sophisticated dramas for the companies employing them. The various children's troupes available to the court at its London-area palaces, other than the children of the royal chapels, would presumably have been available to at least some of the companies as well, along with any London parish-based troupes of boy choristers.[94]

Finally some fifteenth-century types of entertainment not included in what has been already described for the sixteenth century continued into the 1500s and would presumably have been available to companies: saint/miracle plays at least until *c.* the early 1530s,[95] and types of folk drama such as Robin Hood entertainments (encouraged for London players by Bishop Gardiner in 1545[96]). *The Interlude of Johan the Evangelist* (before 1520; printed *c.* 1550 and perhaps by 1520;[97] 653 lines), an odd work consisting of long speeches by the saint intermingled with comic and serious discussions of salvation and damnation, and requiring three to four actors, is difficult to place in terms of auspices but is an example of the kind of saint play which could conceivably have been associated with a craft guild (St. John the Evangelist was a company-sponsored pageant figure in some London Midsummer Watches); and Robin Hood, also a court preoccupation for a time under Henry VIII, should also have interested the city.[98] A disguising is recorded at Skinners' Hall in January 1519 (when a Skinner was mayor);[99] and we also know that, beyond the company's own halls, civic entertainment annually at the Christmas season included "disguisinges, Maskes and Mummeries" in the households of the mayors and sheriffs (always, of course, members of companies); historian John Stow, in his *Survey of London* (first published 1598; second edition 1603), writes of this as a continuing tradition, in his comments on civic misrule festivities and lords of misrule (organizers of parodic/burlesque entertainments, activities, and games) during the regular, extended seasonal festivities of 31 October through 2 February.[100] Stow unfortunately does not tell us much more about the normal hall components of such seasonal entertainment in the mayor's and sheriffs' households (and a city record of 1527 also refers only very generally to sports, singing, and pastimes);[101] and other contemporary sources for sixteenth-century civic misrule festivities focus upon the outdoor/street and royal components of what were apparently unusually elaborate, specific misrule activities in the early 1550s, involving two visits of the king's Lord of Misrule to London.[102] In 1555 the city's Common Council, addressing the issue of costs, forbad the further keeping of lords of misrule by the mayor and sheriffs.[103]

In the small world of early sixteenth-century civic London, the livery company memberships and family interrelationships of some of the major play lovers and play writers of the time should finally be emphasized. One set of memberships and relationships, already mentioned in part, will suffice as an example. Thomas More's reputation as a lover of drama is emphasized in the late sixteenth-century play *Sir Thomas More*; More had begun his political career as a youth in the 1490s in the household of Cardinal Morton, Medwall's patron, supposedly acting extemporaneously there;[104] and More was at one time involved in London's civic government as an under-sheriff, and was a member of the wealthy and prestigious Mercers' Company.[105] William Crane, master of the royal Chapel Children 1523–45, was first a Draper but transferred to the Mercers in 1526 in order to receive, at the king's request, the office of Weigher of Raw Silks, which was the Mercers' to give.[106] John Heywood, court entertainer, musician, and playwright, became a Mercer in 1530: transferring from the Stationers to obtain an office – Meter [i.e., Measurer] of Linen Cloth – requested for him by More.[107] Lawyer, pageant-maker, playwright, and printer John Rastell, who also had a stage at his house in the London suburbs and rented out theatrical costumes, was More's brother-in-law as well as Heywood's father-in-law; and his son William printed four plays of Heywood's in the 1530s.[108] John Rastell's friend Henry Walton, whom Rastell sued in the 1520s over Walton's renting out of Rastell's stock of playing costumes while Rastell was overseas for six months, was probably a Mercer; an inventory of the goods of one Henry Walton, Mercer, when he died in 1540 included a chest "wher in the players garmentys lye".[109] Such linkages and circumstances suggest that the Mercers were not as devoid of feast-time entertainments as their extant sixteenth-century court minutes would suggest. The company had members more than able to provide it with such entertainments, without the arrangements having to be set down in the court minutes.[110] More broadly, such linkages raise the question of whether some of the London companies might not deliberately have enrolled among their members those with the abilities or connections to provide feast-time entertainments by special arrangements which did not have to be recorded in accounts or court minutes.[111] We see such an entertainment deal being worked out in 1522–26 between the city itself and Thomas Brandon, a general entertainer to the king.[112] The king would frequently request – and the city grant – that the freedom of the city (essentially London citizenship, allowing an individual to work and to exercise other legal rights within the city) be given by redemption (i.e., by the paying of a fee) to an individual serving the king in some capacity (as a court administrator, musician, etc.), in some cases without actual payment of the fee; and in 1522 Brandon, at the king's request, was made free of the city, though not without a charge.[113] The city records show, however, that subsequently, in 1526, the city arranged to return this fee to Brandon, on condition that he henceforth provide annually, free of charge, entertainment at the mayor's oath-day feast (at the Guildhall every 29 October: the most important feast of the civic year) and before the mayor on every Monday after Epiphany (i.e., in the Christmas season).[114] Brandon thus officially, in return for his London citizenship, became a regular entertainer of the city (that is, of its civic officials and their guests and servants): through an arrangement which might never have appeared at all in the civic records had there not been a fee return involved. The city was interested in being regularly entertained; it made a *quid pro quo* arrangement with Brandon, a professional entertainer. How often might it have made similar arrangements, initially rather than, as here (and thus recorded), after the fact, with others: producers, actor/managers, playwrights? In 1510 John Chamber, marshall of the king's minstrels, was admitted to the freedom of the city in the Minstrels' Company, with the City Chamberlain to "charge him self *with* xl s in his accom*m*pt. and he to take no more of hym but xiij s iiij d for his said lib*er*tie."[115] Furthermore, in order to be free of the city, Brandon also had to belong to a livery company (the Leathersellers are named in the 1522 entry): which then could have availed itself of his entertainment services as well. Theatrically-connected members, more-over, would presumably have been important to the companies not only for feast-time entertainments but also for arranging the street pageantry that increasingly became a major form of company display from the late fifteenth century on.[116] One record of a "Brandon-type" arrangement between a company and a drumplayer, in relation to the Midsummer Watch, has survived from 1539. "Robert Wayt dromslade" was made free of the Painters' Company "vpon con*dici*on that he on mydsomer evyn & saynt peters evyn take nothynge for hys labo*ur* duryng hys lyffe". Drumplayers were an important part of the Midsummer Watch processions.[117]

In both the fifteenth and the sixteenth centuries players would presum-ably have been hired or arranged for ahead of time (as were the per-formers in the Midsummer Watch), when a play was a normal part of a given, recurring occasion such as the Drapers' election feast or the Blacksmiths' cony feast. Possibly, however, on occasions not regularly re-quiring a play, players might sometimes have turned up "on spec" and been hired, as portrayed in *Sir Thomas More*. And, presumably, players might also have been hired, regularly or occasionally, to participate in the Christmas-season mayors' and sheriffs' household disguisings, masks, and mummeries mentioned by Stow (as noted above) – certainly ongoing in the sixteenth century and probably in the fifteenth century as well – unless the mayors' and sheriffs' company members and special theatrical connections themselves provided enough participants other-wise. How prevalent, indeed, were seasonal disguisings, masks, and the like theatrical entertainments in London's civic (household or company) halls? – both in the fifteenth and in the sixteenth centuries?[118] Certainly in the early fifteenth century the companies commissioned, for presen-tation to the mayor in the Christmas season, mummings by John Lydgate, to which we will now turn.

CHAPTER 6

Civic theatre and John Lydgate

The surviving texts of at least three of seven so-called mummings by the prolific fifteenth-century poet John Lydgate (c. 1371–1449) – writer of both regular and occasional poetic works, large and small, for a wide variety of patrons (royal, noble, religious, merchant-class) – are linked in their fifteenth-century manuscripts with London civic officials and craft guilds. These texts provide our only extant, concrete examples of what besides plays, or perhaps sometimes even included within the term "plays," might be performed as occasional entertainments within London civic halls in the early fifteenth century.[1]

Lydgate's mummings – three for the court, three for London's civic officials and guilds, one for an occasion and audience not yet agreed upon by scholars[2] – largely consist of verses written to be recited by a presenter of a costumed spectacle (of, for example, a classical, biblical, or allegorical nature), with gift-giving at least sometimes involved, and sometimes music.[3] Of the three specifically civic mummings, one, *A Mumming at Bishopswood*, was written for performance at a May Day dinner (of uncertain date) of the sheriffs of London and "theire bretherne" at Bishop's Wood, a manor of the Bishop of London at Stepney.[4] Another, *A Mumming for the Mercers of London*, was apparently commissioned by the Mercers' Company for presentation before London's mayor (himself a Mercer), William Estfeld, on Twelfth Night (6 Jan.) 1430.[5] A third, *A Mumming for the Goldsmiths of London*, was apparently commissioned by the Goldsmiths' Company for presentation before the same mayor on Candlemas night (2 Feb.) 1430 after supper.[6] These details of occasions and, for two of the texts, of performance dates are provided in rubrics, at the start of each manuscript text, by the texts' fifteenth-century copyist (and Lydgate contemporary) John Shirley.[7] For neither of the mayoral mummings do we know the location, but presumably they took place within mayor Estfeld's own hall (the early mayors of London had houses of "size and consequence"[8]), or in the halls of the Mercers and the Goldsmiths (but the Goldsmiths could have sent their mumming to a Mercers' supper, if not to the mayor's own house, instead of presenting it to the mayor as a guest at a Goldsmiths' Candlemas supper).[9] Performance at London's Guildhall is not likely, since there were no kitchens at the Guildhall, for food service, until the beginning of the sixteenth century.[10]

The Bishop's Wood mumming (called a "balade" in Shirley's manuscript rubric), on the subject of rejoicing at the coming of spring, involved an uncharacterized reciter/presenter of sixteen verse stanzas, evidently one to three silent characters/mummers (perhaps the goddess Flora, Ver [spring], and the personified month of May if a separate character from Ver),[11] and possibly a musical interlude by figures from classical mythology. Stanza 15 refers to the muses, Venus and Cupid, song, and Orpheus playing his harp, though all this is likely verbal elaboration only. The Goldsmiths' mumming (called all of a "balade," a "mommynge," and a "desguysing" in Shirley's manuscript rubric) was presented by Fortune and featured singing Levites bringing in the Ark of the Covenant, containing a didactic moral writing, as a gift for the mayor.[12] The Mercers' mumming (a "lettre," "balade," by "mommers desguysed"), presented by Jupiter's herald sent from the east to London, appears to have featured allegorical ships wheeled into the hall and probably a group of mummers as merchants.[13] All three pieces, clearly written by Lydgate on special commission, would thus appear to have featured visual display, allegory, mythology/history, and, once or twice, music. The performers could have been amateurs and/or professionals, adults and/or children. Suzanne Westfall has suggested that Lydgate's court mummings may have been performed by adult and boy choristers, as in the street pageantry of London royal entries.[14]

Bishopswood was clearly not, in honourees or in location, an internal London company feast production, but a special presentation to the two sheriffs – who in any given year usually belonged to two different London companies – at Stepney. *Goldsmiths* was a gift to the mayor, on a special occasion (Candlemas), by a company other than his own.[15] *Mercers* is also reasonably to be interpreted as a special Twelfth Night gift to the mayor, albeit by his own company. All are formal commissioned presentations; and none are called in Shirley's fifteenth-century manuscript rubrics, despite the variety of terms he uses there, a play.[16] In large part these presentations simply demonstrate a kind of entertainment, other than plays, available for London's civic leaders and their associates, and the London companies, on special occasions: just as such mummings/disguisings were available also for entertainment at court;[17] and all three are seasonal, two falling within the period of Christmas-season festivities. They do, however, also raise the important question of just how common such special (and seasonal) entertainments might have been in civic London; and a related question, since two of them were commissioned by London companies, is whether such entertainments might ever have been referred to in company records as plays, since so seldom do the terms mumming, disguising, and ballad occur in company records. Their texts date from the time – the mid 1420s to 1430s[18] – when we begin to find play references in company ordinances and accounts; and entertainment terms in the period seem to have been notably unstable, as Shirley's rubrics demonstrate.[19] Lydgate's *A Mumming at Hertford*, for example, written for performance before the king and called by Shirley a "disguysing," features twelve non-allegorical, non-classical, rustic characters (six husbands and six wives) quarrelling about mastery in marriage.[20] The six wives seem to have their own spokeswoman, different from the main presenter, and yet another person (though it may again be the presenter) may speak for the king in the entertainment's final scripted lines. Here we thus approach – or reach – characters with speaking parts. The courtly *Hertford*, with its large cast of largely silent performers, is clearly beyond the size of the usual four-actor London company play;[21] but the civic *Bishopswood* may have featured four performers (a presenter and perhaps three mutes) – a group, that is, of the size of the performing companies we normally find paid in London company accounts for plays.

We cannot, of course, be sure of what the companies might have entered in their records as "plays," when no titles or descriptions of the works concerned have come down to us; but at least regularly recurring "play" performances (for example, at a company's annual feast), as mandated in company ordinances or recorded in company accounts, would not seem likely normally to have involved specially designed or commissioned displays. Extant company accounts and minutes do not indicate such a practice; and presumably professionals or semi-professionals, paid to perform, would have had their own repertoire of performance pieces: though the companies doubtless had some choice, and special arrangements would always have been possible for special occasions. And although probably performed visual displays were not uncommon as London civic entertainments on Twelfth Night, Candlemas, or May Day – given Stow's comments on the tradition of disguisings, masks and "Mummeries" in the mayor's and sheriffs' households during the Christmas season, as noted in chapter 5 – Lydgate's three extant civic mummings, specifically, do after all appear to have been special. This special status relates to the matter of their dates.

The most recent datings, in Lydgate scholarship, for two of Lydgate's three London civic mummings, *Mercers* and *Goldsmiths*, are 6 Jan. 1429 and 2 Feb. 1429 respectively. Shirley's manuscript rubrics to their texts provide the basis of the datings: the Mercers' mumming was performed "vpon the twelffethe night of Cristmasse" (i.e., on 6 Jan.) for mayor William Estfeld, and the Goldsmiths' mumming, "vpon Candelmasse day at nyght, affter souper" (i.e., on 2 Feb.) for the same mayor. In his 1997 *Bio-bibliography* Derek Pearsall tells us that "William Eastfield was twice Mayor, in 1429 and 1437, and it is clearly to his first year of office that Shirley must allude. Mayors of London took office at Michaelmas but their year of office was counted as the calendar year following, so the *Mumming for the Mercers* was performed on 6 January 1429. Less than a month later, the *Mumming for the Goldsmiths of London* . . . was mummed . . . on 2 February 1429."[22]

William Estfeld, however, was first elected (13 Oct.) and sworn (28–29 Oct.) as mayor of London in the fall of 1429.[23] Performances before him as mayor on Twelfth Night and at Candlemas, during his first term of office were therefore performances in 1430. Estfeld's second term as mayor was from 29 Oct. 1437 to 29 Oct. 1438.[24] Pearsall does not say why the Mercers' (or Goldsmiths') mumming must have been during Estfeld's first term of office; there is no internal evidence, either in Shirley's rubrics or in the texts themselves, pointing towards one of Estfeld's terms of office over the other; and the argument by Rudolf Brotanek in 1902 that the first term must be involved, because otherwise Shirley in his rubrics would have mentioned that it was Estfeld's second term, is not valid.[25] Shirley was not concerned in his rubrics with carefully dating Lydgate's mummings for future historians. Perhaps, however, Pearsall's assumption is based on the dates between 1425 and 1429 (as he has worked them out) of the three court mummings written by Lydgate and copied out by Shirley in the same manuscript as the three civic mummings.[26] Lydgate's mummings in general might reasonably – though not necessarily – be assumed to have been composed within the same period in his writing career: a period Richard Green describes (and dates 1425–*c.* 1432) as Lydgate's time as a government apologist.[27] Certainly it was a time when Lydgate seems to have been heavily involved in political society.

A Mumming at Bishopswood, before London's sheriffs, Pearsall puts in 1429 because of the three other Lydgate mummings (as well as other works) which he places in that year: *A Mumming at Windsor* (before the king at Christmas), and supposedly *Mercers* and *Goldsmiths*.[28] With two of the three (*Mercers* and *Goldsmiths*) now moved, however, to likely 1430 (as opposed to 1438), *Bishopswood* at the least should be tentatively assigned to 1 May (May Day) 1429 *or* 1 May 1430, and perhaps indeed to a wider time span such as 1425–30 (the span of years now of Lydgate's seven mummings, after the dating adjustments made here).

May Day 1430 might be a likely date for *Bishopswood*, however, for almost certainly the reason that Lydgate was commissioned to write both *Mercers* and *Goldsmiths* in the first place, and, if so, certainly for performance in 1430 (not 1438) – and therefore indeed during Estfeld's first term as mayor. The young king Henry VI had been crowned in London on 6 Nov. 1429 (St. Leonard's Day), i.e., only eight days after the start of Estfeld's mayoralty. He was soon also to be crowned in France, and eventually left England for France on 23 April 1430.[29] There were probably special festivities taking place in London, as well as at the court, throughout the first half of Estfeld's mayoralty, because of the king's just-past and upcoming coronations; and the usual annual festivities, during times of seasonal celebration, were probably raised to a higher level than usual. One way for a London company to have marked the special circumstances would have been to have commissioned a writer of Lydgate's stature and court connections to compose special entertainments for seasonal occasions during the celebratory period. Lydgate was apparently the writer of choice for the 1429–30 coronation festivities: with three poems specially written for the coronation itself,[30] as well as the Christmas mumming, for the young king at Windsor, on subject matter related to the upcoming coronation in France.[31] No wonder that the Mercers and the Goldsmiths, and perhaps also the givers of the mumming to the London sheriffs,[32] commissioned Lydgate to write what were thus very likely special coronation-time entertainments for civic feasts at Twelfth Night and at Candlemas, and perhaps on May Day 1430 as well. *A Mumming at London* – with its presenter and five allegorical mute performers representing Fortune, Prudence, Righteousness, Fortitude, and Temperance, the last four of whom end the piece with a song – might also fit into this time period, for its auspices (royal, noble, religious, or civic) and date are not known beyond the fact that it was performed "to fore the gret estates of this lande, thane being at

London".[33] Parliament was in session at Westminster from 22 September 1429 to 23 February 1430.[34]

Lydgate's London-associated mummings, then, were probably special versions of normal seasonal entertainments for civic London, at the time of Henry VI's coronation. And other of Lydgate's writings raise the question of how prevalent in civic London, as a norm, might have been other types of commissioned occasional entertainments, for other kinds of special occasions. Other Lydgate works which have civic performance associations or possibilities are the so-called poems "Bycorne and Chychevache" and "The Legend of St. George."[35] The first, according to a manuscript rubric by Shirley, was made at the request of a London citizen, and is "the deuise of a peynted or desteyned clothe for an halle a parlour or a chaumbre."[36] The nineteen stanzas of verse may therefore simply describe a wall hanging or have been written for inclusion in it in some way,[37] but they seem to have been written to be recited, perhaps by several different voices, and it is possible that either the wall hanging came to life, as it were, in a visual and vocal display, or that Shirley's reference to a "desteyned clothe" is metaphorical and that the piece was entirely a performed recitation. Another manuscript text of the poem does not have Shirley's rubric but instead, as running titles, "The couronne of disguysinges", "The maner of straunge desguysinges, the gyse of a mummynge."[38] Dealing with henpecked husbands and dominating wives, "Bycorne and Chychevache" is on the same subject as *A Mumming at Hertford*, and also requires a large cast if performed. Who was the London citizen Shirley mentions? And is there a possible company entertainment connection? There need not be such a connection; but perhaps well-off individual company members not only commissioned works for themselves but also sometimes, for special occasions, acted for their companies in commissioning entertainments – or simply designs – or made a gift of an entertainment (musical performance, recitation, play, visual display) to their fellows. Company accounts and minutes sometimes do note when a company member has provided a dinner, at his own cost, for the membership.

Suggestively Lydgate's narrative poem "The Legend of St. George" is described in a Shirley manuscript rubric, recalling the "Bycorne and Chychevache" rubric, as "the devyse of a steyned halle of the lyf of Saint George . . . /and made with the balades at the request/of tharmorieres of London for thonour of theyre brotherhoode and theyre feest of Saint George," the text beginning with the direction, "thee poete first declarethe."[39] This "device", written on commission, thus seems to have been recited or sung for the Armourers, perhaps at a feast in honour of the company's patron saint (whose feast day was 23 April), perhaps in relation to a company wall hanging or mural;[40] and although seemingly purely narrative (and whether related or not to an actual wall hanging), the poem – though without the internal "stage directions" which in "Bycorne and Chychevache" may indicate recitation/performance – would have permitted an accompanying mimed performance of some of the elements described, such as a lady, leading a lamb, being rescued by St. George. In 1585 (as we have seen in chapter 5), on the Armourers' election day in August, after the election "a boye armid with a virgine following hime leading a Lamb came in with a drome and flute before theme/and after marching thrisse aboutt the hall their tables all sett they marched to the high tabill with a speache".[41]

Just what were "Bycorne and Chychevache" and "The Legend of St. George"? For what kinds of occasions, special or recurring, might Lydgate have been called upon to compose them? Might he have been commissioned at various times, by various London companies or by their members, to create "speaking-picture" designs or to compose visual and verbal entertainments (other than the mummings we have already noted)? Lydgate's involvement otherwise in performed London civic spectacle, or at least in its recording, is also demonstrated by his poem relating to the annual Corpus Christi procession of the Skinners' Company, and by his verse description of the royal entry pageants provided by the city for Henry VI's return from France in February 1432.[42] Might the Skinners have commissioned Lydgate to record, for posterity or for their own practical purposes, what the opening manuscript rubric calls "an ordenaunce of a precessyoun of the feste of corpus cristi made in london"?[43] The civic-recording provenance of Lydgate's royal entry description is indicated in its final stanza, addressed to the mayor and citizens of London, saying that Lydgate's "wille were goode fforto do yow servyse."[44] (Scholarship today denies that Lydgate's involvement in the entry was as more than a describer.[45]) At the least, given Lydgate's authorship, these poetic pieces, like Lydgate's civic mummings, strengthen our sense of the cultural connections between city and court at this time, and of the variety of possible types of designs, descriptions, and entertainments available, from the same "professional" writers (such as Lydgate), to paying patrons and audiences: royal, noble, religious, or civic.[46]

"A Pageant of Knowledge" (attributed to Lydgate), though with no known civic associations, should nevertheless be considered here briefly because it has no other known associations either and so nothing is ruled out.[47] It seems to begin with a recitation by the seven estates (princes, priests, merchants, knights, plowmen, artisans, and judges – one line each, plus a line by "Rycheman"), then becomes possibly a recitation by a presenter of various allegorical and classical figures, philosophers, and the signs of the zodiac, and finally becomes seemingly not dramatic but a didactic poem only. Pearsall sees the work as "clearly a tableau-presentation" to the end of the signs of the zodiac;[48] H. N. MacCracken compares it to a school play;[49] current thinking is that the "Pageant" may be a compilation of different poems,[50] in which case perhaps one or two are performance entertainments but there is no further information on any of them and hence no grounds on which to speculate. The work(s) may or may not be relevant to civic entertainment.[51]

Lydgate's verses on "The Soteltes at the Coronation Banquet of Henry VI" are not civic but should also briefly be mentioned.[52] Consisting of three stanzas written to accompany three allegorical decorative pieces which were constructed out of sugar and carried in for three different courses of the banquet, they show another kind of typical period mix of visual spectacle and verbal entertainment. The verses presumably accompanied each decorative piece in writing (like the writings used with tableaux on street stages in royal entries), but were probably also recited aloud, to make them known to everyone in the hall. Henry's coronation banquet was of course a royal occasion; but civic leaders would have been present; and special London company feasts would also have had subtleties, with or without verbal explanations. (Subtleties would probably not, however, normally have appeared in court or civic records under any other label or term.)

We learn eight major points from Lydgate's extant texts: some of them perhaps limited to these works, but others generally applicable to fifteenth-century London civic entertainments. One: Lydgate's texts both contain performance variety and prompt terminological uncertainty; but, two, the term "play," used by London companies in their fifteenth-century accounts and ordinances, is not used by Lydgate's contemporary, John Shirley, to describe any of the Lydgate pieces he copies. Despite the uncertain boundaries doubtless also further blurred from time to time between various entertainment forms, plays appear to have been to Shirley, at least, something other than what these texts represent. Three, there is good reason to believe that Lydgate's 1430 entertainments written for the Mercers and Goldsmiths – and perhaps his entertainments as well for the London sheriffs at Bishop's Wood, and for the "gret estates of this lande" at London – were unusual in their circumstances, commissioned and written in celebration of Henry VI's immediately-past English and upcoming French coronations: although such *kinds* of entertainments at festive times such as the Christmas season were probably not at all unusual in civic London. Four, other works by Lydgate associated with civic London and some form of designed picture or entertainment ("Bycorne and Chychevache," "The Legend of St. George") were perhaps commissioned and/or written for practical or commemorative purposes (such as a design blueprint or annual recitation), as might also have been Lydgate's poem about the Skinners' annual Corpus Christi procession; and such kinds of writings were perhaps also not at all uncommon in medieval civic London.[53]

Five, although both the Mercers and the Goldsmiths have manuscript accounts still extant today for the 1420s and 1430s, and early fifteenth-century court minutes as well for the Goldsmiths, no references to the commissioned Lydgate mummings of 1430 appear in any of these company manuscripts. Relying, indeed, only on extant company records, we would erroneously conclude that neither the Mercers nor the Goldsmiths – both important and wealthy companies – had anything much to do with special or even ordinary performance entertainments in the early fifteenth century; their extant records for 1400–1450 are almost devoid of entertainment references.[54] This paucity of entertainment records in the manuscripts of the Mercers and the Goldsmiths continues in fact to 1558; as previously noted, we know, for example, only from non-Mercer sources about the Mercers' lavish street pageantry at midsummer in the 1530s.[55] This dearth of Mercer and Goldsmith information, as we have seen in chapter 4, is explicable. Some London companies may have recorded details of matters such as entertainments in accounts separate from their main ones, to be treated as ephemeral and discarded in time; some companies instead, or in addition, doubtless had ways of acquiring entertainments – through special collections from the membership, gifts from individual members, probably also through personal connections with some writers/performers and/or their patrons – which did not, by their nature, find their way into official company documents. As has been previously stated, therefore, absence of records is no proof of absence of performances. It is probably safe instead to assume that for any record or indication of a play, mumming, disguising, and so forth that we have today, there are many other performances which have gone unrecorded, and that the London guilds in both the fifteenth and sixteenth centuries – to say nothing also of the households, in any given year, of the mayor and the sheriffs – were in general prime territory, at various annual feasts and on other special occasions, for both amateur and professional performances of all kinds.

Six: the variety of Lydgate texts with definite or possible civic auspices and entertainment purposes surely indicates that occasional entertainment generally, in fifteenth-century London, was widely varied; and, seven, Shirley's term "balade" for some of Lydgate's pieces raises the spectre of theatrical performances likely lurking behind some fifteenth-century records of music only, where we have no means today of detecting such performances.

Eight: the varied auspices of Lydgate's entertainments – both court and civic in his mummings – provide another clear illustration of the close entertainment connections in the early fifteenth century between the city and the court. Plays, mummings, disguisings, ballads, musical performances: whatever was performed before royalty and nobility was doubtless also performed in civic halls, where royalty, nobility, and important churchmen also were often guests. The paucity of records and especially of surviving texts has created a near-blank where we should have a full picture of fifteenth-century London civic hall entertainments; but Lydgate's works, along with the few records of civic payments to troupes of actors and mummers associated with royalty and the nobility, begin to fill the empty canvas. It should be noted, for example, as already mentioned in chapter 4, that the Duke of Gloucester's mummers were at Merchant Taylors' Hall in the Christmas season of 1440–41 (and that Gloucester himself was a member of the Merchant Taylors),[56] that the Grocers paid Gloucester's players in 1431–32[57] (a time when Grocer John Welles was mayor, 29 Oct. 1431–29 Oct. 1432), and that Gloucester was one of Lydgate's patrons.[58] Lydgate's *Mercers*, *Goldsmiths*, and perhaps *Bishopswood* and *Mumming at London*, as special coronation-time works, may be unusual in their authorship and occasions but not unusual in their kind, as forms of entertainment common to both court and city in the first half of the fifteenth century.

Richard Green has written, in relation to the non-dramatic literature of the period, that "any attempt to differentiate between the reading habits of the bourgeoisie and the court as distinct entities will in all probability prove chimerical . . . ; it is inherently improbable that the city merchant would aspire to cultural models essentially different from those of his superiors."[59] Green's assumptions surely hold true for the theatre as well as for non-dramatic literature and, when applied to the theatre, are well supported by examination of Lydgate's civic writings involving performance. A better-known close theatrical relationship between the city and the court, however, in the fifteenth and sixteenth centuries as in the thirteenth and fourteenth, is that exhibited in the royal and other such formal entries put on by the city at the behest of and for the honour of the Crown. These entries are the subject matter of the next chapter.

CHAPTER 7

Land entries

As we move from fourteenth-century entries into London, as described in chapter 3, to the fifteenth and sixteenth centuries, we find that formal entries into the city – royal and otherwise – gradually come to incorporate additional display;[1] but also manuscript records and chronicles providing information on London events become more numerous and give more information about entry ceremonial and spectacle. Some texts of speeches written and/or recited during entries have also survived: for the 1432 reception of Henry VI from France, for the 1445 coronation entry of Margaret of Anjou, for the 1501 reception of Katherine of Aragon, for the 1522 reception of Charles V, for the 1533 coronation entry of Anne Boleyn, and for the 1547 coronation entry of Edward VI.[2] Where not anonymous, these speeches are linked with some of the major writers of the day: with Lydgate as their recorder/describer in 1432, and with William Lily and with Nicholas Udall and John Leland as writers in 1522 and in 1533 respectively.[3] John Rastell was also involved in the 1522 entry,[4] and John Heywood in the 1553 coronation entry of Mary,[5] although no texts they wrote or spoke have survived. Finally the master of St. Paul's grammar school in 1554, Thomas Freeman, was the translator into Latin of the City Recorder's still-extant welcoming speech to Philip of Spain at Philip's entry;[6] and John Palsgrave, then City Clerk, made the short speech in French to the entering Great Admiral of France, in 1546, the text of which is to be found in city Letter Book Q.[7]

Accordingly more has been written, by general historians and by theatre historians, about post-1400 entries (and especially post-1500 entries) than about pre-1400 entries, but often with three unfortunate tendencies: to assume that, where we have little or no pageant information, little or no pageantry occurred; to read back late sixteenth and early seventeenth-century patterns into earlier entries; and to ignore important differences among entries even of the same type. But chroniclers, it would appear, recorded what was politically important or otherwise of special interest to them, rather than trying to make a complete and consistent record of events as they occurred, year by year and reign by reign;[8] patterns can be expected to change over time; and individual circumstances will alter individual events otherwise alike. None of the generally known chronicles, for example, refers to pageants on London Bridge for the entry into London of Elizabeth Woodville, queen of Edward IV, arriving for her coronation in 1465; we would know nothing about these theatrical pageants – which included angels, saints (played by actors) and choristers – had the London Bridge House annual accounts for 1465 not survived and included payments for them.[9] Elizabeth's entry was apparently not important to chroniclers. The tradition from *c.* 1533, as Lawrence Manley describes it, of the city's presentation in Cheapside of a gift to the honoured entrant did not exist (as Manley notes) before that date in relation only to Cheapside;[10] other locations, such as the Tower and Westminster, could be used, and also days other than that of the main entry procession.[11] Variation, not consistency, was the pre-1533 norm. And Elizabeth of York's coronation entry in 1487, as we will see, was significantly different from Elizabeth Woodville's in 1465: despite both entries being of queens coming through the city to Westminster to be crowned, a few years into their husbands' reigns. A major shift in entry practice had taken place between 1465 and 1487. London entries before 1558, in short, are more varied – harder to codify, as ritualistic spectacles – than is often recognized.[12]

Furthermore a tendency exists in modern scholarship to focus on major entries only, and to ignore smaller civic occasions similar in some aspects, ranging from ambassadorial (or sometimes minor royal) visits calling for courtesy civic escorts through the city, to visits by dignitaries, such as papal emissaries, requiring a major effort in decorating the streets, positioning musicians along them, calling out the livery companies to line them, and providing a formal escort of major civic officers, to "accession entries" (a monarch entering London immediately upon accession to the throne and welcomed also by a civic escort, street decoration, music, and the livery companies lining the monarch's route). These smaller occasions, although not actually "theatrical" (they do not seem usually to have involved constructed pageants), may help us to understand, through similarities and differences, some of the practical detail and meanings of the larger ones;[13] and perhaps some of them, as well, were not as small as surviving records of and references to them might lead us to assume. Above all they demonstrate, when grouped together with the major entries, how London was constantly experiencing – and having to welcome, entertain, dine, sometimes lodge – not only visiting monarchs and lesser royalty, native and foreign, but also emissaries from foreign courts and from the Pope. Small-scale "entry" ceremonial, music, and display was a continuing civic norm; and major entries could also sometimes occur unpredictably, in rapid succession, within a short time span, as in 1483–87 when London contended with all of the 1483 coronation entry of Richard III, the 1485 welcome ("accession entry") of Henry VII immediately after his defeat of Richard at Bosworth Field, the 1485 coronation entry of Henry VII, and the coronation entry of Henry's queen, Elizabeth of York, in 1487. The street display of entries in London was a continuing experience for both display/ceremony makers and for display/ceremony participants and spectators.[14]

This chapter is concerned, not with listing and describing all London royal entries and/or modern scholarship on them, for the period 1410–1558, but with pointing out the importance of entries as a constant, continuing part of London civic theatre over these one hundred and forty-eight years, and above all with noting the "practical" differences (of scheduling, gift-giving, and the like), often not discussed by theatre historians, among different entries at different time periods and in response to different entry circumstances.[15] Appendix A provides a table of all known major entries, and of selected minor ones, 1400–1558, listing some of their practical similarities and differences. Two of the nine or so well-known London royal entries from the period 1400–1558, for example, are those of Henry VI in 1432, returning from his 1431 coronation in France, and of Katherine of Aragon in 1501, coming to finalize her marriage to Prince Arthur, heir to Henry VII.[16] Both entries conform to what is today thought of as the typical London royal entry pattern. Henry entered London from Southwark, moving across London Bridge and up and along the traditional entry route through the city as it has been outlined in chapter 3: Gracechurch St., Cornhill, Poultry, and Cheapside, to St. Paul's. Elaborate wood-and-canvas pageant constructions were positioned at traditional stations along the route: the Bridge itself (two pageants: at the south entrance [a giant], and at the drawbridge), the Cornhill conduit, the Great Conduit, the Cross in Cheapside, and the Little Conduit near St. Paul's, with representations of locations such as a temple, a castle, and Paradise, of allegorical figures such as Nature, Grace, and Fortune, and of religious images such as the Trinity. Music played; choirs sang; at least one conduit ran with wine. The same route, many stations with pageants, provision of instrumental and vocal music, and conduits running with wine greeted Katherine of Aragon some seventy years later, and a similar mix of different types of representations, though with appropriately different emphases: for example, Sts. Katherine and Ursula (and no giant) on the Bridge, and the figure of Prince Arthur at the Great Conduit. Despite their similarities, however, the two entries were also different. Gordon Kipling, in his recent book demonstrating the liturgical, typological complexity of English and other European royal entries *c.* 1370–*c.* 1550, has persuasively argued for Christian typological differences as well as similarities among various London (and European) entries, including Katherine's and Henry's;[17] and there were also practical differences, involving different practical and political situations and meanings. Henry, for example, was met by the mayor and other important Londoners outside the city, on Blackheath, and formally escorted to the city; and after a religious service at St. Paul's, he processed out of the city to his palace at Westminster, where two days later the mayor and other Londoners presented him with a gift.[18] Katherine, coming from Lambeth, was met by the mayor perhaps at the Bridge and certainly in Cheapside, and was given gifts, and a speech of welcome by the Recorder, in Cheapside at the entrance to Paul's churchyard; and Katherine did not then move on to Westminster but entered the palace of the Bishop of London, at St. Paul's, where she was lodged until her wedding (also at Paul's) two days later.[19] Such practical differences from one entry to another, 1400 to 1558, should be considered as potentially significant, on the civic level, in terms both of entry structures and of overall entry meanings.

A focus on the ritualistic sameness of London royal entries – the pattern varying only, as Lawrence Manley has suggested for the period from 1485 on, according to whether a coronation is involved, with a coronation entry beginning at the Tower of London (and moving along Tower St. and up Mark Lane to Fenchurch St., and along Fenchurch to its meeting with Gracechurch St. and the main entry route as already described), and a non-coronation entry beginning at the Bridge[20] – is illuminating in important respects but, at least for the period pre-1559, obscures some details of difference from one entry to another that may affect our overall interpretation both of each entry individually and of the politics and structures of entries as a whole. Also the Christian typological differences among entries, as persuasively argued by Gordon Kipling, demonstrate the conceptual and visual sophistication of medieval and early Tudor street pageantry but do not include some of its practical aspects such as the particular role of the mayor in each entry and – as outlined below – the division of civic coronation entries into two stages. Both ritualistic and typological approaches are valuable; a closer look at practical civic details is also necessary. Such a look reveals potentially significant points, two examples of which will suffice.

First, it seems from the records available to date that, Richard III possibly excepted, no English or foreign monarch, or monarch's spouse, made a major formal entry into London from 1400 to 1500 without being ceremonially met outside the city, usually at Blackheath, by the mayor and an entourage (sometimes very large[21]) of other important Londoners, in full livery dress and normally with musicians, and being then escorted inside the city's walls.[22] Such a reception of the entrant can be read as a sign of respectful civic subservience and/or as a mark both of civic courtesy and of civic power and privilege; the entrant was welcomed, but entered the city only with the escort of its citizens. London both acknowledged the entrant and asserted, in the manner of its acknowledgement, its own civic wealth and importance, its latent king-making power.[23] The mayor then normally rode through the city with the entering king or queen, as part of the royal procession.[24] In the 1432 "welcoming" entry of Henry VI, for example, as we have seen, the king was met at Blackheath and then accompanied by the mayor not only through the city but – as was normal in fifteenth-century royal entries – all the way to Westminster.[25] Past 1500, the situation is unclear for Katherine of Aragon in 1501: but of course Katherine had not come to England to marry a king but was a princess arriving to celebrate her marriage to a prince.[26] The pattern may have been varied. The king's Council planned that the mayor would meet the entering Katherine in Cheapside;[27] and major MS accounts of her entry also seem at first to suggest that the mayor did not appear on this occasion until Katherine had reached Cheapside;[28] but a closer reading of one manuscript suggests the possibility that the mayor met her at the Bridge and rode in the royal procession, eventually stopping in Cheapside near Paul's churchyard for civic ceremonies there. Another source, however, suggests that the mayor may have processed separately into Cheapside.[29] When, however, in his chronicle Hall tells us that at the 1509 coronation entry of Henry VIII the mayor met the king in Cheapside, during the royal procession from the Tower to Westminster, Hall is merely leaving out the detail (found elsewhere) that the mayor rode in the procession (as usual for coronations) and stopped in Cheapside for ceremonies there:[30]

just as the mayor also rode, subsequent to 1509, in the coronation processions, from the Tower, of all of Anne Boleyn in 1533, Edward VI in 1547, and Mary in 1553, and in the entry procession, as well, of Philip of Spain in 1554.[31] Did the mayor also meet Henry VIII outside the city when the king first came to the Tower before his coronation? – as he met both Anne Boleyn, and Mary?[32] (Edward VI remained in the Tower from his accession until his coronation.) Any change in the details of the mayor's formal role from one major entry to another would presumably involve a significant political shift, from a civic perspective, also affecting entry structure and meaning, as would also variances, such as those noted above, in the place and time of the city's giving of one or more gifts to the honoured entrant.[33]

Second, attention to practical detail shows that civic coronation entries 1400–1558, unlike other types of entries, were not the one-day civic processional events they are normally described as today, and in terms of which their pageant texts (when these have survived) and over-all designed structures are today analyzed. They were, in fact, usually two-day civic events. This would seem especially important to take into account when considering and evaluating multiple-pageant entries as de-signed political and/or religious wholes. In coronation entries 1400–1482, it seems that invariably the king or queen, having been met ceremonially outside the city by the mayor and other Londoners, then en-tered the city over London Bridge, where the first (and often very elabo-rate) pageant displays of the entry were located;[34] but the entrant then normally proceeded not directly along the rest of the traditional pageant route but to the Tower of London (royal, not city, territory), where s/he spent the night.[35] The next day came Part Two, as it were, of the entry: from the Tower along Tower St., up Mark Lane, and along Fenchurch St. to Gracechurch St., up to Cornhill, and along Cornhill, Poultry, and Cheapside to St. Paul's, and then on to Westminster. (The mayor also met the entrant at the Tower, for this Part Two of the coronation entry, and became a member of the entry procession.[36]) For all of Henry IV's queen Joan in 1403, Henry V in 1413, his queen Catherine of Valois in 1421, Henry VI's queen Margaret of Anjou in 1445, Edward IV in 1461, and his queen Elizabeth Woodville in 1465, London entry took place on one day over the Bridge and on the following day from the Tower through the rest of the city.[37] (Henry VI in 1429 may possibly have un-usually crossed the Bridge in the morning, had dinner at the Tower, and proceeded along the rest of the entry route in the afternoon.[38]) Even after 1483, Henry VII in 1485 and Henry VIII in 1509 followed this two-stage coronation entry pattern, with the variation that they came to the Tower two days (not one) before the main entry procession through the city.[39] Bridge pageants – where they occurred for fifteenth-century coronation entries (and we have records of them for all of 1413, 1421, 1429, 1445, and 1465;[40] they seem to have been usual at least by 1413[41]) – thus almost invariably preceded the rest of the entry by at least a day (though for Henry VI perhaps only by a dinner break). The surviving texts of the speeches recited in the 1445 entry do not specify the day-separation of Bridge pageantry from the rest, and at first glance some of the chronicles do not indicate it either; but upon closer examination the chronicles do make clear the different days of the crossing of the Bridge and of the procession through the centre of the city.[42] Also there are no major entries between 1400 and 1482, coronation or otherwise, for which we have records of post-Bridge pageants but not of Bridge pageants (although there are entries – in 1413, 1426, and 1465 – for which we have accounts of Bridge pageants only[43]). The crossing of the Bridge was clearly a special, pageant-marked, liminal event for major entrants into the city, to 1483; and for coronation entrants, to that date, Bridge pageantry may have had a further special status and meaning, given that it was separated by a day from the pageantry of the entry procession through Cornhill and Cheapside to St. Paul's and on to Westminster.

From 1483, civic coronation entries are still two-stage events, but gradually in a way not involving the Bridge. Richard III in 1483 came to the Tower, the day before his coronation entry through Cheapside, not across the Bridge but by water.[44] And although both Henry VII and Henry VIII made the traditional coronation-entry "land" crossing of the Bridge to the Tower (two days before further London entry), all of Elizabeth of York (Henry VII's queen) in 1487, Anne Boleyn (Henry VIII's second queen) in 1533, and Mary in 1553, like Richard III, for their London coronation entries came to the Tower by water.[45] This did not, however, at least for Elizabeth and Anne, turn their coronation entries into one-day events. Bridge pageantry was, for both Elizabeth and Anne, changed into extensive water pageantry; and all three queens were escorted on the water to the Tower by the mayor and a fleet of civic barges.[46] By the later fifteenth century the Thames had begun to become – or had begun to be recorded as – an important venue for ceremonial display on various kinds of occasions: reducing the traditional importance of the Bridge as a coronation-entry point, although the Bridge was still featured in one-day, non-coronation entries such as the welcomes for the Emperor Charles V in 1522 and for Philip of Spain in 1554.[47]

It should also be noted that the royal entries of 1400–1558 about which we have the most detailed information are all unusual in some respect: which raises the question of whether we know so much about them only because they were unusual and hence perhaps generated both the attention of chroniclers and the survival in some cases of the texts of speeches. How far can we make assumptions, from them, about other entries – such as that of Henry IV's queen, Joan, in 1403 – for which we have little information?[48] It can be argued, however, that every royal entry has its own unique circumstances. Henry VI, for example, was crowned in 1429, some seven years after his accession and when he was a child of eight. His 1432 "welcoming" entry into London was then also unusual: as in part an English competitive response to the elaboration coronation entry into Paris that he had been given in 1431.[49] Katherine of Aragon in 1501 was, as we have seen, not an entering monarch, a queen consort, or a coronation entrant; she was a princess entering to finalize a marriage with England's expected future king. Unusually London also had two years to prepare for Katherine's entry; the first record of city preparations is in November 1499.[50] Henry V in 1415 had won a miraculous victory at Agincourt; Anne Boleyn's political situation in 1533 was far from normal; Edward VI in 1547 was, like Henry VI, a child at his coronation.[51] Mary had had to defeat Jane for the crown in 1553; and much of England was opposed to her marriage to Philip of Spain in 1554. Lawrence Manley has usefully emphasized the similar patterns of pageantry and ceremony from one royal entry to another: finding in the patterns depths of ritual meaning for all participants, including the watching crowds.[52] Gordon Kipling, however, has equally usefully focused on the differences in religious patternings and meanings of pageants from one entry to another, given entries' differing circumstances;[53] and differences in processional detail are also potentially important, relating to the particular circumstances, both civic and royal, of each individual entry.

There were also elaborate non-royal entries, at least one of them involving pageants, 1400–1558. These are not usually focused upon by theatre historians, in part because we know comparatively little about them and in part because most are not recorded as having been pageant-centred; but they raise significant points and questions in relation to royal entries. In 1426, for example, the Duke of Bedford – then Lord Protector of England, during the minority of Henry VI – returned to London, with his Duchess, from France, and was welcomed by the mayor and other Londoners in Surrey and escorted to the city, where the Bridge provided elaborate pageant display: two towers with children as angels singing, with organs playing, with effigies of various figures such as Abraham, Isaac, Moses, Joshua, the Duke of Bedford, Hector, and Hercules, and with virgins dressed in white.[54] We know about this display – comparable to some royal entry Bridge display – only because of the survival of some early Bridge House records; chroniclers do not mention it. Was there other pageant display, similarly unmentioned by the chroniclers, in other parts of the city? Furthermore, was this entry an unusual event for the Bridge or might the Bridge have provided "entry" pageantry, as a norm, on other occasions too that we might not expect to include it and for which records have not survived? How does this entry thus affect our views on royal-entry Bridge pageantry? In 1546 the Great Admiral of France arrived by water at London; the Bridge was thus not involved, but were any welcoming pageants prepared elsewhere, on the water or in the city, given that chroniclers do not necessarily provide information on entries in which they themselves – or their patrons – do not have a special interest and that the civic records tell us that "con*n*yng plasterers" were employed by the city to work on the various pageant stations (beginning at the Gracechurch St. conduit) along the usual entry route (the conduits and the Standard are to be "newly ffloresshed & trym*m*ed")?[55] The plasterers, of course, may only have been working to repair and otherwise spruce up the conduits and the Standard where, the records tell us, minstrels and singing men and children were positioned for the entry.[56] In 1549 there was elaborate musical display for Edward VI coming through the city from Southwark to Westminster, after he had had dinner in Southwark and had knighted one of the London sheriffs;[57] and minstrels and singing men and children, on stages, were also pressed into service for the accession entry of Elizabeth I on 28 November 1558.[58]

Entries immediately upon a monarch's accession, for which we have no evidence of constructed pageants (the time would presumably have been insufficient) but which could involve extensive musical performances (with minstrels playing, and choirs of men and boys on stages), could also involve a very different route from the usual royal entry route through the centre of the city via Cornhill, Poultry, and Cheapside. We saw in chapter 3, for example, that Bolingbroke entered London in 1399, shortly after his capture of Richard II, via Aldgate;[59] and Henry VII in 1485, after his victory over Richard III at Bosworth Field, came into the city from Shoreditch and processed through Cheapside to St. Paul's. (He was then lodged in the Bishop of London's palace there).

Mary entered the city at Aldgate on 3 August 1553, and passed through Gracechurch St., Fenchurch St., Mark Lane, and Tower St. to the Tower (i.e., she followed in reverse a part of the usual post-Tower coronation entry route). Elizabeth I entered at Cripplegate and moved along the wall to Bishopsgate, and then proceeded to the Tower, also via Mark Lane.[60] Were these routes largely practical, or did they too, like the standard coronation entry route, have special ceremonial meaning (as has been suggested for Bolingbroke's in 1399)? When the Bishop of York and others in 1471 attempted to shore up Henry VI's grasp on his crown, they processed him through London's streets along, significantly, a route normally taken by London's religious "general procession."[61] (The ploy, however, did not work.)

Moreover, ridings of the monarch through the city on more ordinary occasions also sometimes involved gravelling the streets (to prevent the horses from slipping), decorating houses along the route with rich hangings, and providing a civic escort (including the mayor): for example, for Henry VIII, Queen Jane and the Princess Mary on 22 December 1536, riding from Westminster to the Bridge (reversing the usual major-entry route) on their way to Greenwich because the Thames was frozen over and did not allow them to make the trip by water.[62] The companies on this occasion also lined the streets, and friars and priests censed the king and queen as they passed. The city streets were also decorated, and lined by the livery companies, on other kinds of occasions: as for the entry of an emissary of the Pope in 1496;[63] and in 1498 not only did the crafts line the streets for an entry by Prince Arthur but also a speech to the Prince was delivered by the Recorder, as similarly in 1518 when Cardinal Campeius came from the Pope to process through the lined streets of London and to be welcomed in a speech in Cheapside delivered on the city's behalf by Thomas More.[64] At the least these kinds of displays demonstrate that major royal entries, to repeat the point made earlier, were not so much unique, unusual events as points on a continuum stretching from ordinary ridings through the city of the king or other royalty or nobility simply moving from point A to point B (any land journey from Westminster to the south, for example, involved the crossing of the Thames at London Bridge), to the heightened ceremonial of welcoming a foreign ambassador, to accession entries, to finally the major theatrical display involved at times such as Henry V's 1415 Agincourt victory, the 1522 visit of the Holy Roman Emperor, and the coronations of several queen consorts and, before 1460 and then by at least 1547, of the new monarch himself.[65] The mayor and aldermen would ride with and/or meet the dignitaries; the livery companies would line the streets for a variety of kinds of entries; the streets would be gravelled for a very large movement of horses along them; rich hangings on buildings would be easily supplied; musical performers, instrumental and vocal, could also be assigned to various street locations at quick notice.[66] For some occasions some of the display forms of the Midsummer Watch (see chapter 9) could be utilized: as in July 1519, when bonfires, cresset lights, and armed watchmen were provided for an ambassadorial visit.[67] Only the construction of wood and canvas castles, temples, and the like would require some time: and not as much as might be thought, given both London's fixed structures – such as conduits, and the Cross in Cheapside – upon which and around which structures could be erected, and London's practice in the frequent necessary constructings of such pageants. Henry V's Agincourt entry pageants, for example, were supplied in less than one month.[68]

From the perspective of this examination of London civic theatre to 1558, royal and other entries 1410–1558 are above all important for three reasons. One, they demonstrate simply in their existence, as does so much else in London civic theatre, the intertwined fortunes of civic London and the court, since they involve the city in frequent (compulsory) display for royalty and other court-related visitors. Two, as irregular, required outbursts of sometimes theatrical and usually musical activity – in the former case involving the constructing of stages and figures, the setting up of special effects machinery, the making and hiring of costumes, the designing of pageants and writing of speeches, and the reciting of speeches – they show the ongoing existence in fifteenth and sixteenth-century London, ready to be called upon at very short notice, of considerable professional musical and theatrical expertise. (Court revels and city pageantry may have used, to a large extent, a common group of stagecraft professionals.[69]) Three, as a major preoccupation of the London civic government – given their range and consequent frequent occurrences – they are both a significant part of London's civic theatre (and its ceremonial context) in general and an important part of London's difference from other English cities in its patterns of civic theatre. Major entries, especially, were expensive: and I have already suggested in chapters 3 and 4 that their costs may have been a factor in the disappearance of the major London Clerkenwell play. Other English towns did not live to the same extent under the imperative of constant readiness to respond to court-initiated reception and display needs. Given the importance of entries to London civic theatre, they deserve further detailed exploration with attention to practical civic details (such as schedulings, gift locations, the role of the mayor, and the routes of lesser entries) which may add to our understanding of their political and ceremonial meanings and effects. They should also be examined as parts of a civic continuum from minor to major, and with attention not only to individual entry differences but also to more general changes over time.

To consider London's major and minor land entries 1410–1558 further, examining from a civic perspective both their practical details and the practical differences from one entry to another, would require a separate study. Given, however, the focus of most recent entry scholarship on the land aspects of London's pageantry, and what I have suggested to be a shift in coronation entry patterns from 1483, related to Richard III's coronation-entry arrival at the Tower by water rather than over the Bridge, we should briefly consider what seems to have been the greatest change in the nature of London entries from the fifteenth to the sixteenth century: the move from land to water, in the second half of the fifteenth century, as an alternate normal processional highway for an entrant into the city.

CHAPTER 8

Water shows

As we have partly seen in chapter 1, London was originally founded, shortly before 60 AD, because of the economic and political importance of its location on the Thames; and for the past twenty centuries this economic and political importance of the river to London has been self-evident. Not so much recognized is that the Thames, perhaps from the time of its founding but certainly from the twelfth century, has also been of continuing importance to London as an entertainment location and political display space. In Roman times, naumachia – mock sea battles – may possibly have been staged on the water, given their popularity as civic entertainments in Rome and elsewhere, though we have no evidence for their performance specifically in London;[1] but we do know, from William Fitz Stephen's late twelfth-century description of London, that at least by *c.* 1170–82 the Thames was a war-games entertainment venue for the city: a place where young men

In Easter holy dayes . . . fight battailes on the water, a shield is hanged vpon a pole, fixed in the midst of the stream, a boat is prepared without oares to bee caried by the violence of the water, and in the fore part thereof standeth a young man, readie to giue charge vpon the shield with his launce: if so be hee breaketh his launce against the shield, and doth not fall, he is thought to have performed a worthy deed. If so be without breaking his launce, he runneth strongly against the shield, downe he falleth into the water. . . . Vpon the bridge, wharfes, and houses, by the riuers side, stand great numbers to see, & laugh therat.[2]

Four hundred years later, in his *Survey of London* – a nostalgic, loving look at the city of both his boyhood and his manhood – the aging historian John Stow quoted Fitz Stephen's description and updated it. Commenting on Fitz Stephen's account of battle sport on the Thames, Stow noted the continuity from the late twelfth to the late sixteenth century: "I haue also in the Sommer season seene some vpon the riuer of Thames rowed in whirries with staues in their hands, flat at the fore end, running one against another, and for the most part, one or both ouerthrowne, and well dowked."[3] By the mid sixteenth century, it is generally recognized, the Thames at or near London was a space not only for citizens' games but also for politically oriented, special-occasion water shows, usually featuring fireworks and sponsored by the city or by the court for the entertainment especially of Elizabeth I (but also of all others who could watch);[4] and by 1609 the annual late-October water procession of London's newly elected mayor from the city to Westminster and back, for his oath-taking at the Exchequer, had become an elaborate spectacle involving, in that year, twenty "waterwoork*es*" including a whale "rounded close w*i*thout sight of the boate and to row w*i*th ffins/open for ffireworke*s* at the mouth and water vented at the head," and "A ffoist 60 ffoote longe well rigged and furnished w*i*th . . . powder and fireworke*s*."[5] As with the land processions discussed both in earlier and later chapters, mayoral water display emphasized the wealth and status of the city, and the importance of the livery company to which the mayor belonged.

Leaving aside the centuries before Fitz Stephen, how far back, before the Elizabethan period, can we trace London civic water shows? – elaborate spectacles on the Thames, sponsored for entertainment and political purposes directly or indirectly by the London civic authorities, and involving more than simply impressive processions, with music, up or down the river? Since the Thames was a major highway, ordinary journeys up and down the river, between London and Greenwich, for example, or London and Westminster, were as common as land journeys both for members of the court and for London citizens. City and livery company record books from the fifteenth century include many entries concerning city and company boats or barges escorting or meeting royalty (and other important personages, such as ambassadors) on the Thames (indeed, sometimes travelling down the river to Greenwich, or up it to Putney, in order to provide a water escort);[6] and it is probably safe to assume that normally (as the records do indicate on many such occasions) the citizens wore full livery dress and decorated their barges with banners and streamers, and that very often – as is frequently recorded – musicians were paid to play on one or more of the barges. Such water display would have been routine. But how often might more elaborate, "theatrical" water shows have taken place on the Thames under civic sponsorship, and on what kinds of occasions, for the period from 1276, when the first extant series of London civic manuscript records begins, to the 1558 accession of Elizabeth I, who appears herself to have watched a good number of water entertainments? Such civic water shows appear to have begun in the fifteenth century – although perhaps only records of them begin then – and to have been of two basic types: civic shows for the formal entry into London, by water, of royalty or of other figures of major political importance; civic shows involving the annual oath-taking at Westminster in late October, at the Exchequer, of London's newly elected mayor.[7]

ENTRY WATER SHOWS

There are early records of routine civic water display – as when in 1392 the mayor, aldermen, and other citizens of London accompanied Richard II and his queen on the Thames, going from London to Westminster after a city banquet, in barges with music;[8] but in 1486 we find what appears to be the first record in the civic manuscripts of what could be an actual civic water show for a formal entry, when Henry VII, returning from a progress in the north, was met by London's mayor and citizens at Fulham or Putney, as he came from his palace at Sheen, and was escorted to London by water with "schotyng of wyldfyr"[9] – i.e., with some kind of special pyrotechnical display.[10] The city may have felt obliged to provide unusual spectacle, given the civic welcomes offered to the king elsewhere during his progress.[11] Civic records provide no further details of this water show, other than over half a dozen livery companies' payments for barges and for music (both instrumental and vocal);[12] and no chronicle mentions it either. An elaborate civic water show, however, is recorded – in a non-civic, non-chronicle source – as taking place some eighteen months later, at the 1487 entry of Henry VII's queen, Elizabeth of York, processing by water from Greenwich to the Tower of London on 23 November, the day before her land procession from the Tower to Westminster for her coronation. Four years earlier, Richard III may have been the first English monarch (at least he was the first since before 1377) to go to the Tower by water, rather than by land across London Bridge, for his coronation entry through London;[13] and in 1487 the city provided, for the queen's water journey from Greenwich to Tower Wharf, not only the usual escort of livery company barges with onboard minstrelsy but also "a Barge . . . garnysshed and apparellede, passing al other, wherin was ordeynede a great red Dragon spowting Flamys of Fyer into Temmys. Also many other gentilmanly Pajants wele and curiously devysed to do her Highnesse Sport and Pleasure with."[14] (The description, by an unknown author, is in a manuscript now in the British Library's Cotton collection.[15]) Might the wildfire provided for Henry VII's entry eighteen months earlier have been at all similar to the dragon's "Flamys of Fyer" provided for Elizabeth's entry? – especially since a red dragon was a badge of the Tudors and a symbol already closely linked with the king in his 1485 coronation celebrations?[16] Might there have been one or two "gentilmanly Pajants" (of whatever sort) on the water for Henry also? – since the civic records and chronicles are as silent on such matters for Elizabeth as they are silent on details of Henry's reception?[17] What, moreover, did the 1487 gentlemanly pageants involve? – for the term "pageant" in this period is a slippery one indeed, used for every kind of display from a single ornate banner to a constructed stage with large set pieces and actors.[18]

Further information on elaborate civic water pageantry for London entries does not come until 1533 and the water show provided by the city – on the orders of Henry VIII – for Anne Boleyn processing by water, like Elizabeth in 1487, from Greenwich to London for her coronation. Again the details come not from the civic records but from elsewhere, though this time from the chronicles: Grafton, Hall, and Holinshed describe Anne's water entry in detail, and thus we learn that the mayor's barge escorting the queen was preceded by a foist or wafter (i.e., by an accompanying barge or other vessel) full of ordinance,[19] and with a great dragon "continually moving, and casting wildfire," and with onboard monsters and wildmen also casting fire and making hideous noises. To the right of the mayor's barge was another with trumpets, and decorated with cloth of gold, silk, and small bells; to the left of the mayor's barge was another "in the whiche was a mount & on the same stode a white Fawcon crouned vpon a rote of golde enuironed with white roses and red, which was the Quenes deuise: about whiche mount satte virgyns singyng & plaiyng swetely." Another source tells us that a "Moorish" diver was also featured. The usual fleet of company barges followed, with music and banners; and vast numbers of people watched (if we can believe the hyperbole – but the spectacle was certainly elaborate and also the political interest in Anne was high).[20]

Both the water show for Elizabeth of York in 1487 and that for Anne Boleyn in 1533 thus featured a fire-spewing dragon and what are called in 1487 "other gentilmanly Pajants." Was the 1533 separate foist carrying the constructed display of the mount and falcon therefore a type of water pageant going back at least to 1487, as Sydney Anglo has suggested?[21] Reading backwards from 1533 to 1487 and to 1486, and noting that our sources of detailed information for 1487 and 1533 do not include the civic records themselves (which are almost entirely devoid of water show references[22]), we have three main choices: we may suspect that elaborate civic water shows of the 1533 kind (though perhaps not as elaborate as in 1533) were not unusual after all in earlier times, but that merely the reporting of them was unusual (and dependent on the politics of the occasion concerned); we may believe that the 1486 entry of Henry VII may indicate an earlier low-key beginning or norm of this kind of display (perhaps above all of a military type), which was unusually elaborated in 1487 for Elizabeth of York and then further elaborated for Anne Boleyn's spectacular 1533 entry; or we may think that only ordinance was involved in 1486 and that the first actual water show records are, after all, for Elizabeth's 1487 coronation. As noted in chapter 7, from 1483 all of Richard III, Elizabeth of York (1487), Anne Boleyn (1533), and Mary (1553) came by water to the Tower – rather than crossing into the city by land, over London Bridge – before their coronation entries one to three days later from the Tower through Cheapside and on past St. Paul's to Westminster: thus permitting a substitution of water display for traditional Bridge land display, although we have records of civic pageant-oriented water display for only Elizabeth of York and Anne Boleyn. How might such civic water entry display, which we know to have existed in both 1487 and 1533, have been related to that other kind of London civic water display of the fifteenth and sixteenth centuries: the mayor's annual oath-taking journey by water to Westminster? – which, as already mentioned, by the early seventeenth century involved a lavish water show indeed, as detailed in extant texts and records of that period.

CIVIC OATH-TAKINGS BY WATER

As discussed in chapter 3, from earlier times both the annually elected mayor of London and the two also annually elected sheriffs were accustomed to process by land from the city to Westminster, to the Exchequer there, to be accepted into office by the king or his representatives a day or two after the civic oath-taking ceremonies in the city's Guildhall itself. Gradually, however, from the late fourteenth to the mid fifteenth century, the land processions of the sheriffs and of the mayor – which involved livery companies on horseback, in full ceremonial dress and with minstrels playing – became water processions, also involving the companies, still in full livery dress and with hired musicians, but now on barges.

The shift from land to water as the normal route for the sheriffs going to Westminster might have largely occurred in 1389, when the city ordered the sheriffs henceforth, as a cost-cutting measure, to go to their Westminster presentations either by land on foot or by water; they were not to go by land on horseback.[23] Given a choice between walking or taking a boat, most if not all sheriffs would probably have chosen a boat; and clearly, given the city's cost concerns, no water show was contemplated.[24] We cannot assume, however, that the sheriffs obeyed, either sporadically or regularly, the order to go to their presentations on foot or by water. The city record books, over the centuries, contain a number of orders which apparently were never implemented or which sooner or later fell by the wayside unobeyed; and in 1422 the records of the Brewers' Company clearly refer to the sheriffs as though they were intending, at least in that year, to ride to their Westminster presentations on horseback.[25] The same 1422 Brewers' records, however, also show the sheriffs again ordered in that year to process to Westminster by water (for reasons to be discussed shortly); and from several livery companies' accounts of payments for barge hire, 1423–1453, we can be sure that at least from 1435 the sheriffs were going annually to Westminster by water.[26] Apart from musicians, however, and the display furnished by the doubtless decorated barges themselves, there appears to have been no additional display: nothing that we can call a water show[27] – though it is worth noting that barges were hired, for accompanying the sheriffs, not only by the sheriffs' own companies in any given year but also by other companies, so that the flotilla was not a small one.[28]

When did the mayor begin making his oath-taking trip from the city to Westminster by water rather than by land? – for we would expect the mayoral water procession, rather than the sheriffs', eventually to involve a water show, as we know it did by the early seventeenth century. Traditionally London has elevated mayoral display above display for the sheriffs: often formally limiting the sheriffs' display in order to achieve this end. The first recorded oath-taking mayoral trip by water to Westminster, from the early fifteenth century on, may have been in 1422; in that year both the sheriffs and the mayor were obliged by the city to use barges, perhaps in part for reasons of cost and in part for reasons of political and religious respect. Henry V had died in France on 31 August; the body was brought home to England; and an elaborate funeral was scheduled for early November. Processions of the sheriffs and of the mayor to Westminster for their respective presentations, on 30 September and on 29 October, with elaborate festive display and accompanying musicians, doubtless seemed inappropriate under the circumstances, and probably also unduly costly, given the unexpected civic expenses now of a funeral procession (with special dress) and then of the accession of a new king. The accounts of the Brewers' Company record the order, for the mayor as for the sheriffs, for a water procession rather than a land procession to Westminster; and in relation to the mayor it is also specified that the journey should be without music and with the companies dressed in black and/or russet garb which should be used again for the November funeral.[29]

The 1422 experience does not seem, however, to have inspired the city or future mayors at once to begin regularly using the Thames for the mayoral Westminster oath-taking journey; not until 1453 is there again a clear record of a mayoral oath-taking procession by water, although there is some ambiguous evidence for 1423 and 1424;[30] and in some fourteen of the twenty-five years between 1425 and 1449 (inclusive) there is evidence of a land procession.[31] In 1447 an order was passed by Common Council that the mayor make the oath-taking journey by water;[32] but the order was either for one year only (the manuscript wording is unclear) or was ineffectual; Grocers' Company records show the mayor going to Westminster by land in all of 1449 to 1452.[33] Another such order, however, this time clearly for a permanent change, was passed in 1453;[34] and from 1453, London's mayors, as well as sheriffs, are invariably recorded as making their presentation trips each year by water.[35] The status and efficacy of the 1453 order was doubtless in part responsible for the declaration by a number of chroniclers that the mayor first went to his Westminster oath-taking by water in 1453: but in fact mayoral oath-taking water processions might have occurred, between the early fifteenth century and 1453, only in 1422 and perhaps in 1423–24 and 1447. This statement runs counter to most academic statements on the matter, over the past century: but determining with accuracy when the mayor went by water to his oath-taking, before 1453, is problematic in ways that have not previously been realized. First, the terms "the mayor's riding" and "the sheriffs' riding" by the fifteenth century had become so much descriptions of the presentation occasions concerned, rather than of the transportation method utilized (i.e., horses), that they became used in civic records as occasion references only: so that one finds in livery company accounts phrases equivalent to "paid for the barge for the sheriffs' riding."[36] A record simply of the mayor's or sheriffs' "riding" thus tells us nothing about whether the mayor or sheriffs concerned actually rode a horse or took a barge. Second, the mayor and sheriffs sometimes went by water to Westminster on occasions other than inaugurations into office: for example, on city business, or for a presentation of the mayor to the king at some time later than the Exchequer oath-taking, as required when the king was not present at the oath-taking itself.[37] Thus a company record of payment for a boat for the mayor or sheriffs to Westminster cannot be assumed to refer to a formal inauguration journey unless a more specific reference is also made, or unless the context clarifies that an inauguration ceremony is involved. Further to complicate matters, annual commemoration of the death of Henry V, for many years after his 1422 funeral, involved at least some of the companies in annual barge hire to Westminster for that occasion.[38] It thus becomes difficult or impossible to determine, from company records simply of unspecified and uncontextualized barge hirings, whether in a given year the mayor went to his oath-taking by water or by land:[39] although the land records previously noted, together with the 1453 opposition of the Crown to the city's decision to move, then, entirely to the water, indicates that there were no regular mayoral oath-taking journeys by water (at least in the fifteenth century) before 1453.

Whatever, though, the details of when mayoral oath-taking journeys by water began, *how* did the mayor then take his water journey? – with minimal, modest, or elaborate display? Was there anything beyond a large escort of livery company barges, appropriately decorated, and musicians playing? – for the records do make clear that there was indeed a large barge escort and that the companies regularly hired minstrels to play on board as everyone processed. A water procession may indeed in 1389, for the sheriffs, have been considered cheaper than a land procession on horseback; but the history of civic ceremonial and display in London to 1558 is one of a repeating cycle of modest beginnings, rising spectacle and costs, attempts to cut back, and rising spectacle and costs again.[40] How elaborate did the mayor's oath-taking journeys become, in the mid to late fifteenth and early sixteenth centuries? And do mayoral oath-taking water processions relate in any significant way to the city's royal-entry water shows of 1486, 1487, and 1533?

Here the records of both the Grocers and the Mercers – two of London's Great Companies – become useful. The records of the Grocers' Company, which supplied two mayors of London in the 1450s, include two 1450s inventories listing items (including a griffin) belonging specifically to what the records call a "bachelors' barge;"[41] and the Grocers' bachelors – like the bachelors of any company at this time – were company members just below the rank of the livery (the highest company level),[42] who with their leaders (or "masters") were customarily responsible for much of the ceremonial involved when a company member became mayor. We thus know from the Grocers' records that by at least the 1450s the company's bachelors were specifically involved in ceremonial barge display; moreover, some mid to late fifteenth-century bylaws of the Mercers' Company specify that the Mercer bachelors must regularly provide such a barge when a Mercer mayor takes his oath, and that this is the custom of all the companies when they have a mayor.[43]

Just what was the bachelors' barge? Here we must return to the royal entry water shows of 1487 and 1533: as for both shows the records mention a bachelors' barge (the bachelors concerned being the bachelors of the mayor's company in each year). In 1487 the bachelors' barge is the very barge upon which is situated the great red dragon spouting flames of fire; in 1533 it is separate both from the dragon barge and from the barge carrying the mount, falcon, and virgins; it is the barge decorated with cloth of gold, silk, and bells hanging from cords, and carries musicians. It would appear that the bachelors' barge was basically a display barge provided by the bachelors, and that the type of display could vary.[44] In 1487 it involved dragon fireworks; in 1533 it did not. But in both years there were indeed fireworks/wildfire as part of the overall processional display; and the 1533 chronicle accounts further tell us that the bachelors' barge "with a wafter and a foyst garnished with banners and streamers" (i.e., with the fireworks vessel and the mount vessel) was provided "likewyse as they vse to dooe when the Maior is presented at Westminster."[45] It is unclear from the chronicle wording whether all of the bachelors' barge, wafter, and foist, with various elaborate decorations, were usual features of the mayor's oath-taking procession, or only the decorating of such vessels – or simply of the bachelors' barge – with banners and streamers. We would be wrong to assume that fireworks and constructed pageants on barges were a usual feature of the mayor's ceremonial water journey to Westminster before 1558.[46] But certainly in 1533 the chronicles are drawing parallels between Anne Boleyn's entry and the usual mayoral oath-taking procession; and so the question, which the records do not allow us to answer and which nineteenth-century historians tried to answer in very different ways, is one of how far the parallels were intended to go.[47] Should we add now, for example, to the three royal-entry water shows already mentioned (in 1486, 1487, and 1533), a civic water show at the 1540 (Greenwich) entry of Anne of Cleves? – for the civic records tell us that when London sent a fleet of vessels to welcome Anne at Greenwich, a bachelors' barge was provided, and also one or more foists; and the *Chronicle of the Grey Friars of London* states that the companies went in their barges "with all their best araye as the mayer is wont to goo to Westmyster."[48] (The queen was met on land at Blackheath by the mayor, aldermen, and others, and then escorted by land to Greenwich, not to London, for her marriage;[49] but London's water display welcomed her at Greenwich.) Anne was also later escorted by the city from Greenwich to Westminster, on the water, though not into London itself; but no reference to a bachelors' barge or foist is made on this occasion.[50] Is there also a possibility of at least some civic water pageantry honouring Katherine Howard in 1541, during a royal water passage from Westminster to Greenwich? – some special display was provided, but we have no details.[51] Perhaps significantly also, in relation to both royal and mayoral civic water displays, the records of the Goldsmiths' Company, for the 1545 mayoral oath-taking at Westminster, comment that the masters of the company's bachelors "had the ouerseyght off payment off all the charges off the pagenttes for the barge with all the other charges therto belonggyng".[52] Were these constructed pageants, as in 1533 and probably 1487, or were they just banners and other such kinds of decoration? If constructed pageants (though we cannot know), in which direction would the pageantry influences have been flowing? – from the mayoral water show to the royal-entry water show, or vice versa? – and when had the influencing begun?[53] When, for example, the mayor and other Londoners were to meet the king in 1463, coming by water from Sheen, they were to meet him in barges decorated as for the mayor's oath-taking.[54]

Unfortunately display nomenclature before 1558 is unstable. In 1487, as already noted, the bachelors' barge carried the fire dragon; but in 1533, decorated with streamers, cloth, and bells, it carried musicians; and by the 1550s the term bachelors' barge seems to have become defined in opposition to fire effects, for company records of the mayor's oath-taking ceremonial can give a company's bachelors the choice between providing a bachelors' barge and providing a foist, and the latter involves ordinance (and hence at least the potential for pyrotechnical display), so that the former presumably does not.[55] Either the bachelors' barge terminology was wrongly used by the author of the 1487 description, or the term had not yet then become fixed, or the terminology had changed by the 1550s: all of which makes it impossible to work backwards or forwards, from terms only, to ascertain what was actually being displayed on the water in any given year between 1453 and the 1550s.

For the period before 1558, therefore, what we can say, to date, about London civic water shows is more a matter of weighing probabilities than of drawing firm conclusions. First, it seems unlikely, though possible, that fireworks on the Thames were an innovation in the late 1480s: since fire effects are always popular as entertainment, since the 1487 effects were so elaborate, and since the water has, of course, always been the safest possible place to put on fire displays. Second, it also seems unlikely, though possible, that civic "curiously devised" gentlemanly pageants (whatever the term may mean – but it seems to mean more than banners) were being used on the water at London for the first time in 1487, given that both portable and stationary constructed or costumed displays – of towers, saints, fish, and the like – had been in use in processions on land in the city since at least the thirteenth century, and that the river had become regularly used, by at least the mid fifteenth century, for formal processions.[56] Third, it also seems unlikely that, once used, fireworks and/or constructed pageants on the water, as in 1487, would have been displayed by the city only once every fifty years or so, for the occasional royal entry; and fourth, the involvement of the bachelors of the mayor's company – who from the 1450s usually provided a special display barge of some sort for the mayor's oath-taking water procession to Westminster – in the provision of special water display for royal entries in at least 1487 and 1533 suggests that there could have been some similarity in the kinds of spectacle provided, albeit the royal entry display would doubtless have been more elaborate. Against the possibility of any elaborate pageantry on the water for mayoral oath-takings, however, at least from 1550 to this book's closing date of 1558, is the fact that Henry Machyn does not mention any in his *Diary* while nevertheless noting 29 October vessels (foist/pinnaces) with streamers, trumpets, drums, and guns, 1553–56,[57] and providing details of other kinds of pageantry such as pyrotechnical displays for the Queen after 1558.[58] Also, extant 1541 and *c.* 1558 orders of the Mercers' Company, for how mayoral oath-taking ceremonial should be managed, include no instructions for special pageant or fireworks display on the water,[59] nor for 1556 does a special pageantry manuscript of the Merchant Taylors' Company (although there is a foist and ordinance).[60] On the other hand again, arrangements for the bachelors' barge in the early sixteenth century were apparently so elaborate that twice when a Draper was to be sworn in as mayor, in both 1520 and 1528, the Drapers' bachelors were given two eight-to-nine-leaf quires of barge information (from 1514–15 and from 1511–12, the two most recent years, before 1520, in which a Draper had been mayor); and in 1528 a third, twelve-leaf quire was added (from 1521–22, another Draper mayoral year).[61] The quires unfortunately have not survived. There may have been changes back and forth in mayoral water display – as there were in mayoral land display – during the years from 1453 to 1558.

Three points should be kept in mind. One: from 1453 to 1558 is a hundred and five years – and we cannot assume, in any search for patterns and evidence, simple continuity of water show characteristics and terminology over such a long period of time. Two: from the reticence of the civic records themselves on the matter of water shows before 1558 we can safely infer nothing. The civic records tell us nothing about the fire-spewing dragon and gentlemanly pageants on the water in 1487 (our information comes from a non-civic manuscript); they also say nothing about the water displays – apart from decorated barges and music – for Anne Boleyn's 1533 entry (our information comes from chronicles – and not even all of the chroniclers covering the event describe the water show, despite its spectacular nature). The civic records before 1558 tend to deal largely with the unusual, rather than with the usual: which is of little help when one is trying to ascertain what was routine; and the chroniclers, as already noted, report on events according to their own interests and sense of priorities and of politics, rather than aiming at the creation of a complete and accurate historical record. Three: manuscript survival and non-survival presents a special problem for investigating water shows, given the involvement of the livery companies' bachelors' groups in company ceremonial displays, and the non-survival of most bachelors' manuscript records pre-1559. If pre-1559 manuscript ceremonial and account books kept by the Great Company bachelors had generally survived – such as the several quires of ceremonial instructions we know that the Drapers' bachelors had in 1520 and in 1528, or the separate "pageant" accounts the records tell us were kept by the Goldsmiths' bachelors in 1545[62] – we might be very much wiser today about civic water shows before 1559.[63]

It is finally worth noting that by the late fifteenth and early sixteenth centuries royal water entertainments on the Thames had become generally popular; there were mock battles on the Thames at Westminster, for example, in 1489 as already noted, and in 1539, and at York Place in 1536; and animal baitings also were staged in the water.[64] Once again, at least by the evidence of the 1487 and 1533 civic water shows for royal entries, court and city entertainment interests and presentations appear to have been significantly similar.

CHAPTER 9

The Midsummer Watch

The largest and most important annual or near-annual civic spectacle in London, in the first part of the sixteenth century, was the Midsummer Watch: grown beyond its pre-1400 beginnings (as discussed in chapter 3) into a procession or parade, on the eves to early mornings of the festivals of St. John Baptist (24 June) and of Sts. Peter and Paul (29 June), of men in armour, musicians, cresset-bearers, giants, wildmen, morris dancers, swordsmen, and a varying number of "pageants," i.e., of wood and canvas constructions, carried through the streets by porters, depicting characters and events largely from the Bible, much less frequently from English history, and from classical mythology and allegory. The spectacle moved through the city along a traditional fixed route (as described in chapter 3); the pageants (apparently present in most years) varied somewhat in size and in number, from year to year; and the costs of the event were borne in part by the city government itself but in more significant part – this latter part including the costs of supplying pageants – by the livery companies, especially the companies each year to which the annually elected mayor and two sheriffs for that year belonged. Pageant display in the annual Midsummer Watch was both a responsibility and an opportunity for the companies: a responsibility to the civic government and to the city at large; an opportunity for formal display of individual company power and prestige through elaborate public spectacle.

Since 1954, with the publication of the Malone Society's *Collections III*, "A Calendar of Dramatic Records in the Books of the Livery Companies of London, 1485–1640," we have had available in print a part-calendar, part-edition of the extant manuscript records of arrangements and of payments for Midsummer Watch pageantry, from the first half of the sixteenth century, of eleven of the twelve Great Companies of London: the twelve companies to which, by this period, London mayors invariably, and sheriffs almost invariably, belonged. The records of the twelfth

Great Company were added in 1960.[1] For some of these companies, no pageant records have survived; for others, only a few references or payments can be found in the surviving company records series. For still others, however, extensive manuscript records of Midsummer Watch pageantry are extant. And we also have had, since 1598, the printed nostalgic account of the (then) elderly city (and national) historian John Stow, who set down in his *Survey of London* a description of the Midsummer Watch as he remembered it from his boyhood days. Stow's account of the Watch has largely determined historical views of the event from 1598 to the present; and the records in *Collections III* have largely been treated by theatre historians as elaborations on or as minor qualifications to what they already knew about the nature of the Watch from Stow.[2]

In the Moneths of Iune, and Iuly, on the Vigiles of festiuall dayes, and on the same festiuall dayes in the Euenings after the Sunne setting, there were vsually made Bonefiers in the streetes, euery man bestowing wood or labour towards them . . . . On the Vigil of Saint *Iohn Baptist*, and on Saint *Peter* and *Paule* the Apostles, euery mans doore being shadowed with greene Birch, long Fennel, Saint Iohns wort, Orpin, white Lillies, and such like, garnished vpon with Garlands of beautifull flowers, had also Lampes of glasse, with oyle burning in them all the night, some hung out braunches of yron curiously wrought, contayning hundreds of Lampes light at once, which made a goodly shew, namely in new Fishstreet, Thames streete, &c. Then had ye besides the standing watches, all in bright harnes in euery ward and streete of this Citie and Suburbs, a marching watch, that passed through the principal streets thereof, to wit, from the litle Conduit by Paules gate, through west Cheape, by ye Stocks, through Cornhill, by Leaden hall to Aldgate, then backe downe Fenchurch streete, by Grasse church, aboute Grasse church Conduite, and vp Grasse church streete into Cornhill, and through/it into west Cheape againe, and so broke vp: the whole way ordered for this marching watch, extendeth to 3200. Taylors yards of assize, for the furniture whereof with lights, there were appointed 700. Cressetes, 500. of them being found by the Companies, the other 200. by the Chamber of London: besides the which lightes euery Constable in London, in number more then 240. had his Cresset, the charge of euery Cresset was in light two shillinges foure pence, and euery Cresset had two men, one to beare or hold it, an other to beare a bag with light, and to serue it, so that the poore men pertayning to the Cressets, taking wages, besides that euery one had a strawne hat, with a badge painted, and his breakfast in the morning, amounted in number to almost 2000. The marching watch contained in number about 2000. men, parte of them being olde Souldiers, of skill to be Captains, Lieutenants, Sergeants, Corporals, &c. Wiflers, Drommers, and Fifes, Standard and Ensigne bearers, Sword players, Trumpeters on horsebacke, Demilaunces on great horses, Gunners with hand Guns, or halfe hakes, Archers in coates of white fustian signed on the breast and backe with the armes of the Cittie, their bowes bent in their handes, with sheafes of arrowes by their sides, Pike men in bright Corslets, Burganets, &c. Holbards, the like Bill men in Almaine Riuets, and Apernes of Mayle in great number, there were also diuers Pageants, Morris dancers, Constables, the one halfe which was 120. on S. *Iohns* Eue, the other halfe on S. *Peters* Eue in bright harnesse, some ouergilte, and euery one a Iornet of Scarlet thereupon, and a chaine of golde, his Hench man following him, his Minstrels before him, and his Cresset light passing by him, the Waytes of the City, the Mayors Officers, for his guard before him, all in a Liuery of wolsted or Say Iacquets party coloured, the Mayor himselfe well mounted on horseback, the sword bearer before him in fayre Armour well mounted also, the Mayors footmen, & the like Torch bearers about him, Hench men twaine, vpon great stirring horses following him. The Sheriffes watches came one after the other in like order, but not so large in number as the Mayors, for where the Mayor had besides his Giant, three Pageants, each of the Sheriffes had besides their Giantes but two Pageants, ech their Morris Dance, and one Hench man their/Officers in Iacquets of Wolsted, or say party coloured, differing from the Mayors, and each from other, but hauing harnised men a great many, &c.[3]

How did the London Midsummer Watch become such a major pageant spectacle? The Watch, as we have seen in chapter 3, was a marching event which had begun to incorporate decorative display by at least the late fourteenth century; and as early as 1379 the Watch is recorded as contributing to the honour of the king as well as of the city; but from 1400 to 1474 the civic records and chronicles contain no details of further elaboration, although in 1445 there took place, according to the chronicler Bale, "the royallest wacche that ever was seyn ther a fore and the King the queen and the lordes wer present the same evenes [i.e., 23 and 28 June] in the citee."[4] No information is provided as to what spectacle the city provided: but significantly the Watch followed closely upon the 30 May coronation of Margaret of Anjou, hence perhaps a special civic effort was made. Might a similar special Watch have been presented at midsummer 1465, after the 26 May coronation of Elizabeth Woodville?[5] By the 1470s the Watch appears to have existed in two forms: a regular Watch and a "greater" Watch, the latter presumably incorporating significantly more display than the former. The Mercers' records tell us that in 1477 the king commanded the city to put on the "gretter wache", on the eve of Sts. Peter and Paul, because of the presence in London then of the ambassadors of France and of Scotland;[6] and Journal 8 tells us that twenty-six companies provided a total of five hundred and ten men for this Watch, while the Drapers' records reveal that the Drapers' Company – which had a mayor in office at midsummer

1477 – paid for a morris dance and for a portable pageant (it required fourteen men to carry it) involving gold and silver paper and, it seems, the nine worthies (unless the worthies were a different part of the spectacle from the pageant; the record is unclear).[7] In 1474 there was also, according to *A Chronicle of London*, a "grete watche" on St. Peter's night (i.e., eve).[8]

What did the elaboration of display in a "greater Watch" usually involve? The records do not say, but presumably at least an unusually large number of marching men were provided; compared to the five hundred and ten men for 28–29 June in 1477, only two hundred and fifty men were provided by the companies for what seems to have been an ordinary Watch (on both the usual midsummer-show eves) in 1504.[9] The Drapers' pageant in 1477 may also have been unusual; but in 1504 we have – thanks to the survival of so many of the early records manuscripts of the Drapers' Company – a summary of elaborate pageant display which seems unlikely to have appeared suddenly out of the rare display of one pageant, only, at the time of a "greater Watch": unless "greater" Watches had become frequent and pageant display at them had been gradually increasing. The Drapers – with a mayor in office – record thirteen pageants in the 1504 Watch, at a total cost of £38 13s 10d and 1/2d (no cost breakdowns are provided);[10] these pageants cannot all have been large wood and canvas constructions, some must have been simply elaborate banners or images,[11] but presumably at least some were wood-and-canvas pieces. How long had such pageantry been developing within the Watch? Did it significantly precede 1500? Or was early sixteenth-century Watch pageantry perhaps given a special boost by the example of the elaborate 1501 royal entry of Katherine of Aragon to her marriage? The city sold off its 1501 Aragon entry pageant stuffs in 1502;[12] did some of the companies, or individuals involved in pageant work, buy some of them up for Watch use? The companies liked to maximize the use of their prepared spectacles, for reasons both of economics and of public relations; about a hundred years later, for example, when in 1605 a Lord Mayor's Show was severely rained on, the Merchant Taylors repaired and processed with their pageants again on All Saints' Day (1 November);[13] and in the first half of the sixteenth century companies routinely recycled their Watch pageants from one year to the next.[14]

In the 1520s the Watch was at the heights of display now well known from Stow's description: which is a description not specific to any one Watch but covering the type. In 1521, for example, the Drapers (with a mayor in office) provided fifty men with morrispikes, fourteen gunners, eight archers, four wood-and-canvas portable pageants (the Castle of War, the Story of Jesse, St. John the Evangelist, the Assumption) carried by thirty-one porters, a king of the Moors (with a "stage" and wildfire) and sixty-one other Moors (with scutcheons and darts), a morris dance, a giant, and musicians.[15]

For over thirty-five years, and perhaps for much longer, the Midsummer Watch was London's pre-eminent civic pageant spectacle, recurring annually or near-annually; and apparently even stationary pageants could become part of the spectacle. The Mercers had one at the Great Conduit in Cheapside, just outside their hall, in both 1536 and 1537.[16] Companies vied to outdo one another in display; in 1541, when the Drapers felt that expenses were getting out of hand because of the large sums of money being expended by the Mercers, they paid up regardless ("what remedy but go through wyth all"[17]). By the time Stow wrote his 1598 *Survey*, however, the Watch no longer existed. When did London's Midsummer Watch end, and why? The question gains special importance in that Midsummer-Watch-type pageants (portable canvas and wood constructions, as outlined above) sometime before the Elizabethan period would appear (as historians have assumed for years) to have migrated into another annual civic spectacle, the London Lord Mayor's Show (the subject of chapter 10). Stow would at first seem to have definitively answered, in his *Survey*, both the first question, when, and part of the second, why: in a paragraph immediately following the one quoted above.

This Midsommer Watch was thus accustomed yearely, time out of mind, vntill the yeare 1539. the 31. of *Henry* the 8. in which yeare on the eight of May, a great muster was made by the Cittizens, at the Miles end . . . , to the number of 15000. which passed through London to Westminster, and so through the Sanctuary, and round about the Parke of S. *Iames*, and returned home through Oldbourne. King *Henry* then considering the great charges of the Cittizens for the furniture of this vnusuall Muster, forbad the marching watch prouided for, at Midsommer for that yeare, which beeing once laide downe, was not raysed againe till the yeare 1548. the second of *Edward* the sixt, Sir *Iohn Gresham* then being Mayor, who caused the marching watch both on the Eue of Sainte *Iohn Baptist*, and of S. *Peter* the Apostle, to be reuiued and set foorth, in as comely order as it had beene accustomed, which watch was also beautified by the number of more then 300. Demilances and light horsemen, prepared by the Cittizens to be sent into Scotland, for the rescue of the towne of Hadington, and others kept by the Englishmen. Since this Mayors time, the like marching watch in this Citty hath not been vsed, though some attemptes haue beene made thereunto, as in the yeare 1585. . . .[18]

Stow thus states that the Watch ended (apart from a one-time-only 1548 revival) in 1539: cancelled in that year by Henry VIII himself, in his concern for the citizens' financial wellbeing (although Stow does not tell us why the one year's cancellation, caused by the expenses of an "vnusuall Muster" on 8 May 1539, should then have become permanent); and his 1539 date is still quoted by many today. In 1954, however, the publication of *Collections III* made generally available the proof that Stow had been mistaken about the closing date of the Watch, and therefore also implicitly called into question Stow's (limited) account of the cause of the Watch's end; for *Collections III* printed livery company records of payments for elaborate Midsummer Watch pageantry in 1541, and also records of what seemed to its editors to be company Watch pageants as well in both 1544 and 1545. No more Watch records appear, however, in *Collections III* after 1545: not even for 1548, the year in which Stow tells us there was a one-time-only revival of the Watch, much less for 1585, the year of a proposed revival only.[19]

When, then, *did* the London Midsummer Watch end? And what put a stop to what had been clearly, for a considerable length of time, a major festive occasion (in fact, two occasions within six days) in the lives of Londoners? First let us clarify again the term London Midsummer Watch: for theatre historians then and now can use it with different meanings.[20] As we have seen in chapter 3, "standing" watches (i.e., set watches in specific locations) had been normal, for security reasons, from early times in London, not only at midsummer but also at other such festive times, as well as dangerous times, of the year; and a decorative "marching watch" (i.e., watchmen moving in a parade or procession through the streets of London, along a pre-set route) appears to have existed at midsummer since at least the later fourteenth century. When, however, the editors of *Collections III* use the term London Midsummer Watch they mean – as do most other cultural and theatre historians today – the midsummer watch from the time that it began, as a festive parade, to include wood-and-canvas pageants carried through the streets, until the time those pageants ceased. This time span is normally considered to be 1504–45, the period for which *Collections III*'s editors turned up Great Company records of payments for what appeared to be Watch pageants: although we have now seen that such pageants began well before 1504. Understanding the terminology is important; the revival of the Watch in 1548, for example, as mentioned by Stow, would not be considered by most theatre historians to have been a true revival of the festive event unless it included pageants;

and *Collections III* provides no pageant records. Stow's account of the 1548 revival is minimal; it tells us only that the Watch was revived "in as comely order as it had beene accustomed" (though one would normally assume that this would have included pageants), further augmented by troops intended for immediate military service in Scotland. The urged 1585 revival (as mentioned by Stow) did include plans for pageants;[21] but these are not found in the livery company records because this proposed revival, as Stow also indicates, indeed did not take place. By the usual definition today, therefore, of the term London Midsummer Watch, and according to the records printed in *Collections III*, we should take 1545 as most probably the final year, indeed, of the Midsummer Watch as the kind of complete pageant-spectacle Stow has described so vividly; and further initial investigation moves that final year back from 1545 to 1544, for the 1545 single record printed in *Collections III* is meagre indeed (simply a payment by the Grocers' Company, to which the mayor in June 1545 belonged, for the carriage of pageants to the Greyfriars: perhaps a storage matter[22]) and is moreover in *Collections III* wrongly dated, coming in fact from the 1543–44 Grocers' wardens' accounts (not the 1544–45 accounts), which ran from May 1543 to June 1544 and therefore could include expenses having to do with the Watch either of 1543 or of 1544 but not of 1545.[23] The *Collections III* record entry of 1544 pageants is also short – but is from the manuscripts of the Mercers' Company, which commonly contain little information about Company-sponsored pageantry and so do not automatically invite a question as to whether the pageantry, because dealt with so briefly, did in fact take place.[24] And indeed a second 1544 Midsummer Watch pageant record (from the manuscripts of the Clothworkers, who had a sheriff in office in 1543–44) is printed in the Addenda to *Collections III* – consisting of Clothworkers' dramatic records not available to the Malone Society editors in 1954 – included in *Collections V*.[25]

Accepting, for the time being (but see below), the ending date of 1544, as indicated by the records in *Collections III* and *Collections V*: why did the pageant-bearing Midsummer Watch cease at that time? Its period of decline was not long, given the large numbers and costs of pageants provided by the Drapers, Grocers, and Goldsmiths in 1541;[26] it apparently did not gradually lose popular or civic governmental favour, and accordingly slowly wind down as a public spectacle.[27] Rather, its ending appears to have been comparatively sudden: from elaborate spectacle in 1541 to virtual non-existence by the mid 1540s.

There are at least two significant post-1954 theories, one older and one more recent, which can be taken separately or combined together as to the cause of the mid-1540s demise of the London Midsummer Watch: that it was suppressed by Henry VIII himself (his attack beginning in 1539), or by the city, because of the growing strength of the Reformation and the traditional Roman Catholic associations (saints' days performances) and subject matter (the Assumption, St. John Baptist, etc.) of Watch pageantry;[28] that it was suppressed, or allowed to die, by civic authorities who, looking for a way further to augment their growing political power and its public image, began in the mid 1530s politically and financially to privilege the annual public display associated with the secular 29 October occasion of the inauguration of a new Lord Mayor over the traditional public June display of the Midsummer Watch.[29] These theories are partly grounded in historical facts. The early 1530s did indeed bring the Reformation – with its growing hostility towards images and saints – to England; the Midsummer Watch, with portable pageants on religious subject matter including saints, traditionally took place on the eves to mornings of major saints' festivals; Henry VIII did indeed, as Stow tells us, cancel the Watch in 1539; and a "pageant," provided by a livery company, is first recorded as carried in a mayoral 29 October swearing-in procession (the Lord Mayor's Show, as theatre historians call it from this date) in 1535 and again in 1540.[30] 29 October Midsummer-Watch-type company pageant records, as printed in *Collections III*, are brief through the 1540s (found indeed, after 1540, only in 1543 and 1546); but by the 1550s and 1560s, detailed records begin to be found, and company Watch pageant records have ceased. The facts, however, are more complex than might at first seem to be the case.

First, as already pointed out, Midsummer Watch pageantry in 1541 was as elaborate as in any year of the 1530s – including in 1535 and 1536; and in 1537 and 1538 the mayor at Watch time was a Mercer, so that the absence of detailed Watch records is no indication of an absence of elaborate pageantry, especially given other indications of ongoing elaborate display.[31] Indeed, the civic government in June 1537 issued an order that each sheriff from that time should have no *more* than three Watch pageants.[32] No gradual real decline in Watch pageantry, from the mid-1530s (the first occurrence of a "pageant" in a London Lord Mayor's Show), can be effectively argued.[33] And in 1544 the Mercers are shown by the records still to be planning to provide what looks like normal Watch pageantry ("well for the woorshipse of my Lorde mayere and the Compenye also").[34] But then the pageant Watch records abruptly cease.

Second, as is argued in chapter 10, there is in fact no evidence that the company "pageant" carried on 29 October in both 1535 and 1540 was an elaborate, Midsummer-Watch-type wood and canvas construction; it may on both occasions have been simply an elaborate company banner or other such device; and (also as discussed in chapter 10) the 29 October procession in both years was an unusual, truncated one – as again in 1543, when next we find a 29 October "pageant" being carried – so that in any case we cannot assume that, whatever the "pageant" was, it was any kind of 29 October norm in other years at this time. (And the pageant record printed for 29 October 1546 in *Collections III* is in fact, as the editors themselves point out, probably not a 29 October 1546 record at all.[35]) An account by the Mercers of mayoral ceremonial display in 1541, when a Mercer mayor was sworn into office, also says nothing about wood-and-canvas constructions (though of course this does not prove that they did not exist);[36] and it is not until the 1550s that conclusive evidence is found of Midsummer-Watch-type pageants being carried – perhaps on a regular basis – in sixteenth-century 29 October processions. And by the 1550s the festive Midsummer Watch, as a parade with company-sponsored pageants, appears to have been dead for some years, although with occasional subsequent flare-ups of some different kinds of unspecified display (perhaps only additional armed men), in relation to standing watches, in some years past 1558.[37]

Third, Henry's cancellation of the Watch in 1539 was, as Stow states (and as is sometimes overlooked), for one year only, and at least ostensibly not for religious reasons but for financial ones.[38] The stated reason given by Stow is the king's concern that the June Watch expenses would be too great for Londoners, given that he himself had required them to spend lavishly for 8 May 1539 on a massive military muster. Henry, whose excommunication by the Pope had been published in November 1538 and who in January 1539 had found himself in considerable military danger from a Catholic alliance against him (involving France, the Holy Roman Empire, and Scotland), wanted his nation prepared for a possible invasion;[39] importantly, too, a massive military display by London would send the appropriate message abroad, via foreign ambassadors posted to London/Westminster, of England's military readiness. In the past, Henry had made use where appropriate of the Midsummer Watch to impress foreign ambassadors with London's wealth and power;[40] in 1539 he needed an entirely military display, not festive pageantry. Historians, however, have looked for another, unstated reason for Henry's cancellation of the Watch: probably above all since Londoners themselves – the supposed beneficiaries of the cancellation – do not seem to have greeted the king's action with resounding approval. John Husee wrote to Lord Lisle on 22 June 1539 that, at the Watch's cancellation, "some of the citizens, having prepared for the same, are not very well pleased;"[41] Wriothesley's *Chronicle* notes that the cancellation came late, after the mayor and sheriffs had already prepared their pageants, and "was a great losse to poore men."[42] Henry, it has been suggested, must have had a larger political agenda in mind when cancelling the Watch; and the Roman aspects of the Watch – its occurrence on the eves and mornings of the festival days of major saints, together with its pageants often representing figures such as St. John Baptist himself, or the Assumption of the Virgin – might have led to his targeting of the Watch for religious reasons but under the cover of financial considerations. Such a targeting might well have been welcomed by some Londoners, though certainly not by others.

Pageant content, however, could easily have been changed if religious/political problems about it had arisen (the Drapers' 1477 Watch pageant, as we have seen, probably featured the religiously unproblematic nine worthies); and the 1540 "pageant" (whatever it was) carried in a Lord Mayor's Show was an Assumption pageant – not a logical choice (unless, perhaps, minimal indeed) by the livery company concerned (the Drapers) if such religious subjects in public display had been starting to pose difficulties with the king or his council. The Midsummer Watch also was, significantly, at a celebratory secular, as well as religious, time of the year, so adaptations would have been possible if politically required; livery companies concerned, for example, in the 1540s-50s with the religious implications of continuing to date (as they had been doing) their accounting years by saints' days simply switched to dating their accounts instead by the equivalent secular days – such as midsummer instead of St. John Baptist – or by religious days other than those of saints; they did not change processes, only names, as they adapted to new circumstances.[43] Finally Henry, at least in 1536 when anti-Roman sentiment and actions were stronger than in 1539, far from targeting the Watch as a civic event with strong Roman associations had himself attended it as a spectator.[44] And further, by 1539, concerned about where more extreme anti-Roman measures might be taking him, Henry had begun to backtrack on some of the more zealous moves and sentiments of the mid-1530s.[45] 1539 would have been an unusual time, it would seem, for him – or anyone else – to have decided to begin suppressing the Watch for religious reasons. And indeed there is no need to posit a religious motive (either of Henry himself or of anyone urging or advising him) for Henry's 1539 Watch cancellation: for his 14 June letter to London's mayor, sheriffs, aldermen, and Common Council, cancelling the event, has survived in the city's records, and makes clear his (at least main) motive: the pressuring of London into the replacement of the annual, traditional, festive Watch by an annual purely military spectacle. Civic Watch money would thus become used, annually, entirely for Henry's military benefit.

Ryght trustie & welbelovyd & trustie & welbelovyd we grete you well lating you wytt that calling to our remembraunce howe of late vpon knowlege of our pleasure gyven vnto you ye have putt yourselfes in redynes & furnyture of Armes bothe to serve vs & to defende your selfes in case of necessytie ageinst all suche persones as wold any evyll to vs or to the comen welthe of this our Realme/And to your great charge you have effectually shewed your selfes therin in your late generall musters moche to our contentement & agreable acceptacion wherof we most hartely thanke you ffor asmuche as in consyderacion therof we tendre to dyscharge you of suche further burden as for this present yere dothe nevertheles depend vpon you we have thought not onely by these our lettres to dyscharge you for this yere of those accustomed watches which have bein solemply vsed heretofore at Mydsomer and saint Peters even/But also bycause the same have bein accustomed to be donne in the nyght tyme moche to the dymynytion of the reputacion of the thing And that by reason of the importunytie of the tyme sundrye occasyons of evyll have bein taken & chaunsed thervpon/to leve yt to your Arbytres whyther you wyll herafter contynue the said watches as hath bein vsed or elles to convert bothe the same watches by an ordre to be taken amonges you whervnto we woll be glad to be pryvie & to gyve you our advyse therin before it shuld be fully concluded into A generall muster to be yerely made at A tyme for the same convenyent thinking that suche A generall muster shuld be nomore chargeable to you than the said watches And yet the purpose therof nothing to be regarded nor of any lyke effecte as the said musters shuld . . . [46]

Henry, deeply involved in military manoeuvres and apparently pleased with the effect of the May 1539 London muster, had found a better way – from his perspective – for the Londoners to spend their money annually than on the traditional Midsummer Watch, which was only in part a military exercise of benefit to him.[47] He may also, of course, have been concerned about potential disorders surrounding the Watch – as one line in the above quotation indicates, and as Ronald Hutton has pointed out; but London's response to the king (as outlined below) would seem to indicate that security was not a major factor in the matter, since the city in its reply apparently did not think it necessary even to mention security.[48]

The response of the civic authorities to Henry's 1539 Watch cancellation, and to his suggestion of its permanent replacement by a military muster, is especially interesting in light of the suggestion that the London oligarchy in the 1530s was intent on privileging the annual October mayoral oath-taking at Westminster, in terms of civic spectacle, over the also-annual Watch. Not only, as already noted, was lavish civic spending on the Watch still taking place, but the Common Council in 1539 reacted to Henry's Watch cancellation and annual muster suggestion by the tried and true method with which administrators typically handle difficult political problems: they sent the matter to an ad hoc committee;[49] and the committee reported back with a defence of the Watch which would certainly have undercut – whether they believed their own rhetoric or not – any attempt by the civic authorities themselves either to cancel the Watch permanently or to reduce its display significantly and to transfer its pageantry to the day of the mayoral oath-taking.

Consyderacions as we suppose that it were better to have A watche in the nyght tyme as hath bein accustomed than to have A muster in the day tyme/.

ffyrst bycause solempne watches be & have bene kepte alwayes in the nyght tyme in all the good Townes of England in the vygylles of the Natyvytie of seint Iohan Baptyst & seint Peter aswell as within the Cytie of london And alwayes have beine laudably vsed after that maner/.

Item by reason of the said nyght watches aswell goyng watches as hath bene accustomed afore this tyme within the Cytie of london as by the Standing watches awayting vpon Counstables of this Cytie in their seuerall wardes/A great multytude of people have bene well & clenly harnyssed by reason wherof aswell their harnes as other habylymentes of warre mete for the defence of this Roylme have bene alwayes kept clene & in A redynes for the defence of the Royalme as the same shuld be in case A generall muster shuld be kepte in the day tyme/.

Item by reason of the said watches many poore people be hyred & sett on worke moche to their great commodyties & profyttes by bering of lyghtes & many other wayes/And by the generall muster the same shuld be an vniversall charge aswell of the poore as of the Ryche to their importable charges as of late the same hath beine well knowen within this Cytie/Whyche muster (yf the same shuld be nowe newly establysshed) the same can not be kept/as of late yt hath bene sene to the grett emblemysshing & dyshonour of all the Cytezens of the seid Cytie And to the great defacing of the lawde & estymacion of the seid last generall muster/.

Item by mustre kepte in the day tyme many mysfortunes may chaunce by reason of the heate of the day & otherwyse to suche as shuld be in the ˏ⌈seid⌉ generall muster/.

Item the musters in the day shall not be so honourable neyther for the kinges maiestie nor his said Cytie as the watches kept in the nyght (as have bein accustomed) which have ben had in great honour pryce & estymacion thorowe all the Realmes of Crystendome/.

Item the watches in the nyght tyme be more honourable forasmuche as A lytle cost done in the nyght tyme shalbe estemed of the double value of the cost & charge that ys done in the day tyme And that that ys done in the nyght ys A farre better & more plesaunt spectacle to the ye/And the charge therof not half so muche Wherfore we thinke that it were & ys more lawdable & farre better for the honour & comen welth of this Cytie to have A watche in the nyght tyme as it hath beine accustomed than A muster in the day tyme All which premysses we most humbly remytt vnto your hygh dyscrecions & wysedomes/[50]

The committee and the civic government might not, of course, have believed their own report; the basic purpose of the report might simply have been to prevent a royal takeover of how London decided annually to spend its Midsummer Watch money. The city might conceivably even, originally and privately, have urged Henry VIII to cancel the 1539 Watch: on financial grounds or indeed as part of a covert civic political strategy for transferring Watch pageantry to the Lord Mayor's Show. But genuine community interest in maintaining the traditional Midsummer Watch cannot be ruled out and certainly seems plausible;[51] and at the least it would have proved difficult, after the specifics of Henry's 1539 cancellation and then of the civic response, for the civic government on its own to have shut down the traditional festive Watch, or even to have reduced the public display of the Watch to any significant extent. And the king in 1539 apparently backed off; the Watch, as we have seen, was staged as usual in 1541 (the absence of 1540 Watch pageant records is not surprising, and does not necessarily indicate an absence of Watch pageants, given that a Mercer was then mayor), and probably also in 1542 (Mercer mayor again), and perhaps 1543 (Salter mayor; no Salters' accounts or court minutes for this period have survived).[52]

What then happened? We have seen that the pre-1954 assumption of a 1539 death of the civic-pageant Watch was incorrect; and post-1954 theories of a gradual decline and death of the Watch, from the mid-1530s to the mid-1540s, also are not supported by the records. What the records do support is the demise of the civic-pageant Watch over the course of three years, 1544–46, for financial reasons having to do with Henry VIII's wars. The 1540s were a time of enormous military activity by Henry, especially in France: a time when Henry repeatedly turned to London for the money with which to support his wars. And in all of

1544, 1545, and 1546, Henry again appears to have cancelled the London Midsummer Watch (perhaps at the urgings of the city) – for one year only, each time – because of the wars and their costs. Henry needed military money from London; and perhaps he and/or the civic government also were now more concerned than before about security, at a time of intensive military activities and unpopular financial demands. Wriothesley's *Chronicle* tells us that in 1544 the king cancelled the London Midsummer Watch because the city had been charged with the costs of men for his wars (the May 1544 records from the Mercers' Acts of Court and the Clothworkers' Court Books must thus refer to arrangements made before the cancellation);[53] and a similar cancellation took place in 1545. "This yeare, by reason the Kinge had thre great armies, on the sea one, another in Scotland, and the 3d at Boloyne, there was no watch kept at Midsommer in London but with constables in theyr wardes."[54]

In 1546 yet another such cancellation took place, for one year only. A letter from the Privy Council to Coventry, dated 5 June 1546, discharges it of the 1546 Midsummer Watch "for this yeare in like sorte as hath been doone to Lundon and Bristow,"[55] although no cancellation letter for London itself has survived. Wriothesley gives a somewhat different cancellation account, but one not incompatible with what is said in the Privy Council letter to Coventry. In June 1546, according to Wriothesley, food in London was very dear; and the king charged the city to take 20,000 quarters of wheat and rye he had provided for his troops abroad. The Lord Mayor had "to levie great sommes of money of the company of the said cittie for the payment of the same".[56] A mid-June peace was then celebrated not only with a religious service and processions but also with bonfires in the streets, banqueting, and drinking.[57] "This yeare the watch was laid downe by a court of aldermen for eaver, but my lord major rode on Midsommer Even and Sainct Peeters" with the sheriffs, one hundred constables and their men, cresset lights, the mayor's officers, and so forth, at the mayor's cost except for the constables' lights.[58] This presumably would have been a compromise aimed at providing at least some of the traditional elements of the Watch, including the Watch's support for the poor in the city's employment of Watch cresset bearers. There is no record in the city's Letter Books, Journals, or Repertories of the Watch being "laid downe," temporarily or "for eaver," by the Court of Aldermen in 1546; but these records series are not all-inclusive; a form of Watch was continuing (in the riding of the mayor with a large number of men and lights, with standing watches in the wards); and certainly Wriothesley's account would explain the absence of records – in either livery company manuscripts or city manuscripts – of London Midsummer Watch pageants (with one exception: see below) from 1545 on. And there is certainly no reason to disbelieve Wriothesley's indications of wars and money as the basic causes of the 1544–46 cancellations of the London Midsummer Watch. Indeed, even in the late 1530s and in 1540 the money required to put on the Watch had clearly been causing some restiveness among the London livery companies. In 1537 a civic order held down Watch costs in several ways (limiting, for example, the numbers of city waits, trumpeters, and giants, and also limiting the sheriffs to no more than three pageants each[59]), and in 1540 company members had rebelled against an order for the provision by the companies of large numbers of cresset lights for the Watch.[60] The city does not seem, however, to have been then trying gradually or quickly to eliminate the Watch. In 1538 and 1540 it was concerned with improving the Watch's lights; in 1542 it was busy affirming governing rules for the Watch, specifying again, for example, that the sheriffs were free to provide Watch pageants as long as these did not exceed three per sheriff in number.[61] But the war expenses of the 1540s took a heavy toll; and in 1546 – the year, according to Wriothesley, of permanent Midsummer Watch cancellation – there was also an attempt made by the civic government to reduce mayoralty costs by eliminating, also "for eaver," the traditional 29 October banquet provided by the mayor at the Guildhall.[62] The dinner traditionally given by the mayor on the Monday after Twelfth Day *was* eliminated by the Court of Alderman in 1546–47.[63]

Of course it could be argued that the London civic authorities, for religious reasons, might have been pleased to carry out Watch cancellations for ostensibly financial reasons in the mid-1540s. But the fact remains that the stated financial/political reasons are, on their own, altogether credible, and that the cancellations are consonant with other civic expense-reduction measures – clearly non-religious – which were taking place at the same time. As for the suggestion that the London oligarchy in the 1530s and 1540s would have been pleased to transfer Watch pageantry to the 29 October mayoral inauguration ceremonies, for its own political purposes: perhaps it would have been pleased to have done so, but there is no definite evidence, as chapter 10 will demonstrate, that elaborate Watch-type pageantry was used on 29 October in London in the 1530s and 1540s (although absence of evidence does not mean that such pageantry could not have taken place); and furthermore non-Watch expense reductions in the 1540s also affected (as noted above) mayoral inauguration ceremonies. Only in the 1550s – when the

traditional civic-pageants Watch had been dead for about a decade
(except for the 1548 revival) – do we have definite evidence of Midsummer-Watch-type company pageants regularly appearing in mayoral inauguration shows in London, and then only at the apparent rate of one
per year, to the end of the century.[64] Meanwhile elaborate May games
may have become Watch substitutes: perhaps to some extent, at least at
times, merging with the reduced, ongoing civic non-pageant watch at
midsummer. London citizen Henry Machyn in his *Diary* mentions several May games in London in the 1550s, all with guns, drums, and morris dances, and in 1555 (on 26 May) also with a giant and hobbyhorses, in
1557 (on 30 May) with the nine worthies, speeches, a sultan, an elephant
and castle, young Moors with shields and darts, and the lord and lady of
the May, and in 1559 – tellingly on 24 June, Midsummer Day – with the
nine worthies again, a giant, a pageant with a queen, St. George and the
dragon, and Robin Hood with Little John, Maid Marian, and Friar
Tuck.[65] In 1559 also "thay had spechys rond a-bowt London" – which
sounds like a midsummer procession.[66] Had May games in London always been well developed (companies in the earlier sixteenth century
sometimes borrowed or hired from parishes their Midsummer Watch
giants and also religious pageants; presumably these parishes had ongoing May games[67]), and/or did May games become especially well developed in London with the demise of the pageant-oriented Midsummer
Watch? In March 1553 London sheriff John Maynard (a Mercer), with
other important personages, rode through London with giants, hobbyhorses, armed men, a morris dance, musicians, a devil, a sultan, Jack-of-
Lent and his wife, and a doctor, and more, bringing a withe (a willow
wand or garland, traditionally in this period brought ceremonially into
great houses at Easter time) through the city.[68] Was all of this display
usual civic custom, or a kind of elaboration, beyond the traditional, related at least in part to the loss of the Watch? At midsummer 1567 the
city's standing watch was augmented with constables and "diuers prety
showes done at the charges of yongemen in certayne Parishes" – perhaps
parishes with elaborate May games? – who "aweighted on the Lorde
Maior, hee rydinge frome the Guildhall through Cheape to Algate and
backe agayne": though Stow tells us that the effect was spoiled "for lacke
of good order in keepynge theyr arraye".[69] Was there at least an occasional merging of May games and the civic midsummer watch, once the
companies' pageant-Watch had been "put down"?[70] In June 1571 the
parish of St. Giles Cripplegate provided for midsummer eve, to go before
the mayor in the watch, a giant, morris dancers with six "calyvers" (light

muskets, or soldiers armed with them), and three boys "on horsback"; E. C. Cawte has suggested that the boys may have been on hobbyhorses.[71] St. Giles was a parish that had rented a giant to the Drapers for the 1536 Midsummer Watch, and had been involved in the provision of a pageant of St. Thomas for the Skinners in the 1519 Watch.[72] We know too little about the relationship between the civic Midsummer Watch, from the late fourteenth or mid fifteenth century through the sixteenth century, and London parish (and other) May and midsummer celebrations.[73]

That rising Protestantism, at least, played little or no part in the demise of the civic-pageant Midsummer Watch is further indicated by the 1548 revival of the pageant Watch: at the express commandment of the Protestant-oriented Council of the young Edward VI.[74] And furthermore, despite the negative evidence of *Collections III* (with no Watch pageant records past 1544), this Watch did include (presumably traditional) pageantry; in June 1548 a Mercer was mayor of London, and another Mercer one of the sheriffs; and the Mercers' MS Acts of Court for this year includes arrangements for Watch pageants for both Mercer officeholders, and also the statement that the king himself may come to Mercers' Hall to view the Watch.[75] Why did revivals not continue? Perhaps because by 1549 the political situation was unstable again; there were rebellions, for example, in July, with martial law being proclaimed in London;[76] and in 1550 (and for several years thereafter) the London companies were financially stretched to the limit by being obliged in March to purchase back the quit-rents of their chantry lands which had been seized by the Crown, and also by purchasing from the king at that time the liberties of Southwark.[77] Wriothesley specifically comments that there was only an ordinary night watch at midsummer in 1550;[78] and Letter Books R and S contain orders for midsummer standing watches, usually without lights or music, in most years from 1549 to 1558.

We can thus imagine a plausible scenario in which the costs of the Midsummer Watch were becoming an increasing problem for the London civic authorities and livery companies in the late 1530s and 1540s; but the authorities to 1539 were nevertheless trying to maintain a controlled but elaborate Watch display. Then, with the king's 1539 suggestion that the Watch be replaced by an annual muster, the Watch had to be maintained, and pretty well at its current level: so as not to give the king indirect control over London civic pageantry funding. Community and charity concerns were also involved. Reduction or elimination of the Watch's elaborate display could only be contemplated if matters could be arranged in such a way as to give the king no further opportunity to suggest or to command an annual muster instead. The king's financial demands for military purposes, in the 1540s, along with probably security concerns, as well, at a time of much military activity and general unrest, then provided the necessity for, or means of, eliminating the traditional, elaborate Watch: along with various other expenses of civic government borne by the mayor. And, given the continuation throughout the 1540s not of the civic-pageant Watch (with the exception of the 1548 revival) but of mayoral inaugurations, a natural or enforced shift perhaps then took place (although also perhaps welcomed and/or manipulated by the civic elite) in Londoners' civic pageantry focus. The Lord Mayor's Show thus by the 1550s became the established venue for previous Watch-type, company-provided spectacle: though apparently to a more much limited extent, until the seventeenth century, than the Watch had been; there is currently no known evidence, for example, although more research needs to be done, that more than one constructed pageant regularly was carried in a London Lord Mayor's Show until after 1600. Meanwhile Watch-type spectacle involving pageants may also have become a more prominent part of (if it had not always been a prominent part of) parish-based May games, and May games may have extended themselves to fill a new display gap at midsummer.

The reasons for the decline and fall of London's Midsummer Watch in the mid sixteenth century, in its company-sponsored, pageant-spectacle form, cannot fully be known today. Political and financial agendas on all sides were complex in the 1530s and 1540s: a period of enormous social/political/religious upheaval throughout England and especially in the capital; and a major civic spectacle such as the Watch could not help but have had a number of political dimensions, some of them perhaps religious. Even, for example, with finances the most probable main reason for the Watch cancellations of the 1540s, some stridently Protestant Londoners might have welcomed the cancellations as puttings-down of an event consisting in part of what they might have considered to be Popish spectacle. And others might indeed have seen (positively or negatively) civic Watch expenses as preventing a higher pageant profile for the Lord Mayor's inauguration ceremonies, with others worrying also about potential major disorders in the London streets.

Whatever the full slate of reasons, however, it appears that wars and money, perhaps together with concerns about potential disorders attendant upon the king's military activities in the 1540s – and not the Reformation or oligarchic manipulation – were the major factors in the civic-pageant Watch's 1540s demise.

CHAPTER 10

The Lord Mayor's Show

During the first half of the sixteenth century in London, as was indicated in chapter 9, two major, traditional civic shows involving ceremonial processions and, with variations, pageantry took place annually in the city streets: one largely before 1550 and one—as this chapter will suggest – largely after.[1] The more elaborate, pre-1550 show was the Midsummer Watch, on the evenings to mornings of 23–24 and 28–29 June; the less elaborate, later show was the Lord Mayor's Show, on 29 October. As we have seen already in chapter 3, annually on the day after his swearing in at the Guildhall on 28 October, the feast of Sts. Simon and Jude, London's new mayor formally journeyed to be sworn also before the king or his representatives, the Barons of the Exchequer, at Westminster.[2] The mayor set out from the city, accompanied by craft guild members in full livery dress, and processed (from the mid fifteenth century, as seen in chapter 8) first by land to the Thames, then by water to Westminster, then back by water to the city, and by land to the Guildhall again.[3] The processions both by land and by water involved music and elaborate display (of banners, for example, and of livery dress), perhaps more elaborate display on the water as well (as discussed in chapter 8: although this is only speculative), and, by the 1530s to 1540s, it has generally been believed, Midsummer-Watch-type (i.e., constructed wood-and-canvas and portable) land pageants, provided by the livery company each year to which the new mayor belonged. The whole display, together with further processions, after a Guildhall dinner, to St. Paul's Cathedral and eventually to the mayor's house, is included by theatre historians today under the term the Lord Mayor's Show: the title being commonly used for the display only from the time of its first inclusion of constructed portable (land) pageants.

The standard view today of the origins of Lord Mayor's Show pageants is that expressed in the Malone Society's 1954 *Collections III*: as previously seen, a part-calendar, part-edition, from the extant manuscript

records of eleven of the twelve Great Companies of London, of drama
and pageantry sponsored by the companies between 1485 and 1640.[4]
Collections III indicates that at the very start of the sixteenth century neither the Midsummer Watch nor the Lord Mayor's Show existed in a
form involving portable, constructed, wood-and-canvas pageants, that
from 1504 to 1534 such pageants were associated with the Watch only,
and that in 1535 and the 1540s the Watch's pageants became transferred
to the Lord Mayor's Show, with the Watch then declining and eventually expiring, while the Show's pageantry gradually became very highly
developed. In the early seventeenth century, for example, major public-
theatre dramatists – contemporaries of Shakespeare such as Thomas
Middleton and Thomas Heywood – wrote scripts for highly elaborate
London Lord Mayor's Shows. This volume's chapter 9 has argued that
Midsummer Watch pageants began well before 1504, and also that no
simple transfer of Watch pageants in the 1530s and 1540s to the mayor's
Westminster oath-taking (thus creating the Lord Mayor's Show) took
place. It has also suggested, leaving the suggestion to be developed in
this chapter, that – at least in the sixteenth century – Lord Mayor's
Show land pageants may not have begun until the 1550s. Lord Mayor's
Show land pageantry therefore now requires a closer look.

The Malone Society's *Collections III* established in 1954 a specific date –
five years earlier than had previously been thought[5] – for the first time that
a Midsummer-Watch type of constructed pageant was apparently carried
through the streets of London as a part of the annual London Lord
Mayor's Show. The date – 29 October 1535 – fits smoothly into a theory, as
discussed in chapter 9, positing a mid-1530s uneasiness, in some quarters,
with the Watch because of its traditional Catholic dates and elements, and
a gradual transferral therefore of typical Watch land pageantry to the secular occasion of the mayor's inauguration. It also suits theories of 1530–40
as a period of a "further consolidation of power by London's leaders,"[6]
and increasing frictions between city and Crown,[7] involving an escalation
in mayoral ceremonial in general. *Collections III* prints a transcription of the
relevant 1540 Drapers' Company manuscript record entry appearing to establish the 1535 date; the editors note that the record, in referring to a
planned 1540 pageant (for mayor-elect William Roche, a Draper) refers to
a mayor's installation pageant on one previous occasion: at the installation
for the second time of mayor John Aleyn, a Mercer.

Item it is aggreed to ˌ⌈haue⌉ the pageaunt of thassumpcion boren before the
mayre from the tower to the gild hall And that by a precydent in the ij^de tyme of
sir Iohan Aleyn beyng mayre[8]

John Aleyn was installed as mayor of London for the first time in 1525 and for the second time in 1535.

The *Collections III* record, and its interpretation by the volume's editors,[9] at first seem straightforward enough. The Drapers, in deciding to use a pageant as part of their ceremonial installation display for their mayor-elect on 29 October 1540, were following a single precedent for the novelty, found in the 29 October pageantry in 1535 of the Mercers' Company: a company elsewhere in the Drapers' records (in 1541) castigated for its financial extravagance in relation to the Midsummer Watch.[10] The Mercers, it seems from the Drapers' 1540 record, began the elaboration, with a portable land pageant, of 29 October display in general; and the Drapers picked up the idea when they next had a mayor installed in office, in 1540: one year after Henry VIII had cancelled the Midsummer Watch for 1539 and had indicated his interest in its permanent discontinuation in favour of an annual military general muster by London's citizens.[11] Gradually or quickly, constructed Lord Mayor's Show pageants, provided by the companies, became a norm.[12]

The 1540 record printed in *Collections III* is, however, after all not as simple to interpret as at first it seems: for, as has not previously been realized, it refers not to an ordinary mayoral installation but to a special, irregularly occurring kind. Although the mayor of London from very early times had been required, on the day after taking his oath of office at the Guildhall, to proceed to Westminster to be confirmed there in his office by the Barons of the Exchequer, occasionally the Barons were not available at Westminster at the time of the October installation; and the mayor was then required to take his "Westminster" oath instead at the Tower of London, before its Constable as the king's representative:[13] a requirement involving a truncation of the usual ceremonial display associated with the oath-taking, since the Tower of London was just down the street, so to speak, from the Guildhall. No river procession took place in Tower-oath years.

The 1540 record from the Drapers' manuscripts, dealing with the mayoral oath-taking of William Roche, involves in 1540 not the usual 29 October land procession to the Thames, water procession to Westminster and back, and land procession again from the water to the Guildhall, but the simpler, land-only ceremonial associated with a Tower oath;[14] and in looking back to 1535 for a precedent for having a pageant carried before the mayor "from the tower to the gild hall" (not from the river to the Guildhall, or from St. Paul's to the Guildhall, as would have been the case in a river-procession year), the Drapers are looking back from

1540 specifically to another year in which the mayor took his oath at the Tower.[15] Are, then, the Drapers in 1540 citing a precedent for having a land pageant carried, at all, before the mayor on 29 October? – or are they citing a precedent connected specifically with Tower-oath pageantry? If the latter, the 1540 record in fact tells us nothing about what might or might not have been done, before – or after – 1535/1540, in the years when the mayor processed not to the Tower and back but to Westminster and back. And that the Drapers are deliberately citing a Tower-oath precedent is made clear in their wardens' accounts covering the October 1540 mayoral installation:

It*em* gevyn to the Clerk of the me*r*cers for a p*re*cydent of the mayr*es* goyng to take his othe at the tow*re* of london*e* xij d[16]

The question thus arises: did the use of constructed land pageants on 29 October begin, after all, in 1535, or did it perhaps begin before – or considerably after – that date, in non-Tower-oath years? Now that we need not accept 1535 as the general originating date, in a re-examination of Great Company records do we find any indications at all – to look first at earlier possibilities – of Midsummer-Watch-type company pageants perhaps having been carried in London mayors' 29 October processions before 1535? A fresh examination of all extant, potentially-relevant manuscript records (accounts, minutes, ordinance books, etc.) of the Great Companies to 1535 turns up no signs of Midsummer-Watch-type pageants on 29 October before 1528, although from silence nothing can with certainty be inferred, given the companies' varying accounting and minuting practices, and given also the many company records volumes that have not survived.[17] We do, however, find indications of possible 29 October land pageants, between 1528 and 1535, in the records of, again, the Drapers, who had a mayor installed in both 1528 and 1533: both years of Westminster, not Tower, mayoral oath-taking.

Within the Drapers' Company, as within other Great Companies at this time, existed a group of members, the bachelors, just below the rank of the livery – as we have seen in chapter 8 – and who were responsible for providing a significant part of the ceremonial display by the company associated with the installation of a member of the company as mayor. They had a special barge (the bachelors' barge), for example, involved – as we have seen – in the river procession to and from Westminster; and they served at the mayor's feast at the Guildhall after the oath had been taken.[18] And in both 1528 and 1533 the Drapers' records refer to the bachelors as not providing their usual barge for the mayor's Westminster progress, and to provision (instead?), at the mayor's landing, after his Westminster river journey, of "the Assumption" and of trumpeters going with him from St. Paul's to the Guildhall.

1528
Also aggreed by thassent of my lord the Maire Mr Rudstone that no Bachillers Barge be had this yere/. but at the Maires landing frome westminster to haue the Assumpcione and the trumpetoures goyng frome poulys to the gyld hall/ . And soo aftir dyner vnto poulys ayene & soo home. . . .[19]

1533
Also Agreed bye thassent of my lord Mayre Mr Askue that no bachelers barge be had this yere butt Att the Maiers landyng frome westminster to have thassumpcion And the trumpetours goyng frome powlis to the guyldhall And so After dynner to powles Agayne & soe home . . .[20]

The nature of "the Assumption" is of key importance here, and why it might have been an alternative to the bachelors' barge, or at least have been specified in relation to the barge.

The bachelors of the Drapers' Company were also involved, as a contributing group, in the early sixteenth-century pageantry of the Midsummer Watch in the years in which at midsummer the mayor of London was a Draper;[21] and in the 1520s, three times when a Draper was mayor at midsummer (in 1521, 1522, and 1529), we find the bachelors providing for the Watch a special pageant which was designated as theirs – not one of the pageants displayed by the company as a whole – and which in the records is called the pageant of the Assumption and sometimes simply "the Assumption."[22] (The Drapers' Company, as noted in chapter 5, was especially associated with the Assumption of the Virgin Mary, being the Fraternity of Our Lady and holding its annual election of officers and general company feast at the time of the Assumption [15 August] each year.[23]) Two relevant company records entries for 1521 and 1522 read in part, for example:

1521
Paymentes for mydsomer watche with oure pagentes besides the Bachillers pagent of the Assumpcione. Sir Iohan Brugge being Maire[24]

1522
The xijth day of may here assembled the hole body of the ffelishipe as moste in Nombre And at the said assembley our ordinaunces were redd openly And after that the hows for there parte and the Bachillers for there parte ˌ⌈onely thassumpcione for the bachillers.⌉ graunted to renewe ˌ⌈&⌉ all the old pagentes

‸[for the hows] & to make ‸[also] on*e* newe pagent of the goldyn*e* fflees for the
Mair*e* ayenst mydsom*er* . . .²⁵

No separate records of the Drapers' bachelors for this period – minutes
of meetings, for example, or accounts – are extant; so we have no details
of the bachelors' Assumption pageant; but the company's surviving
main records make clear the bachelors' specific Assumption pageant
responsibility.²⁶

Since, therefore, it was specifically the bachelors who customarily
provided a special barge (as well as other ceremonial services) for the
29 October oath-takings of Draper mayors, and since the bachelors also
customarily appear in Midsummer Watch records in the 1520s, when
Draper mayors are in office, in association with their own pageant
called "the Assumption," the most obvious conclusion to be drawn from
the 1528 and 1533 29 October records previously quoted is that in both
those years the bachelors' contribution to the installation display was,
instead of their barge (or as usual but without their barge), their pageant
of the Assumption, already in existence and being used, during some
Draper mayoralties,²⁷ for the Midsummer Watch.²⁸ If this is indeed the
correct way to interpret the records, use of Midsummer-Watch-type
land pageants for 29 October processions in London precedes 1535 by a
number of years, perhaps becoming a tradition, at least for Draper
mayors, in Westminster-oath years from 1528.²⁹ An initial 29 October
pageant in 1528 might have been especially likely because the 1528 Midsummer Watch had been cancelled, in all but its most basic elements,
because of plague;³⁰ 29 October use by the Draper bachelors of a major part of their usual Watch pageantry, instead of their barge, might
therefore have seemed appropriate.³¹ 1533 was then the next year of the
installation of a Draper mayor, 1533, with its Tower oath, the next
Draper mayoral year. (The Mercers in 1535 and perhaps earlier³² would
then have imitated the Drapers – but unusually, in 1535, in a Tower-oath
year, and hence the Drapers' reference in 1540, another Tower-oath
year, to the Mercers' precedent.)

The possibility of a 29 October pageant in both 1528 and 1533 is
only a possibility, however, because the records are not specific. The
word "pageant" is not mentioned in either of the 1528 and 1533
29 October records referring to "the Assumption"; and so it is always
possible that this "Assumption" was something different from a Midsummer Watch pageant Assumption. Drapers' Midsummer Watch
records refer to an Assumption pageant which is clearly at times called

merely "the Assumption;" but they also refer to the "Assumption" sometimes without specifying – or without the context making clear – that
the particular Assumption being referred to is a constructed pageant.
Listed, for example, among the company's 1521 Watch costs of, among
other items, their (non-Assumption) pageants and the bachelors' Assumption pageant, is an expenditure "for xxxj porters that bare all our
pagent*es* & the Assumpcion*e*".[33] This Assumption might be the bachelors' pageant, referred to as separate from the general company ("our")
pageants, but it might not be a constructed pageant at all. Why, for example, is the company, rather than the bachelors, paying for its carriage? The Drapers "Assumption" when not specified as a pageant, or as
anything else, might, for example, have been a special company banner
of the Assumption, or a religious image. The company – and the bachelors separately – did own Assumption banners;[34] and in fall 1533 the
company had a new square Assumption banner made for its barge.[35]

Further to complicate matters, the term "pageant" itself even presents problems, for it may not always be used in the records, even of the
same company, with the same meaning. In the sixteenth century (and
earlier), as we have seen before, the term pageant could mean simply a
showy representation or device carried in display;[36] perhaps a display as
simple as an elaborate banner would qualify; and within any one company's records, terms for ongoing matters would not have to be specific,
or even to be used always to mean the same thing, since everyone involved knew the (traditional) details of what was being recorded. The
Drapers' Company as a whole (not the bachelors alone), for example, in
both 1523 and 1536 had an elaborate, constructed Assumption pageant
at the Midsummer Watch; the 1523 pageant, together with one other,
required fourteen porters to carry it, and the 1536 pageant, by itself, required sixteen porters.[37] In 1541, however, the Drapers' wardens' accounts record payment to two men, only, to carry "the pageaunt of the
Assumpc*ion*" in the Watch;[38] this "pageaunt" is clearly something very
different from the 1523 and 1536 Assumption pageants. The Drapers'
minutes covering the 1541 Watch include a record of payment of 8d to
two bearers of "thassumpc*ion* banner";[39] could the two-bearer
"pageaunt" of the wardens' accounts be the two-bearer banner referred
to in the minutes? Could the bachelors' Assumption "pageant" (about
which we have no details) also have been an elaborate banner (unlikely
as that seems in some of the record contexts in which we find the bachelors' Assumption pageant noted[40])? – or could the bachelors also have
had different kinds of Assumption "pageants"? Even if, therefore, the

1528 and 1533 "Assumptions" were indeed bachelors' pageants, we cannot be sure of just what those "pageants" might have been.

But querying the meaning of the term "pageant" in, for example, the Drapers' 1541 records also logically leads to querying its meaning in the 1535/1540 Drapers' 29 October record reproduced above. Is this "pageant" indeed an elaborately constructed device of the 1523 and 1536 Watch kind, as has been previously assumed,[41] or might it have been simply an especially elaborate banner or other comparatively simple device? Was it, for example, the two-bearer (only) "pageant" used by the Drapers in the 1541 Watch? It must have been something more than an ordinary banner, or no precedent for its use in 1540 would have been needed; but what was it? The 1535/1540 record may not after all involve elaborate Midsummer-Watch-type pageants; and the first year of a known Midsummer-Watch-type pageant used processionally on 29 Oct. would then be 1551 or 1553. *Collections III* lists 29 October pageants, between 1535/1540 and 1553, in all 3 of 1543, 1546, and 1551;[42] but the 1543 record is in more or less the same situation as the 1535/1540 record, since it consists simply of a reference to "the pagent" (and 1543 was also a Tower-oath year[43]); and the 1546 record is, as *Collections III* notes, not necessarily to be related to 29 October, although it could be.[44] In 1551 a "Luzerne" (lynx: from the arms of the Skinners' Company) was specially made, and carried by two youths, with two wildmen and a Moor also being part of the procession;[45] was the lynx a substantial constructed "pageant," a single figure (would this also qualify as a pageant?), or a representation on a special banner? It cannot have been very heavy, at any rate, since it required only two young bearers.[46] It is only when we reach 1553 and following years that the known records definitely indicate substantial pageant structures.[47]

The 1535–52 MS records of all Great Companies with mayors in office between those dates, when re-examined for anything *Collections III* might have missed, add only further uncertainties to the 29 October pageant picture drawn above. Mayors 1535–52 are distributed by company as follows: Mercers – eight (installed 1535, 1536, 1537, 1539, 1541, 1547, 1549, plus one later replacement for 1543's deceased Draper mayor); Drapers – two (1540, 1543); Haberdashers – two (1538, 1552); Skinners – two (1550, 1551); Fishmongers – one (1548); Goldsmiths – one (1545); Grocers – one (1544); Merchant Taylors – one (1546); Salters – one (1542). No Salters', Haberdashers', or Fishmongers' minutes or accounts, or other records volumes likely to include material on 29 October displays, have survived for this period; and the extant accounts of the

Merchant Taylors (there are no extant sixteenth-century Merchant Taylor minutes before the 1560s) do not list pageants among definite 29 October 1546 expenses.[48] The Grocers' wardens' accounts covering 29 October 1544 are also silent about pageants on that occasion, though an unspecified number of pageants are noted as having been carried "to the gray ffryers" sometime during spring 1543 to spring 1544.[49] No Grocers' minutes for this period have survived. The Drapers' manuscripts contain nothing helpful beyond what *Collections III* has already provided.

The records of all three of the Goldsmiths, Mercers, and Skinners have material of potential relevance, but involving interpretative problems. The Goldsmiths' combined wardens' accounts and minutes covering 29 October 1545 confusingly refer to the bachelors (as seen above in chapter 8) as having overseen payment of "all the charg*es* off the pagent*tes* for the barge w*ith* all the other charg*es* therto belonggyng"; these pageants are apparently not land-carried constructions, but continue to raise questions about the meaning at this time of the term "pageant."[50] The Mercers' Acts of Court for 2 October 1549 assign two bachelors to "Leade the mayde",[51] clearly as part of the bachelors' provision of display during the year of the Mercer mayor (1549–50); and their Register of Writings, in describing their mayoral installation ceremonial in 1541 and detailing the procession from the river and St. Paul's to the Guildhall, refers to the bachelors as having "their mayde w*ith* them", with twelve trumpets before her, whom they "shewed" to the mayor and others at the Guildhall and later processed with again.[52] Much later (post-1660) Mercer mayoral displays included a maid, representing the crowned virgin of the company's arms, as the centrepiece of a pageant involving a chariot;[53] but whether there was anything in 1541 other than the representative, doubtless elaborately-dressed maid herself, the records do not show. Was she herself, led by two bachelors (as generally in 1549), a "pageant"? – perhaps even the Tower-year pageant of 1535?[54] No Mercers' general wardens' accounts for this period, only renter wardens' accounts, have survived.

The Skinners' 1551 lynx we have already noted; but we should also now look back to an earlier Skinners' record, in relation to the Skinners' 1534 mayor. The Skinners' Receipts and Payments books, extant for this whole period (except for the year 1543–44), unlike the Skinners' minutes (which have survived only from 1551), refer in the account running from spring 1534 to spring 1535 to two pageants being taken to Leadenhall (where companies customarily worked on their Midsummer Watch pageants[55]); these would therefore seem to be portable constructions; and the reference comes at the end of a list of expenses for the October 1534 installation of the Skinner mayor.[56] The reference need not belong, however, with the October expenses; companies did not necessarily keep their accounts chronologically. The pageant entry could relate either to 29 October 1534 or to June 1535; preparations for the Midsummer Watch, for a company with a mayor in office, always began well in advance, and therefore could have fallen this year, for the Skinners, in part into the account ending 27 May 1535 – though otherwise all the 1535 Midsummer Watch expenses of the Skinners are to be found in their 1535–36 account. The Malone Society editors of *Collections III*, in printing this record, have dated it as belonging to midsummer 1535; for them, of course, no question about the date arose, since they believed 29 October pageants to have begun only in October 1535. The Skinners' 1535–36 account, containing detailed information on 1535 Watch expenses, includes costs of two new and two old pageants, and, at the end of the Watch, carriage of pageants from Leadenhall to Skinners' Hall.[57]

Extant Great Company records, therefore, leave considerable uncertainty as to when 29 October pageants of a Midsummer Watch type began and/or became a continuing tradition in sixteenth-century London. And, in turning to the regular, ongoing records of the city itself – to its Letter Books, Journals, and Repertories – we encounter a record creating even further uncertainties. 29 October pageants were the responsibility not of the city itself but of the companies with mayors being sworn into office; but the city had overall responsibility for the mayor's installation; and in 1481 it issued a decree which raises the possibility of 29 October pageants of the sixteenth century being part of a tradition extending back to at least 1480.[58]

Be it Remembred that the xxiijth day of October the xxjth yere of the Reign of kyng Edward the iiijth. It is Accordet by Iohn Broun Mair and the Aldremen of the Citee of london. that from hensfurthe in the Goyng and Commyng. of the Mair to or from westmynster when he shall take his Othe. there shall no disguysyng nor pageon be vsed or hadde from the Maires house to the water nor from the water to the Maires house. like as it hath been used nowe of late Afore this tyme vppon payn of xx li. to be lost by the ffeolashipp that shall hapne to do the contrary herevnto to thuse of the Chambre &c'[59]

Given the questions previously raised about the term "pageant," we cannot be sure, of course, as to how the word "pageant" is being used here; but the pageants are being linked with disguisings, i.e. with costumed performances, and are part of the land displays involved in regular

29 October processions by both land and water to Westminster and back. These pageants would seem no more nor less likely to be constructions than those of, for example, 1535/1540; a large constructed pageant, after all, was carried in the Midsummer Watch, on St. Peter's eve, at least as early as 1477 by the Drapers.[60] Were they perhaps elaborate, and therefore costly, constructions? (Costs are often a key factor in civic display prohibitions.) When had they begun? – apparently fairly recently ("of late"), but the record is not more specific.

The 1481 Letter Book record thus raises the possibility (though, again, not any certainty) that, if the Drapers did use portable constructed land pageants on 29 October in 1528 and 1533, they may have done so in an interrupted tradition extending back to the later fifteenth century; and in 1540 they may have required a pageant precedent only because the tradition did not include Tower-oath years. Or, if 1528 and 1533 involved only elaborate banners, images, or the like, and the pageants prohibited in 1481 were constructions, possibly the Mercers in 1535 (and then the Drapers in 1540) reintroduced 29 October land pageants (elaborate or limited; and perhaps, for the Mercers, involving a maid?), after their banning in 1481, by providing a pageant first in an unusual, Tower-oath year when indeed the device would not be processed "to the water nor from the water" as part of the proceedings. In such a case, Tower-oath pageants in both 1535 and 1540 might have provided the thin end of the wedge opening the door more generally again, in the mid sixteenth century, to a late fifteenth-century practice. The 1481 record – perhaps but not definitely involving portable constructed pageants – extends our uncertainty about the starting date of 29 October Watch-type land pageants to some seventy-five years between the 1470s and 1553.

We are finally left, then, not with any old or new certainties about the starting dates and causes of Midsummer-Watch-type pageants in London Lord Mayor's Shows, but instead with a variety of alternative possibilities. Although other variations can be posited as well, four basic, alternative scenarios can be outlined: the first two assuming that where, in the sixteenth-century records, we find a reference to a "pageant" on Lord Mayor's Day, a Midsummer Watch type of land pageant is meant, the third assuming this for the fifteenth-century records as well, and the fourth not making any such assumptions.

The first scenario consists of the traditional theory that a Midsummer Watch type of land pageant was first carried in the London Lord Mayor's Show on 29 October 1535 and 1540, and from 1540 became (slowly or rapidly) a fairly regular feature of 29 October display. Given, however, that Henry VIII did not cancel any Midsummer Watch until 1539 (and then for 1539 only), that the 1540 29 October pageant was on the (religious) subject of the Assumption, that the city, as we have seen in chapter 9, seems to have been eager in the late 1530s and early 1540s to continue the Watch, and that the Watch was still going strong in at least 1541 (when the mayor had four pageants and each sheriff had three)[61] and was revived in 1548, in this scenario we must reconsider – as already indicated in chapter 9 – the theory that Lord Mayor's Show pageantry began (although it may eventually have continued) because of the gradual religious suppression or natural decline of the Watch.[62] Also to be reconsidered is the argument that such pageantry began (although, again, it may have continued) as a deliberate expression of increasing civic governmental power. It seems much more likely that a Lord Mayor's Show pageant in 1535 and 1540 emerged simply from a company's or an individual mayor's desire for some additional visual display in Tower-oath years when the mayor's procession on 29 October was perforce less flamboyant, without its river component, than in Westminster oath years. We might note especially that Mercer John Aleyn, sworn in as mayor for the second time in 1535, had had the bad luck to have been sworn in also at the Tower for his first mayoralty, in 1525. Faced with no river procession for the second time around, a perhaps frustrated Aleyn may have wanted some addition to the usual Tower-oath processional display. And then, although Tower oaths had previously not happened often (there were none, for example, between 1525 and 1535), by 1540 there had been three within six years (in 1535, 1536, and 1540[63]): certainly providing an incentive to the Drapers in 1540 to continue a provision of pageant display in a Tower-oath procession.[64] In 1540, furthermore, the Drapers were having their first mayor installed since 1533 – and only their second mayor in thirteen years, after they had had four mayors during the ten years of the 1520s. The opportunity for company display may have been important to them. By the time of yet another Tower oath in 1543 (with a Draper mayor again) – when we find another single-pageant record – the Lord Mayor's Show precedent may have become set for 29 October more generally, or have become so as the Midsummer Watch then indeed did disappear, at least in its traditional civic festive form, in the mid-1540s. (The 1535, 1540, and 1543 pageants may or may not have been ones also used in the Midsummer Watch.)

Scenario 2 assumes (with Patricia Lusher) that the 1520s Assumption pageant of the Draper bachelors is indeed the Assumption referred to in the 1528 and 1533 Drapers' Lord Mayor's Day records, and that a pageant on 29 October therefore either began with the Drapers in 1528 (perhaps because of the cancellation that year of the Midsummer Watch) – thus ironically making it the Drapers, and not the supposedly lavishly-spending Mercers, who began this particular 29 October expense – or began with the Mercers in 1526, or, less likely, with the Vintners in 1527. (For neither 1526 nor 1527 do we have any records evidence.) There are, as already noted, no references to a pageant in Draper mayoral installation records for 1520, 1521, or 1524; and 1525 was the year of Mercer John Aleyn's first Tower oath. Use of a pageant in 1535 would still, within this scenario, have been unusual, because involving a Tower oath: hence the Drapers' citing of the 1535 precedent in another Tower-oath year, 1540. Even more in this scenario than in the first one, initial uses of a land pageant on 29 October would not have grown out of the demise of the traditional Midsummer Watch, though they could have resulted from growing civic governmental power.

Scenario 3 starts with the 1481 prohibition of disguisings and pageants "used nowe of late" on 29 October, going *to* the water and *from* the water when the mayor takes his oath at Westminster, and posits the second half of the fifteenth century as the time when Lord Mayor's Show constructed land pageants began. We do not know how long the 1481 prohibition was in effect, or what caused it; all we know is that by the mid sixteenth century, at least, the pageants had resumed. From the non-existence of evidence for the intervening period of time, nothing can with safety be inferred, given the many variations in different companies' record-keeping and also the many company manuscripts which have not survived. To reverse the usual argument: might the elaborate Midsummer Watch pageantry of the early sixteenth century have developed in part as a result of the demise of mayoral inauguration pageantry in 1481?

Scenario 4 points out that the first definite evidence we have of a substantial, constructed pageant being used on land on 29 October is in 1553 (by the Merchant Taylors), and that although the Midsummer Watch type of pageants may indeed have been used before that date in mayoral oath-taking processions, given the range of meanings of the word "pageant" in the early sixteenth century (and earlier) we cannot pinpoint any earlier date with certainty. A beginning of the Midsummer Watch type of pageantry on 29 October in the 1550s would, of course, fit nicely with the demise in the 1540s of the traditional civic form of the Watch: especially given that the Catholic Queen Mary came to the throne in July 1553. The 29 October 1553 Merchant Taylors' pageant was of St. John Baptist (the company's patron saint); and by 1553, with no traditional civic Midsummer Watch in existence, the only formal London civic venue for this type of pageantry – a type perhaps back in special favour with the new regime – was the Lord Mayor's 29 October oath-taking. Earlier "pageants" on 29 October (in 1535, 1540, 1543, 1551) would by this scenario have been devices such as elaborate banners or single figures (the Mercers' maid in 1535, an especially elaborate Drapers' Assumption banner, or equivalent, in 1540, a Skinners' figure of a lynx in 1551: all devices referring to their companies' coats of arms), but perhaps gradually increasing in scope (there were also wildmen and a Moor in 1551) and leading to substantial Midsummer-Watch-type pageants on 29 October in 1553 and following years. The 29 October 1541 display by the Mercers' Company, *if* fully described in the company's Register of Writings, might then be a typical example of transitional 1540s (and 1535? and 1470s–1480?) Lord Mayor's Shows.[65]

For a final generalized overview, some mixing of these four scenarios may tentatively be attempted: some kind of 29 October special visual land displays – "pageants" – having come into existence before 1481, prohibited in 1481, reintroduced – as elaborate constructions or as simple devices – in the 1520s or 1530s for reasons of company and/or individual mayoral interest in or rivalry over visual display, and certainly having become elaborate constructions by at least 1553, this last because of a combination of factors including perhaps evolving custom and political/religious necessity and/or opportunism (including the mid-1540s demise of the civic Midsummer Watch in its traditional form). Greater specificity does not seem possible from the records known to date: and the Lord Mayor's Show thus becomes a demonstration of the mix of fact and speculation involved – despite, or even perhaps because of, the use of manuscript records – in all aspects of any attempt to construct a history of pre-Elizabethan London civic theatre.

Indeed, the more we know, the more we realize the complexities of the civic theatrical past in London, and how much we do not know about it. Paradoxically we move forward in understanding by moving backward: discarding previous certainties for new uncertainties, and postulating more than one speculative new pattern in relation to a wide variety of civic theatrical activities.

Appendix A Royal and other entries 1400–1558

This list (a work in progress) includes all major royal entries into London, 1400–1558, and a few selected other entries (ones of special interest in relation to entry pageantry, providing examples of different levels of ceremonial activity and display), in terms of specific date, entry type, general route, pageants or not, conduits running with wine or not, and the placement of the mayor: according to information found. Pageants are noted only in terms of whether they occurred at London Bridge and/or elsewhere in the city and/or on the Thames; and it is not noted whether the mayor was accompanied by the aldermen and/or other civic officials, although normally in any formal meeting of an entrant outside the city (as well as on some other types of occasions) the mayor was indeed so accompanied. Only the most informative sources for each entry, including those providing the kinds of factual details recorded here, are cited; this is not intended to be a complete list of sources for each entry. Dating is a special problem, given the frequent date disagreements among sources such as chronicles; date disagreements are noted (without all sources being cited).

For general entry procedures see, for queen consorts (from at least the late fifteenth century), "A Ryalle Book" (printed from manuscript in Francis Grose's *The Antiquarian Repertory*, 1 [London: Edward Jeffery, 1807]; see pp. 302–303; for the late fifteenth-century date see pp. 296–297, n.) and, for monarchs, the fourth recension of the *Liber Regalis* (extant from the time of Richard II but probably first used for the coronation of Edward II) and the fifteenth-century "Forma et Modus" and "Little Device." The last three, and their dates, are available in Leopold G. Wickham Legg, *English Coronation Records* (Westminster: Archibald Constable, 1901); see, for entry matters only, pp. 82–83, 172, and 219–225. Some of the details of the specific entries listed below are discussed above in chapters 7 and 8.

A line across columns 3 and 6 indicates a break between one day and the next. A civic coronation entry usually took place over two separate days: the first day involving a procession to the Tower, and the second day (not necessarily consecutive to the first) beginning at the Tower, where the king or queen had spent at least one night, and involving a procession through the city to Westminster. The mayor normally participated in the procession on both days, so this may be assumed where there is no information to the contrary.

Blank spaces indicate merely absence of information, not necessarily (or, often, even likely) absence of activity.

ENTRY	TYPE	ROUTE	PGTS	WINE	MAYOR
1400[1] (21 Dec.) (Tues.)	Welcome of Emperor Manuel II	Blackheath "London"			
1403[2] (?23–24 Feb.) (?Fri.–Sat.)	Coronation of Queen Joan	Blackheath ———— City/Cheapside Westminster			Blackheath ———— With queen through City to Westminster
1413[3] (7–8 Apr.) (Fri.–Sat.)	Coronation of Henry V	Bridge Tower ———— City/Cheapside Westminster	Bridge		With king to Tower ————
1415[4] (23 Nov.) (Sat.)	Welcome of of Henry V	Blackheath Bridge City/Cheapside Paul's Westminster	Bridge City	yes	Blackheath to Westminster

1. The city's involvement in Manuel's welcome is unclear; the king met him at Blackheath and brought him to London. See p. 213 of Donald M. Nicol's "A Byzantine Emperor in England," *University of Birmingham Historical Journal* 12.1 (1969), 204–225.

2. Chronicles disagree on the year; but the Grocers' records (GL MS 11570, p. 91) confirm the year as 1403 (John Walcote, e.g., was mayor) and also establish the two-day route. Joan was married to Henry IV at Winchester on 7 Feb. 1403 (Holinshed, III.21; Stow, *Annales*, p. 522) and was crowned on 26 Feb. according to Stow – though 26 Feb. 1403 was a Monday and coronations were usually on a Sunday (or a holy day: see *Liber Regalis*, p. 113). Stow may be wrong. City entry was likely on Fri. and Sat., 23–24 Feb.; the fifteenth-century norm (see other entries below) was a procession across the Bridge to the Tower on one day (usually Fri.), and through the city to Westminster on the next day (usually Sat.), with the coronation normally on the following day, Sun. See also Flenley, pp. 99–100 (Longleat MS), and John Silvester Davies, ed., *An English Chronicle of the Reigns of Richard II., Henry IV, Henry V, and Henry VI.* (Camden Society, os 64, 1856), p. 29.

3. BH Weekly Payments, Series 1, vol. 2, p. 26; *Vita & Gesta*, pp. 17–20; *A Chronicle*, p. 95; Holinshed, III.61. Coronation on Sun. 9 Apr.

4. *Gesta*, pp. 100–113 (and see also pp. xxxvii and 191–192); *A Chronicle*, pp. 103 and 230–232; *Vita & Gesta*, pp. 71–73; Usk, pp. 258–263; *Brut*, pp. 380 and 558. City's gift presented Sun. 24 Nov. at Westminster (Usk, pp. 260–261, places it in Cheapside). Wylie, *Reign*, II. 257–268, creates an account by putting together various historical sources, and provides useful footnotes; see also *EP*, I.132–137. Kipling, *King*, p. 205, n. 54, lists sources.

ENTRY	TYPE	ROUTE	PGTS	WINE	MAYOR
1416[5] (7 May) (Th.)	Welcome of Emperor Sigismund	Blackheath City Paul's Westminster			Blackheath to Westminster
1421[6] (21–22 Feb.) (Fri.–Sat.)	Coronation of Queen Catherine of Valois	Blackheath Tower ——— City Westminster	Bridge City	yes	Blackheath Tower ——— through City to Westminster
1426[7] (10 Jan.) (Th.)	Welcome of Duke and Duchess of Bedford	Merton Southwark Bridge City Westminster	Bridge		Merton to Westminster
1429[8] ([?4–]5 Nov.) ([?Fri.–]Sat.)	Coronation of Henry VI	Kingston Tower [Dinner] ?——— City/Cheapside Westminster	Bridge City	yes	met king coming from Kingston Tower ?——— through City to Westminster

5. *Gesta*, pp. 130–131 (dating it before 4 May); Kingsford, *Chronicles*, p. 124; *A Chronicle*, pp. 103–104; *Brut*, pp. 380–381. The king accompanied the Emperor. A version of the *Brut* printed in Kingsford, *EHL*, says (p. 299) the mayor and commonalty brought the Emperor to St. Thomas Watering where the king met him.

6. BH Weekly Payments, Series I, vol. 2, pp. 457–468, 478, 480, 488, 496; Grocers' GL MS 11570, p. 138; *Brut*, p. 426; *Vita & Gesta*, pp. 297–299; *Great Chronicle*, p. 115; Fabyan, p. 586; Wylie, *Reign*, III.268. The king came to London a week before the queen; Wylie, *Reign*, III. 267, n. 8, suggests perhaps as early as by 8 Feb. but the specification of a week in GL MS 11570 would seem to deny this. (*Great Chronicle* has 14 Feb.) Wylie, *Reign*, III.268, suggests elaborate pageants, as in 1415. City's gift presented at Tower (Jor. 1, f. 88r). Coronation on Sun. 23 Feb. (Thomas Rymer, *Foedera, Conventiones, Literae*, vol. 10 [London: A. and J. Churchill, 1710], p. 63; *A Chronicle*, p. 108; and see Wylie, *Reign*, III.268, n. 7). (Mon. 24 Feb., St. Matthew's Day – Grafton, I.543, Holinshed, III.125; Stow, *Annales*, p. 581 has 14 Feb., as does the Latin *Brut* version in Kingsford's *EHL*, p. 337.) *DTR* no. 923 dates as 14, 24 Feb.; *Great Chronicle* incorrectly calls 24 Feb. both Sun. and St. Matthew's Day. For Sun. 2 March, see Kingsford, *EHL*, p. 295. See above, chapter 7, n. 43.

7. BH Weekly Payments, Series I, vol. 3, f. 170r–v; Gregory, p. 160; Fabyan, p. 596. Misdated 1427 in *DTR* no. 929 (from Charles Welch, *History of The Tower Bridge* [London: Smith, Elder, 1894], pp. 120–121). City's gift presented 11 Jan.

8. BH Weekly Payments, Series I, vol. 3, f. 278r; *Brut*, pp. 450–451. *Brut* reads as though Henry's entry perhaps took place in one day, 5 Nov., with a dinner break at the Tower; but the text is

ENTRY	TYPE	ROUTE	PGTS	WINE	MAYOR
1432[9] (21 Feb.) (Th.)	Welcome of Henry VI	Blackheath Bridge City/ Cheapside Paul's Westminster	Bridge City	yes	Blackheath With king to Westminster
1445[10] (28–29 May) (Fri.–Sat.)	Coronation of Queen Margaret	Blackheath Tower ——— City/ Cheapside Paul's Westminster	Bridge City	yes	Blackheath ——— With queen to Westminster
1461[11] (26–27 June) (Fri.–Sat.)	Coronation of Edward IV	Sheen/ Lambeth Tower ——— City/ Cheapside Westminster			Lambeth Tower ———

somewhat confused and this is probably a conflation of a normal two-day entry, 4–5 Nov. Coronation on Sun. 6 Nov. (Bertram Wolffe, *Henry VI* [London: Eyre, Methuen, 1981], p. 48, is certainly wrong in assuming a Tower-to-Westminster entry and a coronation – and a coronation banquet – all on 6 Nov.)

9. LB κ, ff. 103v–104v (printed in *MG*, III, Appendix 3, pp. 457–464); Kingsford, *Chronicles*, pp. 97 116 (Lydgate's descriptive poem), nn. on pp. 301–303; *Brut*, pp. 461–464; *A Chronicle*, p. 119 (and Lydgate's poem, pp. 234–250); *Great Chronicle*, pp. 156–170 (Lydgate's poem); Fabyan, pp. 603–607; Gregory, pp. 173–175 (14 Feb. date); see also *EP*, I.142–147. City's gift at Westminster 23 Feb. (Fabyan, p. 607, says Sat. 23 Feb.; Lydgate's poem says Sat., as does *Brut*, p. 464; Stow, *Annales*, p. 602, dates gift 24 Feb.). Kipling, *King*, p. 143, n. 59, lists sources; see also *DTR* no. 933.

10. Gregory, p. 186; Flenley, p. 103 (from Bodleian Library MS Rawlinson B.355); Bale, pp. 119–120; *Brut*, p. 489 (misdates Fri. as 26 May); *Short English Chronicle*, in James Gairdner, ed., *Three Fifteenth-Century Chronicles* (Camden Society, NS 28, 1880), p. 64 (misdates Fri. as 29 May; incorrect marginal 1444). For the general reliability of the *Brut* see Keith Dockray, *Henry VI, Margaret of Anjou and the Wars of the Roses: A Source Book* (Phoenix Mill, Gloucestershire: Sutton, 2000), pp. xiv–xv (and pp. 13–14 for a reprinting of the *Brut* account of this entry). Fabyan, p. 617, misdates 28th as 18th, as does Holinshed, III.207–208 (following Fabyan). (*Great Chronicle*, pp. 177–178, is somewhat confused.) For text of pageants, see: Carleton Brown, "Lydgate's Verses on Queen Margaret's Entry into London," *Modern Language Review* 7 (1912), 225–234; Robert Withington, "Queen Margaret's Entry into London, 1445," *Modern Philology* 13.1 (1915–16), 53–57; Gordon Kipling, "The London Pageants for Margaret of Anjou: A Medieval Script Restored," *Medieval English Theatre* 4.1 (1982), 5–27. Text misascribed in Stow's *Annales*, p. 624, to Lydgate. Coronation on Sun. 30 May.

11. Jor. 6, f. 43r/photo 496 (deteriorated MS available at CLRO only in photographic form); *Brief Latin Chronicle*, p. 174; Fabyan, p. 640 (misdates Fri. as 27 June); Kingsford, *Chronicles*,

ENTRY	TYPE	ROUTE	PGTS	WINE	MAYOR
1465[12] (24–25 May) (Fri.–Sat.)	Coronation of Queen Elizabeth	Bridge Tower ———— City/Cheapside Westminster	Bridge		met queen; with her through Southwark and Gracechurch to Tower ————
1483[13] (4–5 July) (Fri.–Sat.)	Coronation of Richard III	To Tower (by water) ———— City Westminster			———— to process from Tower[14]

pp. 175–176 (misdates 26 as 16 June); *Chronicles of the White Rose of York* (London: James Bohn, 1845), p. 10 (Th. 26 and Fri. 27 June). BH Annual Accounts 3, ff. 16v and 19r, confirm the king's entry from Lambeth on the Fri. (and see also Stow, *Annales*, p. 681). Coronation on Sun. 28 June (Gregory, p. 218; Stow, *Annales*, p. 681).

12. BH Annual Accounts 3, ff. 94v–95r (printed in *EES*, I.324–331); William of Worcester, p. 784; Fabyan, p. 655. Misdated 1464 in *DTR* no. 942 (following *EES*). Coronation on Sun. before Whitsunday, 26 May (LB L, f. 37v; Fabyan, p. 655 [wrongly calling it Whitsunday]; *Brief Latin Chronicle*, p. 180; Stow, *Annales*, p. 687; Grafton, II.7 [has 16 May]). Fabyan places the king's creation of Knights of the Bath at the Tower the night before the coronation; but the city entry and the coronation would not have been on the same day. William of Worcester, pp. 783–784, places this creation at the Tower, by the king, on Thurs. 23 May, as does Stow, *Annales*, p. 687.

13. Grafton, II.113–115; Hall, p. 375, Holinshed, III.397–398, and Stow, *Annales*, pp. 761–762 (all with some confusion in dates); George Buck, *The History of the Life and Reigne of Richard The Third*, intro. A. R. Myers (Totowa, NJ: Rowman and Littlefield, 1973), pp. 24–25; Dominicus Mancinus, *The Usurpation of Richard the Third*, ed. and tr. C. A. J. Armstrong, 2nd edn. (Oxford: Clarendon Press, 1969), pp. 99 and 101 (and n. 104 on pp. 132–133). Anne F. Sutton and P. W. Hammond, *The Coronation of Richard III: the Extant Documents* (Gloucester/New York: Alan Sutton/St. Martin's Press, 1983/84), provide a partly conjectural chronology of the events leading up to the coronation, dealing with 4–5 July on pp. 27–34, and print the procedural document (the "Little Device") drawn up for the entry (pp. 213–215) and coronation. Buck states, p. 24, that 4,000 gentlemen from the north (in addition to the southern nobility) rode with the king from the Tower to Westminster; Richard had met with them outside the city on 3 July and ridden in with them to St. Paul's (see the Mercers' MS Acts of Court 1 [Lyell-Watney, pp. 155–156]). Coronation on Sun. 6 July (see Sutton and Hammond, *Coronation of Richard III*, p. 215).

14. I set this down here only because it is a requirement of the "Little Device" specifically prepared for Richard's coronation. See Sutton and Hammond, *Coronation of Richard III*, p. 214. I have found no record or reference, to date, as to whether the mayor participated in the king's journey *to* the Tower. Sutton and Hammond speculate, p. 28, that there may have been a civic water escort.

ENTRY	TYPE	ROUTE	PGTS	WINE	MAYOR
1485[15] (3 Sept.) (Sat.)	Accession of Henry VII	Shoreditch City Paul's Bishop's palace[16]			Shoreditch (and to Bishop's palace?)
1485[17] (27 & 29 Oct.) (Th. & Sat.)	Coronation of Henry VII	Lambeth Bridge Tower ——— City Westminster			Bridge ——— With king through City
1486[18] (5 June) (Mon.)	Welcome of Henry VII	Sheen Westminster (by water)	Thames (wildfire)		Putney Westminster (by water)
1487[19] (3 Nov.) (Sat.)	Welcome of Henry VII	Hornsey Park Bishopsgate Paul's	?Paul's		Met king

15. See Sydney Anglo, "The Foundation of the Tudor Dynasty: The Coronation and Marriage of Henry VII," *Guildhall Miscellany* 2.1 (1960), 4, and also pp. 9–10 of his *Spectacle*. Fabyan, p. 675, says the mayor met the king (at Hornsey Park) 28 Aug., and Stow, *Annales*, p. 784 (at Shoreditch) has 27 Aug. (as do *Great Chronicle*, p. 238, and Kingsford, *Chronicles*, p. 193), but the Mercers' MS Acts of Court 1 show (Lyell-Watney, pp. 290–291) that the king still had not reached there by 31 Aug. DeLloyd J. Guth suggests that Henry entered through Aldersgate; see his "Richard III, Henry VII and the City . . . ," in Ralph A. Griffiths and James Sherborne, eds., *Kings and Nobles in the Later Middle Ages: A Tribute to Charles Ross* (Gloucester/New York: Alan Sutton/St. Martin's Press, 1986), p. 196. The blind Bernardus Andreas, Henry VII's poet laureate, wrote celebratory verses (for which, see *Bernardo Andrea*, pp. 35–36).

16. Bishop of London's palace, by St. Paul's.

17. See Anglo, "Foundation," pp. 5–8 (and *Spectacle*, pp. 13–15), Stow, *Annales*, p. 785, Legg, pp. 221–223 ("Little Device"). Coronation on Sun. 30 Oct.

18. Merchant Taylors' GL MS 34008/1, f. 5r; Leathersellers' MS Liber Curtes 1, p. 56 (wildfire used); *Collectanea*, IV.202–203. See above, chapter 8, pp. 143–145.

19. Stow, *Annales*, p. 788; *Collectanea*, IV.217–218; Anglo, *Spectacle*, p. 49. McGee-Meagher, pp. 36–37, and *DTR* no. 949.5 both record this as a theatrical occasion because an angel descended from Paul's roof to cense the king; but this may in fact have been a religious ceremony. *Liber Albus* (early fifteenth century) notes, p. 26, that as a regular part of a customary religious procession (involving the mayor, sheriffs, and aldermen) at Pentecost, those processing entered St. Paul's and "came to a stand in the nave, while the hymn *Veni Creator* was chaunted by the Vicars to the music of the organ in alternate verses, an angel meanwhile censing from above." Riley (ed., *Liber Albus*) suggests that this angel was a costumed church official, and states that the practice was not uncommon "on great occasions and public ceremonials" (p. 26, n. 3).

ENTRY	TYPE	ROUTE	PGTS	WINE	MAYOR
1487[20] (23–24 Nov.) (Fri.–Sat.)	Coronation of Queen Elizabeth	Greenwich Tower (by water)	Thames ?City		Greenwich Tower (by water)
		City/Cheapside Westminster			With queen
1496[21] (31 Oct.) (Mon.)	Welcome of Pope's emissary	Bridge City Paul's			Bridge
1498[22] (30 Oct.) (Tues.)	Welcome of Prince Arthur	Cornhill City/Cheapside Westminster			Cheapside
1501[23] (12 Nov.) (Fri.)	Welcome of Katherine of Aragon (to marriage)	Lambeth Bridge City/Cheapside Paul's Bishop's palace	Bridge City	yes	Bridge? Cheapside
1509[24] (21 & 23 June) (Th. & Sat.)	Coronation of Henry VIII	Greenwich Tower (by land) City/Cheapside Westminster			With king to Westminster

20. *Collectanea*, IV.218–222; Stow, *Annales*, p. 788 wrongly indicates that the water journey to the Tower was on Sun. 11 Nov. The city's land display may have consisted entirely or largely of costumed singing children. Coronation on Sun. 25 Nov.
21. Kingsford, *Chronicles*, p. 211.
22. Kingsford, *Chronicles*, p. 224. City's gift presented Weds. at Bishop of Salisbury's palace in Fleet St.
23. Rep 1, ff. 61v, 62r, 87r; *L&PH7*, 1.409–411 (king's Council's plans; from BL Cotton MS Vespasian c.xiv, f. 81); Kipling, *Receyt*, esp. pp. 10–36 (authoritative text) and 50; Jor. 10, f. 238r; Kingsford, *Chronicles*, pp. 234–248 (text) and 250, nn. on pp. 332–335; *Great Chronicle*, pp. 297–310 (partial text); Grafton, II.222; Stow, *Annales*, pp. 805–807; *Grey Friars*, p. 27; Hall, p. 493. (Initial plans in *The traduction & mariage of the princesse* [*RSTC* 4814; 1500].) Marriage on Sun. 14 Nov. (Subsequent to a 16 Nov. river procession to Westminster, the mayor also escorted the king, queen, prince, and princess, with music, by water [Fri. 26 Nov.] from Westminster Bridge to Mortlake [see esp. Kipling, *Receyt*, pp. 69–70]). See also *EP*, 1.166–168, Sydney Anglo, "The London Pageants for the Reception of Katharine of Aragon: November 1501," *Journal of the Warburg and Courtauld Institutes* 26 (1963), 53–89, and Anglo, *Spectacle*, pp. 57–97. Kipling, *King*, p. 209, n. 58, discusses sources; *DTR* no. 963 and McGee-Meagher, pp. 44–48, provide listings. (*DTR*'s no. 962, dated 1499, actually concerns the 1501 entry.) Kipling in *Receyt* explains the highly complex relationships of the various extant accounts of the entry. For interpretation problems concerning the mayor's part, see above, chapter 7, p. 133.
24. Hall, pp. 507–509; Stow, *Annales*, p. 813 (wrongly calling Sat. 24 June); *Great Chronicle*, pp. 339–340; BH Annual Accounts 4, f. 304v; BL Cotton MS Tiberius E.viii, f. 101r–v.

ENTRY	TYPE	ROUTE	PGTS	WINE	MAYOR
1518^{25} (29 July) (Th.)	Welcome of Cardinal Campeius	Blackheath Southwark City/Cheapside Paul's Bishop of Bath's at Temple Bar			Cheapside
1522^{26} (6 June) (Fri.)	Welcome of Emperor Charles V	Deptford Southwark Bridge City/Cheapside Paul's Blackfriars	Bridge City		Deptford Southwark through City
1533^{27} (29 & 31 May) (Th. & Sat.)	Coronation of Queen Anne Boleyn	Greenwich Tower (by water) ———— City/Cheapside Paul's Westminster	Thames City	yes	Greenwich Tower (by water) ———— With queen

(Holinshed, III.547–549, has 11 instead of 21 June, and calls Fri. and Sat. 22 and 24 June); Coronation on Sun. 24 June. For the mayor's part, see above, chapter 7, pp. 133–134.

25. Wriothesley, I.12; Holinshed, III.627. Speech by Thomas More.

26. Grafton, II.322–323; Hall, pp. 638–640 (text); *CSPV,* III.236, no. 466; *Grey Friars,* p. 30; *EP,* I.174–178, Sydney Anglo, "The Imperial Alliance and the Entry of the Emperor Charles V into London: June 1522," *Guildhall Miscellany* 2.4 (Oct. 1962), 131–155; Anglo, *Spectacle,* pp. 186–202. (Wriothesley, I.13, says Thurs. [5 June].) Numerous sources are listed by McGee-Meagher, pp. 79–80, and by *DTR* no. 998. See also C. R. Baskervill, "William Lily's Verse for the Entry of Charles V into London," *Huntington Library Bulletin* 9 (1936), 1–14, Jean Robertson, "L'Entrée de Charles Quint à Londres en 1522," in Jean Jacquot, ed., *Fêtes et Cérémonies au Temps de Charles Quint* (Paris: Centre National de la Recherche Scientifique, 1960), pp. 169–181, and *Of the tryumphe/and the verses that Charles themperour/& the most myghty redouted kyng of England/were saluted with/passyng through London* (*RSTC* 15606.7; [1522]) (text).

27. Grafton, II.448; Hall, pp. 798–805; Stow, *Annales,* pp. 948–954; Wriothesley, I.19; Grose, II.232–239; Arber, *Garner,* II.41–60 (text: from *The noble tryumphaunt coronacyon of quene Anne* [*RSTC* 656;1533]); Frederick J. Furnivall, ed., *Ballads from Manuscripts,* I.1 (Ballad Society, 1868), pp. 364–401 (text included, from BL Royal MS 18 A.lxiv); *EP,* I.180–184; Anglo, *Spectacle,* pp. 247–261; *DTR* no. 1017; McGee-Meagher, pp. 88–90. Anglo, *Spectacle,* dates the river procession 19 May, as do Grafton and Hall (followed by Holinshed); but *Grey Friars, RSTC* 656, and some other contemporary sources say 29 May (see, e.g., *EP,* I.181, n. 3 – the Thurs. before Pentecost, i.e., 29 May in 1533), which would be expected from entry date norms; also Hall describes the river procession and city entry as on the Thurs. and the Sat. of what he clearly means to be the same week (and 19 May 1533 was Mon., not Thurs.). Even Grafton describes Whitsun eve (31 May in 1533) as the day after (clearly an error for two days after) the river procession. City's gift presented in Cheapside. Coronation on Sun. 1 June.

ENTRY	TYPE	ROUTE	PGTS	WINE	MAYOR
1536[28] (22 Dec.) (Fri.)	Passage of Henry VIII and queen through city	Westminster City/Cheapside Bridge			Knighted at Westminster; rode with king
1540[29] (3 Jan.) (Sat.)	Welcome of Anne of Cleves	Blackheath Greenwich	?Thames		Blackheath Greenwich
1540[30] (4 Feb.) (Weds.)	Welcome of Queen Anne of Cleves	Greenwich Westminster (by water)	?Thames		Greenwich Westminster (by water)
1546[31] (21 Aug.) (Sat.)	Welcome of Great Admiral of France	Tower Wharf (by water) City/Cheapside Bishop's palace	?City (music)		On river and in Cheapside
1547[32] (19 Feb.) (Sat.)	Coronation of Edward VI	[from Tower] City/Cheapside Paul's Westminster	City	yes	Rode with king
1549[33] (17 Oct.) (Th.)	Passage of Edward VI through City	Bridge City/Cheapside Paul's Temple Bar	(music)		

28. Wriothesley, I.59–60. Jane Seymour was queen. See also Muriel St. Clare Byrne, ed., *The Lisle Letters*, vol. 3 (Chicago and London: University of Chicago Press, 1981), pp. 576–579.

29. *Grey Friars*, p. 43; Wriothesley, I.111; Hall, pp. 833–836; Grafton, II.468–471. The mayor and aldermen met and accompanied Anne on land, Blackheath to Greenwich, but company barges etc. were also sent to Greenwich for a civic water display. See chapter 8, pp. 149–150.

30. Rep. 10, f. 161r; Wriothesley, I.112; Hall, p. 837; Grafton, II.472. Probably only a civic water escort provided, given the 3 Jan. water display at Greenwich.

31. Rep. 11, f. 276r (to land at Billingsgate) (and LB Q, f. 181r); Wriothesley, I.172 (21 Aug.; Tower Wharf); Grafton, II.497 (20 Aug.; Tower Wharf); Holinshed, III.859 (date not specified; Tower Wharf); Fabyan, p. 708 (21 Aug.; Tower). For 21 Aug., see also LB Q, f.183r. Plasterers were set to work, in advance, on stations in the city from the Gracechurch St. conduit on to Paul's. City's gift presented same afternoon (Wriothesley) or same night (Rep. 11).

32. *Collectanea*, IV.310–322 (9 Feb.)(text); John Gough Nichols, ed., *Literary Remains of King Edward the Sixth*, 2 vols. (Roxburghe Club, 1857; rpt. New York: Burt Franklin[, 1963]), I.cclxxviii–ccxci (19 Feb.; better version of *Collectanea* material); *Grey Friars*, p. 53 (20 Feb.); Wriothesley, I.182; Fabyan, p. 709; Holinshed, III.866 (24 Feb.); Rep. 11, ff. 309v–310r; LB Q, f. 195v. Also *EP*, I.185–187, and Anglo, *Spectacle*, pp. 283–294. McGee-Meagher, pp. 97–98, lists sources. Edward had been at the Tower since his accession. City's gift presented in Cheapside. Coronation on Sun. 20 Feb.

33. Rep. 12(1), ff. 154r, 156r–v; Wriothesley, II.28–29; Holinshed, III.1021; see also Nichols, *Literary Remains*, II.244, n. 2, for date and some sources.

ENTRY	TYPE	ROUTE	PGTS	WINE	MAYOR
1553[34] (3 Aug.) (Th.)	Accession of Mary	Aldgate Leadenhall Tower	(music)		outside Aldgate; then with queen
1553[35] (27 & 30 Sept.) (Weds. & Sat.)	Coronation of Mary	To Tower (by water) ——— City/Cheapside Paul's Westminster	City	yes	To Tower (by water) ——— Rode with queen
1554[36] (18 Aug.) (Sat.)	Welcome of Philip of Spain	Southwark Place Bridge City/Cheapside Paul's Westminster	Bridge City		Rode in procession
1558[37] (28 Nov.) (Mon.)	Accession of Elizabeth I	Charterhouse Cripplegate Bishopsgate Leadenhall Tower	(music)		Charter- house; then with queen

34. Rep. 13(1), f. 70v; Wriothesley, II.93–95; *Grey Friars*, pp. 81–82; Machyn, pp. 38–39.
35. Rep. 13(1), f. 79v; *Chronicle of Queen Jane*, pp. 27–30; Holinshed, IV.6–7; Stow, *Annales*, pp. 1043–1044; Machyn, pp. 43–45; *Two London Chronicles*, pp. 29–30; *EP*, I.188–189; Anglo, *Spectacle*, pp. 319–322. McGee-Meagher, pp. 104–105, *DTR* no. 1083, and Kipling, *King*, p. 345, n. 115, list sources. Coronation on Sun. 1 Oct. See also C. V. Malfatti, ed. and tr., *The Accession Coronation and Marriage of Mary Tudor* (Barcelona: C. V. Malfatti, 1956), pp. 151–153. BL Royal MS Appendix 89 (formerly BL Cotton MS Appendix XXVIII) dates Mary's water journey to the Tower on Thurs. 28 Sept. (f. 93r), a date followed by others such as Anglo (*Spectacle*, p. 319).
36. John Elder, *Copie of a Letter sent into Scotlande* (1555; rpt. Amsterdam and New York: Da Capo Press, 1971), B4r–C5r (text); *La Solenne et Felice Intrata delli Serenissimi Re Philippo . . .* (1554) (text); *Chronicle of Queen Jane*, pp. 78–81 (+rpt. of Elder's letter); *Grey Friars*, p. 91 (19 Aug.); Holinshed, IV.62–63 (Sat. 19 Aug.), John Foxe, *The Acts and Monuments of John Foxe*, vol. 6, ed. George Townsend (London: Seeley, Burnside, and Seeley, 1846), pp. 557–559; *Two London Chronicles*, pp. 37–38. Elder's 18 Aug. date is also given by Wriothesley, II.122, Fabyan, p. 716, and (indirectly) *Chronicle of Queen Jane*, p. 78. See also *EP*, I.189–194, and Anglo, *Spectacle*, pp. 327–339. McGee-Meagher, pp. 106–107, *DTR* no. 1089, and Kipling, *King*, p. 347, n. 120, list sources. The attitude of the English to Philip is noted in Malfatti, *Accession Coronation and Marriage*, pp. 92–93. Philip came to Southwark Place from Richmond by water on 17 Aug.
37. Holinshed, IV.156; John Hayward, *Annals of the First Four Years of the Reign of Queen Elizabeth*, ed. John Bruce (Camden Society, os 7, 1840), p. 10 (19 Nov.; see nn. on pp. 9–10); Machyn, p. 180.

Appendix B   *Selected civic records*

Several of the records included in this Appendix have not previously been published; and all are significant to our understanding of early civic theatre in London. The original MS lineation (including spaces between lines) has largely not been preserved; and entries have been spaced for ease and clarity in reading. Marginal signs and the like, not affecting content, have not been reproduced. For transcription practices in general, see above, p. xix. The Latin expansions have been provided by Dr. Abigail Young, Records of Early English Drama project; but, as not in REED editions, marginal notes are not here reproduced, punctuation is given to pounds, shillings and pence abbreviations only when such punctuation appears in the manuscripts, the abbreviation for "demi" is expanded ("de*mj*") and the abbreviation "&c" is given an abbreviation sign ("&c'").[1] Records transcriptions from Corporation of London Record Office manuscripts (Bridge House Weekly Payments, Series 1, vols. 2 and 3, Letter Books H, N and O, and Journal 5) appear by kind permission of the Corporation of London; those from livery company manuscripts appear by kind permission of the Brewers' Company (4), Drapers' Company (8), and Mercers' Company (9C and 11).

1. *The London Midsummer Watch*: 1378: the earliest known record, to date, of a London midsummer watch involving non-practical, decorative display. Letter Book H, f. 79v (from a bill sent to each alderman).[2]

... Et outre ce vo*us* mandons qe vous ensemblement oue les bones gentz de vo*st*re garde soiez bien & suffisantement armes vestuz de rouge & blanc pa*r*ty

1. Dr. Young has also checked and corrected the Latin entries in general; and Professor Brian Merrilees (University of Toronto) has kindly checked the one Anglo-Norman entry. Errors, however, are mine alone, as their checks had to be made from microfilm.
2. The list of wards in the manuscript is not arranged as it is here, in this transcription, but is spread across the page in columns (with groups 1 and 3 on the left, 2 and 4 in the centre, and 5 on the right; 6 is in a single line across the page below the others). Also, in the manuscript, spacings are irregular; and groups, except for the sixth, are bracketed together. The entry ends at the bottom of the page, apparently unfinished. Henry Thomas Riley has printed an English translation in his *Memorials of London and London Life in the XIIIth, XIVth, and XVth Centuries* (London: Longmans, Green, 1868), pp. 419–420, and says (p. 420, n. 6) that the "description abruptly closes." The twenty-three wards listed are the same twenty-three as in a list on f. 84r of wards electing aldermen. Portsoken ward is missing; its non-elected, *ex officio* alderman (hence the ward's non-appearance on f. 84r), until the dissolution of the monasteries and religious houses under Henry VIII, was the Prior of Christ Church or Holy Trinity, Aldgate. (See Beaven, 1.179 and 181.)

p*ar*dessuz v*os*tre armure p*ur* faire les gaites es veilles del Nat*ivit*e seint Iohan & seintz Piere & Paul p*r*ocheinz venantz en man*ere* come Auntdit[3] feut faite p*ur* honestete de la Cite & la pes garder. Et ce ne lessez sur p*er*il qapent & come v*ous* voles lonur de la Cite sauuer

Et Sur ce p*ar* auys des Maire & Aldermens la dite gayte feut faite en man*ere* q*e* sensuyt cest assauoir q*e* touz les Aldr*emens* oue les bones gentz de lur gardes sasembleroient en Smythefeld la veille seint John*a*n vestuz come auant est dit & de illeoq*es* irroient p*ar*my la ville p*r*im*er*ement les Aldr*emens* & gentz des gards de

P*r*im*er*ement	Tour Billyngesgate Algate lymstret	oue cressetz les launces blanches poudres oue esteiles rouges
Secoundement les gardes de	Pount Candelwykstret Dougate Walbroke	oue launces touz rouges
Tiercement	Bisshopesgate langebo*ur*ne Cornhull Bradstret	oue launces blanches enuirones cest assauoir Wrethes de rouge
Quartement	ffarndon*e* Chastel baynard Aldrichesgate	oue lances noires poudres desteiles blanches
Quintement	Chepe Crepulgate Colmanstret Bassyeshawe	oue laun*c*es touz blancs
Sysmement	Bredstret Ryue la Royne Vinet*r*e Cordewan*er*stret oue launces	

2. *Entry of Henry V*: 1413: London Bridge House record of entry pageant details. The record has been referred to, but not printed, in Charles Welch's *History of The Tower Bridge* (London: Smith, Elder, 1894). BH Weekly Payments, Series 1, vol. 2, p. 26*.

It*em* sol*utum* p*ro* diu*er*s*is* expens*is* videl*ice*t Steynyng*e* peyntur*a* pann*o* lineo. plat*es* & al*ijs* p*ro* Gigante vna c*um* al*ijs* op*er*arijs & chauntours c*um* eor*um* app*ar*atu fac-tis in aduentu Reg*is* nu*n*c tempo*re* Coronaci*on*is sue apud Pontem londoni*ensis* pr*ou*t patet in vna cedul*a* p*er* p*ar*cellas inde s*umm*a ix li xiiij. s. x d

3. *Entry of Catherine of Valois*: 1421: London Bridge House records of entry pageant details. The entry was known only through chronicle description until

3. Should be "Auantdit".

the publication of selected Bridge House records, including these, in translation in Vanessa Harding and Laura Wright, eds., *London Bridge: Selected Accounts and Rentals, 1381–1538* (London Record Society, 1995); see that volume's pp. 77–88, 97–99, 105, and 112 for complete entry records in translation. Five short examples are reproduced here, from BH Weekly Payments, Series 1, vol. 2, pp. 457 (A below), 463 (B below), 464 (C below), 465 (D below), 480 (E below).

(A)   Item W Goos kervere pro factura capitum Gigantum pro Ponte per ij dies erga. aduentum ˏ[Regis] xviij d

(B)   Item solutum I. Oliuer pro iijMl demj iij halpenynailles iijMl Patynnailles & xxvjMl de [patyn] latys nailles emptis pro ordinacione dicti Regis &c' precio in toto xxj s xj d ob
Item pro xx duodenis Goldpaper emptis pro eodem xl s
Item pur vij plates ferri nigri & demjC fyn gold iij s viij d. ob
Item pro ijC [& demj] duodenis ˏ[& demj] siluerpaper. pro eodem ij s vj d

(C)   Item quibus laurencio & Henrico Taillours pro factura de xix garnementes de panno lineo steyned pro virginibus super Pontem [star] &c' xv s x d
Item eisdem pro I. virga de blanket. pro eisdem xij d

(D)   Item pro imposicione des Pysens pro les Geauntes ix d
Item Ricardo Carletone & socio suo. Paviatoribus per vnum diem super Pontem xiiij d
Item factura ij. Garnementes pro les Geauntes pro dicta ordinacione ij s

(E)   Item pro factura I. ymaginis sancte Petronille pro Ponte in aduentu Regis ij s

4. *Mayor's Oath-Taking by Water*: 1422: Brewers' Company record of a city order that the mayor's oath-taking will be by water because of the death and funeral of Henry V. Brewers' ancient account and memoranda book: GL MS 5440, f. 71r. (The sheriffs were also ordered to go to Westminster by barge to take their charges: f. 70v.) Printed in R. W. Chambers and Marjorie Daunt, eds., *A Book of London English 1384–1425* (Oxford: Clarendon Press, 1931), p. 143; the order to the sheriffs is printed on pp. 142–143.

And after þis William Walderne þe day of seint Edward nexte folwynge was chosen to be Mair of londone as for þe nexte ȝer suynge vpon þe whiche day hit was ordeyned þat þe Mair and þe Aldremen sholden wer blac and also to riden yn barge to Westmynster þere to take his charge with craftes of londone in diuerse barges yn blac clothinge with outen any mynstrall⁴ or eny other solempnite ffor on þe day of seint Edward hit was ordeyned þat eueryche housholder of euery Crafte beinge of power sholde ordeigne hym a blac goune with an hood of blac/or ellis a russet goune with a blac hood ridinge yn barge with þe for said Mair to Westmynster/And after þat yn þe same clothinge of

---

4. Possibly "mynstralles": the barred double l in this MS seems to indicate sometimes a singular and sometimes a plural.

blac or ellis russet*e* to be pr*e*sente atte þe enterement of our said king*e* henr*e* þc
v^te And on þis maner hit was ordeyned and doon . . .

5. *Entry of the Duke and Duchess of Bedford*: 1426: London Bridge House
records of pageants for a non-royal entry. (Also originally referred to by Welch,
see above, 2.) The longest of several records is reproduced here, from the BH
Weekly Payments, Series 1, vol. 3, f. 170r-v. The various expenses here detailed
are totalled, on f. 170v, at £9 3s 3d.

It*e*m solut*um* pr*o* ordinac*i*one pr*o*posita & infra br*eue* spacium p*er*acta erga
aduentum d*omi*ni Ducis Bedfordie & Ducisse sup*er* Pontem london*iensis* c*er*to
temp*ore* aduentus sui nescito. Videl*ic*et in pr*i*ore accessu in cornib*us* angulatis.
ad fine*m* Pontis vertibilis. ij Turres sing*u*lares cu*m* ang*e*lis infantulis psallentib*us*
pr*o*pe aures audiend*as* cu*m* organis &c' Vlt*er*ius q*ue* in vno ordine directo p*er*
spacium long*itudinaliter* domor*um* vltra & iuxta archum Porte intus edifica-
c*i*onem contrafact*am* cu*m* batellament*is* honesto m*o*do xij^cim. Duces. Principes.
nobiles. famosi. quilibet ab alio spacio debito. Medio autem sede vacuo vt
digne pr*e*parato pr*o* ip*s*o duce Bedfordie associand*o* ad ip*s*am turbam Ducum
nobilium cu*m* sede cathedrata puluilib*us* & veste status aurei. ornat*is* & vlt*ra*
caput cuiuslibet ducis &c' Arme in Scutis pendentes. cu*m* nom*i*nib*us* suprascrip-
t*is* I^mo videl*ic*et Abraham patriarcha/ij^do. Ysaac Patriarcha./. iij^o. Iacob
Patriarcha./.iiij^to Ioseph Princeps Egipti./v^to. Moyses Dux Hebreor*um*/vj^to
Iosue Dux filior*um* Israel vij^mo. Iohannes Dux Bedfordie/viij^uo. Iudas
Machabeus Dux &c'./ix^no Centurio Dux Senat*us* Romanor*um*/x^mo S*anctu*s
Albanus. Princeps./xj^mo. Henricus pr*i*mus Dux lancastrie/xij^mo Ector
Princeps Troianor*um*⁵/xiij^mo. Ercules valens pr*i*nceps Quorunq*ue* in ordine
sup*er*iore consim*i*liter contrafact*a* cu*m* batelment*is* In medio loco pr*i*ncipali virgo
Pr*i*ncissa decent*er* ornata cu*m* pluribus asstantib*us* virginib*us* Iunioribus tunicis
albis crinib*us* circumbentib*us* &c'. Subscript*is* v*er*bis Dauid psal*m*o <blank>
Dux Itin*er*is fuisti in conspectu eius & Plantasti Radices/Quor*um* custus &
expens*a* pr*o* quibuscumq*ue* inde accumbentib*us* Primo videl*ic*et sup*er* huiusmo-
di pr*e*parata vt pr*e*dicitur pr*o* aduentu ducis & ducisse Bedfordie pr*o* p*ar*uis
clauis pr*o* emendac*i*one batellamentor*um* vj d It*e*m de ip*s*o Custode Robert*o*
Colbrok pr*o* C patynnaill*es* lib*er*at*is* Ioh*ann*i Stanle j d ob It*e*m eidem pr*o* C spyk
pr*o* inferiorib*us* batellament*is* ad Pontem v*er*tibilem xij d It*e*m eidem pr*o* M^l ij^C
Cardnaill*es* viij d It*e*m M^l dem*j* booteuetnaill*es* xxij d ob It*e*m Henr*ic*o Mondon*e*
pr*o* Ioh*ann*e Middelton*e* & Ioh*ann*e Whetele pictoribus p*er* iiij^or dies op*er*antib*us*
vtroq*ue* ca*p*iente p*er* diem [viij d] ⌐viij d. v s iiij d⌐ It*e*m pr*o* xlj vlnis sailkloth pr*o*
vln*a* ij d ob empt*is* de Ric*ar*do Gosselyn. viij s vj d ob. It*e*m in allocac*i*onib*us*
diu*er*simode fact*is* viij Carpentarijs & v^e laborarijs op*er*antib*us* & auxiliantib*us*
p*er* vic*es* noctantib*us* sup*er* pr*e*missa v s v d It*e*m pr*e*fato Henrico Mondon*e* pr*o*
pr*e*fat*is* Ioh*ann*e Melton*e* & Ioh*ann*e Whetele p*er* iiij^or dies & I noctem/Ric*ar*do
Coyfott p*er* iij dies & I noctem. & Ioh*ann*e Peyntour p*er* ij dies & I. noctem.
quol*ibet* ca*p*iente p*er* diem siue p*er* noctem viij d xj s iiij d It*e*m s*ib*iip*s*i Henr*ico*

---

5. Should read "Troianor*um*" but seems to read "Troianar*um*;" readers disagree.

Mondon p*ro* vadijs suis p*er* quindenam cu*m* regardis <u>xx s</u> It*em* eidem p*ro* p*aru*-
ulo suo regardat*o* <u>viij d</u> It*em* eidem quibuscumq*ue* colorib*us* papir*o* aureo &
argenteo. & alijs diu*er*sis p*er* bill*am* inde computat*am* <u>xxxix s viij d</u> It*em* dat*um*
leonell*o* Cantatori p*ro* se & p*aru*ulis suis cantantib*us* <u>vj s viij d</u> It*em* sol*utum*
Thome Edward ex compact*o* pr*e*parand*o* p*ro* ornamentalib*us* quor*um*cumq*ue*
pr*e*dictor*um* p*er* vices sibi solut*um* [lx] in grosso manucaptu*m* <u>lxvj s viij d</u> It*em* in
I kynderkyn c*er*uisie empt*o* & pr*e*parat*o* p*ro* s*er*uientib*us* pr*e*dict*is* in turre <u>xix d</u>
<u>ob</u> It*em* alias allocat*um* p*ro* expens*is* fact*is* p*er* Nichol*au*m Holford p*ro* eisd*em* <u>iij</u>
<u>s I d</u> It*em* de consim*i*lib*us* expens*is* p*er* Thomam Hakun scriptore pr*e*sencium <u>ij</u>
<u>s v d</u> It*em* p*ro* iiij costis carnium bouinar*um* vltra se p*er* ip*su*m R*o*bert*o* Colbrok
<u>xij d</u> It*em* regardat*um* Thome Hakun p*re*dict*o* p*ro* sua diligencia. & p*re*ordina-
c*i*one pr*e*dictor*um* ex considerac*i*one Custodum <u>vj s viij d</u>

6. *Entry of Henry VI*: 1429: London Bridge House records of pageants on the
Bridge for the king's coronation entry. (Also referred to by Welch, see above, 2.)
BH Weekly Payments, Series 1, vol. 3, ff. 278r and 279v.

(A) f. 278r
It*em* solut*um* p*ro* expens*is* fact*is* circa erectionem vni*us* turris sup*er* Pontem londoni*ens*is erga coronac*i*onem dom*i*ni Reg*is* Henrici vj^ti. ut in Carpent*arijs* laborarijs conduct*is* & iij puell*is* conduct*is* ad sedend*um* in ear*um* apparat*u* quar*um*
vna tenebat*ur* I ceptr*um* in manu no*min*e Regine. cum filio stante ante ea*m* cum
corona in manib*us* suis & xij pu*er*is Iuuenilib*us* conduct*is* ad stand*um* ante dicta*m* Reginam iij Cl*er*icis & viij pueris conduct*is* ad Cantand*um* & in pane s*er*uisia
piscib*us* Carnib*us* & pranis empt*is* p*ro* dict*is* Carpent*arijs* & laborarijs & alijs
&c'. Necno*n* in Claui*s* spintris patellis [terris] terreis. & alijs in toto iiij li j d ob
Et solut*um* Guidoni lincoln*e* pictori p*ro* pictura. vni*us* angeli ij egelis & p*ro* pic-
t*ura* turris sup*er* Pontem & p*ro* victualib*us* s*er*uorum suor*um* p*er* idem tempus iiij
li iiij s^6

(B) f. 279v
It*em* solut*um* eid*em* p*ro* pane & s*er*uisia dat*is* Carpent*arijs* & laborarijs [de]^7 tem-
p*or*e deponenc*ibus* turr*em* sup*er* Pontem vertibil*em* post coronac*i*onem dom*i*ni
Reg*is* v d

7. *Mayor's Oath-Taking by Water*: 1453: Journal 5, ff. 124v and 126r. The original order (f. 124v, 8 Oct.) apparently met with some opposition from the Crown
or Council, also recorded (f. 126r, 18 Oct.). Because of this 1453 decision, from
this year on, the mayor's annual oath-taking journey to and from Westminster
took place by water.

(A) f. 124v, 8 Oct.
Isto die cons*titutum* [est] p*er* Maiorem Aldr*e*mann*os* supradictos q*uod* p*ro* equi-
tac*i*one Maioris apud Westm*o*nasterium 〔ad sacramentu*m* suu*m* pr*e*standu*m*〕
ad petic*i*onem communitat*is* ad vltimu*m* commune concilium desideratu*m* &

---

6. The total given for all these expenses, at the right of the entry, is "viij li iiij s j d ob".
7. Possibly not cancelled.

mactitat*um* qu*o*d de cet*er*o Maiores Ciuitat*is* pr*ed*ic*te* qui p*ro* tempore erunt Ibunt & quili*b*e*t* eor*um* ibit p*er* bargeas ad sacr*amen*tu*m* vt pr*e*dicit*ur* pr*e*stand*um* &c'

(B) f. 126r, 18 Oct.

In isto Comm*un*i Concilio administrat*ur* mat*er*ia p*ro* conducc*i*o*ne* Maioris v*er*sus Westm*onasteri*um p*er* Bargeas p*ro* eo qu*o*d dom*inu*s Cardinal & Cancellar*ius* Anglie ac dom*inu*s dux Som*er*setie miser*unt* Maiori & Aldremann*is* Thoma*m* Belgr*au*e Seruient*em* ad Arma [retul] qui quid*em* Thomas retulit pr*e*fat*is* M*aiori* & Aldremann*is* qu*o*d intencio dom*inorum* fuit qu*o*d Maior & Aldremann*i* moueant & instigant Comm*un*itatem Ciui*ta*t*is* qu*o*d ip*s*i conduc*ant* M*aiorem* v*er*sus Westm*onasteri*um equestr*em* pr*o*ut antea temp*or*ib*us* retroact*is* vsi fuer*unt* ad capi-end*um* sacr*amen*tu*m* suum qui quid*em* Comm*un*itas Nullo modo adhoc consen-tire voluissent s*ed* qu*o*d conduceret*ur* p*er* bargeas &c'

8. *Midsummer Watch Pageant*: 1477: earliest known record, to date, of a con-structed portable pageant carried in the Watch. Drapers' MS +403 (Wardens' Accounts), f. 9r−v. Also printed in A. H. Johnson, *The History of the Worshipful Company of Drapers of London*, 5 vols. (Oxford: Clarendon Press, 1914–22), II.273–274.

Paymente*s* of the costis don on seint Petre Nyght for the wache wayting vppon the Meyre

ffirste paide for þe morisse daunce and for the cost*es* of the ix worthi as it aperith by a bille of parcell*es* of the same xxviij s ix d
Item paide to Braban Carpent*er* for his labour for a day and a nyght and iij men with him iij s.
Item for xvj foote of quart*er* boorde v d.
Item for vj quarters of Oke xij d.
Item paide to the groc*er* for gold papir and silu*er* papir and oth*er* diu*er*s thing*es* belongyng to þe pageant as it shewith clerely by A bill of þe p*ar*cell*es* therof ix s j d.
Item paide to xiiij men for their labour þat bare þe pageant iiij s viij d.
Item paide for lxx Iakett*es* for Archers that wayted uppon þe Meire S*umm*a iij li iij s. vij d.
Item paide to william ffyner for him self and for v personys w*ith* him for A day iiij s iiij d.
Item paide for the bering of A Cresset iiij d
Item paide for drynke to the wachemen when the wache was don viij d
S*umm*a v li xv s x d

9. *John Heywood*: 1523 and 1530: John Heywood in 1523 is made free of the city at the king's request, first at the newly established fee and then, after recon-sideration, at the previous (lower) fee ("haunse") level. He also becomes a Mercer in 1530. Letter Book N, ff. 222r (3 Mar. 1523) and 239r (22 May 1523) (and also in Journal 12, ff. 213v and 235v); Mercers' Acts of Court 2, f. 27r (30 Jan. 1530) and Letter Book O, f. 206v (also in Repertory 8, f. 83v). The Chancellor whose letters are referred to in (C) is Sir Thomas More.

(A) Letter Book N, f. 222r, 3 Mar. 1523
Item as to Iohan heywode and Thomas Tyrwhytte for whome the kyng directed his seueralle le*tt*res to be made ffremen/been denyed to be made ffre
Excepte they paye eche of theym x li Accordynge to the newe Acte therof Late
made and prouyded &c'./.

(B) Letter Book N, f. 239r, 22 May 1523
It*e*m At the Contemplac*i*on of the Kyng*es* L*ett*re Iohan heywoode ys admytted
into the liberties of this Citie payinge the olde haunse./

(C) Mercers' MS Acts of Court 2, f. 27r, 30 Jan. 1530
Where as the Lord Chancelier directed his le*tt*res to the wardeyns and feli-
ship/Instansyng and hartely requyryng them by the same/to graunte vnto his
coseyn Iohan haywood/the parte of thoffice of meter of Lynen cloth*e* Lately
exercised by william Byrche gentilman/And after that the said wardeyns
Assistent*es* and generaltie had well*e* vnderstonde and p*er*ceyued the tenure of
the same le*tt*res/they w*ith* oon Assent condessended and graunted therun-
to/And ordeyned that the said Iohan Haywood shall*e* haue and enjoye the
same office w*ith* all*e* com*m*odities profites and aduantaiges to the same office
apperteynyng in as ample maner as the said william birche enjoyed the
same/Moreou*er* the said day/henry Pepwell*e* and lewes Sutton wardeyns of
the feliship of Stacioners/p*er*sonally appered bifore the wardeyns of this feliship in their hall*e* at seynt Thomas of Acon/knowleigyng there howe the company of Stacioners aforsaid/w*ith* oon Assent were very well*e* contented to
departe w*ith* the said haywood/and that he shuld be admytted of this feliship
of the Mercery/concideryng it was for his preferment/wherupon the same
Iohan haywood by consent of all*e* the whole company was admytted to the lib-
*er*ties of the same grat*is*/

(D) Letter Book O, f. 206v (the first f. 206, not the repeated one), 1 Feb. 1530
Johan heywoode Citezein and Stacyoner of london and oon of the kyng*es* s*er*u-
aunt*es* ys pr*e*sented by Maister Rauff waren Maister Wardeyn of the Mercers
to this Courte As Com*en* Mesurer or Met*er* of lynnen Clothes to occupie by
hym or his Suffic*ient* Depute and to doo Right and equally betwene all p*ar*-
ties/And also he ys Transmuted from the saide Crafte of Stacyon*er* vnto the
Mist*er*e of Mercers by thassent of bothe the said Misteres./.

10. *Thomas Brandon, Entertainer*: 1526: Thomas Brandon, the king's entertainer, is granted the London freedom (citizenship) in return for providing entertainment at civic banquets. Letter Book N, f. 305r, 11 January (and also in
Repertory 7, f. 78v). (The previous act referred to in this record is on f. 195r of
Letter Book N and has been printed in Anna Jean Mill, ed., "Dramatic
Records of the City of London: The Repertories, Journals, and Letter Books,"
in the Malone Society's *Collections II.3* [1931], pp. 286–287.)

Where afore this by thauctorite of Com*en* Counsell At the Conttemplac*i*on of
the kyng*es* le*tt*res Thomas Brandon the kyng*es* player with lieger de Mayn was
admytted into the liberties and ffredome of this Citie he payinge to the

Chamberleyn the olde haunce/As by the said Acte more playnely Apperith/Nowe at this Courte it is agreed and graunted that the said olde haunse shalbe clerely Remytted and for geven to the said Thomas with this Condicion that he shalle fromhensforthe yerely at the Maiers ffeaste/And also the Munday next after the ffeast of the Epiphanie of our lord before the Maire then beynge Mynystre suche beste playe & disporte As concerneth his ffacultie without eny takynge therfore &c'/

11. *Mayor's Oath-taking Ceremonial*: 1541: two extracts from the Mercers' MS Register of Writings, vol. 2, ff. 137v and 138r, the whole entry seeming to be partly an account of the specific ceremonial activities when Mercer mayor Michael Dormer was sworn into office in October 1541 and partly a directive for like occasions in the future. The extracts are here in reverse chronological order, as in the MS; the second deals with the initial activities of 29 October 1541, and the first, with the following activities. The first is also preceded in the MS by some details (not here transcribed) concerning the waits and the trumpeters (twelve of the latter were the king's trumpeters).

(A) f. 137v

Memorandum that the Master of our barge whiche went with Master Wardeins and the Commpeny called Ieorge Percevall had a Redde hatt and a tepet and we toke our barge by the Crane in the Vyntre at dyhowse stayd and paid hir iiij d for Warfage and so sent a dosen of Cushyns ij bankers and a carpett ij stremers to the sayd barge and so went to Westmynster and from thens came to powlys Warff and there we Landed and sent vp our stremers to be borne afore the bachelers and my Lorde Mayour Landed at beynerd Castell and the bachelers were at my Lorde of Huntyngtons place by and they set fourthe toward powles vp the hyll with theire men that they gaff gowns afore theym in copyll euerye man bering a Iavelynge in hys necke and some tergates and Master Wardeins folowinge the bachelers and our compeny after them the bachelers had their mayde with them and xij trompettes afore hyr and our compeny had xij trompetters afore the Wardeins and my Lord Mayour had the vj Wayghtes afore hym and so we went to the Guyld hall the bacheleres standynge with oute in the courte hard to the vtter dore of the hall tyll the Compeny went in and my Lorde Mayour and all the aldermen and then the bacheleres went in with theire mayde and shewed hir to my Lorde Mayour and other noble men and to all the Ladyes and then caryd hir home to Robert Longes in seint Lavrens Lane where she dined and the viij Master bachelers and the Rest was at the yeld hall & serued

Item after dynner the bachelers with their Mayde stode at seynt Lavrens churche corner and so went to Powlys our commpeny followynge their torches born afore theym ij & ij to gether one Lyghte/our commpeny had vj torches born by them and euery man that bore them had ij d/and at our retorn from powlys in perdone churche yard we Lyted all the torches & so went home to my Lord Mayours thorowe Mylkstrete the bachelers standynge with oute at the gate in order the commpeny went in to the court & stode in ij Rynges tyll my Lorde was come in and then we toke our Leve and

browght*e* home o*ur* iij Wardeins Levyng at eu*er*y one of their howses ij
torches of o*ur*s whiche should haue ben caryed to o*ur* haull & o*ur*
Alderman*e* Wardein shold haue bene browght*e* home w*ith* ij of the said
torches when he went from my lord mayo*ur*

(B) f. 138r
Memorand*um* that the morowe after Symond and Iude daye at viij of the
clocke all*e* the Compeny of the Laste L*e*u*er*ey Assembled at seint Thomas and
all*e* the bachelers and so went from thens to the Mayo*ur*s place the Wardens
afore the com*m*peny followinge and the bachelers after them and from thens
the bachalers went afore to the yeld hall dore ther standinge arowe on the west
syde the court and o*ur* wardens and compeny followinge them they goynge in
to the hall next xij tro*m*pett*es* afore the bachelers and xij afore o*ur* Wardens the
vj Wayght*es* afore the Mayo*ur* the compeny went into the hall and stode in two
ryng*es* the Wardens next the stayers and after my Lord Mayo*ur* is gone into the
haule and Aldermen then all the bachelers to retorn in order to baynerd*es*
Castell or where theire barge Lyethe w*ith* their sorte of trompett*es* w*ith* them
and another sorte of trompett*es* must tary and wayte vpon the compeny the
bachelers in the meyne tyme muste make them Redy to wayte vppon my Lord
Mayo*ur* in their barge and to make suche pastyme as shalbe devysed when my
Lord mayo*ur* and thaldermen come downe out of the Counsell Chamber then
the Compeny muste set fourthe in order w*ith* there trompet*es* afore them & so
pas to their barge/[8]

---

8. Later in the same MS volume, f. 149r–v, comes an undated description of the process to be followed for the Westminster oath-taking when a Mercer mayor is being installed. It provides
more detail in areas not covered in the above record (for example, about the process at Westminster itself), and largely avoids detail in areas extensively covered by the above record. It
contains no reference to a maid, or to a pageant; and it immediately precedes, in the MS, a list
of plate for the 1558 mayor's feast. Mercer mayors 1541–58 were installed in 1541, 1544 (in
April, replacing a deceased Draper mayor), 1547, 1549, and 1558.

Notes

INTRODUCTION

1 David M. Bevington, *From 'Mankind' to Marlowe: Growth of Structure in the Popular Drama of Tudor England* (Cambridge, MA: Harvard University Press, 1962), *passim*. The book deals with the structure of the popular drama, and the eventual permanent locating of theatre in London, but emphasizes the itinerant nature of pre-Elizabethan professional troupes. *Mankind*'s traditional status as a touring play, though not its provincial provenance, has since been called into question; see, e.g., Richard Southern, *The Staging of Plays before Shakespeare* (London: Faber and Faber, 1973), pp. 21–43 and 143–145, Tom Pettitt, "*Mankind*: An English *Fastnachtspiel?*" in Meg Twycross, ed., *Festive Drama* (Cambridge: D. S. Brewer, 1996), pp. 190–202, and Greg Walker, *The Politics of Performance in Early Renaissance Drama* (Cambridge: Cambridge University Press, 1998), p. 54, n. 9.

2 Richard Beadle, ed., *The Cambridge Companion to Medieval English Theatre* (Cambridge: Cambridge University Press, 1994; rpt. 1995).

3 Lois Potter, gen. ed., *The Revels History of Drama in English*, vol. 1: *Medieval Drama* (London and New York: Methuen, 1983).

4 Alan H. Nelson, *The Medieval English Stage: Corpus Christi Pageants and Plays* (Chicago and London: University of Chicago Press, 1974), pp. 170–178.

5 A. R. Braunmuller and Michael Hattaway, eds., *The Cambridge Companion to English Renaissance Drama* (Cambridge: Cambridge University Press, 1990).

6 Neither the *Cambridge Companion* volume for medieval theatre nor the Renaissance one seems to take responsibility for theatre originating in the early sixteenth century (although the medieval theatre volume deals with, e.g., cycle drama continuing into this period). John Heywood's work, e.g., "lie[s] outside the remit of this book," says the medieval volume (p. 66).

7 Lois Potter, gen. ed., *The Revels History of Drama in English*, vol. 2: *1500–1576* (London and New York: Methuen, 1980).

8 Gordon Kipling, "Wonderfull Spectacles: Theater and Civic Culture," in *New History*, pp. 153–171. See List of Abbreviations: *New History*.

9 Alan Nelson's edition of *The Plays of Henry Medwall* (Cambridge/Totowa, NJ: D. S. Brewer/Rowman and Littlefield, 1980), p. 1, untypically sees

Medwall's work as significantly connected to London – although Nelson also typically comments on the English drama as *shifting* in the sixteenth century from the provinces to London.

10 One major source of theatrical records, e.g., are the histories of the various London craft guilds/livery companies, which often include (though not always with accuracy) some or many excerpts (some volumes are almost entirely excerpts) from pre-1559 company MSS of accounts, minutes, regulations, and the like, some of which concern theatrical activity. (Company historians normally include in their volumes at least one chapter on company ceremonials, celebrations, and entertainments.) Some major, complete pre-1559 company MSS, and complete MSS beginning before 1559, have also been published in modern editions (I here exclude the also useful and usually private company printings of early ordinances, charters, and the like): *Records of the Worshipful Company of Carpenters*, vols. 2–4, ed. Bower Marsh (Oxford and London: The Company, 1913–16); *Wardens' Accounts of the Worshipful Company of Founders of the City of London 1497–1681*, ed. Guy Parsloe (London: University of London, Athlone Press, 1964); *Facsimile of First Volume of MS. Archives of the Worshipful Company of Grocers of the City of London, A.D. 1345–1463*, 2 parts, ed. John Abernethy Kingdon (London: The Company, 1886); *Acts of Court of the Mercers' Company 1453–1527*, ed. Laetitia Lyell assisted by Frank D. Watney (Cambridge: Cambridge University Press, 1936); *The Merchant Taylors' Company of London: Court Minutes 1486–1493*, ed. Matthew Davies (Stamford: Richard III and Yorkist History Trust, in association with Paul Watkins, 2000); *Scriveners' Company Common Paper 1357–1628, With a Continuation to 1678*, ed. Francis W. Steer (London Record Society, 1968); *A Transcript of the Registers of the Company of Stationers of London; 1554–1640 A.D.*, ed. Edward Arber, vol. 1 (London: privately printed, 1875). A volume of early Goldsmiths' Company accounts and minutes is now forthcoming. One private printing of special note is the Drapers' Company's *Drapers' Company: Transcripts of the Earliest Records in the Possession of the Company* (London: Chiswick Press, 1910).

11 A recent exception is Michael D. Bristol's socioeconomic analysis, in *New History*, pp. 244–248, of why permanent playhouses were probably built in later 16th century London (the full chapter is entitled "Theater and Popular Culture"); and Greg Walker in *Plays of Persuasion: Drama and Politics at the Court of Henry VIII* (Cambridge: Cambridge University Press, 1991) demonstrates, pp. 28–31, the comparatively new scholarly attitude to early sixteenth-century civic play regulation as based more in public nuisance concerns than in hostility to theatre *per se*.

12 See List of Abbreviations: *DTR*.

13 *DTR* also includes for London a few miscellaneous listings past 1558 to 1623.

14 See List of Abbreviations: Manley, *Culture*; and see also Manley's 1986 edited collection of early writings (some of them from before 1559) specifically on London, *London in the Age of Shakespeare: An Anthology* (London and Sydney: Croom Helm, 1986).

15 Most of the craft guilds also eventually became incorporated by royal charter, beginning in the fourteenth century; see George Unwin, *The Gilds and Companies of London* (London: Methuen, 1908), pp. 157–159. Unwin's work, despite its date, is still largely reliable on London guild/company history generally. For the complex origins of craft guilds and of their included religious fraternities, see Unwin's pp. 28–109 and Caroline M. Barron, "The Parish Fraternities of Medieval London," in Caroline M. Barron and Christopher Harper-Bill, eds., *The Church in Pre-Reformation Society: Essays in Honour of F. R. H. Du Boulay* (Woodbridge, Suffolk, and Dover, NH: Boydell Press, 1985), pp. 14–17. For the livery, or common distinctive clothing, worn by guild members, see Unwin, pp. 189–192, and *Cal. LB L*, pp. xxv–xxx.

16 I avoid the term "bourgeois" because of its pejorative and theoretical baggage.

17 See Williams, p. 193, Beaven, 1.329, and *Historical Charters*, pp. 46–47. Steve Rappaport, *Worlds Within Worlds: Structures of Life in Sixteenth-Century London* (Cambridge: Cambridge University Press, 1989), has demonstrated that by the middle of the sixteenth century (see p. 28) some three-quarters of the city's adult males were freemen (i.e., citizens); see his chapter 2, "The nature and extent of citizenship," pp. 23–60. "Except for the family," declares Rappaport, p. 26, "companies were the most important social organisations in sixteenth-century London, directly responsible for much of the work of collecting taxes, maintaining the peace, organising pageants, providing poor relief, and so on."

18 Caroline Barron has pointed out (*Atlas*, p. 44) that the ward, not the guild, was the basic unit of early London civic government: each ward was administered by an alderman, chosen to serve – for life, throughout most of this period – on the city's Court of Aldermen; the mayor (from 1435) had to come from among the aldermen (and before 1435 was usually an alderman as well); and the wards also elected members to the city's Common Council. (See Rappaport, *Worlds Within Worlds*, pp. 32–34.) The aldermen themselves, and their nominators, were all, however, at least from the early fourteenth century, citizens and members of guilds (see Rappaport, p. 35); from around that time all Common Council members also had to be freemen, and therefore guild members, as well (p. 35); and from 1475 company liverymen (the companies' senior members) controlled the annual elections of the mayor and of the two sheriffs (Beaven, II.xxiv; Reginald R. Sharpe in *Cal. LB L*, pp. xxix–xxx and 73, provides the 1467 beginnings of the 1475 move, as well as the 1475 order on p. 132). Unwin, *Gilds and Companies*, pp. 66–67, emphasizes the importance of craft guilds as a political force in the fourteenth century.

19 Such a kind of theatre is described by David Chaney as collective, ritualized, and spectacular, rooted in the ideological construction of social order and its idealization; see his *Fictions of Collective Life: Public Drama in Late Modern Culture* (London and New York: Routledge, 1993), pp. 16–29.

20 The order of the companies on ceremonial occasions was a matter of some controversy from time to time; and in 1484 the Skinners and Merchant Taylors were awarded alternate-year precedence in relation to one another (see *Cal. LB L*, pp. xl–xli). The order was finally settled (including the Skinners/Merchant Taylors arrangement) in 1516 (*Cal. LB L*, pp. xli–xlii), what were then the Shearmen becoming the Clothworkers in 1528.

21 The mayor, as noted above, had to be chosen from among the aldermen; and customarily, to be nominated and elected, from the fifteenth century an alderman had to belong to, or agree to be transferred to, a Great Company. See Beaven, I.329–331. In the late 1550s the rule was relaxed for aldermen but not for the mayor.

22 See Beaven, II.xxv, xxxvii–xxxviii. Also, from 1386 (by a Common Council ordinance of Dec. 1385), no one could be chosen mayor who had not previously been a sheriff (Beaven, II.xxv).

23 The title Lord Mayor was not commonly used for London's mayor until the sixteenth century (see *Cal. LB L*, pp. xiii–xiv); and throughout this book I use it rarely for the mayor himself but normally in the now-traditional title of the Lord Mayor's Show, the visual display surrounding the annual oath-taking, at Westminster, of London's newly elected mayor, which had become a significantly theatrical event by at least the middle of the sixteenth century and is discussed below in chapters 3 and 10.

24 Excellent books covering the structures, civic privileges and responsibilities, and general internal workings and external contexts of the London companies are, for 1300–1500, Thrupp, *London*, and, for the sixteenth century, Rappaport's *Worlds Within Worlds*. For a summary of London's internal governing structures above all by the middle of the sixteenth century, see Manley's *London in the Age of Shakespeare*, pp. 2–6.

25 A very recent exception to this statement is Claire Sponsler's "Alien Nation: London's Aliens and Lydgate's Mummings for the Mercers and Goldsmiths," in Jeffrey Jerome Cohen, ed., *The Postcolonial Middle Ages* (Houndmills, Basingstoke, Hampshire, and London: MacMillan Press, 2000), pp. 229–242.

26 See, e.g., David M. Bevington's *From 'Mankind' to Marlowe, passim*, and Greg Walker's *Politics of Performance*, pp. 6–50. Barbara A. Mowat, "The Theater and Literary Culture" (in *New History*), has recently reminded us (p. 215) of the traditional view that early play printings had "acting companies as a primary market;" but that market has largely been seen in terms of travelling troupes, not of London-based ones.

27 Anna Jean Mill, ed., "Dramatic Records of the City of London: The Repertories, Journals, and Letter Books," in *Collections II.3* (Malone Society, 1931), pp. 285–298; *Collections III*, pp. xlvi–xlviii, 132–139, 183–184. (Both collections also include post-1558 records.) Jean Robertson's "A Calendar of Dramatic Records in the Books of the London Clothworkers' Company (Addenda to *Collections III*)," *Collections V* (Malone Society, 1960 for 1959), includes only one pre-1559 record, p. 9, which is not of a play but of a

pageant. The much earlier (1907) Malone Society publication of the city's Remembrancia (E. K. Chambers and W. W. Greg, eds., "Dramatic Records of the City of London. The Remembrancia," in *Collections I.1*, pp. 43–100) includes no material before 1580, as the Remembrancia did not begin until about that date. Despite the limited number of livery-company MS records of plays, however, Alan Nelson in his *Medieval English Stage* assumed (correctly, as demonstrated in chapter 4, below) that such plays were "common" (p. 176) in early London.

28 E. K. Chambers, *The Mediaeval Stage*, 2 vols. (Oxford: Oxford University Press, 1903) II.166–173.

29 See List of Abbreviations: *EP*. Vol. I includes two pages (I.106–108) on Lydgate's mummings.

30 Withington's interpretative views, of course, have become outdated: e.g., his statement (II.302) that older pageantry was pure popular entertainment, "innocent of an ulterior motive."

31 For *Collections III*, see List of Abbreviations; for *Collections V* (though with only one pageant record before 1559), see n. 27, above.

32 See List of Abbreviations: *EES*.

33 Wickham's work on pageant stagecraft was preceded by George R. Kernodle's in *From Art to Theatre: Form and Convention in the Renaissance* (Chicago and London: University of Chicago Press, 1944), but Kernodle took a broadly European view and was primarily interested in royal entry stages as static, architectural art (see his pp. 58–108).

34 The 1465 entry record is in *EES*, I.324–331. Wickham misdates the entry as in 1464 (see this book's Appendix A, under 1465).

35 See List of Abbreviations: Anglo, *Spectacle*.

36 Gordon Kipling, in his 1998 *Enter the King: Theatre, Liturgy, and Ritual in the Medieval Civic Triumph* (see List of Abbreviations: Kipling, *King*), provides on p. 1 a footnote listing the major studies of court festivals over the past fifty years; as Kipling himself notes, they are largely focused on the Renaissance.

37 For Kipling's books, see *The Triumph of Honour: Burgundian Origins of the Elizabethan Renaissance* (The Hague: Leiden University Press for the Sir Thomas Browne Institute, 1977), ed. *Receyt* (see List of Abbreviations: Kipling, *Receyt*), and *King*.

38 For Bergeron's books, see *English Civic Pageantry 1558–1642* (Columbia, SC: South Carolina University Press, 1971), ed. *Pageantry in the Shakespearean Theater* (Athens, GA: University of Georgia Press, 1985), ed. *Pageants and Entertainments of Anthony Munday: A Critical Edition* (New York: Garland, 1985), ed. *Thomas Heywood's Pageants: A Critical Edition* (New York: Garland, 1986), *Practicing Renaissance Scholarship* (Pittsburgh: Duquesne University Press, 2000).

39 Gordon Kipling, "Richard II's 'Sumptuous Pageants' and the Idea of the Civic Triumph," in Bergeron's *Pageantry in the Shakespearean Theater*, pp. 83–103.

40 Arthur F. Kinney, ed., *Renaissance Drama: An Anthology of Plays and Entertainments* (Malden, MA, and Oxford: Blackwell, 1999). The three pageant texts

are those of the royal entries of 1559 (Elizabeth I) and 1604 (James I) and of the Lord Mayor's Show of 1605. Kinney's introduction to each text also ends with a brief bibliography of recent relevant published work on Elizabethan and Jacobean pageants. Modern texts of all of Thomas Dekker's civic shows are also included in Fredson Bowers's *The Dramatic Works of Thomas Dekker*, 4 vols. (Cambridge: Cambridge University Press, 1953–61), and Thomas Middleton's will appear in newly edited texts in the forthcoming Oxford edition of Middleton's dramatic works.

41 See also (above, n. 14) Manley's edited collection of early writings on London, and his "Of Sites and Rites," in David L. Smith, Richard Strier and David Bevington, eds., *The Theatrical City: Culture, Theatre and Politics in London, 1576–1649* (Cambridge: Cambridge University Press, 1995), pp. 35–54.

42 See Greg Walker, *Plays of Persuasion, passim,* and *Politics of Performance, passim.*

43 Anne F. Sutton and P. W. Hammond, *The Coronation of Richard III: the Extant Documents* (Gloucester/New York: Alan Sutton/St. Martin's Press, 1983/84).

44 See, e.g., R. Malcolm Smuts, "Public Ceremony and Royal Charisma: The English Royal Entry in London, 1485–1642," in A. L. Beier, David Cannadine and James M. Rosenheim, eds., *The First Modern Society: Essays in English History in Honour of Lawrence Stone* (Cambridge: Cambridge University Press, 1989), pp. 65–93.

45 After some two decades of an emphasis on theory in English literary and theatrical studies in general, a movement generally back towards historical field work may now be signalled by 1997's *New History* volume. Its introduction notes, p. 2, the importance of historical facts, and many of the individual chapters rely on archival research.

I ROMAN LONDON

1 Details about London's newly discovered amphitheatre, here and below, are taken largely from N. C. W. Bateman, "The London Amphitheatre: Excavations 1987–1996," *Britannia* 28 (1997), 51–85. (The amphitheatre site was directed by Bateman for the Museum of London Archaeology Service; his article is a report on and analysis of the findings to date.) Information on the amphitheatre's larger urban context comes above all from Dominic Perring, *Roman London*, The Archaeology of London Series (London: Seaby, 1991), and Gustav Milne, *Book of Roman London: Urban Archaeology in the Nation's Capital* (London: B. T. Batsford/English Heritage, 1995), both of whom also discuss the amphitheatre but at earlier stages in its excavation and study and without Bateman's special familiarity with and study of the site. Where special details are involved, specific citations are supplied. Perring and Milne both synthesize what archaeological discoveries over many years, but especially since 1973, have demonstrated about Roman London in general: its beginnings, development, and ultimate decline and disappearance. Earlier excellent sources such as Peter Marsden's *Roman London*

(London: Thames and Hudson, 1980) and Ralph Merrifield's *London: City of the Romans* (London: B. T. Batsford, 1983) did not have as extensive archaeological findings with which to work, given the operations 1973–91 of London's Dept. of Urban Archaeology (created 1973, closed 1991; see Milne, pp. 24–31). Merrifield's essay on Roman London in *Atlas*, pp. 10–19, immediately follows the amphitheatre's discovery but unfortunately predates much of the excavation work. In Nov. 2000 the Museum of London Archaeology Service brought out Bateman's *Gladiators at the Guildhall: The Story of London's Roman Amphitheatre and Medieval Guildhall*: a lavishly illustrated account of the amphitheatre discoveries, for the general reader but containing post-1997 analysis; this present chapter had already been largely finalized, but especially where Bateman's 1997 details as used here have been revised in the 2000 book, citations to *Gladiators* have been incorporated. Illustrations from the new book have not been specifically cited, but a number are extremely useful. Much more will be learned about the amphitheatre over the next 3–4 years as MoLAS continues its analyses.

2 See, e.g., John H. Humphrey, *Roman Circuses: Arenas for Chariot Racing* (London: B. T. Batsford, 1986), p. 3, Margarete Bieber, *The History of the Greek and Roman Theater* (Princeton: Princeton University Press, 1939; 2nd edn. 1961), p. 190 (for theatres), John Morris, *Londinium: London in the Roman Empire*, rev. Sarah Macready (London: Weidenfeld and Nicolson, 1982; new edn. 1998), pp. 245, 249–251, and Marsden, *Roman London*, pp. 56–57 (for amphitheatres); all four books were written before the discovery of the London amphitheatre. Morris's book is essentially a social and political rather than archaeological history, and draws for its descriptions of Roman London and the activities of its inhabitants on what is known more generally about ancient Rome itself and its Empire.

3 See, e.g., Marsden, *Roman London*, pp. 56–57 (amphitheatre), John Wacher, *The Towns of Roman Britain*, 2nd edn. (London: B. T. Batsford, 1995), pp. 55–56 (theatre), and Morris, *Londinium*, pp. 240–251.

4 For the unexpectedness of the location, see Bateman, "London Amphitheatre" (1997), pp. 51–52. For photographs of the excavated amphitheatre beneath the Yard, see Perring, *Roman London*, p. 62 (fig. 27), and Milne, *Book of Roman London*, p. 60 (illustration 35). Nicholas Bateman, "The London Amphitheatre," *Current Archaeology* 137 [12.5] (Feb./Mar. 1994), 164–171, provides a photograph of the site in relation to the Guildhall now (p. 164) and to former medieval buildings around Guildhall Yard (p. 167), as well as close-ups (pp. 165, 169) of specific amphitheatre features. The remains of the eastern amphitheatre entrance have now been preserved in the lowest level of the new Guildhall Art Gallery, constructed on the site, and will eventually be exhibited.

5 See Perring, *Roman London*, and Milne, *Book of Roman London*, *passim* (though the decline was not steady; see, e.g., Perring, p. v). Archaeological findings have led now to the dismissal of medieval traditions of a pre-Roman history for London; see, e.g., Perring, pp. viii, 1–3, and Milne, p. 41. Geoffrey

of Monmouth's noting of "ludos" performed at London in 55–54 BC (see *DTR* no. 1754, under "Doubtful Texts and Records") may therefore be disregarded.

6 The quotation is from Perring, *Roman London*, p. v. For the importance of London's site, see Perring, pp. 3–5 (including fig. 2), 16–21; for its public buildings *c.* 70–*c.* 120, see Perring, pp. 23–38, 42–43, and Milne, *Book of Roman London*, pp. 48, 52–70. The population figure of up to perhaps 60,000 is calculated from Perring, pp. 16 and 70, and may be too high. The road system and water pipes had existed by 60–61: see Perring, pp. 10–11.

7 All Roman theatres and amphitheatres (both definite and possible) known in Britain to 1983 are listed in *DTR*. For *DTR*'s theatres (by modern location) see item nos. 413 (Brough-on-Humber), 490 (Canterbury), 518 (Catterick), 542.5 (Cirencester), 550–551 (Colchester), 1349 (St. Albans), and, as possibilities, 847 (Lincoln) and 1754.5 (Wycomb); for amphitheatres see item nos. 1593 (Caerleon), 1597 (Carmarthen), 523 (Chester), 538 (Chichester), 542 (Cirencester), 606 (Dorchester), 680.5 (Frilford), 1325 (Richborough), 1398 (Silchester), and, as possibilities, also 1596 (Caerwent), 1755 (Charterhouse-on-Mendip), 656 (Exeter), 847 (Lincoln), 1349.5 (St. Albans), 1600 (Tomen-y-Mur). See also no. 1546. The sites range all over England and Wales; and Wacher (*Towns*, pp. 56, 246–247) has recently suggested another amphitheatre or theatre at Caistor-by-Norwich. *DTR* also includes records of likely theatrical masks found in a number of locations (nos. 358, 518, 751.5, 877 – Londinium [see below], 1489, 1594), and of the names of perhaps a pair of travelling entertainers (no. 826 – Verecunda the "ludia" [player or dancer?] and Lucius the gladiator) recorded on a pottery shard found at Leicester. (Roman theatrical masks, however, have recently become associated also with brothels – as in a find of early 1998 in Salonika, Greece – and so no longer can be taken necessarily as indications of theatre *per se*; see *The Globe and Mail* (Toronto, Canada), 17 April 1998, p. A14, cols. 5–6.) Bateman, whose 1997 London amphitheatre report also most usefully places the Londonium structure within the context of what is now known about other British amphitheatres, cites ("London Amphitheatre" [1997], p. 74) a more recent (1989) amphitheatre-only list by Michael Fulford (in his *The Silchester Amphitheatre: Excavations of 1979–85*, *Britannia* Monograph Series 10 [London: Society for the Promotion of Roman Studies, 1989], p. 177, and map, p. 178) which includes, beyond *DTR*, Aldborough, Caistor St. Edmund, London, and (queried) Winterslow (but does not include *DTR*'s queried Exeter, Lincoln, and St. Albans); Bateman questions, pp. 74–75, Aldborough, Charterhouse-on-Mendip, and Winterslow, while tentatively adding Catterick, Newstead, and (p. 76, n. 125) York. (He both mentions and dismisses, in addition, Woodcutts.) His fig. 6, p. 75, provides in map form his own listing of both certain and uncertain theatres and amphitheatres throughout Britain as of 1997; believing that mixed-use performance space was the norm in Roman Britain (pp. 76–77), he maps nineteen amphitheatre and mixed theatre/amphitheatre sites, five "uncertain" sites, and only

one definite theatre-only site (at Colchester), though he also mentions (p. 76 and, on p. 77, n. 131), the possibility of separate theatre and amphitheatre buildings at Cirencester. In *Gladiators* he mentions (p. 38) Gosbecks.

8 See Marsden, *Roman London*, pp. 56–57, Morris, *Londinium*, pp. 240–241, 250–251, and on the situation in Rome itself, Oscar G. Brockett, *History of the Theatre*, 7th edn. (Needham Heights, MA: Allyn and Bacon, 1995), pp. 53–54, 61, and Wickham, *History*, p. 50. In the time of Augustus, over 60 days a year in Rome were designated for public festival spectacles (plays and amphitheatre and circus events), and by 354 AD, 175 days, 100 of which were for plays (Bieber, *History*, p. 227).

9 On amphitheatre entertainment generally, see Morris, *Londinium*, pp. 245–249, and Brockett, *History*, pp. 59–60. (Bateman, "London Amphitheatre" [1997], pp. 82–83 and 85, discusses some of its political purposes.) Significantly, "theatrical spectacle seems to have been imported increasingly into amphitheatres" (Brockett, p. 60), with use of music, sound effects, costuming, and scenic elements for gladiatorial contests, and sometimes added presentations of dance-drama. (See also Brockett, p. 67.) Bateman includes a discussion of amphitheatre entertainment in *Gladiators*, pp. 14–19.

10 John Wacher, *Roman Britain*, 2nd edn. (Stroud, Gloucestershire: Sutton, 1998), has pointed out (p. 289), however, that gladiatorial shows were expensive and that no British training centre has yet been identified.

11 Bateman, "London Amphitheatre" (1997), p. 58 and n. 24, who also notes that bear bones have not to date been found in association with any other British amphitheatres.

12 Naumachia (mock sea battles) were also popular amphitheatre entertainments at Rome and elsewhere (see Brockett, *History*, p. 60), though not usually mentioned by historians in connection with Londinium: but see Kevin Flude, "The Roman London amphitheatre" [letter], *London Archaeologist* 7.7 (Summer 1994), 189–190 (possibly naumachia and other water spectacles in the amphitheatre). Given Londinium's location, however, the Thames itself might logically have been used for water shows. For the probable kinds of entertainments in Londinium's amphitheatre, see especially Marsden, *Roman London*, p. 56, who also names a first-century troupe of gladiators perhaps popular in Britain (glass cups with their crested helmets have been found in London as well as on the Continent) and points out that the three-pronged point of an iron trident found decades ago in Southwark probably was part of a gladiator's weapon. See also Humphrey, *Roman Circuses*, pp. 1–3, for general information on the architecture of amphitheatres, theatres, circuses, and stadii, and on the types of entertainments performed in each kind of structure at different periods. Morris's *Londinium*, chapter 12, "Sports and Leisure" (in which the terms stadium and circus are used interchangeably for what Humphrey defines as a circus) is also useful. Bateman, "London Amphitheatre" (1997), pp. 81–82, although arguing against use of amphitheatres for military training, suggests executions of

criminals as another possible British amphitheatre function; and see also his *Gladiators*, p. 39.

13 This is possible, given the increasing Roman use (see above, n. 9) of theatrical effects in amphitheatre shows of the period; also theatrical spaces could be adapted for amphitheatrical shows: see Brockett, *History*, p. 63, Peter D. Arnott, *The Ancient Greek and Roman Theatre* (New York: Random House, 1971), p. 136, and Bieber, *History*, p. 190. For theatrical presentations BC in circuses – even larger structures than amphitheatres – see Bieber, pp. 167–168. Arnott notes, p. 136, that Roman entertainment forms tended to merge under the Empire. Bateman, "London Amphitheatre" (1997), points out, pp. 76–77, that mixed-usage performance spaces were common in Rome's western provinces, and believes (as noted above) that mixed usage was the norm in Britain.

14 See Brockett, *History*, pp. 57–59. (Wacher, *Roman Britain*, has somewhat inexplicably suggested that British theatres were intended primarily for religious ceremonials [p. 81] but that in urban centres mime and pantomime would have been the performance norm [pp. 286–287].) Mime (for which actors normally did not wear masks: Brockett, p. 69) was usually comic or satiric, involved large casts and spectacle, often included violence, and dealt with everyday life (e.g., money, love, sex, politics); and mime performers also presented entertainments such as juggling, tightrope walking, singing, and dancing. Pantomime involved narrative music-dance, usually on mythological or historical subjects. Both mime and pantomine became gradually more sensational during the Empire. For extensive information on the various kinds of late Roman theatrical forms (tragedy, comedy, farce, mime, pantomime, satyr play), see Bieber, *History*, pp. 227–253, and also, for mime and pantomime only, Arnott, *Ancient Greek and Roman Theatre*, pp. 138–147. Famous performers toured the Roman provinces (Morris, *Londinium*, p. 250; also Bieber, *History*, p. 239).

15 For Hadrian's tour of Britain, see Marsden, *Roman London*, pp. 97–98. Bateman, "London Amphitheatre" (1997), p. 83, speculatively links the early second-century rebuilding of Londinium's amphitheatre with Hadrian's visit; see also his *Gladiators*, p. 24.

16 See Bateman, *Gladiators*, pp. 20–25, for various measurements and calculations; for previous detailed work on size, see Bateman, "London Amphitheatre" (1997), pp. 69–73.

17 Milne points out, *Book of Roman London*, p. 71, that London was probably more densely populated in the early second century than for another 1000 years; and Perring comments, *Roman London*, pp. 73–75, on its prosperity then. See Perring's chapter 4, "The city in its prime (*c.* AD 100–150)," pp. 57–75.

18 Perring, *Roman London*, dates the amphitheatre's construction *c.* 120, as a provisional date, p. 63; the site was still being analyzed as he wrote his 1991 book. He also suggests, p. 35, the possibility of an earlier amphitheatre on the same site. Milne in 1995 asserts, *Book of Roman London*, pp. 53, 59–60, a rebuilding, between *c.* 90 and 120, of an earlier structure dating from after 70.

Bateman, "London Amphitheatre" (1997), has now reported, pp. 66–67, 70–71 AD as the definite date of initial construction and, p. 67, *c.* 125 as provisionally the date of the second construction phase. Both Perring, pp. 57–66, and Milne, e.g., p. 70, note the extensive public works program in Londinium *c.* 90–120; and, as noted above (n. 15), Bateman has suggested, "London Amphitheatre" (1997), p. 83, and *Gladiators*, p. 24, a possible link between the rebuilding of the amphitheatre and the 122 visit to Londinium of the Emperor Hadrian.

19 Bateman, "London Amphitheatre" (1997), p. 55.

20 Perring (*Roman London*, p. 61, fig. 26), Milne (*Book of Roman London*, p. 61, illustration 36), and Bateman ("London Amphitheatre" [1994], p. 166) provide slightly different plans of the overall amphitheatre. Bateman in "London Amphitheatre" (1997) provides plans (figs. 2, 3, 4, 5) of its various specific features.

21 Perring, *Roman London*, provides overall plans of Londinium, from *c.* 95 to *c.* 300 (figs. 15, 31, 40, 50), which include the amphitheatre location (see also Bateman, "London Amphitheatre" [1994], p. 166); Milne's amphitheatre plan (*Book of Roman London*, p. 61, illustration 36) places the amphitheatre in relation to the streets and buildings immediately around it today (see also Bateman, "London Amphitheatre" [1994], p. 164), and another broader plan (p. 121, illustration 80) places various surviving features of Londinium, including the amphitheatre, in relation to the modern city's street system.

22 See Bateman, "London Amphitheatre" (1997), pp. 78–82, who discusses earlier suggestions about the military associations of the amphitheatre (and military amphitheatres in general), and who also notes, p. 68, n. 90, that the fort may have remained in military use as late as *c.* 250 AD.

23 See Perring, *Roman London*, pp. 76–113. One notable mark of the turn from public to private concerns is the construction in the mid third century of a temple of Mithras: a private temple "dedicated to the mysteries of a cultic sect; a place where the initiated few could engage in rituals which set them apart from the rest of society" (pp. 104–105).

24 Bateman, "London Amphitheatre" (1997), p. 68.

25 The quotation is from p. 113 of Perring's *Roman London*. One logical explanation for the survival of the amphitheatre would be, of course, a need for such a location for communal entertainments on important civic occasions such as the suggested visits to Londinium by the Emperor Constantine in 310–312 and 314. For these possible visits, see Merrifield, *London*, pp. 209–210 (citing the work of John Casey).

26 Milne, *Book of Roman London*, pp. 87–88 (provisional findings); noted as possible by Bateman, "London Amphitheatre" (1997), p. 68, n. 90.

27 Bateman, *Gladiators*, p. 40.

28 See, e.g., Milne, *Book of Roman London*, pp. 17–18 (political troubles), 79–81 (Thames water-level changes), 88 (Roman administrative changes), 88–89, and Perring, *Roman London*, p. 130.

29 See Milne, *Book of Roman London*, especially pp. 88–89.

30 See, e.g., Wickham, *History*, p. 51, and chapter 2, following.

31 For the physical characteristics of the typical Roman theatre, see Brockett, *History*, pp. 61–64. Wacher, *Towns*, discusses, pp. 55–56 and 60, different types of Roman theatres found in Britain, and provides plans of several, pp. 57–59, as does also Guy de la Bédoyère, *The Buildings of Roman Britain* (London: B. T. Batsford, 1991), pp. 102–107.

32 Guy de la Bédoyère, *Roman Towns in Britain* (London: B. T. Batsford/English Heritage, 1992), p. 49, suggests that London might even have had two theatres, one being an odeon (a covered performance area) for events such as literary readings. Merrifield, *Atlas*, notes, p. 19, that at least one London theatre is likely.

33 Perring, e.g., has suggested, *Roman London*, p. 63, that a theatre might have been located in the area of the modern Knightrider St., as part of a religious complex; Roman theatres were commonly attached to religious complexes. See also T. F. C. Blagg, "Monumental Architecture in Roman London," in J. Bird, M. Hassall and H. Sheldon, eds., *Interpreting Roman London: Papers in Memory of Hugh Chapman*, Oxbow Monograph 58 (Oxford: Oxbow Books, 1996), p. 46. Nicholas Fuentes, "Some Entertainment in Londinium," *London Archaeologist* 5.6 (Spring 1986), 144–147, with reference above all to medieval urban topography has suggested the St. Andrew's Hill area as a theatre site. Tim Williams, however, in *The Archaeology of Roman London*, vol. 3: *Public Buildings in the South-West Quarter of Roman London*, CBA Research Report 88 (London: Museum of London and CBA, 1993), p. 28, has found no archaeological evidence of a theatre, though he does not entirely dismiss the possibility that one did exist. The recent archaeological link made generally between theatrical masks and brothels (see above, n. 7) also raises interesting questions about possible combinations of temples, religious rites, theatres, and prostitution (see, e.g., John Arthur Hanson, *Roman Theater-Temples* [Princeton: Princeton University Press, 1959], p. 16, and also de la Bédoyère, *Buildings*, p. 107).

34 In London, of course, given its present building density and past construction patterns, finding a Roman site such as a theatre presents considerable difficulties; numerous Roman sites in London will have been completely obliterated over the centuries, and others will still exist but under more recent buildings where exploratory excavations cannot be carried out. De la Bédoyère, *Buildings*, has suggested, p. 102, that British theatres largely may have been temporary structures built of timber and so now be difficult for archaeologists to trace; but one would expect a London theatre to have incorporated at least some stone, since the amphitheatre did.

35 G. D. Marsh, "Three 'theatre' Masks from London," *Britannia* 10 (1979), 263–265 (cited in *DTR* no. 877); the article is highly speculative, drawing on Continental examples, and the drawings provided show how fragmentary indeed are the mask pieces found.

36 It has been suggested both that the Walbrook was a recipient of votive offerings and that there were attempts to build up its banks by dumping rubbish collected from across London. See, e.g., Tony Wilmott, *Excavations in the Middle Walbrook Valley. City of London, 1927–1960* (LMAS Special Paper 13, 1991), pp. 170–171, Ralph Merrifield, "Roman Metalwork from the Walbrook – Rubbish, Ritual or Redundancy?" in *TLMAS* 46 (1995), 27–44, and Martin Millett, "Evaluating Roman London" [book review], *Archaeological Journal* 151 (1994), 429–430. See also above, nn. 7 and 33, which raise different questions about theatre-location speculations based solely or primarily on artefacts such as theatrical masks.

37 Morris, *Londinium*, p. 241, takes for granted the existence in London of what he calls a stadium; but by stadium he means what, following Humphrey, *Roman Circuses*, I here call a circus.

38 Humphrey, *Roman Circuses*, p. 3.

39 For the typical size of a circus, and the kinds of events normally held in one, see Humphrey, *Roman Circuses*, pp. 1–2, 71–72.

40 Humphrey, *Roman Circuses*, pp. 4–5.

41 Humphrey, *Roman Circuses*, pp. 295–296, 322, and 332–333 (on makeshift circuses in North Africa), 388, 428–437. See also de la Bédoyère, *Roman Towns*, pp. 50 and 52. Wacher, *Towns*, however, has proposed a possible circus in Wroxeter: see pp. 54, 61, and 375, and also Wacher, *Roman Britain*, pp. 291–292.

42 Humphrey, *Roman Circuses*, pp. 431–432. His chosen location involves archaeological remains proposed hesitantly by Morris, *Londinium*, p. 241, as those of a theatre. Fuentes has also suggested, "Some Entertainment," pp. 145–147, the Knightrider St. area.

43 See Williams, *Archaeology*, pp. 86–87. Merrifield in 1989 (*Atlas*, p. 19) still supports the possibility of a London circus.

44 See Brockett, *History*, p. 54. Wacher, *Roman Britain*, notes, p. 280, that readings, recitations, dancing, juggling, and acrobatics were customary Roman dinner entertainments.

2 LONDON c. 410–1200

1 See Allardyce Nicoll, *Masks Mimes and Miracles: Studies in the Popular Theatre* (London: George G. Harrap, 1931), pp. 135–213, and Wickham, *History*, pp. 56–65. An example of the opposite point of view is Grace Frank, *The Medieval French Drama* (Oxford: Clarendon Press, 1954; rpt. 1967), pp. 1–17: because she is concerned with the earlier Roman drama, e.g., Plautus' plays, and not with the later Roman theatre. Recent work such as Lawrence Clopper's "English Drama: From Ungodly *ludi* to Sacred Play," in David Wallace, ed., *The Cambridge History of Medieval English Literature* (Cambridge: Cambridge University Press, 1999), pp. 739–766, also does not so much disagree with Nicoll and Wickham as focus specifically on (religious) plays rather than on broadly-defined (secular) theatre (though Clopper suggests the latter was merely games,

sports, and parodic activities); indeed Clopper views religious plays as having developed in part in opposition to a secular, irreligious tradition of festive games-playing.

2 In any discussion of pre-medieval and early medieval theatre, it is difficult to distinguish between "theatre" and non-theatrical entertainment; the same performers juggled, danced, sang, and role-played in a variety of ways, and society did not then distinguish, as we try to do now, among the various kinds of "games." For a useful treatment of this issue of game-playing, see Glynne Wickham, *The Medieval Theatre*, 3rd edn. (Cambridge: Cambridge University Press, 1987), pp. 2–4; and John Southworth, in *The English Medieval Minstrel* (Woodbridge, Suffolk, and Wolfeboro, NH: Boydell Press, 1989), deals with English early medieval entertainment in general rather than attempting distinctions.

3 Significant specific evidence of the survival in (or reintroduction into) Britain of Roman playing-place traditions, for example, is a seventh-century theatre of the Northumbrian kings, at Yeavering (Northumberland), modelled on a Roman theatre. See *DTR* no. 1554.

4 See, e.g., Gustav Milne, ed., *From Roman Basilica to Medieval Market: Archaeology in Action in the City of London* (London: HMSO, 1992), p. 38.

5 Brian Hobley, "Lundenwic and Lundenburh: Two Cities Rediscovered," in Richard Hodges and Brian Hobley, *The Rebirth of Towns in the West AD 700–1050* (CBA Research Report 68, 1988), p. 69; Alan Vince, ed., *Aspects of Saxo-Norman London: II. Finds and Environmental Evidence* (LMAS Special Paper 12, 1989), p. 409.

6 See Hobley, "Lundenwic," p. 69; Alan Vince, *Saxon London: An Archaeological Investigation*, The Archaeology of London Series (London: Seaby, 1990), pp. 59, 61–62; Martin Biddle, "A City in Transition: 400–800," in *Atlas*, p. 22. Both Hobley, "Lundenwic," p. 69, and Vince, *Aspects*, p. 412, note the seventh-century practice by Saxon kings of giving abandoned Roman forts and towns to religious communities.

7 See, e.g., Hobley, "Lundenwic," p. 73, Vince, *Aspects*, pp. 413–414, Biddle, *Atlas*, pp. 22–23, and Vince, *Saxon London*, pp. 54–56; see also Tony Dyson and John Schofield, "Saxon London," in Jeremy Haslam, ed., *Anglo-Saxon Towns In Southern England* (Chichester: Phillimore, 1984), pp. 307–308. Biddle argues for a royal enclave ongoing from the time of the Roman withdrawal, and calls the Saxon Lundenwic (pp. 27–28) one part of a dual entity, the other part being the walled (royal and ecclesiastical) Lundonia, as he names it. Lyn Blackmore concurs; see "From Beach to Burh: New Clues to Entity and Identity in 7th- to 9th-century London," in Guy De Boe and Frans Verhaeghe, eds., *Urbanism in Medieval Europe*, Papers of the 'Medieval Europe Brugge 1997' Conference, vol. 1 (Zellik: Institute for the Archaeological Heritage, 1997), p. 130.

8 See, e.g., Dyson and Schofield, "Saxon London," p. 287, and Brian Hobley, *Roman and Saxon London: A Reappraisal* (London: Museum of London, 1986), p. 18.

9 See, e.g., Biddle, *Atlas*, pp. 23, 27, and Hobley, *Roman and Saxon London*, p. 18.
10 See Biddle, *Atlas*, pp. 23–24.
11 See Nicholas Bateman, "The London Amphitheatre," *Current Archaeology* 137 [12.5] (Feb./Mar. 1994), 170–171, and Ralph Merrifield, "Roman London," in *Atlas*, p. 19. As in the preceding chapter, Bateman's *Gladiators at the Guildhall: The Story of London's Roman Amphitheatre and Medieval Guildhall* (London: Museum of London Archaeology Service, 2000) should also be consulted for the most recent information on (and illustrations of) the Roman amphitheatre site, in this case past the Roman period. Archaeological analysis in this area, as for the Roman period, is ongoing, and in another three to four years a great deal more should be known.
12 See Biddle, *Atlas*, pp. 23–24, who writes that this "imposition of one place of public assembly [the Guildhall] over another is remarkable," and points out that in other parts of the former Roman empire public buildings, even when in ruins, remained public sites down into the early Middle Ages. Francis Sheppard, *London: A History* (Oxford: Oxford University Press, 1998), pp. 60–61 (and see also p. 78), cites and agrees with Biddle.
13 Bateman, *Current Archaeology*, p. 171; and see also Dyson and Schofield, "Saxon London," pp. 307–308.
14 Bateman, *Current Archaeology*, p. 171.
15 Biddle, *Atlas*, p. 24.
16 Bateman, *Gladiators*, p. 40; also personal communication to this author, Oct. 2000.
17 Gina Porter, "An Early Medieval Settlement at Guildhall, City of London," in Guy De Boe and Frans Verhaeghe, eds., *Urbanism in Medieval Europe*, Papers of the 'Medieval Europe Brugge 1997' Conference, vol. 1 (Zellik: Institute for the Archaeological Heritage, 1997), p. 148; Bateman, *Gladiators*, pp. 40–41, 46.
18 See Milne, *Medieval Market*, pp. 34–35, though Vince, *Saxon London*, pp. 18–20 and 25, declines to assume that the raids were the cause of the settlement's location change. Blackmore, "From Beach to Burh," has recently suggested, pp. 130–131, that the resettlement was gradual.
19 See Gustav Milne, "King Alfred's Plan for London?" *London Archaeologist* 6.8 (Autumn 1990), 206.
20 Bateman, *Current Archaeology*, p. 170, with a Saxon building plan provided on p. 171; Porter, "An early medieval settlement," pp. 148–150.
21 Bateman, *Current Archaeology*, pp. 167–170, including a plan, p. 167, of the medieval Guildhall area.
22 See Porter, "An Early Medieval Settlement," p. 149.
23 For the dates of Cheapside's origin (certainly by 1104 and perhaps by *c.* 1067 or even earlier), see *Atlas*, Gazetteer, s.v. Cheppes syed. Brooke, *Atlas*, p. 33, suggests Cheapside may even date back to the ninth century; Nightingale, p. 28, does not think this likely. Tim Tatton-Brown, "The Topography of Anglo-Saxon London," *Antiquity* 60 (1986), 26, states that it was probably created in the tenth century.

24 Vince, *Saxon London*, pp. 17, 25.

25 See Vince, *Saxon London*, pp. 61–62.

26 Vince, *Saxon London*, p. 13, points out that, despite the 604 Lundenwic reference by Bede in his eighth-century *Ecclesiastical History of the English Nation*, we cannot be sure of when in the seventh century Lundenwic began to flourish as an international port. Hobley, "Lundenwic," p. 70, assumes Bede is talking about Lundenwic as a trading centre in the early eighth century, but points out other evidence for it as a trading centre by the late seventh century. Derek Keene, summarizing recent Lundenwic scholarship in "London in the Early Middle Ages 600–1300," *London Journal* 20.2 (1995), 9–21, comments (p. 10) "it has become apparent that in its complexity and market orientation . . . [Lundenwic's trade] probably . . . resembled city commerce in the central and later Middle Ages."

27 The norm of the solitary travelling entertainer is perhaps best represented by the probably apocryphal story of Alfred the Great, disguised as a minstrel performing interludes and songs, visiting the camp of the invading Vikings, in the late ninth century, to gain knowledge of their battle plans. See *DTR*'s doubtful record no. 1758. Southworth, *English Medieval Minstrel*, warns, pp. 2–3, against the popular image today of the minstrel as a wanderer, although certainly medieval minstrels travelled.

28 Wickham, *History*, pp. 56–57, points out the continuing importance, before the major urbanization of Britain, of festivals tied to the seasonal rhythms of the agricultural year, and discusses, pp. 60–62, Church efforts to Christianize annual non-Christian events such as midsummer ritual celebrations. Midsummer festivities in the London area continued to involve traditional pre-Christian elements, such as bonfires (in the streets) and representations of giants (carried in procession), into the 1540s; for the fifteenth to sixteenth-century London Midsummer Watch, see below, chapter 9.

29 From the tenth century, London was perhaps the largest town in England, with "remarkable" eleventh-century growth and much wealth (Keene, "London," pp. 11–12). Nightingale discusses, pp. 6–19, London's tenth-century and early eleventh-century international trade; and see also John Schofield, *The Building of London from the Conquest to the Great Fire*, 3rd edn. (Phoenix Mill, Gloucestershire: Sutton, 1999), pp. 32–33, for London's power and wealth by 1000. For the invasions, see Vince, *Saxon London*, pp. 30–32.

30 For the folkmoot, see Biddle, *Atlas*, p. 24, who also points out a possible relationship between the folkmoot, the amphitheatre, and the civic Court of Husting (indoor assembly), the court meeting in the medieval period in the Guildhall but first "reliably" mentioned in 1032 and probably then simply with a new Danish name for a much older institution. (Biddle suggests that this court and its ancestor[s] were perhaps based in the old Roman amphitheatre; and Porter, "An Early Medieval Settlement," has suggested, pp. 151–152, that the eleventh-century settlement in the amphitheatre area may have been Danish. For further discussion of Danish settlement in eleventh-century London, see Bateman, *Gladiators*, pp. 59–61.) See also

Christopher N. L. Brooke, assisted by Gillian Keir, *London 800–1216: The Shaping of a City* (London: Secker and Warburg, 1975), p. 249.

31 I omit the thorny problem of the relationship between theatre and the Christian liturgy. See, e.g., Axton, *European Drama*, chapter 4, pp. 61–74.

32 See *DTR* nos. 191 (679: bishops and clerics in England are ordered not to allow "jocos vel ludos" before them), 192 (799: Alcuin refers in a letter to "spectacula et diabolica figmenta"), 193 (9th–10th centuries: attack on pagan practices such as "lusa diabolica"), 197 (1005–07: the Archbishop of York requires the secular clergy to abstain from heathen songs and "deofles zamena" on feast days). Clopper, "English Drama," has recently argued that all such terminology refers to sports and games (secular or religiously-parodic).

33 See *DTR* nos. 194–196. William Tydeman, for example, indicates in *The Theatre in the Middle Ages: Western European Stage Conditions c. 800–1576* (Cambridge: Cambridge University Press, 1978), p. 26, the difficulty in believing that none of this terminology was related to what we might call theatre, although he also discusses, pp. 185–188, its non-specificity in relation to performers.

34 In the twelfth century, e.g., John of Salisbury in his *Policraticus*, dedicated to Thomas Becket, wrote with (much-)qualified approval of the drama of Plautus, Menander, and Terence, while entirely condemning the frivolous theatre of his own day (although stories and spectacles of virtue and utility were acceptable). See *Frivolities of Courtiers and Footprints of Philosophers. Being a Translation of the First, Second, and Third Books and Selections from the Seventh and Eighth Books of the 'Policraticus' of John of Salisbury*, ed. and tr. Joseph B. Pike (Minneapolis/London: University of Minnesota Press/Humphrey Milford, Oxford University Press, 1938), book 1, chapter 8 (pp. 36–39). For the Latin text of chapter 8, see John of Salisbury, *Policraticus* I–IV, ed. K. S. B. Keats-Rohan, Corpus Christianorum, Continuatio Mediaevalis 118 (Turnholt: Brepols, 1993), pp. 52–55.

35 For the founding date(s) of Westminster Abbey, see Vince, *Saxon London*, pp. 66–67.

36 See Vince, *Saxon London*, p. 65. Sheppard, *London: A History*, p. 76, speaks of a "tremendous concentration of religious foundations" in the London area by the twelfth century. The contents of medieval British religious libraries demonstrate Church knowledge of Roman drama; *DTR* no. 1526 notes, e.g., for the eleventh century, a MS of Terence in a list from Keynsham Abbey, Somerset, which was perhaps originally from Worcester Priory; and by the twelfth and thirteenth centuries we have records of at least six more MSS of Roman drama in ecclesiastical libraries in Britain (see *DTR* nos. 421, 491, 619, 1297, 1341, 1350).

37 See: *DTR* nos. 1493–4 and its Dramatic Texts, nos. 3–4 (tenth century: tropes, Winchester) and no. 5 (11th century); no. 616 and Dramatic Texts, no. 6 (early twelfth century: a St. Katherine play, probably for Henry I at Kingsbury Regis); no. 673 (late twelfth century: an Easter play, Eynsham);

no. 843 and Dramatic Texts, no. 12 (late twelfth century: Christmas and Easter drama, Lichfield); and also doubtful items nos. 1759 and 1761 (an early twelfth-century Easter play at Malmesbury and late twelfth-century miracle plays supposedly seen by Henry II near Dublin). Also no. 620 and Dramatic Texts, no. 9 (mid twelfth century: a dramatic dialogue). An eighth-century fragmentary Harrowing of Hell dialogue is listed (Dramatic Texts, no. 1, and no. 1756) as doubtfully a dramatic text.

38 Vince, *Saxon London*, pp. 72, 75–76; Vince, *Aspects*, p. 429.

39 See Schofield, *Building of London*, pp. 41–50, who discusses (pp. 37–56) London building in general from *c.* 1066 to 1200, and also his *Medieval London Houses* (New Haven and London: Yale University Press for the Paul Mellon Centre for Studies in British Art, 1994), p. 14.

40 See Brooke, *Atlas*, p. 30.

41 For an excellent overall treatment of London's wealth, and of its close connections (economic, political, administrative, personal) with the Crown at this time, see Nightingale, chapters 2 and 3, *passim* (pp. 23–60). Brooke's general history of the city 800–1200, in *Atlas*, pp. 30–41, is also extremely useful.

42 R. H. Britnell, *The Commercialisation of English Society 1000–1500* (Cambridge: Cambridge University Press, 1993), pp. 8 and 167.

43 See Brooke and Keir, *London 800–1216*, pp. 278–282. A Pipe Roll list of 1179–80 includes nineteen guilds of various kinds, the wealthiest being the Goldsmiths'. See also George Unwin, *The Gilds and Companies of London* (London: Methuen, 1908), pp. 47–55.

44 Brooke and Keir, *London 800–1216*, p. 121.

45 See Brooke, *Atlas*, p. 38 (citing Fitz Stephen, see below); see also Schofield, *Building of London*, pp. 52–56 (specifically on the houses), and also his *Medieval London Houses*, p. 34. Chris Phillpotts, "The Metropolitan Palaces of Medieval London," *London Archaeologist* 9.2 (Autumn 1999), 47–53, describes in detail the late twelfth-century residence in Southwark of the bishops of Winchester; and Caroline M. Barron includes some twelfth-century material in her "Centres of Conspicuous Consumption: The Aristocratic Town House in London 1200–1550," *London Journal* 20.1 (1995), 1–16.

46 *Atlas*, Gazetteer, s.v. London Bridge.

47 See *DTR* no. 673, and its Playing Places and Buildings, no. 22.

48 Brooke and Keir, *London 800–1200*, p. 121.

49 *DTR* no. 878.

50 William Fitz Stephen, "Descriptio Londoniae," tr. H. E. Butler ("A Description of London"), in F. M. Stenton, *Norman London: An Essay*, new edn. (London: Historical Association Leaflets 93–94, 1934), p. 30.

51 Brooke, e.g., in *Atlas* calls Fitz Stephen's *Description* "a picture inflated with rhetoric and mythology," and showing Fitz Stephen's "hazy knowledge of classical models" (p. 39), but then goes on to accept Fitz Stephen's information as largely correct. John Scattergood has recently placed Fitz Stephen's work, more precisely, in a tradition of written "city laudation" going back

to classical times; Fitz Stephen's description is deliberately (and intertextu-
ally) laudatory in its foci and emphases; but it is not to be disbelieved in
terms of information, only to be approached with care in terms of information selection and presentation. See Scattergood's "Misrepresenting the
City: Genre, Intertextuality and William FitzStephen's *Description of London*
(c. 1173)," in Julia Boffey and Pamela King, eds., *London and Europe in the Later
Middle Ages*, Westfield Publications in Medieval Studies 9 (London: Centre
for Medieval and Renaissance Studies, Queen Mary and Westfield College,
University of London, 1995), pp. 1–34.

52 It is also certain that performances of miracles and martyrdoms would
have provided the opportunity for – though need not have used – Roman-
like spectacle and violence. They may have been of special interest to Fitz
Stephen in this *Description* because of its context: Fitz Stephen's life of (martyr
and saint) Thomas Becket.

53 Schofield, *Medieval London Houses*, p. 14.

54 *DTR* no. 879; see *The Chronicle of Richard of Devizes of the Time of King Richard
the First*, ed. and tr. John T. Appleby (London: Thomas Nelson and Sons,
1963), pp. 65–66: "whatever evil or malicious thing that can be found in any
part of the world, you will find in that one city [London]. Do not associate
with the crowds of pimps; do not mingle with the throngs in eating-houses;
avoid dice and gambling, the theatre and the tavern. . . . Actors, jesters,
smooth-skinned lads, Moors, flatterers, pretty boys, effeminates, pederasts,
singing and dancing girls, quacks, belly-dancers, sorceresses, extortioners,
night-wanderers, magicians, mimes, beggars, buffoons: all this tribe fill all
the houses. Therefore, if you do not want to dwell with evildoers, do not
live in London." Although the term "histriones," translated by Appleby as
"actors," could be used to refer not just to actors but also more broadly to
general-purpose entertainers, the separate naming of mimes, jesters, etc.,
would seem to indicate that the author is differentiating among different
types of entertainers.

55 Further complicating our use of Devizes, however, is the fact that his narrative is likely tongue-in-cheek (the one city of which the villain approves,
Winchester, is where the young man he is warning is subsequently mur-
dered); and also Devizes may slyly be reproducing, for parodic purposes,
merely a list of the typical moral objects of Christian social attack, and so
not be dealing after all with the actualities of twelfth-century London. Recently Scattergood, "Misrepresenting the City," has stated (p. 9) that part of
Devizes' list of evildoers is based on Horace's *Satires*, I.ii.1–3: although if
Horace is Devizes' part-source, Devizes is considerably expanding and
recontextualizing Horace's brief list of flute girls, pedlars, mendicants, fe-
male mimes, and buffoons, all of whom mourn the death of the generous
Tigellius. See Horace, *Satires I*, ed. and tr. P. Michael Brown (Warminster:
Aris and Phillips, 1993), p. 27.

56 For the texts of these two plays, both in the original Anglo-Norman and
in English translation, and for useful introductions to them, see David

Bevington, ed. and tr., *Medieval Drama* (Boston: Houghton Mifflin, 1975). Quotations are from *Adam*, pp. 94 and 105. A brief discussion of the sophistication and appeal of both plays, in their twelfth-century context, is also found in Richard Axton and John Stevens, eds. and trs., *Medieval French Plays* (Oxford: Basil Blackwell, 1971), pp. xiii–xvi; and Axton also treats *Adam* at length in his *European Drama*, pp. 112–130, as does M. Dominica Legge in *Anglo-Norman Literature and its Background* (Oxford: Clarendon Press, 1963), pp. 312–321.

57 Two examples of Anglo-Norman civic record-keeping, though from past the twelfth century, are the early city Letter Books, A to L (1276–*c.* 1498), which contain a good deal of Anglo-Norman, and the earliest extant accounts of the Mercers' Company (MS Wardens' Accounts 1347–1464), which are largely in Anglo-Norman. (For the 1276 date, see chapter 3, n. 11.)

58 See Bevington, *Medieval Drama*, pp. 78 and 122, Axton and Stevens, *Medieval French Plays*, pp. 3 and 47, Legge, *Anglo-Norman Literature*, pp. 321–328, and Lynette Muir (who does not, however, accept *Adam* as significantly English), "Medieval English Drama: The French Connection," in Marianne G. Briscoe and John C. Coldewey, eds., *Contexts for Early English Drama* (Bloomington and Indianapolis: Indiana University Press, 1989), pp. 57–58. Bevington translates the Paris MS text of *Holy Resurrection* (fourteenth-century Bibliothèque Nationale MS fr. 902), and *Medieval French Plays*, the longer Canterbury one (BL Add. MS. 45103). Elizabeth Salter, *English and International: Studies in the Literature, Art and Patronage of Medieval England*, ed. Derek Pearsall and Nicolette Zeeman (Cambridge: Cambridge University Press, 1988), p. 31, notes that for most of the thirteenth century French was the dominant literary language in England.

59 Axton, e.g., in *European Drama* suggests, p. 113, performance of *Adam* possibly at a cathedral school (in northern France or in southern England).

60 Axton and Stevens have noted, e.g., in *Medieval French Plays*, that it is "clear from the existence of these two plays [*Adam* and *Holy Resurrection*] that there was a fully developed vernacular religious drama in England in the second half of the twelfth century" (p xiii). For twelfth-century England as international generally in its culture, see Salter's first chapter (in *English and International*), pp. 4–28.

61 A notable production took place at New York's The Cloisters (of the Metropolitan Museum of Art) in Jan. 1958, by the New York Pro Musica under the direction of Noah Greenberg. See Noah Greenberg, ed., *The Play of Daniel* (New York: Oxford University Press, 1959), esp. p. ix.

62 All three are edited and translated in Bevington's *Medieval Drama* anthology.

63 Two fifteenth-century surviving examples of saint plays are the lengthy Digby *Mary Magdalene* and the Croxton *Play of the Sacrament*, both in Bevington's *Medieval Drama* anthology. Saint plays became an endangered species in England at the Reformation, and very few of such texts from any pre-Reformation period have survived. An early twelfth-century play of

St. Katherine has been recorded, probably for performance before
Henry II: see *DTR* no. 616 (under Dunstable, Bedfordshire).

64 John of Salisbury's condemnation of contemporary actors, mimes, and the
like, in his 1159 *Policraticus*, does not mention London but would seem to
point broadly to an active secular entertainment profession (including
jesters, jugglers, and storytellers) in twelfth-century England (and therefore
surely including London): although John's statements are very general, and
Nicoll, *Masks Mimes and Miracles*, suggests (p. 151) that he is working from
classical literature rather than from experience. See Pike's translation, *Frivolities of Courtiers*, pp. 36–39, for John of Salisbury's text, and pp. 3–4 for his
life (he spent some twenty years in Canterbury).

65 See *DTR*, Dramatic Texts, no. 10, and Keith Bate, ed., *Three Latin Comedies*,
Toronto Medieval Latin Texts 6 (Toronto: Centre for Medieval Studies and
Pontifical Institute of Medieval Studies, 1976), introduction, pp. 1–2, 7–8,
and text, pp. 35–60. Axton, *European Drama*, pp. 29–30, argues for recitation
and mime. For extensive information on Map see the *Dictionary of National
Biography*, ed. Leslie Stephen and Sidney Lee, 22 vols. (Oxford: Oxford University Press, 1921–22; rpt. 1963–64), XII. 994–997.

66 Nightingale notes, p. 375, e.g., that the London Grocers from the twelfth
century had three good city schools where their sons could learn French
and Latin.

67 *Babio* has three characters and perhaps a separate presenter: resulting in a
cast size, if performed rather than recited by one narrator, equal to those of
the plays routinely performed before London guild audiences in the fifteenth and sixteenth centuries (see below, chapters 4 and 5).

68 See *DTR*, Dramatic Texts, no. 16, and J. A. W. Bennett and G. V. Smithers,
eds., *Early Middle English Verse and Prose* (Oxford: Clarendon Press, 1966),
pp. 77–95 (introduction and text for *Dame Sirith*), especially pp. 78–79 on
likely performance. Axton believes (*European Drama*, pp. 21–22) that the text
requires both a solo human performer and a performing dog.

69 We also have what is doubtless a fragment of a religious play, dealing with
a king and his messenger; see *DTR*, Dramatic Texts, no. 20, and Norman
Davis, ed., *Non-Cycle Plays and Fragments* (EETS, Supplementary Texts 1,
1970), pp. 116–117.

70 See *DTR*, Dramatic Texts, no. 19. Bennett and Smithers, *Early Middle
English Verse and Prose*, provide an introduction and text (pp. 196–200), call it
"the oldest secular play extant in English" (p. 196), and suggest (p. 79) that
Dame Sirith may be its specific source. Axton, *European Drama*, pp. 19–21, believes *Interludium* to have been acted by several performers, perhaps between
the courses of a banquet.

71 For French texts, see Axton and Stevens, *Medieval French Plays*.

72 Interludes had both elite and popular audiences; see Bennett and Smithers,
Early Middle English Verse and Prose, p. 196, who also equate English interludes
with French farces in this period.

73 See above, n. 41, and especially Brooke, *Atlas*, pp. 31–32.

74 See Fitz Stephen, in Stenton's *Norman London*, p. 30, and also Brooke, *Atlas*, pp. 34 and 39, and Nightingale, p. 45.

3 LONDON 1200–1410

1 See *DTR* nos. 205, 208–11, 367, 422, 513–14, 539–40, 582, 626, 670, 822, 870–71, 1237, 1371, 1408, 1506, 1535, 1584, 1601; 1342, 1602; 848; 1241; 1604; 375, 1218, 1473, 1556; 684. See also nos. 360, 403, 516, 765, 1364, 1763, and J. Alan B. Somerset, ed., *Shropshire*, REED (Toronto: University of Toronto Press, 1994), 1.10–11 (singers), 73–74 ("ludos alios inhonestos").

2 For more about the uncertainties and inconsistencies of performance nomenclature in this period than has already been indicated in chapter 2, see, e.g., William Tydeman, *The Theatre in the Middle Ages: Western European Stage Conditions c. 800–1576* (Cambridge: Cambridge University Press, 1978), pp. 17–19, 26.

3 For a detailed look at thirteenth-century London, although with a focus on the London Pepperers (later Grocers), see Nightingale, chapters 4 (pp. 61–80) and 5 (pp. 81–107). Christopher Brooke, *Atlas*, pp. 31–32, summarizes the city's economy and trade 800–1270, stating, p. 30, that by 1270 London was one of the major commercial capitals of north-west Europe. John Schofield, *The Building of London from the Conquest to the Great Fire*, 3rd edn. (Phoenix Mill, Gloucestershire: Sutton, 1999), discusses, pp. 59–79, London's material constructions.

4 *DTR* nos. 1148, 1149.

5 See Caroline M. Barron, "Centres of Conspicuous Consumption: The Aristocratic Town House in London 1200–1550," *London Journal* 20.1 (1995), 1–16, who discusses the town house phenomenon and the lavish spending associated with it, and mentions records of musicians hired, though not records of any other entertainers and not specifically in relation to the thirteenth century.

6 William Fitz Stephen, "Descriptio Londoniae," tr. H. E. Butler ("A Description of London"), in F. M. Stenton, *Norman London: An Essay*, new edn. (London: Historical Association Leaflets 93–4, 1934), p. 30. Thrupp, *London*, suggests (see pp. 1–2) that itinerant entertainers would have moved in and out of London with the waves of visitors for law terms, parliaments, etc. See also *EES*, 1.181–185, on groups of entertainers, especially in the fourteenth century.

7 The higher population estimate (of "80,000 or more inhabitants, twice the traditional estimate") is Derek Keene's; see his "London in the Early Middle Ages 600–1300," *London Journal* 20.2 (1995), 12, citing his own recent work. Nightingale, however, argues, pp. 194–195, for the more traditional, lower estimate in the years following 1320 (which she sees as involving a population reduction from the earlier fourteenth century). At 100,000, London would have been about the size of Florence: see Keene, *Cheapside before the Great Fire* (Economic and Social Research Council, 1985), pp. 19–20.

8 See, e.g., Gervase Rosser, *Medieval Westminster 1200–1540* (Oxford: Clarendon Press, 1989), pp. 16–17, 20, 36–37, who also provides information (pp. 16–32) on the late twelfth and early thirteenth-century settling in Westminster of court officials and lords; and see also S. B. Chrimes, *An Introduction to the Administrative History of Mediaeval England* (Oxford: Basil Blackwell, 1952; 3rd edn. 1966), especially pp. 31–32, 48, 198, and Barron, *Atlas*, p. 42.

9 See *Atlas*, Gazetteer, s.v. King's Wardrobe, and Francis Sheppard, *London: A History* (Oxford: Oxford University Press, 1998), p. 99.

10 See Williams, p. 193, and George Unwin, *The Gilds and Companies of London* (London: Methuen, 1908), pp. 51–52.

11 In *Cal. LB A*, Sharpe uses the starting date of 1275 for the manuscript because he is using the designation 1275–76 for the period modern-dated 1 January–24 March 1276. The same is true for LB B; Sharpe's *Cal. LB B* title dates are *c.* 1275–1312.

12 See below, e.g., on the London puy, the late thirteenth-century statutes of which are preserved in the early fourteenth-century *Liber Custumarum*; and see Hugo Deadman and Elizabeth Scudder, eds., *An Introductory Guide to the Corporation of London Records Office* (London: Corporation of London, 1994): a listing of custumals, with dates and contents, is on pp. 9–11. The other kinds of city records surviving for the thirteenth century and earlier – charters, deeds, wills, pleas in the Court of Husting and Mayor's Court, and other legal documents – would not be expected, except perhaps at very infrequent intervals, to include information about civic theatre; and although, therefore, some few potentially important items might in the end be found among such documents, the amount of MS material extant has precluded, for the present, a check of all but the printed calendars (where these exist) of such sources.

13 See above, chapter 2, p. 31 and n. 43; also Unwin, *Gilds and Companies*, pp. 47–65.

14 Company ordinance books – containing regulatory bylaws – are also a potential source of information on company theatrical activities (since the social/religious/fraternal aspects of the companies are normally included); but I have found, to date, no theatrically relevant company ordinances before the fifteenth century, when such ordinances do become an important information source. Charters, being general legal documents, are most unlikely to be relevant: although, to be sure, I have examined company charters as well. Given the quantities of documents involved and the law of diminishing returns, I have not also searched through company property deeds, wills, and the like (as noted in the Introduction), except where pointed to an individual item by another source; the theatrically important documents from such categories thus remain to be found.

15 For palace and abbey see, e.g., Brooke, *Atlas*, p. 37, and Sheppard, *London: A History*, p. 68. Derek Keene notes ("London," p. 15) the abbey's importance to English kings from the thirteenth century on.

16 The Bridge House manuscripts covering the late fourteenth century are the Bridgemasters' account rolls 1381–1405.

17 The Goldsmiths unusually have combined wardens' accounts and court minutes, from 1334 (Goldsmiths' MS 1518 is the earliest of such volumes); normally the two kinds of records are kept in separate MSS. The Grocers' so-called Black Book (GL MS 11570) contains various company membership lists, ordinances, memoranda, and (incomplete) accounts 1345–46 to 1462–63. The Mercers' earliest MS accounts (Wardens' Accounts 1347–1464) begin *c.* 1392–94, with one earlier year, 1347, also included; and a MS of the accounts of the Merchant Taylors (GL MS 34048/1) begins at the century's end, in 1398–99.

18 Its port was assessed in the mid fourteenth century, e.g., at over three times as much as that of its nearest English rival, Bristol (see Gustav Milne, ed., *From Roman Basilica to Medieval Market: Archaeology in Action in the City of London* [London: HMSO, 1992], p. 130).

19 See Nightingale, pp. 138–163.

20 Nightingale, p. 194.

21 For the text of the puy's articles, see *MG*, II.1 (*Liber Custumarum*), pp. 216–228, trans. in II.2, pp. 579–94.

22 For information on both puys in general and the London puy in particular, I am almost entirely indebted to Anne F. Sutton, "Merchants, Music and Social Harmony: the London Puy and its French and London Contexts, circa 1300," *London Journal* 17.1 (1992), 1–17. Sutton notes, p. 2, that the articles of London's puy are the oldest to survive for any puy.

23 The sophisticated secular plays of mid-to-late thirteenth century Arras writer, musical composer, and (Sutton, p. 3) puy member Adam de la Halle are discussed in detail by Axton, *European Drama*, pp. 140–158, who notes, p. 140, their appeal to both courtly and popular audiences. De la Halle did not hesitate to tackle political topics in his work: as in his satiric *Le Jeu de la Feuillée*.

24 For additional possible reasons for its demise, relating to the individuals who were some of the puy's important members, see Sutton's "The *Tumbling Bear* and its Patrons: A Venue for the London Puy and Mercery," in Julia Boffey and Pamela King, eds., *London and Europe in the Later Middle Ages*, Westfield Publications in Medieval Studies 9 (London: Centre for Medieval and Renaissance Studies, Queen Mary and Westfield College, University of London, 1995), pp. 85–110. (Sutton here suggests London taverns in the Mercers' area of Cheapside as possible venues for the puy.)

25 Barron, *Atlas*, pp. 42–43.

26 See *Atlas*, Gazetteer, s.v. Guildhall Chapel, and Sutton, "Merchants," p. 4; one relevant city record is found in LB E, verso of first original unnumbered leaf. Williams, p. 60, notes the special association of the Mercers with this chapel.

27 Unlike a number of other scholars (see, for some examples, Suzanne R. Westfall, *Patrons and Performance: Early Tudor Household Revels* [Oxford: Clarendon Press, 1990], p. 33, n. 21), I do not attempt to distinguish

between these two terms but consider them to refer to the same kinds of activities, with "disguising" as the more "elite" term (though not invariably so). Westfall notes the medieval and early Tudor blurring of such terms.

28 1334 – LB E, f. 2*r, 14 Dec.; 1352 – LB G, f. 2r [30 Nov.-Dec.].

29 For example: 1370 – LB G, f. 262r (no one with a visor or false face is to walk the streets or to enter people's houses to play at dice) [Dec.]; 1372 – LB G, f. 298r, 24 Dec.; 1376 – LB H, f. 54r [Dec.].

30 LB H, f. 127v.

31 LB H, f. 224r.

32 See, e.g., LB H, ff. 138v–139r, 8 Jan. 1382.

33 Wearing visors to play at dice or for any other reason was also generally forbidden, not only in a Christmas-season prohibition, in 1378; see LB H, f. 98v; and in 1512 a national statute prohibited persons from disguising themselves as mummers (*DTR* no. 266). Mumming ceases to be specified in the usual Letter Book Christmas-season "false faces" prohibitions after 1387, until 1418, when an English version of the prohibition for that year replaces the formulaic Latin one used from *c.* 1404, and also adds plays and interludes as part of the problem: "no man*ere* pe*r*sone . . . be so hardy in eny wyse to walk by nyght in eny man*ere* mo*m*myng/pleyes/enter-ludes/or eny oþer disgisynges with eny feynyd berdis peyntid visers disfourmyd or colourid visages in eny wyse . . ." (LB I, f. 223r). Jor. 1 (beginning in Oct. 1416) includes in 1417 a Christmas-season explicit mumming prohibition (as well as a separate prohibition of visors and false faces); see f. 41r.

34 The palace was demolished in 1531 to provide materials for Whitehall (*DTR*, Playing Places and Buildings, no. 70).

35 See *A-ND*, s.v. debler, = "devil(?)". This phrase is quoted.

36 Any processional riding from Cheapside to London Bridge would presumably have followed the city's major entry route in reverse: from Cheapside through Poultry and Cornhill, and down Gracechurch St. to the Bridge; see below, 3, Royal and Other Entries, pp. 46–47.

37 See *Anon. Chronicle*, pp. 102–103, and also Stow, *Survey*, I.96–97, Kingsford's note (to Stow's *Survey* description), II.283, and E. K. Chambers, *The Mediaeval Stage*, 2 vols. (Oxford: Oxford University Press, 1903), I.394–395. After the dice play, the prince called for wine and minstrels, and the prince and courtiers danced on one side, and the mummers on the other. Wickham, *EES*, III.49, suggests a 1 or 6 Jan. date, because of the gift-giving involved.

38 See *DTR*, Playing Companies to 1558, no. 302, and also no. 224 (for Richard's favour towards mummers).

39 Mercers' MS Wardens' Accounts 1347–1464, f. 12r; Caroline M. Barron, "The Quarrel of Richard II with London 1392–7," in F. R. H. Du Boulay and Caroline M. Barron, eds., *The Reign of Richard II: Essays in Honour of May McKisack* (London: University of London, Athlone Press, 1971), p. 195 and n. 91; see also Malverne, p. 278 (around Epiphany Londoners came

with "glorioso apparatu," and presented the king with a dromedary with a boy sitting on top of it, and a bird also to the queen). (See also *Westminster Chronicle*, pp. 510–511; the editors suggest, p. 511, n. 4, with thanks to Dr. Diana Greenway, that the bird was a pelican.) London ironmonger Gilbert Maghfeld made a loan of 40s – to his company or to the city? – for mumming expenses: see Edith Rickert, "Extracts from a Fourteenth-Century Account Book," *Modern Philology* 24 (1926–27), 117.

40 Malverne, p. 281 ("diverso apparatu," dancing, singing); a longer description in the *Westminster Chronicle* notes, pp. 516–517, choruses, songs, and "a mock ship remarkably crammed with spices and other gifts."

41 Mercers' MS Wardens' Accounts 1347–1464, f. 19v; the location of the mumming is not specified either. The particular account including the mumming expenses (without itemization) is for the accounting year 24 June 1395 to 24 June 1396; the Mercers pay more than twice as much as for the Christmas-time 1392–93 mumming at Eltham.

42 See *A Chronicle*, p. 87; also Stow, *Survey*, 1.97 (fifteen aldermen and their sons). Were the aldermen the mummers or merely the subject matter? The Mercers' collection of contributions for a mumming for the king at Eltham, recorded in their wardens' accounts for 1400–01, is doubtless for this occasion; see Mercers' MS Wardens' Accounts 1347–1464, f. 32v.

43 *DTR* no. 912; the Merchant Taylors (see their GL MS 34048/1, f. 11r) make a payment "a le Guyhalle *pur* le Momyng a Nowell*e*".

44 *DTR* no. 1510; but see also Chambers, *Mediaeval Stage*, 1.395 and n. 1.

45 *DTR*, p. xx and nos. 1510 and 635. For Henry IV's treatment in general of Manuel II, see Donald M. Nicol, "A Byzantine Emperor in England: Manuel II's Visit to London in 1400–1401," *University of Birmingham Historical Journal* 12.1 (1969), 204–225, especially 211–216.

46 See *DTR* nos. 887, 889, 884, 891.

47 Henry Thomas Riley, ed. and tr., *Chronicles of the Mayors and Sheriffs of London, A.D. 1188 to A.D. 1274* (London: Trübner, 1863), p. 25 ("the City being handsomely hung with tapestry"). The coming of the prince is placed during the time of the sheriffs for 1255–56, and is dated as the vigil of St. Andrew, i.e., the day before 30 Nov.

48 Riley, *Mayors and Sheriffs*, p. 24 ("the City of London being most nobly tapestried and arrayed"); this is said to have happened on a Sunday, the feast of St. Eldreda (i.e., Etheldreda), in the year (Sept. – Sept.) of the 1255–56 sheriffs. Riley gives 23 June as her feast day, thus placing the entry in 1256. 23 June was on a Friday, however, in 1256; and St. Etheldreda had a second feast day in each calendar year, 17 Oct. (the day of her translation), which during the term of the 1255–56 sheriffs fell on a Sunday, 17 Oct. 1255. See also, for the 1255 date, Fabyan, p. 338.

49 Riley, *Mayors and Sheriffs*, p. 25 ("the City being decorated and hung with tapestry"); they came to London the Sunday before the feast of the beheading of St. John Baptist, which in the year of the sheriffs for 1255–56 would have been 27 August 1256. Fabyan, however, has 29 August (p. 339).

50 Riley, *Mayors and Sheriffs*, pp. 43–44 ("the City being excellently hung and arrayed"), the vigil of the Purification of Mary; see also Fabyan, p. 345.

51 For another reference simply to decoration or display, in 1243, see Robert Withington, "The Early 'Royal-Entry,'" *PMLA* 32 (1917), 619 (citing Matthew Paris).

52 Matthew Paris, *Historia Anglorum*, ed. Frederic Madden, vol. 2, RS 44 (London: HMSO, 1866), pp. 108–109. The city is also decorated with flowers, hangings, "et facibus et cereis." The civic welcome is said to be by royal precept ("ex praecepto regis"). In *Annales Londonienses*, ed. William Stubbs in *Chronicles of the Reigns of Edward I. and Edward II.*, vol. 1, RS 76 (London: HMSO, 1882), Otto's welcome is merely said to have involved rich cloths/hangings and other decorations (p. 13 – "pallis et aliis ornamentis").

53 Matthew Paris, *Chronica Majora*, ed. Henry Richards Luard, vol. 3, RS 57 (London: HMSO, 1876), pp. 336–337. These adornments, like those for Otto, were other than the banners, hangings, and crowns also specified as decorations.

54 Stow, *Survey*, I.95.

55 See *OED*, s.v. Pageant, *sb.*, 1.d ("A scene represented on tapestry, or the like"), 3 (". . . any kind of show, device, or temporary structure, exhibited as a feature of a public triumph or celebration"), and below, chapter 10, pp. 177–178.

56 Riley, *Mayors and Sheriffs*, p. 220 (a later insertion in the original MS). The date given is the Sunday before St. Edward; and although there are five different feast days associated with a St. Edward (see C. R. Cheney, *Handbook of Dates for Students of English History* [London: Royal Historical Society, 1945; rpt. 1970], "Saints' Days and Festivals," s.v. Edwardus [pp. 49–50]), the only one coming shortly after Margaret's marriage date of 10 Sept. 1299 is 13 October. The Sunday before 13 Oct. in 1299 was 11 October. The Anglo-Norman word "bretasches," translated by Riley as "wooden towers," is defined in *A–ND* as wooden parapets on a fortress; see s.v. "bretesche." A second meaning probably not applicable here, because of the outlets for wine, is wooden platforms for watching processions, although spectator stands with wine outlets cannot be entirely ruled out. Fabyan, pp. 401–402, mentions only rich hangings.

57 For the Great Conduit's date, see *Atlas*, Gazetteer, s.v. Great Conduit. Stow tells us (*Survey*, I.17 and 264) that the Great Conduit was built and castellated *c.* 1285.

58 Henry Knighton, *Chronicon Henrici Knighton, vel Cnitthon, Monachi Leycestrensis*, ed. Joseph Rawson Lumby, vol. 1, RS 92 (London: HMSO, 1889), p. 270; *Croniques de London, depuis l'An 44 Hen. III. jusqu'à l'An 17 Edw. III.*, ed. George James Aungier (Camden Society, OS 28, 1844), p. 13 (also p. 237 of Riley's edition of *The French Chronicle of London* – this same chronicle – in the same volume as *Mayors and Sheriffs*). Edward succeeded to the throne in 1272 while abroad, and did not return to England (from the crusades) until

August 1274; see Michael Prestwich, *Edward I* (London: Methuen, 1988), p. 89. For Edward's coronation date of 19 Aug., see also *Croniques*, p. 13.

59 Riley, *Mayors and Sheriffs*, p. 214 (a later insertion in the MS); Cheapside is not named, just "the Conduit," but its Great Conduit is intended, as specified in LB D. In the fourteenth century wine runs from the Great Conduit in all of the celebrations for the birth of Prince Edward (later to become Edward III) in 1312 (LB D, f. 168r), the entry of King John of France in 1357 (*Anon. Cant.*, p. 205), and the two main royal entries of the reign of Richard II, in 1377 (*Anon. Chronicle*, p. 108) and in 1392 (see the reference in Maidstone's contemporary poem, *EES*, 1.69).

60 Our information on thirteenth-century London entries comes mainly from brief references in Riley, *Mayors and Sheriffs*, and in Matthew Paris. Older scholarship assumes a general developmental process from little civic pageantry in earlier centuries to a flowering under Richard II; this is not necessarily the case. Robert Withington's view, e.g., of early fourteenth-century "spontaneous dancing" by Londoners, for the coronation of Edward II, as "a natural folk procedure" (*EP*, 1.125) leading on in that century to true "pageantry" (1.126), was developed without knowledge of the sophistication of earlier London. See, e.g., Wickham, *EES*, 1.xxv.

61 *Annales Londonienses*, p. 152. The deceased John de Triple is recorded in 1325 in LB E, f. 158v, as still owing money to the city for what appears to have been a civic assessment for the entry (among several assessment debts for the early fourteenth century is one for the queen's first coming to England). For the New Jerusalem motif as common in royal entries throughout medieval Europe, see, e.g., Kipling, *King*, p. 15.

62 R. E. Latham's *Revised Medieval Latin Word-List* (London: Oxford University Press for The British Academy, 1965; rpt. 1973) defines "catasta" as birdcage, though Latham's examples are both from the fifteenth century; he also lists the spelling "catesta," *c.* 1410, as a scaffold. Scaffold/platform is almost certainly the meaning here, see the similar entries described below. (*DTR* no. 891 accepts cage as the likely meaning.)

63 See *Anon. Chronicle*, p. 41, and *Anon. Cant.*, pp. 204–205 (from which the "catasta" quote is taken). John of Reading's chronicle (in the same vol. as *Anon. Cant.*) provides, pp. 126–127, the information that the entry procession came across London Bridge; the Canterbury work notes, p. 205, that past Cheapside and St. Paul's the procession rode through Ludgate and via Fleet St. to Westminster. Henry Knighton, *Chronicon*, is interested (p. 93) only in the military might displayed in the entry; he says nothing about any other kind of display (nor does he mention anything about Richard II's elaborate 1377 entry).

64 See *Anon. Chronicle*, pp. 107–108, and Thomas Walsingham, *Historia Anglicana*, ed. Henry Thomas Riley, vol. 1, RS 28 (London: HMSO, 1863), pp. 331–332; Walsingham's account is partly reproduced in Latin, and translated, in *EES*, 1. 54–55. (The same account occurs in *Chronicon Angliae*, ed. Edward Maunde Thompson, RS 64 [London: HMSO, 1874], pp. 155–156.) Walsingham's

description indicates the angel to be a mechanical one; but in 1392 (see below) an angel who offers drink from a gold cup to the king and the queen is a human actor, as is a maiden (played by a boy) who is also mechanically lowered with the angel. Walsingham's description also points to the tower/castle as being constructed so as to incorporate the conduit, while the *Anon. Chronicle* seems to indicate that the tower/castle is a separate structure. The Goldsmiths' early MS 1519 includes, p. 21, col. b, a few payments for the tower/castle.

65 Withington, for example, in 1918 (*EP*, 1.128–129) accepted the suggestion that the castle was derived from the tournament, despite the "New Jerusalem" chronicle reference even for the 1308 entry and the common use of the castle in medieval art as an image of the heavenly city. Today scholars emphasize religious interpretation; but Manley, *Culture*, typifies the late twentieth-century approach, in seeing, p. 242, typological symbolic display in London entries as beginning "with the single pageant constructed for the coronation of Richard II in 1377" (and see also Nigel Saul, *Richard II* [New Haven and London: Yale University Press, 1997], p. 342): whereas we have two Cheapside towers, with eight outlets running with wine, in Queen Margaret's 1299 entry some seventy-eight years earlier, and gold scattered by maidens from a high platform, as in 1377, in the Black Prince's 1357 entry. Gordon Kipling also essentially starts at 1377; see his "Richard II's 'Sumptuous Pageants' and the Idea of the Civic Triumph," in David M. Bergeron, ed., *Pageantry in the Shakespearean Theater* (Athens, GA: University of Georgia Press, 1985), p. 83. (Kipling's excellent interpretative article deals extensively with the religious and political symbolic meanings of the entry displays in both 1377 and 1392.) Wickham, *EES*, 1.54, also begins his analysis of street stages in royal entries with 1377's entry.

66 *OED*, s.v. Summer-castle: (1) a movable tower used in sieges (first usage example, 1400); (2) an elevated structure on a ship (first usage example, 1346). Most scholars have assumed a structure resembling a castle, given the towers/castles of 1299 and 1377; but the military/nautical term suggests use of military or shipbuilders' construction techniques. The base of the device might, e.g., have been a (concealed) wheeled cart, with rigging above to hold the tower, as with the portable ship pageant displayed by the Fishmongers' Company in 1313 (see below). For a lengthy discussion of this castle, and possibly also those of 1377 and 1392, as based on movable military siege towers, see Richard H. Osberg, "The Goldsmiths' 'Chastell' of 1377," *Theatre Survey* 27.1–2 (May and Nov. 1986), 1–15.

67 *DTR* no. 901 (with an erroneous date of 1383), citing William Herbert, *The History of the Twelve Great Livery Companies of London*, 2 vols. (London: privately printed, 1834–37; rpt. Newton Abbot: David and Charles, 1968), II. 217–218 (but Herbert's account contains errors). Herbert's source is Goldsmiths' MS 1518, p. 57, col. b.

68 Fish St.: now Fish St. Hill. (Old) Fish St. was south-east of St. Paul's; this (New) Fish St. ran north from the Bridge, from the top of Bridge St., and

led into Gracechurch St. See *Atlas*, s.v. Olde Fysshestrete (Knightrider Street), Knyghtryderstrete, Newe Fysshestrete, and Briggestrete, and Map 3 of the four *c.* 1520 London maps.

69 *DTR* no. 907; Stow, *Annales*, p. 483. The most detailed description of the entry is a poem by Richard Maidstone, a Carmelite friar and court favourite; see his "The Reconciliation of Richard II with the City of London," in Thomas Wright, ed., *Political Poems and Songs Relating to English History*, vol. 1, RS 14 (London: HMSO, 1859), pp. 282–300. Maidstone's poem is translated in part in *EES*, I.64–71. Without it we would know nothing of the gold leaves/coins, the distinction between the angel and the maiden, the cloud machine/effect, the suspension of the tower on cords, and the two following pageants at Paul's and at Temple Bar; this raises the significant question of how much we do not know about earlier entries simply because they did not have a (surviving) celebratory poem written about them. See also, for the 1392 entry: *Brut*, p. 347 (largely reproduced in *EP*, I.130); Knighton, *Chronicon*, pp. 319–320; Malverne, p. 275; Fabyan, pp. 537–538; *Westminster Chronicle*, pp. 504–507 (the only account which tells us about the censing). The angel and maiden were played by boys (Malverne; *Westminster Chronicle*). For analyses see Kipling, "Sumptuous Pageants," pp. 83–103, and *King*, pp. 12–20, and Manley, *Culture*, pp. 242–243. Scholars now routinely suggest an elaboration of all ceremonial during Richard's reign (see, e.g., Saul, *Richard II*, pp. 333–358, and Kipling, "Sumptuous Pageants," p. 83); and the elaborateness of the 1392 entry has been suggested to have been influenced by an earlier elaborate Parisian entry (see, e.g., Saul, *Richard II*, pp. 351–352).

70 There was lavish display by Richard in France at the formal handing-over of Isabella (then aged 6) to him (see Saul, *Richard II*, pp. 229–232); but chroniclers say little about her welcome to London or her coronation. Her age – see Saul, p. 457 – was also doubtless a factor. When she first came to London in Nov. 1396, she was greeted on Blackheath by Londoners with minstrels, and accompanied by them to Southwark; but she and the king then rode to Kennington (and a number of persons who had turned out to watch were crushed to death in the crowds on London Bridge). Subsequently in early January she processed through London, from the Tower to Cornhill and Cheapside and then to Westminster, but the chronicles give no details. See *Historia Vita Et Regni Ricardi Secundi*, ed. George B. Stow, Jr. ([Philadelphia]: University of Pensylvania Press, 1977), pp. 136–137, *Brut*, pp. 350–351, and *Great Chronicle*, p. 47. (Stow, *Survey*, I.25, has conflated her journeys to Kennington in Nov. and to the Tower in Jan.)

71 See, e.g., Mary-Rose McLaren, "The Aims and Interests of the London Chroniclers of the Fifteenth Century," in Dorothy J. Clayton, Richard G. Davies, and Peter McNiven, eds., *Trade, Devotion and Governance: Papers in Later Medieval History* (Stroud, Gloucestershire, and Dover, NH: Alan Sutton, 1994), pp. 158–176; her remarks are applicable beyond the fifteenth century.

72 See, e.g., *Brut*, p. 339.

73 See Maidstone's account in Wright, *Political Poems*, p. 291.

74 See, e.g., Keith Dockray, *Henry VI, Margaret of Anjou and the Wars of the Roses: A Source Book* (Phoenix Mill, Gloucestershire: Sutton, 2000), p. x.

75 See John Hayward, *The First Part of the Life and Raigne of King Henrie the IIII.* (1599; rpt. Amsterdam and Norwood, NJ: Theatrum Orbis Terrarum, 1975), p. 71. Froissart more credibly describes Henry as processing, before his coronation, through a London decorated with hangings, and with conduits running with red and white wine (see John Froissart, *Sir John Froissart's Chronicles of England, France, Spain, Portugal, Scotland, Brittany, Flanders, and the Adjoining Countries*, tr. John Bourchier, Lord Berners, 2 vols. [London: F. C. and J. Rivington *et al.*, 1812], II.753). Both the Merchant Taylors (GL MS 34048/1, f. 7r) and the Grocers (GL MS 11570, p. 83) record minstrel payments for this occasion.

76 See the Mercers' MS Wardens' Accounts 1347–1464, f. 15v. A 1364 visit of King John of France to London, e.g., also elicited minstrels (Froissart, *Chronicles*, I.279).

77 See, e.g., *Anon. Chronicle*, p. 67. *EP*, though old and containing errors, nevertheless provides material giving a good indication of the many different levels of display, from the simple (merely citizens riding in special liveries) to the complex (the construction of elaborate display stages), which Londoners would provide for various kinds of arriving dignitaries on various different kinds of occasions. For *EP*'s material on fourteenth-century entries, see I.124–132.

78 See John Webb, "Translation of a French Metrical History of the Deposition of King Richard the Second," *Archaeologia* 20 (1824), 180.

79 See above, n. 63, the entry of the Black Prince; and this appears also to have been the route for Richard II's 1392 entry (see Malverne, p. 275).

80 The basic route is set down in the *Liber Custumarum* for the coronation of Richard II (Tower, Cheapside, Fleet St., Westminster; see *MG*, II.2, p. 476); and see also above, n. 70, on Isabella's coronation entry route in 1397. *Anon. Chronicle* also provides (p. 108) Richard II's 1377 entry route.

81 *Atlas*, Gazetteer, s.v. Conduit (Cornhill at Bishopsgate Street). Bishopsgate St. runs north from Cornhill, opposite Gracechurch St.

82 *Atlas*, Gazetteer, s.v. Standard and Conduit (Cheapside), "by 1395–96," also noting Stow's date of "by 1293."

83 *Atlas*, Gazetteer, s.v. Cheap Cross (*or* Great Cross in Cheapside).

84 See, e.g., Barron, *Atlas*, p. 45.

85 *Atlas*, Gazetteer: s.v. Conduit by St. Paul's Gate (in Westcheap, Little Conduit) – begun 1389, rebuilt or completed 1440–42; s.v. Conduit (The Tun) – water cistern 1401–02, enlarged and castellated 1475; s.v. Conduit (at Stocks Market) – *c*. 1500; s.v. Conduit (Gracechurch Street) – begun 1491.

86 Manley, *Culture*, pp. 225–241.

87 For example, the route up Gracechurch St. to Cornhill, and then west along Cornhill to Poultry, involved fewer turns (by 1283, when the Stocks

Market was built at Cornhill and Poultry) and apparently generally wider streets than if the route had run west from Gracechurch St. along Lombard St. to Poultry (see the *c.* 1270 and *c.* 1520 maps of London [2 and 3 for *c.* 1520] in *Atlas*; and see *Atlas*, Gazetteer, s.v. Stocks Market); and also the Great Conduit in Cheapside, as has been seen, was a usual entry feature from the late thirteenth century on. Two Cornhill conduits would also have been bypassed, by *c.* 1500, if Lombard St. had been used instead of Cornhill. For the importance of conduits as "stage" locations, see *EES*, 1.55–58.

88 See Keene, *Cheapside*, p. 8.

89 Keene, *Cheapside*, p. 8. Manley, *Culture*, p. 229, also notes Becket's importance.

90 For a variety of castle associations, see George R. Kernodle, *From Art to Theatre: Form and Convention in the Renaissance* (Chicago and London: University of Chicago Press, 1944), pp. 76–84. Kipling emphasizes religious meaning: see, e.g., *King*, pp. 36–37.

91 Stow, *Survey*, I.95–96. For the importance of the Fishmongers' guild in late thirteenth-century and early fourteenth-century London, see Unwin, *Gilds and Companies*, pp. 38–39.

92 The account in *The Chronicle of Dunmow* is quoted in *EP*, I.124.

93 Cheapside, as has been seen, is central to early London street pageantry; but the Fishmongers were associated with the Thames, and with the parish of St. Magnus (see Thrupp, *London*, p. 34, and Unwin, *Gilds and Companies*, p. 95). The involvement also of other crafts in the procession may make the Cheapside route more likely; on the other hand, the St. Magnus Day occasion may tilt the likelihood towards the route north from St. Magnus Martyr. The church had been established by 1128–33: see *Atlas*, s.v. St. Magnus the Martyr (by the Bridge), Church of.

94 For the Fishmongers' 1313 route (Cheapside to Westminster, and back through the city), and the queen's final Canterbury destination (on pilgrimage), see LB D, f. 168r. The same information is in BL Add. MS. 15,664, f. 176r. Presumably the queen rode from Westminster into the city through Ludgate and along the usual entry route, in reverse, to London Bridge, which she crossed to travel to the palace of Eltham in Kent (see *DTR* no. 886) and then eventually on to Canterbury. *Annales Londonienses*, p. 221, specifies Eltham, not Canterbury, as the queen's destination: presumably it names only her immediate, not ultimate, destination. See also *Croniques de London*, p. 37 (p. 250 of Riley's *French Chronicle* edition).

95 See, e.g., *EES*, 1.163–167. For detailed religious interpretation of the street pageants of royal entries throughout medieval Europe, see Kipling, *King, passim*.

96 For these dates see *DTR* no. 1560 (York cycle), and its Dramatic Texts, nos. 28 (*Castle*) and 75 (*Mary Magdalene*). The sheer entertainment value of medieval pageantry today requires new emphasis, however, having been significantly displaced in contemporary scholarship by a focus upon serious religious and political meanings. Meaning and entertainment were not mutually exclusive.

97 For Roman use of entertainment devices such as towers, a ship construction, and dolphin representations (for counting race laps) in their circuses,
see John H. Humphrey, *Roman Circuses: Arenas for Chariot Racing* (London:
B. T. Batsford, 1986): towers, p. 266 (and also 55, 173–174, 589); ship, p. 116;
dolphins, pp. 262–265.

98 Stow, *Survey*, I.102, gives the sixteenth-century route, which involved a loop
in Gracechurch St. around the conduit at Grace Church: south and then
north again.

99 Stow, *Survey*, I.101–104. See chapter 9, below.

100 Manley, in his "Of Sites and Rites," in David L. Smith, Richard Strier,
and David Bevington, eds., *The Theatrical City: Culture, Theatre and Politics in
London, 1576–1649* (Cambridge: Cambridge University Press, 1995), p. 43,
has suggested an origin for the processional Watch in a ceremony of military service owed to the city by the lord of Castle Baynard, involving a
procession from St. Paul's to Aldgate, as described in Stow's *Survey*,
I.62–64. (See Kingsford's nn. to Stow's I.62 and 65, in II.278–279, which
also correct Stow's dating on I.65.) This ceremony, however, is not necessarily to be connected to the Watch (and Stow does not so connect it), although it may be; it has to do with military service in time of war. The
original record which is Stow's source is printed in *MG*, II.1 (*Liber Custumarum*), pp. 147–151, and is translated in II.2, pp. 554–558; and Riley comments upon it at length in *MG*, II.1, pp. lxxvi–lxxxiv, dating to the reign of
King John (see p. lxxviii) the military procession described. Holy Trinity at
Aldgate may have been especially associated with the city's defence and
general security (see H. C. Coote, "The English Gild of Knights and their
Socn," *TLMAS* 5 [1876–80], 477–493, and Unwin, *Gilds and Companies*, pp.
23–27), and thus have been a natural component of any security/military
procession; see, however, Williams, p. 32 and n. 2.

101 For the Assize of Arms, see William Stubbs, ed., *Select Charters and Other
Illustrations of English Constitutional History*, 6th edn. (Oxford: Clarendon
Press, 1888), pp. 154–156; an English translation is provided in David C.
Douglas and George W. Greenaway, eds., *English Historical Documents*, vol. 2
(1042–1189) (London: Eyre and Spottiswoode, 1953), pp. 416–417.

102 For the likelihood of regular security watches in London from at least the
early thirteenth century, see Mary Bateson, "A London Municipal Collection of the Reign of John," *English Historical Review* 17 (1902), 502 (cited by
Sheila Lindenbaum, "Ceremony and Oligarchy: The London Midsummer Watch," in Barbara A. Hanawalt and Kathryn L. Reyerson, eds., *City
and Spectacle in Medieval Europe*, Medieval Studies at Minnesota 6 [Min-
neapolis and London: University of Minnesota Press, 1994], p. 184, n. 10),
and *Liber Albus*, p. 105.

103 See Stubbs, *Select Charters*, pp. 370–373 and 374–375. Stow, *Survey*, I.101,
mentions the 1253 order for watches. The 1252 order was for the period
from Ascension Day (a movable feast, 30 April–3 June) to St. Michael's
Day (29 Sept.).

104 See, e.g., Riley, *Mayors and Sheriffs* for 1266, p. 92: "dancing and singing of carols . . . , as is the usual yearly custom upon the Feast of Saint John the Baptist;" and A. R. Myers, ed., *English Historical Documents*, vol. 4 (1327–1485) (London: Eyre and Spottiswoode, 1969), notes, p. 1067, that usual curfew rules would be suspended at midsummer. Fire was a special concern; see *Liber Albus*, p. 105: in early times one of the city's three annual folkmoots (in existence from before 1191 – see Unwin, *Gilds and Companies*, pp. 29–30) was held at the Feast of St. John "to protect the City from fire, by reason of the great drought." Bonfires were a feature of midsummer celebrations (for a sixteenth-century description see Stow's *Survey*, quoted below in chapter 9, pp. 154–155, and cresset lights from at least the late fourteenth century (see below).

105 See, e.g., the City's concern over Christmas-season mummings, as described above, p. 41.

106 See Stubbs, *Select Charters*, pp. 469–474 (including an English translation). An English translation is also provided in Harry Rothwell, ed., *English Historical Documents*, vol. 3 (1189–1327) (London: Eyre and Spottiswoode, 1975), pp. 460–462. It may be relevant that in July 1321 a special security watch required of London by the king involved a plan by the civic government not only to place watchmen at the gates and on the walls but also to have at least two hundred armed men moving throughout the city (see LB E, ff. 119v–121r): though it is unclear (see *Cal. LB E*, pp. 141–143) whether the moving men were in the end provided. Moving watches were not new at this time, however: see, e.g., LB C, f. 20r (*c*. Christmas 1294). A compulsory 3 Feb. muster in all cities, towns, etc., recorded in the *Liber Custumarum* (see *MG*, II.2, p. 637), is dated by Riley (*MG*, II.2, p. 636, n. 1) only as probably much later than William the Conqueror.

107 See Lindsay Boynton, *The Elizabethan Militia 1558–1638* (London/Toronto: Routledge and Kegan Paul/University of Toronto Press, 1967), p. 8. Henry VIII's commissions always referred to the statutory obligation of service.

108 See below, chapter 9. London was not alone in this regard; other towns also required royal cancellation permission. See, e.g., R. W. Ingram, ed., *Coventry*, REED (Toronto: University of Toronto Press, 1981), for Coventry's midsummer watch as "the King's watch" (p. lxv), and, for cancellations, John Roche Dasent, ed., *Acts of the Privy Council of England*, NS I (1542–1547) (London: HMSO, 1890), pp. 422 (Bristol) and 447 (Coventry). In 1511 the London Mercers note in their MS Acts of Court 1, f. 210v, that London has a commission to hold a muster and that they will provide twelve armed men for the mayor in the Midsummer Watch "in trust" that this "garnysshing" of the Watch will be in lieu of the muster.

109 LB H, f. 111r. See chapter 9, below: in the fifteenth and sixteenth centuries the king sometimes used the Watch to impress foreign ambassadors and rulers.

110 See, e.g., LB A, f. 135r.

111 Withington implies, in *EP*, I.38, that a decorative watch took place at midsummer 1377, and cites Sharpe's *Cal. LB H*, p. 308; but (1) Sharpe, p. 308, deals with the 1387 watch, with no indication in his calendaring of any special decorative display (and none in the record itself, f. 217r) (2) the 1377 watch at midsummer calendared in *Cal. LB H*, pp. 64–66, is not a special display event but part of an ongoing military effort because of the death of Edward III and the accession of Richard II while the French were threatening England's south coast (see *Cal. LB H*, p. 64, n. 3).

112 LB H, f. 79v. Henry Thomas Riley in his *Memorials of London and London Life in the XIIIth, XIVth, and XVth Centuries* (London: Longmans, Green, 1868), pp. 419–420, prints a translation of the record; for a transcription of the original, see this volume's Appendix B, 1. London's aldermen were the leaders of the ward-based militia: see David Nicholas, *The Growth of the Medieval City: From Late Antiquity to the Early Fourteenth Century* (London and New York: Longman, 1997), p. 238.

113 Charles Pythian-Adams has suggested, in relation to the fifteenth-century midsummer watch in Coventry, that carrying fire (i.e., cressets) through the streets at midsummer was symbolically significant. See p. 72 of his "Ceremony and the Citizen: The Communal Year at Coventry 1450–1550," in Peter Clark and Paul Slack, eds., *Crisis and Order in English Towns 1500–1740* (London: Routledge and Kegan Paul, 1972).

114 See LB H, ff. 111r (1379), 175r (1384), 190v (1385), 200r (1386), 217r (1387). In 1378 and 1379 the marchers assembled in Smithfield, and in 1384–86, at St. Paul's cemetery.

115 The records are sometimes unclear as to whether there are two groups (one of men within the wards, one of men marching with the mayor) or one.

116 See GL MS 11570, p. 67, col. b. Organized recording of expenses is not a feature of livery companies' accounts throughout this period.

117 See below, chapter 9.

118 For the 1406 record, see LB I, f. 48v. It is for St. Peter's eve only, and involves over 300 men to be provided to go with the mayor through the city (numbers of men are specified by ward). The Statute of Winchester had been confirmed in 1383; see *The Statutes at Large*, vol. 1, ed. Owen Ruffhead (London: Mark Baskett *et al.*, 1769), p. 366.

119 The 1379 Midsummer Watch order requires the watchmen to have battle axes ("une hache" – LB H, f. 111r; see *A-ND*, s.v. hache).

120 For historians' suggestions of increasing ceremonial display in general during the reign of Richard II, see above, n. 69.

121 In 1298 a charter of Edward I specified that the mayor could be presented to the Constable of the Tower of London if both the king and his representatives at Westminster, the Exchequer barons, were absent. For all these dates (1215, 1253, 1298), see *Historical Charters*, pp. 19, 34, 43.

122 See Brooke, *Atlas*, p. 39.

123 See *Liber Albus*, pp. 19–20.

124 See Goldsmiths' MS 1518, p. 39, col. b (1369) and p. 69 (1388), and MS 1519, p. 21, col. b (1377).

125 *Liber Albus*, p. 19. Williams, p. 166, also refers to early fourteenth-century oath-takings by water.

126 LB H, f. 95v.

127 Grocers: see GL MS 11570, pp. 78, 81, 83. Mercers: see Mercers' MS Wardens' Accounts 1347–1464, ff. 13v, 23r, 28r, 30v. Merchant Taylors: see GL MS 34048/1 (beginning 1398), ff. 4r, 7r. The years covered by one or more records are 1393, 1396, 1397, 1398, 1399.

128 *Liber Albus*, p. 22.

129 For a description of the early fifteenth-century norm of the mayor's riding, before it became regularly a water journey (from 1453), see *Liber Albus*, pp. 22–24.

130 See Beaven, II.xxxiii, for the changing dates of the sheriffs' elections before 1325 and from 1527.

131 GL MS 11570, p. 67, col. b (1386).

132 The Goldsmiths' May 1383–May 1384 account contains a payment for minstrels to ride with the sheriff (Goldsmiths' MS 1519, p. 30): but a Goldsmith was sworn as sheriff in Sept. 1382, not 1383. Sheriffs sworn in 1383 were an Armourer and a Mercer. Was the 1383–84 accounting a delayed one for a 1382 payment? Did the Goldsmiths pay in 1383 for minstrels for a non-company sheriff? Was the riding for an occasion other than a sheriff's presentation, May–Sept. 1383?

133 LB H, f. 246r.

134 See GL MS 5440, f. 70v: although in the end the journey was made by water.

135 Mercers' MS Wardens' Accounts 1347–1464, ff. 12r, 13v, 23r; Grocers' GL MS 11570, p. 91 (the account is wrongly headed as for May 1401–May 1402).

136 Although under Henry III the city's chosen sheriffs had to be presented to the king's justices, Edward III agreed that they need not take any oath at the Exchequer except upon yielding up their accounts. See *Historical Charters*, pp. 21, 56. Their situation was therefore unlike the mayor's; and *Liber Albus* specifies nothing about any sheriff's presentation journey to Westminster.

137 *Liber Albus* suggests, p. 19, that the expenses of the mayor's presentation – along with those of other mayoral responsibilities – also had begun to increase in the early fourteenth century.

138 Lawrence M. Clopper, "London and the Problem of the Clerkenwell Plays," *Comparative Drama* 34 (Fall 2000), 291–303, has very recently argued, largely on terminological grounds and in relation to provincial norms, against the chronicle and records evidence for recurring and large-scale play performances at Clerkenwell/Skinners' Well. Clopper believes a Clerkenwell play to have been performed only in 1390 and 1409, and to have been "some sort of parish fund-raiser" (p. 300) held in conjunction

with St. Bartholomew's August fair, "just one of the sights among the usual games." The combination of London's large population and wealth, longstanding theatrical traditions in other areas such as royal entries, huge base of parishes and other wealthy religious institutions, and close ties to the royal court (with royal attendance at the play in 1390 and 1409 – see below), together with the slippery nature of theatrical terminology in this period and the accumulation of a variety of references to elaborate Clerkenwell performances 1384–1409, leads me to a more traditional although also cautious interpretation of the records and chronicle references. Most certainly, at the least, performances before royalty would not have been mere parish fundraisers, and would have had lavish resources poured into them.

139 Fitz Stephen, "Descriptio Londoniae," p. 27; also in Stow, *Survey*, 1.15.
140 *DTR* no. 543; see W. O. Hassall, "Plays at Clerkenwell," *Modern Language Review* 33 (1938), 564–567, for a transcription (p. 565) of the undated (*c.* 1300) PRO Ancient Petition 4858 – the prioress' petition to the king for help against the crowds, endorsed as a precept to the constable of the vill, for action.
141 A "wrestlyngplace" at Clerkenwell is mentioned twice in a fifteenth-century document of the priory of St. John of Jerusalem there (Hassall, "Plays at Clerkenwell," p. 567); and wrestling was also a popular activity at August's Bartholomew Fair, held beside and in Smithfield just to the south of Clerkenwell; see, e.g., Stow, *Survey*, 1.104 (who states that "of olde time" August wrestling participants included London's sheriffs and sergeants).
142 Hassall also transcribes ("Plays at Clerkenwell," p. 566) a royal writ dated 8 April 1301 and referring to the prioress' complaint (or to another such complaint by her), to London's mayor and sheriffs, to make a proclamation against wrestlings ("luctas") and "alios ludos" which could damage the prioress' meadows and pastures – the "alios ludos" thus being, given the *c.* 1300 complaint, possibly or probably miracle plays: i.e., plays about miracles performed by God and by his saints. (A miracle play of St. Katherine is recorded at Dunstable some 200 years earlier; see *DTR* no. 616.) The writ is also reproduced in Hassall's edn. of the *Cartulary of St. Mary Clerkenwell* (Camden Society, Series 3, 71, 1949), p. 260.
143 See, e.g., the reference in royal Wardrobe accounts for 1409, cited by James Hamilton Wylie in his *History of England under Henry the Fourth*, vol. 4 (London: Longmans Green, 1898), p. 213, to a timber scaffold built at Clerkenwell for seating for a great play there, and the same 1409 play reported by chroniclers (see below) as having taken place at Skinners' Well. See also *A Chronicle*, p. 91 (including marginal notes).
144 (1) 1384 – Malverne, p. 47 (Skinners' Well, clerks of London, 29 August, 5 days in length); *Westminster Chronicle*, p. 95 (same information). (2) 1390 – Frederick Devon, ed., *Issues of the Exchequer . . . from King Henry III. to King Henry VI. Inclusive* (London: John Murray, 1837), pp. 244–245, payment of a

gift of ten pounds "on account of the play *of the Passion of our Lord and the Creation of the World*" performed "after the feast of Saint Bartholomew last past," Issue Roll, Easter, 14 Richard II [1391] (Skinners' Well, clerks of the parish churches and divers other clerks of London, after 24 August 1390, no length specified). (3) 1391 – Malverne, p. 259 (Skinners' Well, clerks of London, 18 July, 4 days in length, Old and New Testaments); *Westminster Chronicle*, p. 477 (same information); Stow, *Survey*, 1.93 (Skinners' Well, parish clerks of London, 3 days in length, king and queen and nobles present). Stow also records (1.15) a performance in 1390 (Skinners' Well, parish clerks of London, 18 July, 3 days in length, king and queen and nobles present); this would seem either to be the 1391 performance mistakenly recorded as 1390 (at the same two points in his text at which Stow gives the "1390" and "1391" play information – which is otherwise the same save for the lack of a day and a month in the "1391" description – he also provides 1409 performance information [1.15, 1.93], repeated; and the Issue Roll dates the 1390 performance in August) or an erroneous conflation of 1390 and 1391 details (1390 performance length and royal attendance, 1391 day and month; although the king could also have attended in 1391). Since the king paid a gift for the end-of-August 1390 performance, it seems likely that at least he attended then; and Saul's itinerary for Richard II (in an appendix to his *Richard II*, pp. 468–474) has Richard II at Windsor (so at least in the London area) 25–30 August 1390. In summer 1391 Saul has a number of itinerary gaps, though he places Richard in the London area 2–4 August (at Windsor) and 15–16 August (at Eltham). A prohibited 1385 performance (see below) must have been scheduled in August, as the prohibition is dated 12 August.

145 It seems improbable that the five-day "ludum valde sumptuosum" (*Westminster Chronicle*, p. 94) by clerks at Clerkenwell in 1384 was not an earlier occurrence or version of the play performed in 1390; and although the 1390 and 1391 performances might be one performance erroneously recorded as two, they have been recorded with somewhat different details. The subject matter in 1390 should remind us of that of the three-day Cornish *Ordinalia* (also fourteenth-century): see Sally L. Joyce and Evelyn S. Newlyn, eds., *Cornwall*, REED (Toronto/European Union: University of Toronto Press/Brepols, 1999), p. 542, who also suggest that the *Ordinalia* may originally have been a full cycle.

146 *A Chronicle*, p. 91 (Skinners' Well, Weds., Thurs., Fri., ending Sun., i.e., four days; a second MS, BL Cotton MS Julius B.i, names Clerkenwell); Gregory, p. 105 (Skinners' Well); *Great Chronicle*, p. 87 (Skinners' Well; Stow, who owned the original MS [see *Great Chronicle*, pp. xvi and xxiii], has annotated the MS, adding that the play was "of corpus christi" and lasted eight days); Stow, *Survey*, 1.15, repeated 1.93, largely repeated again 11.31 and 11.171 (Skinners' Well, parish clerks of London implied, eight days in length, subject matter from the creation of the world, "most part of the Nobles and Gentiles in England" present). One chronicle apparently misdates the 1409 performance as 1411: from the context (a year of great

jousts in Smithfield), and other date discrepancies, 1409 must be intended; see *Grey Friars*, p. 12 (Skinners' Well, seven days, subject matter from the beginning of the world, most part of the lords and gentles of England present). *DTR* no. 549 lists this *Grey Friars* reference as involving a separate 1410–11 performance. Wylie, *History of England*, IV.213, cites royal Wardrobe accounts for a timber scaffold built in 1409 at Clerkenwell for Henry IV, the prince, barons, knights, and ladies to see a great play there from the creation to the day of judgment, and provides (his Appendix Q) a year-by-year itinerary for Henry IV's reign showing, p. 298, the king at Clerkenwell on 24 July 1409 (a Wednesday; and presumably for the next few days as well); in 1410 and 1411 the king does not seem to be in that vicinity during the summer (see pp. 299–301). *DTR* no. 548, following Wylie, provides 1409 performance dates of 24–28 July.

147 For the French three to four-day norm, see Grace Frank, *The Medieval French Drama* (Oxford: Clarendon Press, 1954; rpt. 1967), p. 170; and the Cornish *Ordinalia*, also dating from the fourteenth century, was performed, as well, over several days, as were also the later Cornish *St. Meriasek* and *Creation of the World*; see Joyce and Newlyn, *Cornwall*, pp. 541–545. London also had other civic theatrical events, at this time, spread over more than one day: e.g., the regular Midsummer Watch (though at this time apparently only decorative rather than theatrical), and in 1403 the coronation entry of Queen Joan (see below, Appendix A). (Royal tournaments in and around London, of course, were also multi-day events; see, e.g.; below, p. 64, for a three-day tournament in London in 1359.) Wickham, *EES*, I.163, speculates that the London play was performed in a circular performance area; Stanley J. Kahrl, *Traditions of Medieval English Drama* (London: Hutchinson, 1974), states, pp. 48–49, that it must have had "place-and-scaffold" staging, as in *The Castle of Perseverance*, with stages around a circular playing area. (Kahrl defines his terms on pp. 29–30.)

148 LB H, f. 195r. The order reads, in part, "Ne q*e* le iew qest ordeine destre fait a skynn*ere*swelle ne null autre tiel ne semblable ne soit iewe en la dite Citee ne dehors".

149 See LB H, f. 195r. A French army was threatening an invasion of England; and some French had gone to Scotland to encourage an invasion from the north as well. See Anthony Steel, *Richard II* (Cambridge: Cambridge University Press, 1941), p. 105.

150 Stow, *Survey*, 1.15. Sharpe in *Cal. LB H* has apparently been influenced by Stow, whom he cites in a footnote, in wrongly calendaring the 1385 prohibition as of "the play that customarily took place" (p. 272). "Customarily" is not part of the LB record, which merely reads (in Anglo-Norman) "le iew qest ordeine destre fait" (the play which is ordered/arranged to be performed). Clopper, "London," argues (p. 299) that there was a real play (as opposed to games, etc.) only in 1390 and 1409.

151 T. Cromwell, *History and Description of the Parish of Clerkenwell* (London: Longman *et al.*, 1828), says, p. 40, he assumes that Fitz Stephen's cited

plays were at Clerkenwell; and the name Clerkenwell (which is found in Fitz Stephen) according to Stow's *Survey* (1.15) came from clerks' perform-ances at the well there, with the late fourteenth and early fifteenth-century performances being "of later time." (Stow could, of course, have been mistaken.)

152 *DTR* nos. 1560 and 554; and see the two relevant REED volumes: Alexandra F. Johnston and Margaret Rogerson, eds., *York*, 2 vols. (Toronto: University of Toronto Press, 1979), and R. W. Ingram, ed., *Coventry* (Toronto: University of Toronto Press, 1981).

153 For the dates of Corpus Christi feast establishment, see Lynette R. Muir, *The Biblical Drama of Medieval Europe* (Cambridge: Cambridge University Press, 1995), p. 22.

154 On Corpus Christi as inspiring the beginnings of English cycle drama, see, e.g., Wickham, *History*, pp. 76–77, 91, and recently Mervyn James, "Ritual, Drama and Social Body in the Late Medieval English Town," *Past and Present* 98 (Feb. 1983), 3–29. (The same material is included in his *Society, Politics and Culture: Studies in Early Modern England*, Past and Present Publications [Cambridge: Cambridge University Press, 1986], chapter 1, pp. 16–47.) James, however, although he sees Corpus Christi as a major force in fourteenth-century English cycle history, does not disallow the possibility of some pre-Corpus Christi play development. Considerable caution has recently been expressed over the notion of the Feast of Corpus Christi as cycle inspiration by William Tydeman, in Beadle, pp. 20–21; and some twenty years earlier Richard Axton, in *European Drama*, wrote, pp. 169–170, of cycles as only part of a wider movement to-wards "contextual completeness," *Adam* and *The Holy Resurrection* (see chapter 2, above) being twelfth-century examples of this trend.

155 Alan Nelson suggested this in 1974: see his *The Medieval English Stage: Corpus Christi Pageants and Plays* (Chicago and London: University of Chicago Press, 1974), p. 172. Nelson also disposed of earlier arguments against London's play as a cycle drama similar to those in the provinces, although James has since assumed ("Ritual, Drama and Social Body," p. 24, n. 79) that London's play was unusual – not a true Corpus Christi play – because directed at non-Londoners, including royalty and nobility, as the primary audience. There is no evidence for this, other than that royalty attended in both 1390 and 1409, although it is possible (and my own argument below, about religious auspices, takes a somewhat similar tack). Royalty also attended provincial cycle performances, as James also notes, p. 12.

156 See above, n. 69, for historians' suggestion of a general elaboration of courtly ceremony and cultural activities during Richard II's reign. Still, London from the twelfth century on was a more sophisticated, wealthy, and sizeable city than any provincial town (for its population and wealth, see, e.g., John Schofield and Alan Vince, *Medieval Towns* [Madison, Teaneck: Fairleigh Dickinson University Press, 1994], p. 19): more likely, early on, than the provincial centres to have become the location of a major biblical

play. In 1334, e.g., no provincial town had one quarter of London's wealth (Susan Reynolds, *An Introduction to the History of English Medieval Towns* [Oxford: Clarendon Press, 1977], p. 62).

157 E. K. Chambers, *Mediaeval Stage*, II.381, believes it continued into the fifteenth century, past 1409, and is even behind a 1498 payment to London players and an early sixteenth-century chronicle's reference to 1508 "spectacula" on St. John's eve (see *DTR* no. 972, citing the *Annales* of Henry VII's poet laureate Bernardus Andreas: see *Bernardo Andrea*, p. 121). Such references would seem unrelated to the Clerkenwell play; the "spectacula," e.g., would instead seem to be associated with the Midsummer Watch. (See below, chapter 9.) A continuation of a major biblical drama or cycle in London would surely otherwise have been recorded at least a few times after 1409, given the growing numbers of chronicles and of other MS records extant from *c.* 1400 on; and the reference in Stow's *Survey*, I.93, to stage plays at Skinners' Well in 1391 and 1409 and to playhouses in Stow's own time is unlikely to be correctly read as a statement of the continuation specifically of a major biblical play or cycle. (Stow seems, rather, only to be suggesting that the earlier plays have their counterparts in the London public playhouses of the mid to late sixteenth century.) There were, however, some religious plays in London in Stow's own time: see, e.g., Machyn, pp. 138 (at the Greyfriars, June 1557) and 145 (in Silver St., July 1557), both of these plays during Queen Mary's reign; and see also Mary C. Erler, "Spectacle and Sacrament: A London Parish Play in the 1530s," *Modern Philology* 91 (1993–94), 449–454. *DTR* also lists, nos. 1007, 1009, and 1010, stage plays at All Hallows in the Wall, at Christ Church, St. Katherine's, and at St. Margaret's, Westminster, in the 1520s.

158 By before 1250 and on into the sixteenth century there were *c.* 100 parishes in London; see Brooke, *Atlas*, pp. 34–35, and Barron, *Atlas*, p. 48. Within those parishes, *c.* the end of the fourteenth century, there were also probably over fifty parish fraternities; see Unwin, *Gilds and Companies*, pp. 367–370.

159 For both St. Mary's and St. John's, see J. S. Cockburn, H. P. F. King, and K. G. T. McDonnell, eds., *The Victoria History of the Counties of England. A History of the County of Middlesex*, vol. 1 (Oxford: Oxford University Press for the Institute of Historical Research, 1969), pp. 170–174 and 193–200, and "London's Monasteries," *Current Archaeology* 162 [14.6] (April/May 1999), 204–206. In 1381 the prior of St. John's was also Treasurer of England, and was executed during the Peasants' Revolt by the angry mob that also burned the priory.

160 For information on St. Bartholomew's Priory, see William Page, ed., *The Victoria History of the Counties of England. The Victoria History of London*, vol. 1 (London: Constable, 1909), pp. 475–480, and on the fair, also Stow, *Survey*, II.27.

161 Henry Morley, *Memoirs of Bartholomew Fair* (London: George Routledge and Sons, 1892), argues, pp. 68–72, that St. Bartholomew's Priory staged

miracle plays at the fair itself. James Christie, *Some Account of Parish Clerks* (London: The Worshipful Company of Parish Clerks, 1893), pp. 61–62, links the Clerkenwell play with the fair.

162 Cockburn *et al.*, *Victoria History of Middlesex*, p. 195.

163 Cockburn *et al.*, *Victoria History of Middlesex*, p. 198.

164 See Webb, "Metrical History," pp. 180–181, 190–191. Misreportings stemming from this source are ultimately responsible for the statement, in Cockburn *et al.*, *Victoria History of Middlesex* (p. 198), and elsewhere (e.g., in H. W. Fincham, *The Order of the Hospital of St. John of Jerusalem and its Grand Priory of England* [London: Collingridge, 1915], p. 16), that Henry stayed at St. John's for the period immediately before his coronation.

165 See Wylie, *History*, III. 246 and IV.213. The king had "corrody" – the right to be housed and fed – in all monastic establishments in England (and could also send his representatives to exercise this right): see L. B. Larking, ed., *Knights Hospitallers in England* (Camden Society, OS 65, 1857), pp. xlix and 99. Numerous monarchs (including Henry V in 1413) made use of this right, over the centuries, at St. John's: see Cockburn *et al.*, *Victoria History of Middlesex*, p. 198, Fincham, *Order of the Hospital*, pp. 16–18, and specifically on 1413, James Hamilton Wylie, *The Reign of Henry the Fifth*, 3 vols. (Cambridge: Cambridge University Press, 1914–29), 1.315. Eleanor of Castile, e.g., stayed at St. John's in 1255: see Fabyan, p. 338.

166 Page, *Victoria History of London*, pp. 477–478.

167 London *c.* 1377 is estimated to have had a population of 35,000 (*Atlas*, p. 56); an older (1982) comparative estimate of the populations of English towns at this date places London at 45,000–50,000, four other towns at 8000–15,000, eight more at 5000–8000, twenty-seven at 2000–5000: see R. H. Hilton, "Towns in English Medieval Society," in Richard Holt and Gervase Rosser, eds., *The Medieval Town: A Reader in English Urban History 1200–1540* (London and New York: Longman, 1990), p. 22. In 1948 Thrupp, *London*, suggested (p. 1) that, at 30,000–40,000 people, London in 1377 was more than three times as large as York or Bristol, almost five times as large as Coventry.

168 The August 1385 city prohibition of the Clerkenwell play involved, however, external danger: for in July 1385 an invasion of England by France and Flanders had been anticipated (LB H, f. 193v), as noted above, and a tax levied on Londoners for defence (ff. 93v–94r); and the play prohibition (f. 195r) is immediately followed in LB H by the declaration that if the enemy should approach, women and children should stay indoors. Overall the 1380s and 1390s were a time of political turmoil for London: see Ruth Bird, *The Turbulent London of Richard II* (London: Longmans Green, 1949), *passim*.

169 Gervase Rosser, *Medieval Westminster*, e.g., notes (pp. 113–115) that in the late thirteenth and early fourteenth centuries the great international, commercial fairs of Europe, annually recurring at specific times of the year, declined because of a shift from seasonal trading at fairs to year-round commercial

trading in developed cities such as Paris and London. John C. Coldewey, "Some Economic Aspects of the Late Medieval Drama," in Marianne G. Briscoe and John C. Coldewey, eds., *Contexts for Early English Drama* (Bloomington and Indianapolis: Indiana University Press, 1989), pp. 77–101, discusses economics in general in relation to medieval plays, though for later in the medieval period and not in relation to London.

170 See below, chapter 4.

171 *DTR*, pp. xvii–xviii and xx. See, however, R. N. Swanson, *Church and Society in Late Medieval England* (Oxford: Basil Blackwell, 1989), p. 342 (a collapse of Lollardry in 1414).

172 The early records of the Parish Clerks' Company were destroyed, along with the company's hall, by enemy action in December 1940; but it is unlikely that any Parish Clerks' records of the Clerkenwell play had survived even into the nineteenth century, given the interest of earlier scholars in Clerkenwell and yet their failure to find any such records.

173 Both the Wakefield and the Ludus Coventriae cycle MSS have an estimated date range beginning *c.* 1450 (*DTR*, Dramatic Texts, nos. 58 and 55); and the York cycle MS is fifteenth-century as well (*DTR* no. 1560). Extant MSS of the Chester cycle (except for one possibly fifteenth-century fragment) begin *c.* 1500: see R. M. Lumiansky and David Mills, eds., *The Chester Mystery Cycle*, vol. 1 (EETS, Supplementary Series 3, 1974), p. ix.

174 See Cockburn *et al.*, *Victoria History of Middlesex*, p. 193, n. 21, and Charles M. Clode, *The Early History of the Guild of Merchant Taylors of the Fraternity of St. John the Baptist, London*, 2 parts (London: privately printed by Harrison and Sons, 1888), I.111–112. The Merchant Taylors also in the fourteenth century acquired a chapel at St. Paul's (Clode, I.111). For the centrality of religious fraternities to the early London craft guilds, see Unwin, *Gilds and Companies*, pp. 52, 93–109, and Caroline M. Barron, "The Parish Fraternities of Medieval London," in Caroline M. Barron and Christopher Harper-Bill, eds., *The Church in Pre-Reformation Society: Essays in Honour of F. R. H. Du Boulay* (Woodbridge, Suffolk, and Dover, NH: Boydell Press, 1985), pp. 14–17.

175 See Clode, *Early History*, I.132. Richard II may also have been a member. Stow, *Survey*, I.182, lists as members all kings from Richard II through Henry VII.

176 Clode, *Early History*, I.4; see also I.63–64. (The Merchant Taylors/St. John's Priory association, in relation to 29 August, continued into the sixteenth century; see Fincham, *Order of the Hospital*, p. 17.)

177 See above, nn. 144 and 146.

178 See Nightingale, pp. 292–294 and 363, and Matthew Davies, "The Tailors of London: Corporate Charity in the Late Medieval Town," in Rowena E. Archer, ed., *Crown, Government and People in the Fifteenth Century*, The Fifteenth Century Series 2 (Stroud/New York: Alan Sutton/St. Martin's Press, 1995), pp. 166–167. Even members of other companies joined the fraternity for its religious life and social and political prestige.

179 In 1455, e.g., the Merchant Taylors' GL MS 34048/2 records, f. 41v, payments for waits at the company's own feast and going to the Hospital of St. John at the feast of St. John Baptist's nativity.

180 See Reginald H. Adams, *The Parish Clerks of London* (London and Chichester: Phillimore, 1971), pp. 13–15.

181 See Adams, *Parish Clerks*, p. 17, who believes the association dates from at least 1406 (p. 19), and also Christie, *Some Account of Parish Clerks*, pp. 27–29. By the sixteenth century the company was performing mass in Guildhall chapel before the annual election of the mayor (Adams, *Parish Clerks*, p. 19).

182 Stow, *Survey*, 1.16.

183 The Skinners' procession is mentioned in the company's 1392 charter as an activity of its fraternity of Corpus Christi: see John James Lambert, *Records of The Skinners of London, Edward I. to James I.* (London: The Company, 1933), p. 51, and also pp. 133–139 for more procession information. Stow, *Survey*, 1.230, mentions the procession but does not provide a starting date for it. He does suggest, 1.16, that the Skinners' early plays at Skinners' Well were replaced there by wrestlings. Mervyn James states (from Stow's reference), in "Ritual, Drama and Social Body," p. 24, n. 79, that the Skinners had "responsibility" for the Clerkenwell/Skinners' Well play; he does not mention the parish clerks, and does not note the Skinners' Corpus Christi procession. The Skinners would seem unlikely to have taken the lead in two such major events in a year as their procession and a major biblical play; and also it would seem unlikely for any single guild – other than perhaps the Parish Clerks, with their multiple parishes throughout London and with the support perhaps otherwise, too, of the Church – to have been responsible for an entire multi-day religious drama.

184 *Grey Friars* says, p. 56, that the year of suppression was 1547–48; but in the Skinners' extant accounts, which begin in 1491–92 (GL MS 30727/1), the Corpus Christi procession reference which appears every year, from the start, is replaced (GL MS 30727/3) by a reference to an election dinner in 1540–41 and 1541–42, and then again in 1547–48 and following years. (The 1543–44 account is missing.) Some parish Corpus Christi processions were revived under Mary (see Machyn, pp. 63–64).

185 Stow states, *Survey*, 1.230, that royal Skinners included Edward III, Richard II, Henry IV, V, and VI, and Edward IV; these are confirmed in Lambert, *Records of The Skinners*, p. 54, as members of the Skinners' Corpus Christi fraternity, along with others such as (p. 55) Humphrey Duke of Gloucester (son of Henry IV) and Richard Duke of Gloucester (who became Richard III). See also Thrupp, *London*, p. 31. Lambert also notes, pp. 82–83, two queens who were members of the fifteenth-century Skinners' yeomanry's fraternity of Our Lady's Assumption.

186 See above, n. 148.

187 *A Chronicle*, p. 80.

188 St. Katherine was the patron saint of the Haberdashers' Company; and several London churches were dedicated to her, as were at least nine London

parish fraternities before 1400 (see Unwin, *Gilds and Companies*, Appendix A, pp. 367–370). Thrupp points out (*London*, p. 34), e.g., that the parish fraternity of St. Katherine at St. Mary Colechurch in Cheapside was supported by well-to-do members of various crafts; this fraternity was founded in 1339 (Barron, "Parish Fraternities," p. 23) and purchased a royal licence in 1400 (Barron, "Parish Fraternities," p. 22 and n. 42). Ian W. Archer, *The History of The Haberdashers' Company* (Chichester: Phillimore, 1991), states (p. 10) that St. Katherine was the second most popular dedicatee of London parish fraternities; and see also Barron, "Parish Fraternities," p. 32. "The cult of St. Katherine was one of the most popular in later medieval England" (Archer, p. 10).

189 Another possibility, of course, is that the Clerkenwell/Skinners' Well play was begun in the 1380s by clerks foiled in an attempt to compete at Christmas time with the Paul's scholars.

190 [Robert Dodsley, ed.,] *A Select Collection of Old Plays*, vol. 1 (London: R. Dodsley, 1744), "Preface," p. xii.

191 Note that the references in Chaucer's late fourteenth-century *The Canterbury Tales* to miracle and mystery plays (see *DTR* nos. 231 and 1244) may well have been inspired, since Chaucer was a Londoner, at least in part by the Clerkenwell/Skinners' Well play, as may also have been his "Physician's Tale" in its apparent drawing on theatrical performance traditions of the presentation of Abraham's sacrifice of Isaac: a standard episode of Old Testament history as presented in all the extant provincial cycles (see Anne Lancashire, "Chaucer and the Sacrifice of Isaac," *Chaucer Review* 9 [1975], 320–326). Alan Nelson, *The Medieval English Stage*, has suggested (see p. 172) that Chaucer might even have been in charge of erecting timber scaffolds for London's 1390 play performance.

192 Perhaps worth noting, e.g., are the groups of clerks who witnessed a number of the deeds in the surviving cartulary of St. Mary's Clerkenwell; Hassall (*Cartulary*, p. xii) comments that they would have worn the tonsure and possibly attended a song school.

193 Caroline Barron has reported that before 1400 only two London companies (Goldsmiths and Merchant Taylors) definitely had their own halls; by 1520 the number had risen to at least 38. See *Atlas*, p. 50.

194 *DTR* no. 895: citing Herbert Francis Westlake, *Westminster Abbey: The Church, Convent, Cathedral and College of St. Peter, Westminster*, 2 vols. (London: Philip Allan, 1923), II.315, from the expenses of the sacrist.

195 *DTR* no. 889; for another fourteenth-century example of costumed tournament role-playing involving a procession through Cheapside to Smithfield, see *DTR* no. 896 (1375).

196 See *Chronica Johannis de Reading et Anonymi Cantuariensis 1346–1367*, ed. James Tait (Manchester: Manchester University Press, 1914), p.151.

197 See, e.g., *Annales Londonienses*, p. 157, and *Annales Paulini* (also in William Stubbs, ed., *Chronicles of the Reigns of Edward I. and Edward II.*, vol. I, RS 76 [London: HMSO, 1882]), p. 267.

198 Stow, *Survey*, 1.268, and *Annales*, pp. 493–494.

199 Sheila Lindenbaum has discussed the economic importance to London of Richard II's 1390 tournament in Smithfield, although she sees the show politically as affirming difference between court and city. See her "The Smithfield Tournament of 1390," *Journal of Medieval and Renaissance Studies* 20.1 (Spring 1990), 1–20. *DTR* cites (no. 884) a court London-area tournament involving Arthurian role-playing (its specific location is not clear); see Roger Sherman Loomis, "Edward I, Arthurian Enthusiast," *Speculum* 28 (1953), 118–121.

200 Such processional accompaniment had the advantage, of course, of being able to be read in two different ways: as a physical indication of the city's subservience to the Crown, the mayor and other important Londoners taking their places as "servants" of the monarch, and as a physical indication of the city's power, the king entering the city only with the agreement and escort of the mayor and his associates. The city needed the king's favour; the king needed the city's financial support. See also below, chapter 7, p. 133.

201 See *Chronica Johannis de Reading*, pp. 131–132, and *Brut*, p. 309.

202 LB H, f. 252r (and printed in translation in Riley's *Memorials*, pp. 521–522). Sharpe in *Cal. LB H* states (p. 353, n. 4), citing both Higden (i.e., Malverne) and Stow's 1592 *Annales*, that these jousts began on 10 October, with many foreign nobles present; an account of them is found in the *Westminster Chronicle*, pp. 436–439 and 450–451, and in Malverne, p. 241.

203 Paul Veyne has written, in another context (in *Bread and Circuses: Historical Sociology and Political Pluralism*, tr. Brian Pearce [Harmondsworth, Middlesex: Penguin, 1992]), about the sociopolitical philosophy of gift-giving by community notables to the community at large. Public entertainments are in some respects socially obligatory gifts.

4 COMPANY HALL PLAYS: PERFORMANCE RECORDS

1 The section of this chapter on the Drapers' Company is a revised version of my "Medieval to Renaissance: Plays and the London Drapers' Company to 1558," in Robert A. Taylor, James F. Burke, Patricia J. Eberle, Ian Lancashire, and Brian S. Merrilees, eds., *The Centre and its Compass: Studies in Medieval Literature in Honor of Professor John Leyerle*, Studies in Medieval Culture 33 (Kalamazoo, MI: Western Michigan University, Medieval Institute Publications, 1993), pp. 297–313, and is used here with the kind permission of the Board of the Medieval Institute, Kalamazoo. Information on the Blacksmiths' and Cutlers' early play records has previously appeared in "Plays for the London Blacksmiths' Company" and "Players for the London Cutlers' Company" in the *REED Newsletter*, 1981:1, pp. 12–14 and 1981:2, pp. 10–11, and is used here with the kind permission of REED.

2 For early London chronicles, in print and in MS, see (to 1911) Ralph Flenley, ed., *Six Town Chronicles of England* (Oxford: Clarendon Press, 1911),

pp. 96–98, and, more recently, Mary-Rose McLaren, "The Textual Transmission of the London Chronicles," *English Manuscript Studies 1100–1700*, 3 (1992), 64–67.

3 See the fifteenth-century originating dates provided for a good number of the London company halls in *Atlas*'s Gazetteer, and see also Barron, *Atlas*, p. 50.

4 By company "feast" I mean the entire formal period (one or two days) of company ceremonial, commemoration, and celebration, and not only the major dinner usually taking place during such a period.

5 The religious and social (fraternal) aspects of a London craft guild, as opposed to its trade aspects, were often organized (until 1545) through a "fraternity" devoted to a particular saint (e.g., St. Loye, for the Blacksmiths). Ordinances could be issued involving the craft guild's trade aspects, or its fraternal aspects, or both together. In some companies, such as the Merchant Taylors and the Skinners, a good number of individuals from other crafts also joined the fraternity (only), without otherwise being members of the company.

6 Merchant Taylors' GL MS 34048/1, f. 57r. I am grateful to Professor David Parkinson, University of Saskatchewan, for his search of Merchant Taylors' GL MSS 34048/1–3.

7 See, e.g., below, for the parish clerks paid for play performances by the Brewers in the early fifteenth century.

8 There were at least twenty-five crafts legally recognized in London by 1328, and fifty-one took part in Common Council elections in 1377 (David Nicholas, *The Growth of the Medieval City: From Late Antiquity to the Early Fourteenth Century* [London and New York: Longman, 1997], p. 286; George Unwin, *The Gilds and Companies of London* [London: Methuen, 1908], pp. 87–88). In 1422 a Brewers' Company MS lists 111 crafts in operation in the city (GL MS 5440, f. 11v), although not all of these crafts may have been organized into self-governing guilds; see Unwin, p. 88 (with the 1422 list reproduced on p. 167 and transcribed and translated on pp. 370–371). In 1488, eighty-two companies were assessed for taxation (Barron, *Atlas*, p. 50); and by *c.* 1500 there were seventy-eight craft guilds in London (Susan Brigden, *London and the Reformation* [Oxford: Clarendon Press, 1989], p. 140; and see also Jor. 10, f. 374r (*c.* seventy-eight). In 1540, fifty-eight were listed as attending the mayor's feast at the Guildhall (Cambridge University Library MS Ee.2.12, ff. 31v–33v). BL Harley MS 5111 includes a list (f. 75r) of "all the craftes" in London in 1533: seventy.

9 Also the companies with Anglo-Norman records use not the Anglo-Norman "ju," "jeu," "juer," etc. (see the *A–ND*), but the English "playe," "pleiers," etc.

10 William Tydeman, in *The Theatre in the Middle Ages: Western European Stage Conditions c. 800–1576* (Cambridge: Cambridge University Press, 1978), pp. 217–219, implies that the term "players," as far as professional entertainers were concerned, had begun normally to mean "actors" by at least the mid fifteenth century.

11 See, e.g., A. H. Johnson, *The History of The Worshipful Company of the Drapers of London*, 5 vols. (Oxford: Clarendon Press, 1914–22), and Tom Girtin, *The Triple Crowns: A Narrative History of The Drapers' Company, 1364–1964* (London: Hutchinson, 1964), *passim*.

12 Drapers' MS +795.

13 The ordinance (Drapers' MS +795, p. 29) comes from a group headed 1418 but including ordinances originating before 1418 (see MS heading, p. 26) and after 1418, with revisions of various dates. At least the final part of the ordinance immediately preceding this one is internally dated 7 August 33 Henry VI (i.e., 1455 – or perhaps 1454 if the start of the new regnal year on 1 September is being anticipated); but the *c.* 1418+ ordinances are apparently not set down in chronological order.

The first group of ordinances in the MS (pp. 19–21), from 1405, were copied down on 19 February 1 Edward IV according to their MS heading on p. 19; and the date 1460/1 has been entered in the margin, i.e. 1461 by our modern calendar. 19 February 1 Edward IV is, however, 1462. Probably the marginal date is a later error.

The *c.* 1418+ ordinances were probably copied down at about the same time as the 1405 ordinances they follow, as the same copying format and red and blue colouring are involved.

14 In this as in following quotations from the MS records, no marginal markings are recorded since none changes the meaning of the text itself.

15 Later correction: letter inserted above.

16 Later mark.

17 The whole section I have placed within square brackets has been cancelled at a later date. (For subsequent changes in feast funding arrangements, see below.) This ordinance has been printed in Johnson, *History*, I. 266–267.

18 See *OED*, s.v. Mess, *sb.*, II.4.

19 The ordinance must be dated no earlier than 1436–39 because it refers to company masters past and present, and we first hear of a master in the early wardens' accounts (1413–14 [?] to 1440–41, incomplete: Drapers' MS +140) in 1439, with the accounts being missing for 1435–36 to 1438–39. It also comes second-to-last in the group of ordinances, not all chronologically ordered, to be dated, overall, *c.* 1418–1462 (see n. 13 above).

20 Drapers' MS +795, p. 39. Also printed in Johnson, *History*, I.273–274.

21 These wardens' accounts (Drapers' MS +140) have been transcribed and printed by Johnson, *History*, I.282–348, and are also published in *Drapers' Company: Transcripts of the Earliest Records in the Possession of the Company* (London: Chiswick Press, 1910).

22 See Drapers' MS +140, ff. F3r, G3r, H3v, I4r, K2v.

23 Girtin, *Triple Crowns*, p. 52.

24 Drapers' MS +795, p. 45. Johnson calendars, *History*, I.278, and misdates as 1476.

25 Drapers' MS +795, p. 44; see also Johnson's calendaring, *History*, I.277 (misdated 1475). See also the ordinance passed on 17 Dec. 1466 (MS +795,

p. 42; Johnson, 1.276), which gives the wardens some Assumption-time fines for funding of their (unspecified) costs and charges.

26 Drapers' MS +795, p. 45.

27 Drapers' MS +795, p. 46; see also Johnson's calendaring, *History*, 1.278 (dated 1477–78).

28 Drapers' MS +403, f. 20r. This specific example is from 1481.

29 See Drapers' MS +403, ff. 41v, 45v, 56r.

30 Drapers' MS +403, ff. 15v, 17v.

31 Drapers' MS +795, p. 48; Johnson calendars, *History*, 1.279.

32 Drapers' MS +795, p. 48; Johnson calendars, *History*, 1.279.

33 Drapers' MS +795, p. 28; Johnson, *History*, 1.265.

34 Drapers' MS +130/1, p. 116.

35 From 1515–16 to 1558, see especially Drapers' MSS +130/1–3 (1515–16 to 1552–53), and also Drapers' MSS +128, +253, +254, +255, +140a, +252.

36 Drapers' MS +130/1, p. 101. There were no regular feast-time dinners 1522–26 (inclusive) and 1536.

37 1517, 1527, 1528, 1532, 1534, 1535, 1541.

38 For English's acting company, see *DTR*, Playing Companies to 1558, no. 267, 1 (where Rutter and Hinstock are also listed). In these Drapers' records, Rutter's company membership follows from English's, and Hinstock's is specified.

39 1516, 1518, 1520, 1530.

40 See, e.g., *DTR*, Playing Companies to 1558, nos. 275 and 267,1.

41 Drapers' MS +130/1, p. 157.

42 Drapers' MS +130/2, p. 607. In the late fourteenth and early fifteenth centuries, of course, a clerks' play would not necessarily have been "amateur" in terms of performance expertise, given, e.g., the large-scale performances at Clerkenwell to 1409; and an active parish clerk's group in early sixteenth-century London might well also have had sufficient paid performance opportunities to have become semi-professional.

43 The Drapers' specific play performance records, from 1485 on, have in large part been printed (though misdated in a number of instances) in the Malone Society's *Collections III*, some in the main body of collected records (under "III. Miscellaneous") and some as Addenda (pp. 183–184). For the misdating problems see Anne Lancashire, "Medieval to Renaissance: Plays and the London Drapers' Company to 1558," in *The Centre and its Compass*, pp. 308–309.

44 See *OED*, s.v. Mess, *sb.* 4 (a mess usually involved four people); also Drapers' MS +252, f. 11r (ten messes as involving forty-two people).

45 Drapers' MS +140, f. F3r.

46 GL MS 5440, ff. 58v and 194r.

47 See below, p. 88.

48 See below, on the Bakers and on the Pewterers.

49 Drapers' MS +254, p. 232. For the two Paul's companies in relation to this dinner, see Anne Lancashire, "St. Paul's Grammar School Before 1580:

Theatrical Development Suppressed?" in John H. Astington, ed., *The Development of Shakespeare's Theater* (New York: AMS Press, 1992), pp. 38–39.

50 See Anne Lancashire, "The Problem of Facts and the London Civic Records, 1275–1558," in Alexandra F. Johnston, ed., *Editing London Records* [provisional title] (Toronto: University of Toronto Press, forthcoming 2003).

51 See the Skinners' Receipts and Payments, GL MS 30727/1, account 1491–92, p. 13 (my count): Corpus Christi expenses, including for the procession, are said to be listed "particulerly in A Boke of the same", although the expense total for the company *is* listed in its main accounts, and a total continues to be entered every year to 1558 (see also the Skinners' accounts in GL MSS 30727/2–3, *passim*); with the Reformation, the reference to a Corpus Christi procession becomes replaced by a reference to an election dinner.

52 Merchant Taylors' GL MS 34105. See also the note in the Blacksmiths' Company's accounts for 1541–43, GL MS 2883/2, f. 305e r–v, that details of cony feast expenses are now in a separate book. Such detailed accountings would not normally survive longterm, as part of a company's permanent financial record.

53 The Mercers in 1540, e.g., ordered a separate accounting, by the wardens, of the company's June wages etc. and of a banquet for the king should he come to Mercers' Hall for the Midsummer Watch; see Mercers' MS Acts of Court 2 (1527–1560), f. 128r, for the order and ff. 111r (1538) and 151v (1542) for the Watch connection. A Mercer was mayor at midsummer in all of 1538, 1540, and 1542.

54 See, e.g., the Drapers' early ordinance, above, and the Blacksmiths' 1426 ordinance, below, both requiring a special feast-time payment from company members; and see also below on the Pewterers. The Brewers' earliest set of accounts (in GL MS 5440) notes in 1430 (f. 170r) that because of dinner costs for the masters, at the annual feast, for the first time dinner money was gathered in the hall at the tables (i.e., a special collection was taken up from company members to help cover the costs of the dinner). The Carpenters (GL MS 4326/1) paid for a barge going to and from Westminster at the mayor's annual oath-taking, from 1453 on, with a collection from members which at first only appeared in their accounts when there was a surplus (1455 – f. 4v) or a deficit (1470 – f. 24r).

55 See below, on the Cutlers' Company and its hired players.

56 For an example of the complex financial arrangements that could be involved for a special company occasion, with contributions from a variety of sources, see, e.g., GL MS 30727/2, Skinners' account for 1518–19, pp. 30 and 36 (a Christmas-season wassail, supper, and disguising, when a Skinner was mayor, paid for by all of individual company members, the religious guild associated with the Skinners, company monies collected in trade searches, and other company funds). In this instance the arrangements are recorded in the permanent accounts. (Skinners' account 1518–19 is wrongly dated on its first page but correctly dated on p. 27.)

57 Once a minstrel is paid 12d (Goldsmiths' MS 1522, Book D, p. 383–1518), and once waits are paid 20d (p. 408–1521); in both cases the eve drinking expenses and day dinner expenses are recorded together. I am grateful to Professor David Parkinson, University of Saskatchewan, for his search of Goldsmiths' MSS 1518 through 1523.

58 See below, chapter 6. The Goldsmiths' accounts contain very little in the way of regular itemized expenses for most of the fifteenth century.

59 See below, chapter 6.

60 See Drapers' MS +130/2, June 1541, p. 646: costs of midsummer minstrels, morris dancers, sword players, etc., have risen "by a wanton and superfluows precydence begon by mayres and Shereffes of the mercery". The Mercers' MS Acts of Court 2 (1527–1560), e.g., tells us (f. 102v) that the company erected a pageant at the Great Conduit for midsummer in both 1536 and 1537 – but provides no detail other than a final payment decision (f. 109v). Such detail presumably was provided outside the Acts of Court: e.g., see above, n. 53, for a separate special-occasion accounting ordered by the Mercers in 1540.

61 Merchant Taylors' GL MS 34048/1, f. 57r.

62 Merchant Taylors' GL MS 34048/1, f. 332v; see also the company's collection for this "Gyfte" for the mummers, f. 331r.

63 Merchant Taylors' GL MS 34048/1, f. 135v ("pur Albright oue mon sieur de Glouceter").

64 For Gloucester's acting troupe see *DTR*, Playing Companies to 1558, no. 279. Might these players also have been, wholly or in part, the mummers of 1440–41? Derek Pearsall, *John Lydgate (1371–1449): A Bio-bibliography*, English Literary Studies (Victoria, BC: University of Victoria, 1997), p. 33, notes that Gloucester in the early 1430s was at the height of his power and influence at court, and wanted a reputation "as a European patron of letters and as the English representative of the new Italian humanist learning;" and two Latin comedies were written in his household, probably in East Greenwich, 1437–38 (*DTR* no. 50). See below, chapter 6.

65 See chapter 3, p. 59 and n. 175.

66 Merchant Taylors' GL MS 34048/4, ff. 165v, 199r, 236r, 260r, 287v, 313v, 339r, 368r. The Goldsmiths employed the Paul's choristers for musical entertainment: see, e.g., *Collections III*, p. 139. These same Paul's children, however, apparently performed an interlude for the Drapers in 1557, as noted above.

67 GL MS 15333/1, pp. 155 ("pley"), 191 ("enterlude"). This Golder was probably the same Robert Golder who instructed four children playing angels in the Drapers' midsummer pageant of St. Margaret in 1541 (Drapers' MS +130/2, p.649). The 1542 occasion also involved a jester named "wyat", separately paid. For the possibility of further theatrical entertainment for the Vintners in this period, see below on the clerk of St. Magnus.

68 GL MS 30727/2, account 1511–12, p. 29 (my count), and account 1518–19, p. 36. See above, however, for the Skinners' major Corpus Christi feast-time

expenses as not detailed in the regular accounts. For disguisings, see above, p. 43, and below, p. 115, and chapter 6.

69 GL MS 11570, p. 213.

70 GL MS 11571/1, f. 26v; GL MS 11571/2, f. 71r.

71 GL MS 11571/2, ff. 137r, 161v, 182v. A tumbler and his man are also paid in 1468.

72 GL MS 11571/3, f. 119v (1514 – 8s), GL MS 11571/4, ff. 153r (1525 – 10s 4d), 225r (1526 – 20d). The 1526 payment of only 20d is specifically to John English, leader of the King's Players at the time (see *DTR*, Playing Companies to 1558, no. 267, 1), and "ye Iugler". Probably only the two performers were involved.

73 GL MS 11571/4, f. 459v.

74 GL MS 15333/1, p. 88.

75 The church of St. Magnus the Martyr, founded by the twelfth century, was (and still is) located at London Bridge; see above, chapter 3, n. 93. Over sixty-five years earlier the boys of St. Magnus had sung for the 1465 royal entry of Elizabeth Woodville: see *DTR* no. 942 (wrongly dating Elizabeth's entry 1464). For further speculation on the clerk of St. Magnus and his children/company, in relation to entertainment for the Vintners, see Lancashire, "The Problem of Facts," forthcoming.

76 GL MS 11571/4, f. 418v. *DTR* no. 1038 states (with references) that "ballett" was "a term commonly used for an interlude;" the *OED*, s.v. Ballet, 1., defines the word as meaning a "theatrical representation, consisting of dancing and pantomime," from the seventeenth century, and also as an obsolete form of "ballad."

77 GL MS 11571/5, f. 30r. These are clearly not the regular (adult) players of Charles Brandon, Duke of Suffolk, for which, see *DTR*, Playing Companies to 1558, no. 222.

78 GL MS 5535, p. 34. The ordinance as quoted here has been corrected in a different ink and hand, presumably at a later date, to read, starting at "ij d" and ending at "a pece &", "iij d the man & ij d the woma*n* whether thei come or come not & [a pece &]". The correction has been made by adding an extra i to the front of the original ij and going over the j again, adding a carat, adding the insertion partly above the line and partly in the righthand margin, and deleting the original three words "a pece &". The entire entry, along with others in the MS, has been cancelled at some later date. The "þey" of line one are the master and wardens of the company.

79 The 1434 ordinances appear in Henry Charles Coote's and John Robert Daniel-Tyssen's "The Ordinances of Some Secular Guilds of London, 1354–1496," *TLMAS* 4 (1871), 32–35.

80 See GL MS 2883/2, pp. 56 and 176, and also the regulation quoted above.

81 See GL MS 2883/1, p. 45. The written account heading gives the date of these accounts as from Michaelmas 11 Henry VII to Michaelmas 13 Henry VII (i.e., 29 September 1495 to 29 September 1497); a later inserted

slip and a marginal note give the dates as Michaelmas 1496 to Michaelmas 1498. I accept the original written account heading.

82 GL MS 2883/1, p. 51. The entry must be for 1496, as a second quarter-day players entry in the 1495–97 accounts is dated (via regnal year) as 1497.

83 GL MS 2883/1, pp. 52, 63, 66. For the 1497 date, see the two notes immediately above. The next set of accounts is similarly double-dated, and again I accept the original written account heading, Michaelmas 13 Henry VII to Michaelmas 15 Henry VII (i.e., 29 September 1497 to 29 September 1499). These 1497–99 accounts contain two play/players quarter-day entries unspecified as to year; but one clearly belongs to each of 1498 and 1499. The accounts also contain (p. 69) a 1499 payment for 2s 4d for "... ij torteȝes for the pley weiyng xix lb wast j lb demi the makyng and wast" – presumably for this same quarter-day play.

84 GL MS 2883/2, pp. 169 (1510: 4s 4d), 171–172 (1511: 4s), 56 (1512: 4s, also recorded on p. 176 but there crossed out), 63–64 (1513: 5s), 76–77 (1514: 4s 4d), 81 (1515: 4s 4d), 89 (1516: 5s), 92 (1517: 5s), 102 (1518: 5s), 104–105 (1519: 4s 8d), 116 (1520: 4s 8d).

85 GL MS 2883/2, pp. 129–130 (1522: 4s 8d), 136 (1523: 5s 4d), 151–152 (1525: 6s 8d), 158 (1526: 5s).

86 GL MS 2883/2, pp. 201–202 (the feast date could be 1529 or 1530 but 1529 is more likely), 215, 228, 238 (apparently wrongly dated 1536 instead of 1535), 250 (the feast date could be 1536 or 1537 but is probably 1537), 270–270a (270a is my numbering of the unpaginated verso of 270), 294–295. In both 1533 and 1535 the payment was 5s 4d instead of 5s.

87 GL MS 2883/2, p. 305e, r–v.

88 GL MS 2883/2, pp. 96–97. The date, from the accounts, could be 1548 or 1549; but at this period the cony feast seems to have been held only every second year, in odd-numbered years.

89 GL MS 2883/2, pp. 122–123. See the note immediately above; the alternate dates here are 1550 and 1551.

90 GL MS 2883/2, p. 168. See the two notes immediately above; the alternate dates here are 1554 and 1555.

91 GL MS 2883/2, pp. 151–152.

92 See above, n. 8.

93 GL MS 7146. The rentals of the hall to the Blacksmiths are to be found in rolls 1–13.

94 Surviving rolls cover the years (from one feast of the Trinity to the next) 1442–45, 1449–51, 1452–54, 1456–57, 1458–60, 1461–63, 1464–66, 1467–72, 1473–81, 1483–87, 1489–90, 1492–93, 1494–95, and 1496–98.

95 The last two (1470–72) of these sixteen, however, simply read "atte Cristmas" without reference to dinner.

96 Charles Welch in his *History of the Cutlers' Company of London*, 2 vols. (London: The Company, 1916–23) both refers to players at the company's annual cony feast, with specific mention of the dates 1492–93 and 1497–98

(1.151 and 177), and reproduces the wardens' accounts of 1442–43 and 1497–98 complete with their players entries (1.304 and 311). Tom Girtin, *The Mark of the Sword: A Narrative History of The Cutlers' Company 1189–1975* (London: Hutchinson Benham, 1975), refers generally, p. 77, to players at the cony feast and also, p. 85, speaks (with slight inaccuracy) of their having performed for over fifty years for a fee of 7s.

97 From 1515 the Drapers paid from 13s 4d to 15s 8d for their two annual plays: i.e., also around 7s per play. Before 1515 the Drapers' payment to players is included in a total payment for a number of items rather than being separately recorded.

98 E.g., 1492–93: "It*em* paid for a messe of mete for the same players xvj d".

99 Girtin, *Mark of the Sword*, notes, pp. 85–86, the new provision of food for the players by 1497.

100 GL MS 5440: ancient account and memorandum book kept by William Porland, company clerk.

101 GL MS 5440, ff. 14r (1419 – players, amount paid not separated), 58v (1421 – players/play, 7s), 80v (1423 – an "Int*er*ludy at Playe", 7s), 137r (1425 – players, 7s), 181v (1431 – players, 3s 4d), 194r (1432 – play, 3s 4d), 218v and 220v (1433 – players/play, 4s 4d), 228r and 229v (1434 – players/play, 5s 4d), 246v and 249r (1435 – players/play, 5s 4d), 258v (1436 – players, 4s 4d), 281v (1437 – play, 4s 2d), 297r (1438 – players, amount paid not separated), 316v (1439 – play, amount paid not separated). For 1430's costs problem and fragmentary folio, see ff. 170r and 171.

102 1421, 1432, 1435, 1437, 1439.

103 1421, 1433, 1434, 1435, 1436, 1437.

104 A mass was also specified and the words then cancelled; the entry reads (square brackets indicate the cancellation) "to the Clerkes of london for apleye and for here labo*ur* atte owre feste [w*ith* the feste Messe of owre lady] x s".

105 GL MS 5440, f. 41v, col. b.

106 GL MS 4326/1, ff. 4r, 53v. The play entry on f. 4r has been added in a different hand (which has also totalled the expenses on the page and made corrections in the text above).

107 GL MS 4326/1, ff. 21r, 36v, 38v, 68r, 70v, 76r.

108 GL MS 4326/1, ff. 91r–167r.

109 The fragmentary account preceding the 1546–47 account in GL MS 4326/2 is for 1545–46.

110 In 1480–81, however, minstrels are paid 3s 4d on an unspecified occasion which may have been the feast, and similarly 2s in 1488–89 (GL MS 4326/1, ff. 37v, 50v).

111 Similarly the Blacksmiths' Company in the sixteenth century consistently pays for players at its winter cony feast and minstrels at its midsummer feast; see GL MSS 2883/1–2, *passim*.

112 Typical induction ceremonial – involving processions and the crowning of the new company officers with garlands – is described in the Ironmongers'

Charter, Ordinance, and Memorandum Book (GL MS 16960), f. 26v; and
see also, among other examples, Drapers' MS +130/2, p. 658.

113 GL MS 4326/1, f. 77r.

114 GL MS 4326/1, f. 118v, 126r. At all of the 1502, 1505 and 1507 feasts, a taborer is paid 4d, and 6d together with a luter in 1503 (ff. 93r, 120v, 132r,
110v); is 1506's "barnard" perhaps a taborer? Also in 1505, however, a
jester/storyteller is paid 4d at May quarter day (f. 118v).

115 GL MS 6152/1, f. 68v. These would probably be the boys of St. Anthony's
(Hospital) school, who performed in a Merchant Taylors' Lord Mayor's
Show pageant in 1556 (Merchant Taylors' GL MS 34105, f. 30v), playing,
singing, and reciting speeches (ff. 1v, 30v, 31r); or perhaps they were the
schoolboy orphans of Christ's Hospital school (founded 1553) or the boys
of St. Thomas of Acon's (Hospital) school.

116 GL MS 6152/1, ff. 68v, 19v.

117 GL MS 6155/1, *passim*. One of the two non-player years occurs where a
MS leaf is missing.

118 GL 7086/2, f. 224r. The deletion is illegible.

119 GL MS 7094, f. 65r.

120 GL MS 1574/1, f. 197r.

121 GL MS 1574/1, ff. 135r, 212v. For St. Clement's Day 1531, 4d was paid to
"A Man that pleyed with A Dogg" (f. 146v).

122 For 1539 the MS notes (f. 213r) that the St. Clement's dinner expenses are
recorded in detail elsewhere. No MS including such details is now extant.

123 See George Norton, *Commentaries on the History, Constitution, and Chartered
Franchises of The City of London* (London: Henry Butterworth, 1829), pp.
457–458. The clerk of the market was a royal officer concerned with
weights and measures; and by Edward IV's first charter to London, "the
clerkship of the market in London was conferred upon the City." The
city's Repertories record a John Wilmot as Common Weigher of Bread in
Oct. 1531 (Rep. 8, f. 183r), as a mayor's officer in July 1534 (Rep. 9, f. 65r),
and (as having kept Aldgate) as late deceased in Nov. 1535 (Rep. 9, f. 135v).

124 Coopers – GL MSS 5614A, 5606/1; Wiresellers/Pinners – BL Egerton
MS 1142 (a photostat copy is in the Guildhall Library, GL MS 6526);
Leathersellers – MS Liber Curtes, vol. 1 (Leathersellers' Hall); Weavers –
GL MS 4646; Armourers and Brasiers – GL MS 12065/1; Founders – GL
MS 6330/1. Liber Curtes also includes audit statements from 1531, plus
receipts of rents and of corn money.

125 GL MS 6330/1, p. 256, GL MS 4646, f. 9r.

126 Wax Chandlers – GL MS 9481/1 (renter wardens' accounts); Butchers –
GL MS 6440/1; Stationers – wardens' accounts 1554–1571 (Register A);
Curriers – GL MS 14346/1.

127 GL MS 9481/1, f. 54r.

128 Some of the non-Great companies also have other kinds of early MSS,
such as the Scriveners' Common Paper (GL MS 5370), which has been
edited by Francis W. Steer, *Scriveners' Company Common Paper 1357–1628, With a*

Continuation to 1678 (London Record Society, 1968); all such MSS have been checked but, apart from the Blacksmiths' GL MS 5535 (a memorandum book), previously dealt with, have yielded no play records. The date spans given above for the extant accounts of the various companies are from the MSS themselves and do not necessarily correspond to the date spans in the MSS titles or under which the MSS have been catalogued.

129 GL MS 12071/1, p. 115. Sydney Hewitt Pitt in *Some Notes on the History of the Worshipful Company of Armourers and Brasiers* (London: The Company, 1930) cites, p. 35, a scaramouch (a stock character from Italian farce) at a 1557 company dinner; but no such entry can now be found. The MS, of course, has been badly water-damaged since 1930; but Pitt also associates the dinner with the death of prominent company member John Richmond (an odd association for a scaramouch), and Richmond died not in 1557 but in 1559 (GL MS 12071/1, p. 553; Beaven, II.29), where no scaramouch MS entry can now be found either. (Sydney Pitt is probably drawing on G. Newton Pitt's transcription of dinner expenses – including for a scaramouch – in his *Notes on the History of the Armourers' & Brasiers' Company* [London: The Company, 1914], p. 13, where the dinner concerned is linked to Richmond's death but is undated. The item immediately above, in Pitt's 1914 work, concerns a 1557 bequest by Richmond.) The *OED* does not provide any examples of the term "scaramouch" in England before 1662.

130 Only the Blacksmiths, however, record regular hall performances by actors into the 1550s: although the Pewterers' records also suggest play performances then. The late 1530s through the 1540s was a period of company hall rentals to players; rentals are recorded by the Armourers and Brasiers (GL MS 12065/1, f. 122v), Founders (GL MS 6330/1, pp. 308, 311, 314, 323, 332), and Weavers (GL MS 4646, f. 17r, ?226r); and the Pewterers (GL MS 7086/2, ff. 60r, 80v, 88r, 118r, 123r, 149v; the last rental was in 1551–52) rented mainly or entirely to a Spaniard with a dancing school. Did players around this time begin performing less at company feasts and more under their own auspices, for political or other reasons? See below, chapter 5, p. 113.

131 *DTR* lists a few late fifteenth-century troupes, with noble patrons, which might have been available for performances in London when their patron was at London or Westminster. See *DTR*, Playing Companies to 1558, Part B, *passim*.

132 It should perhaps be noted that Wriothesley, II.118, though in connection with anti-Roman propaganda, refers in 1554 to one Myles, clerk of St. Botolph's in Aldersgate St. and a player. In 1557–58 players rented Trinity Hall from St. Botolph without Aldersgate (*DTR* no. 1109).

133 See Anne Lancashire, "St. Paul's Grammar School," pp. 29–31.

134 See *DTR* no. 1065, Anne Lancashire, "St. Paul's Grammar School," pp. 30–31, and above, p. 79.

135 William Ingram, *The Business of Playing: The Beginnings of the Adult Professional Theater in Elizabethan London* (Ithaca and London: Cornell University

Press, 1992), argues (see especially p. 75) that the evidence of the mid six-teenth century is of a city "full of stage players." *DTR*, Playing Companies to 1558, no. 107, also lists a number of performances outside London by players associated with the city.

5 COMPANY HALL PLAYS: TYPES AND PERFORMERS

1 A. H. Johnson, *The History of The Worshipful Company of the Drapers of London*, 5 vols. (Oxford: Clarendon Press, 1914–22).
2 Bower Marsh, ed., *Records of the Worshipful Company of Carpenters*, vol. 1 (Oxford and London: The Company, 1913).
3 G. Newton Pitt, *Notes on the History of the Armourers' & Brasiers' Company* (London: The Company, 1914). To 1913, the Armourers and Brasiers' history had so far been dealt with in print in a book by Timothy Morley, *Some Account of The Worshipful Company of Armourers and Brasiers, in the City of London* (London: The Company, 1878), and in two articles in *TLMAS*, NS 2 (1911–13), E. Jackson Barron's "Notes on the History of the Armourers' and Brasiers' Company," pp. 300–319, and (Viscount) [Harold Arthur Lee-] Dillon's "The Arms and Armour at Armourers' Hall," pp. 320–324.
4 For the three works, see the note immediately above.
5 GL MSS 12071/1,12065/1, 12073. A further quick check of Armourers and Brasiers' MSS all the way to 1642 indeed yields nothing resembling Pitt's feast description.
6 The surviving Parish Clerks' Company records are at the Guildhall Library. Printed editions of the records of various London parishes also provide no help with Pitt's possible source(s) (*DTR* has surveyed them to 1984, and I have looked at later printed material).
7 William Herbert, *The History of the Twelve Great Livery Companies of London*, 2 vols. (London: privately printed, 1834–37; rpt. Newton Abbot: David and Charles, 1968), 1.76.
8 William Fitz Stephen's late twelfth-century *Description of London*, e.g., with its reference to London's "holier plays" (see above, chapter 2, p. 31), may be one source for Herbert and/or writers before him, given the tendency of early historians of London theatre to generalize as though *c.* 1200 to *c.* 1550 was a span of only fifty rather than 350 years. See p. 30 of Fitz Stephen's "Descriptio Londoniae," tr. H. E. Butler ("A Description of London"), in F. M. Stenton's *Norman London: An Essay*, new edn. (London: Historical Association Leaflets nos. 93–94, 1934). I have not, however, fur-ther pursued the matter of printed sources for Herbert.
9 Drapers' MS +130/1, p.101. Since the bachelors in a company usually kept their own accounts, it is unusual to find this expense in the regular company accounts; perhaps the 8d involved here was a company addition to a sum already being paid by the bachelors (for a regular play?), other-wise this performer would seem to have been, for some reason, a special company "gift" to the bachelors.

10 "It*em* to hym that playd the ffrere at the Bachillers supper viij d". Susan Brigden, *London and the Reformation* (Oxford: Clarendon Press, 1989), p. 121, cites this record as a likely example of a performance involving conventional satire upon the clergy.

11 See *DTR*, Playing Companies to 1558, Part B, *passim*. The early fifteenth-century listings are especially significant when one takes into account the more limited information surviving from the earlier period than from later ones.

12 See above, chapter 4, pp. 77–78.

13 See above, chapter 4, pp. 91, 90, 86.

14 See above, chapter 4, p. 83.

15 See above, chapter 4, p. 93.

16 See above, chapter 4, pp. 79, 82.

17 Herbert, *History*, I.40–112. One reference by Herbert, I.103, to the Haberdashers may be, but probably is not, a reference directly to their records. Few early Haberdashers' records, however, have survived, and these (largely now on deposit at the Guildhall Library, with a few still at the company's hall) contain, pre-1559, no references to plays or players in any volumes of a type likely to contain such references.

18 Leathersellers' MS Liber Curtes 1.

19 GL MS 5442/1–2, *passim*. Many of the entries do not specify the date or the hall location, but others do, and all seem related to the same recurring occasion.

20 See, e.g., E. K. Chambers, *The Mediaeval Stage*, 2 vols. (Oxford: Oxford University Press, 1903), I.363 and 369–371, *EES*, III.182–3, and James Christie, *Some Account of Parish Clerks* (London: The Worshipful Company of Parish Clerks, 1893), pp. 58–60. Dressing children as priests, bishops, and women, on the feasts of St. Nicholas, St. Katherine, St. Clement, the Holy Innocents, etc., was finally prohibited in England in 1541, although the practice does not seem to have stopped as ordered; see *DTR* no. 289, and Christie, pp. 62–63. The accession of Mary to the throne further complicated such matters. See, e.g., Edward F. Rimbault, introduction to "Two Sermons Preached by The Boy Bishop," ed. John Gough Nichols (Camden Society, NS 14, 1875), pp. xx–xxiii.

21 Herbert does use Drapers' Company records in vol. I of his *History*, for his section on the company itself (pp. 389–498): there once citing, p. 469, a play performance record (from 1516, though he dates it 1514–15) involving Sly and his company (see Drapers' MS +130/1, p. 7).

22 See *DTR* no. 721. The entertainment is not extant.

23 See *DTR* no. 999. These particular schoolboys – of St. Paul's grammar school, not choir school – may not have performed much otherwise; see Anne Lancashire, "St. Paul's Grammar School Before 1580: Theatrical Development Suppressed?" in John H. Astington, ed., *The Development of Shakespeare's Theater* (New York: AMS Press, 1992), pp. 29–56.

24 The Grocers' records, e.g., specify a tumbler in 1456 (GL MS 11571/1,

f. 43r), a "tregetour" (juggler, magician) in 1459 (GL MS 11571/1, f. 91r), and a tumbler and his man, along with players and minstrels, in 1468 (GL MS 11571/2, f. 161v).

25 Suzanne R. Westfall, *Patrons and Performance: Early Tudor Household Revels* (Oxford: Clarendon Press, 1990), believes otherwise, however, stating, p. 33, n. 21, that such differentiation was not normal or clear in this period.

26 Of course, these plays' very survival, in MS or in print, may indicate that they were unusual in some way. It has been suggested, e.g., that some play texts may have been printed when a given troupe's patron felt such printing to be useful for his political purposes; see, e.g., Westfall, *Patrons and Performance*, pp. 113–114.

27 This conforms to David M. Bevington's finding, in *From 'Mankind' to Marlowe: Growth of Structure in the Popular Drama of Tudor England* (Cambridge, MA: Harvard University Press, 1962), p. 79, that pre-Elizabethan adult troupes largely if not always did not include a boy (i.e., were four men, not the "four men and a boy" of the fictional earlier acting troupe of the 1590s play *Sir Thomas More*; for a discussion of *More*, see below). It also matches Westfall's finding (see her *Patrons and Performance*, p. 126, and its Appendix A) of four as the normal size of adult troupes with royal or noble patrons.

28 As previously noted in chapter 4, for an example of such ceremonial, see the Charter, Ordinance, and Memorandum Book of the Ironmongers' Company: GL MS 16960, f. 26v. This particular company act is to be dated after 20 March 1463 and probably after 1498; the MS hand is to be dated some time in the early sixteenth century but the act could be older than its copying into the MS. See also the Drapers' MS +130/2, p. 658 (one of numerous mid sixteenth-century descriptions of the Drapers' election ceremonial).

29 Two-part possibilities in general – not linked to company performances – are indicated by Medwall's two-part *Fulgens and Lucres* and *Nature*, both performed on probably aristocratic occasions in the 1490s, and by the 1530–60 (?) *Resurrection of Our Lord*, divided in MS into the first and second days' plays. For the dates of all three, see *DTR*, Dramatic Texts, nos. 81, 78, and 112. The provincial cycles and the Clerkenwell play were multipart enterprises.

30 Henry Machyn mentions in his *Diary* (Machyn, p. 22) a "skaffold for the play" set up in January 1560 in what appears to be a livery company hall. (The play was followed by a mask.) But T. W. Craik, *The Tudor Interlude: Stage, Costume, and Acting* (Leicester: Leicester University Press, 1958), argues, p. 10, that raised stages for plays in halls were not usual before the later sixteenth century, and, p. 11, that references to a "skaffold" might in any case be to audience seating. See Craik on hall staging in general, pp. 7–26, and also Richard Southern, *The Staging of Plays before Shakespeare* (London: Faber and Faber, 1973), *passim*.

31 For a persuasive argument as to the many plays, now lost, originally

performed in the early Tudor period, see Westfall, *Patrons and Performance*, pp. 110–112.

32 Suitability, of course, could involve political (and, after Henry VIII's break with Rome, religious) interpretation; and David Bevington's *Tudor Drama and Politics: A Critical Approach to Topical Meaning* (Cambridge, MA: Harvard University Press, 1968) long ago demonstrated the political nature of a great deal of late fifteenth and early sixteenth-century drama, while most recently Greg Walker has argued the politics of this drama in both *Plays of Persuasion: Drama and Politics at the Court of Henry VIII* (Cambridge: Cambridge University Press, 1991) and *The Politics of Performance in Early Renaissance Drama* (Cambridge: Cambridge University Press, 1998). I have nevertheless avoided the debates on political meanings, except to note where appropriate that a company norm would probably have been to avoid highly political performance pieces that might create political problems for the guild.

33 Drapers' MS +143, f. 23r (for 1512). For a printed collection of the Drapers' Midsummer Watch records, see the transcriptions from the Drapers' MSS in *Collections III*'s Midsummer Watch section, pp. 1–36.

34 See Beadle, p. xxi.

35 See, e.g., the *Annals*' fifteenth-century listings; and the REED project, with its ongoing series of published volumes, is finding records of more of such plays, as noted by Alexandra F. Johnston (though not for the fifteenth century specifically) in "What if No Texts Survived? External Evidence for Early English Drama," in Marianne G. Briscoe and John C. Coldewey, eds., *Contexts for Early English Drama* (Bloomington and Indianapolis: Indiana University Press, 1989), pp. 6–7 and especially n. 8. See also Johnston's note (" 'Amys and Amylon' at Bicester Priory") in the *REED Newsletter* 18.2 (1993), 15–18, on a record of a miracle play, *Amys and Amylon*, performed at Bicester in 1424.

36 Midsummer Watch saints' pageants dealt with, e.g., Sts. Blythe, Elizabeth, John the Evangelist, George, Margaret, John the Baptist, Thomas Becket, Ursula, and Christopher: see *DTR* no. 969.

37 GL MS 12071/2, p. 483: "And after a boye armid with a virgine following hime leading a Lamb came in with a drome and flute before theme/and after marching thrisse aboutt the hall their tables all sett they marched to the high tabill with a speache".

38 See above, Introduction, n. 1.

39 See David Bevington, ed. and tr., *Medieval Drama* (Boston: Houghton Mifflin, 1975), p. 921, n. to line 503. Bevington's edited text of the play runs to 914 lines.

40 Bevington, *From 'Mankind' to Marlowe*, counts, p. 70, *Nature*'s lines as 1439 + 1421. Westfall, *Patrons and Performance*, points out, p. 56, that twenty-two different costumes are required.

41 See *DTR*, Dramatic Texts, no. 78: also the source of the *c*. 1490–1500 date given here.

42 Westfall suggests, *Patrons and Performance*, p. 56, that it was performed for Morton by a combination of his various household entertainers.

43 *DTR*, Dramatic Texts, no. 78.

44 See *DTR*, Dramatic Texts, no. 81. A particular performance occasion has been suggested (see, e.g., Bevington, *From 'Mankind' to Marlowe*, p. 43): before the ambassadors of Flanders and of Spain at Christmas 1497.

45 The line counts are from Bevington's *From 'Mankind' to Marlowe*, p. 70.

46 Bevington, *From 'Mankind' to Marlowe*, p. 44; Westfall, *Patrons and Performance*, pp. 56–57. Alan H. Nelson, ed., *The Plays of Henry Medwall* (Cambridge/Totowa, NJ: D. S. Brewer/Rowman and Littlefield, 1980), specifically suggests, p. 19, that professional actors were employed but that some of the performers may have been boy choristers from Morton's chapel.

47 Bevington, *Tudor Drama and Politics*, pp. 44–51, comments on the play's political allusions and significance but notes Medwall's tactful use above all of comedy to safeguard against giving political offence.

48 *DTR* no. 1226.

49 For a list of some editions of *Robin Hood and the Sheriff*, see *DTR* no. 1226; an especially good edn. is by W. W. Greg, "Robin Hood and the Sheriff of Nottingham," in *Collections I.2* (Malone Society, 1908), pp. 117–123. Johnston, "What if No Texts Survived?", p. 7, notes the "truly astounding" popularity of Robin Hood as a dramatic subject in the south and west of England and in Scotland, largely for parishes. She does not distinguish between the fifteenth and the sixteenth centuries. For the sixteenth century specifically, at least partly in London, see below. There might also have been fifteenth-century plays, available for London performance, on romance subject matter including material from ballads; but none has survived. In Bermondsey, a play about a knight named Florence was performed in August 1444, probably with abbey auspices; and a play about Sir Eglamour of Artois was in St. Albans in late June 1444 (see *DTR*, nos. 373 and 1353).

50 See Westfall, *Patrons and Performance*, pp. 126 and 210–212.

51 See *DTR*, Dramatic Texts, no. 88, whose dating for the play is also here cited.

52 Here and below, except where footnoted otherwise, all line counts for plays are taken from Bevington's *From 'Mankind' to Marlowe*, pp. 69–70, as are numbers of actors required, p. 72. Bevington explains, pp. 290–291, n. 3, how his counts were done. Line counts by others, of other plays, will not necessarily conform to what the numbers might have been if they had been done by Bevington in 1962, but will provide at least a rough sense of play lengths.

53 For the various datings that have been suggested for *More*, see G. Harold Metz, "'Voice and credyt': The Scholars and *Sir Thomas More*," in T. H. Howard-Hill, ed., *Shakespeare and 'Sir Thomas More': Essays on the Play and its Shakespearian Interest* (Cambridge: Cambridge University Press, 1989), pp. 25–29, and also Scott McMillin's work within the same volume, "*The Book of Sir Thomas More*: Dates and Acting Companies," pp. 57–76.

54 For the titles as given within the play, see *The Book of Sir Thomas More*, ed. W. W. Greg (Malone Society, 1911), lines †919–922.

55 Here and below, dates given for extant early sixteenth-century texts are, unless specifically footnoted otherwise, from *DTR*'s Chronological List of Dramatic Texts, pp. 3–31, as are dates of printed editions of the plays.

56 As performed within *More*, the text of *The Marriage of Wit and Wisdom* also comes in part from other Tudor interludes: *Lusty Juventus*, *The Disobedient Child*, and (for the Vice's name) *The Trial of Treasure*. See John Jowett, "Henry Chettle and the Original Text," in Howard-Hill, *Shakespeare and 'Sir Thomas More'*, p. 133, and Giorgio Melchiori and Vittorio Gabrieli, "A Table of Sources . . . ," in the same volume, p. 199.

57 One – *The Cradle of Security* (*c.* 1570) – exists in a description by a seventeenth-century writer of a moral play he had seen, when a boy, performed by travelling players before the mayor, aldermen and council in a civic hall in Gloucester (see R. Willis, *Mount Tabor*, 1639, as quoted by Bevington, *From 'Mankind' to Marlowe*, pp. 13–14); another, *Dives and Lazarus* (*c.* 1570?), is referred to in other works of the period (see *From 'Mankind' to Marlowe*, p. 19); the third, *Hit the Nail o' th' Head* (*c.* 1570?), is nowhere referred to outside *Sir Thomas More*. Cast sizes and lengths for all three remain a mystery. Dates given here for the three are from the *Annals*.

58 1544: Walker, *Politics of Performance*, p. 234 (but also possibly a now-lost 1534 edn.).

59 Despite the varying political interpretations of many early Tudor plays, Heywood's pieces are generally agreed to be genial, anti-inflammatory, moving towards a reconciliation of differing points of view both within the plays and within their audiences. See, e.g., on *The Four PP*, Alistair Fox, *Politics and Literature in the Reigns of Henry VII and Henry VIII* (Oxford and New York: Basil Blackwell, 1989), pp. 250–251. Greg Walker has analyzed the politics of Heywood's plays in considerable detail in *Politics of Performance*, pp. 76–116, but calls his chapter "John Heywood and the politics of contentment." On *The Four PP*, see his pp. 91–100.

60 All three plays are discussed, as examples of pre-Shakespearean adult professional drama, in Bevington's *From 'Mankind' to Marlowe*, pp. 19–21. *Impatient Poverty* was printed in 1560, and *Lusty Juventus*, perhaps *c.* 1550 (*DTR*, Dramatic Texts, nos. 152 and 148).

61 Actor counts are mine. Walker, *Politics of Performance*, pp. 80–85, sees *The Pardoner and the Friar* as political and as possibly to be dated as late as 1532–33.

62 Bevington, *From 'Mankind' to Marlowe*, suggests (p. 41) they were written to be recited at banquets. Actor numbers for both, and the line estimate for *Witty and Witless* (in *The Dramatic Writings of John Heywood*, ed. John S. Farmer [London: Early English Drama Society, 1905; rpt. New York: Barnes and Noble, 1966]), are mine.

63 The line count is from Richard Axton's edition, in his *Three Rastell Plays* (Cambridge and Ipswich/Totowa, NJ: D. S. Brewer/Rowman and Littlefield,

1979); the play is missing a conclusion but Axton believes that very little has been lost. The publication date is from *DTR*, Dramatic Texts, no. 96 (with a query mark there); Walker, *Politics of Performance*, pp. 17 and 233, gives *c.* 1525–27.

64 For a discussion of the two versions of the play, see Bevington, *From 'Mankind' to Marlowe*, pp. 45–47; and see also Westfall, *Patrons and Performance*, p. 57. Bevington suggests that Rastell wrote the play, according to humanist educational principles, for performance on his own stage (for which, see below, pp. 115–116); but the play and even its printing may date from before Rastell's stage was constructed: see Axton, *Three Rastell Plays*, pp. 8–9, who states that Rastell's stage was constructed in 1524. Rastell was notably connected with both court and city in his professional pageant-making activities: see Axton, pp. 7–8.

65 For disguisings in early sixteenth-century London, see below, p. 115.

66 See Axton, *Three Rastell Plays*, pp. 15–17. The line count is from Axton's text.

67 The line count is from Axton's text (in *Three Rastell Plays*). Fox, *Politics and Literature*, pp. 246–247, argues for Rastell's authorship, and Axton, pp. 20–26, for Heywood's.

68 The actor counts are mine.

69 *Calisto and Melebea*, printed *c.* 1525 (*DTR*, Dramatic Texts, no. 106) or *c.* 1525–30 (Walker, *Politics of Performance*, p. 233); *Gentleness and Nobility*, printed 1533 (*DTR*, Dramatic Texts, no. 98) or *c.* 1529 (Walker, *Politics of Performance*, p. 234). Another play printed by Rastell or by his son William, *c.* 1530 according to *DTR*, Dramatic Texts, no. 110, is extant now only in an eighty-four-line fragment: a lively piece about a husband, a shrewish wife, and a prodigal son. The fragment has four characters and a song, and at least from these eighty-four lines looks like potential court and city theatrical material similar to Heywood's *Johan Johan* and *The Four PP*. See W. W. Greg, ed., "The Prodigal Son," in *Collections I.1* (Malone Society, 1907), pp. 27–30.

70 *From 'Mankind' to Marlowe*, especially pp. 69–73.

71 *DTR*, Dramatic Texts, no. 154.

72 See Bevington, *From 'Mankind' to Marlowe*, p. 53; the title page of the original 1560s printing wrongly states that only four actors are required.

73 See A. Esdaile, ed., "Love Feigned and Unfeigned," in W. W. Greg, ed., *Collections I.1* (Malone Society, 1907), pp. 17–25. The line and actor counts are from this text.

74 See *DTR*, Dramatic Texts, no. 92, from which this date also is taken, and Ian Lancashire, ed., *Two Tudor Interludes: 'The Interlude of Youth', 'Hickscorner'* (Manchester/Baltimore: Manchester University Press/Johns Hopkins University Press, 1980), pp. 49–58.

75 See *DTR*, Dramatic Texts, no. 95, and Ian Lancashire, *Two Tudor Interludes*, pp. 58–64. Lancashire also corrects to four, p. 32, Bevington's counted four to five actors. Walker, *Plays of Persuasion*, bases his analysis of the play, pp. 42–59, on Lancashire's.

76 For examples of three different, highly political interpretations of *Magnificence*, among a good number, see: (1) Robert Lee Ramsay's edn. of the play for the EETS (Extra Series 98, 1908; rpt. 1958), pp. cvi–cxxviii – titular character as Henry VIII, play as satire against Wolsey; (2) Paula Neuss's edn. for the Revels Plays (Manchester/Baltimore: Manchester University Press/Johns Hopkins University Press, 1980), pp. 31–42 – titular character as Wolsey, play as satire against him; (3) Fox, *Politics and Literature*, pp. 237–238 – titular character as Henry VIII, play as commentary on the 1519 expulsion of four of his minions. Neuss says nothing as to why the play would have been performed in Merchant Taylors' Hall; Fox does not say that the Merchant Taylors commissioned it but does state that the play presents the Londoners' point of view and functions as political pressure on the king. One example of a broader interpretative perspective is Seth Lerer's in his *Courtly Letters in the Age of Henry VIII: Literary Culture and the Arts of Deceit* (Cambridge: Cambridge University Press, 1997); Lerer suggests, pp. 57–65, that *Magnificence* criticizes the theatricality of politics and of satiric theatre itself. Walker, *Plays of Persuasion*, pp. 60–101, discusses a variety of interpretations.

77 The two lines upon which Neuss (Revels edn., p. 43) bases her argument are (1)"Measure is meet for a merchant's hall" and, *c.* 1000 lines later, (2) "Ye have eaten sauce, I trow, at the Taylors' Hall" (a sarcastic jibe by the titular character at a virtuous character). "Merchant," of course, was a term covering the members of a number of London companies (and their wealthy foreign counterparts), not simply the Merchant Taylors; and we do not necessarily, for example, place a play at Westminster because its text refers to Westminster. Further close examination of both the text and its historical circumstances is required before placing the play at Merchant Taylors' Hall or anywhere else.

78 See Walker, *Plays of Persuasion*, pp. 88–90 on the play's auspices and pp. 66–101 on interpretation.

79 For a discussion of Bale's plays, especially in performance, see Paul Whitfield White, *Theatre and Reformation: Protestantism, Patronage, and Playing in Tudor England* (Cambridge: Cambridge University Press, 1993), pp. 12–41. White notes that "religious strife and angry opposition are linked with every known production of Bale's plays" (p. 29). On the other hand, White sees Bale's plays as an important part of the political propaganda manoeuvrings of Henry VIII's chief 1530s minister, Thomas Cromwell.

80 See, e.g., the varying political interpretations of a number of early Tudor plays as given by Bevington, *Tudor Drama and Politics*, Walker, *Plays of Persuasion* and *Politics of Performance*, and Fox, *Politics and Literature*. As an alternative to political interpretations, Westfall provides, *Patrons and Performance*, pp. 152–199, more generalized moral interpretations – focused on aristocratic and humanist concerns – of a number of early Tudor plays.

81 For likely disagreement, e.g., within the Mercers' Company over performances by the boys of St. Paul's grammar school (run by the company) –

although not at Mercers' feasts – see Anne Lancashire, "St. Paul's Grammar School," pp. 41–42.

82 See *DTR* nos. 1037, 1042, 1047, 1051; also 1046. Before the 1542 prohibition there was a 1541 playing, initiated by the keeper of Carpenters' Hall, of an interlude against priests (see *DTR* nos. 1035 and 1036). In April 1543 one William Blytheman, a Clothworker, one George Tadlowe (or Gadlowe), a Haberdasher, and one Thomas Hancokkes, a Vintner, were obliged to agree not to permit any interludes or common plays within their London dwelling houses; see Rep. 10, ff. 322v–323r, and, for further information, Anna Jean Mill, ed., "Dramatic Records of the City of London: The Repertories, Journals, and Letter Books," in *Collections II.3* (Malone Society, 1931), p. 289. Also in 1543 Ambrosius Chapman, Draper, agreed to have no more plays or disguisings at Carpenter's Yard in St. Botolph's parish (Jor. 15, f. 23v).

83 See above, chapter 4, n. 130. The city's prohibitions in the 1540s would have pushed players into company halls as a controlled environment under watchful civic eyes. For the freedom provided to players within "the great halls of the political elite," see Walker, *Politics of Performance*, pp. 62–63 and following, although Walker also argues, pp. 226–227, that the city's concerns before 1549 were over general social disruption rather than over particular political ideas.

84 See above, chapter 4, n. 130.

85 For *c.* 1541–42 see *DTR*, Dramatic Texts, no. 128, and for 1540–41, Fox, *Politics and Literature*, pp. 240–245; the play may have belonged in any case to the Chapel Children, who did not perform outside the court.

86 See Walker, *Plays of Persuasion*, pp. 130–132 (auspices); for his dating and interpretation, see pp. 102–132.

87 *DTR* no. 1085. See Walker, *Politics of Performance*, pp. 163–195, for a recent treatment.

88 Bevington, *Medieval Drama*, p. 1030; the line count is from the text in this anthology.

89 *DTR*, Dramatic Texts, no. 153. *Jack Juggler* runs to 1217 lines in the Malone Society edn. by B. Ifor Evans (1937 for 1936).

90 The boys of Westminster School in the 1540s were performing classical plays at Christmas time (*DTR* no. 1044), and one of the Paul's boys' groups (probably the grammar school boys) played Terence's *Phormio* before Wolsey in January 1528 (*DTR* no. 1006; Anne Lancashire, "St. Paul's Grammar School," pp. 30–31).

91 Five garments, collars, "crownetes" and wigs for prophets were kept at St. Magnus church in 1552 (*DTR* no. 1077): although these are not necessarily related to the 1530s children's group.

92 *DTR* no. 639.

93 For the play as a children's piece, see Bevington, *From 'Mankind' to Marlowe*, pp. 40–41, and *Medieval Drama*, pp. 990–991. Walker, *Plays of Persuasion*, pp. 134–136, argues for adult court players as more likely, and,

pp. 136–168, for the play as highly political; see also his *Politics of Performance*, pp. 89–91.

94 Westfall suggests, *Patrons and Performance*, p. 106, that most choirboy play scripts may have been written with household (i.e., private hall to private hall) touring in mind.

95 For a 1530s London parish play possibly a saint play (though not a play likely to turn up in company performance), see Mary C. Erler, "Spectacle and Sacrament: A London Parish Play in the 1530s," *Modern Philology* 91 (1993–94), 449–454. A pageant of St. Margaret was still being displayed in the Midsummer Watch in 1541 (see *Collections III*, p. 33); but by the late 1540s the companies were renaming their election feast times and accounting years by secular or generally religious names rather than by saints'-day names: e.g., the Drapers' accounting year becomes early August to early August rather than Assumption [15 August] to Assumption (see Drapers' MS +130/3, accounts up to 1547–48 and accounts after 1547–48), the Drapers' revised ordinances of 1543 no longer specify the company's feast day as *c.* the Assumption (Drapers' MS +795), and the Goldsmiths after 1547 substitute the feast of the Trinity for the feast of St. Dunstan in their account headings, although they drop the Trinity and reintroduce St. Dunstan once Mary is on the throne (Goldsmiths' MS 1524, Books G, H, and I). The city itself in 1539 set about altering its seal because the seal had on it an image of St. Thomas Becket (LB P, f. 197r–v), and similarly with the Bridge House seal in 1541 (Rep. 10, f. 215v).

96 *DTR* no. 1048; and fifteen Robin Hood coats were inventoried at a London church in 1552, *DTR* no. 1077.

97 For the possibility of an earlier edn. or version, see *The Interlude of Johan the Evangelist*, ed. W. W. Greg (Malone Society, 1907), p. vi.

98 The line count for *Johan the Evangelist* is from Greg's Malone Society edn, and the actor count is mine. For St. John's figure in Watch pageants, see *Collections III*, pp. 5 (Drapers), 8–9 (Drapers), 18–19 (Drapers), 25 (Skinners). For Henry VIII's love of Robin Hood, see, e.g., *DTR* no. 977, Jan. 1510. Two short Robin Hood plays were printed in London *c.* 1560; for the texts and some textual commentary, see W. W. Greg, ed., "A Play of Robin Hood for May-Games," *Collections I.2* (Malone Society, 1908), pp. 125–136. Robin Hood was still popular on stage in London at the end of the sixteenth century; see, e.g., Anthony Munday's *The Downfall of Robert Earl of Huntingdon* and the (probably) Munday–Chettle collaborate *The Death of Robert Earl of Huntingdon* and *Look About You*. We might expect other figures from ballads and romances also to have been popular dramatic subject matter 1500–58, but (as noted above for the fifteenth century) no such play texts have survived.

99 Skinners' GL MS 30727/2, account 1518–19, p. 36.

100 Stow, *Survey*, I.97. Stow parallels civic lords of misrule with those traditionally appointed in royal and noble households for the Christmas season. A lord or abbot of misrule is documented at court most Christmases from

1485 to 1521, and in 1534, 1551–52, and 1552–53 (see Streitberger, p. 8); and a lord of misrule is also documented in a London dwelling at Christmas 1523 (see J. S. Brewer, ed., *Letters and Papers, Foreign and Domestic, of the Reign of Henry VIII.*, vol. 4.1 (London: HSMO, 1870), 390, item 30, p. 170.

101 See below, n. 114.

102 Henry Machyn, London citizen (and Merchant Taylor), writes in his mid sixteenth-century *Diary* (Machyn, pp. 28–29) that a London sheriff's lord of misrule in the Christmas season of 1552–53 on 4 January 1553 met the king's lord of misrule coming to London from Greenwich and landing at Tower Wharf; and there was music, morris dancing, foolery with stocks and fetters, and a procession (along the usual royal entry route) to Cheapside, then dinner with the mayor and visits to other houses before the sheriff's lord saw the king's lord off, back by water to Greenwich. See also *Grey Friars*, pp. 76–77. Holinshed, iii.1033, also describes this occasion though misdating it 1551–52 (he names the mayor, George Barne, and the sheriff, John Maynard, with the lord of misrule ["Vause"] involved; and both Barne and Maynard were in office at Christmas 1552–53, not 1551–52). See also Stow, *Annales*, p. 1029, and Albert Feuillerat, ed., *Documents Relating to the Revels at Court in the time of King Edward VI and Queen Mary.* (*The Loseley Manuscripts.*) (Louvain: A. Uystpruyst, 1914), pp. 89–92, 119, 281 (mock midsummer watch). Streitberger, pp. 198–199, calls the event a mock midsummer watch and mock royal entry. At Christmas 1551–52 the king's lord of misrule also visited London, but we know nothing about any civic lord of misrule on this occasion (see Machyn, pp. 13–14, Streitberger, pp. 198–200, *Grey Friars*, p. 73, and Feuillerat, pp. 59–60). Streitberger notes, pp. 8–9, that the king's lord of misrule had special, unusual support for his activities in 1551–52 and 1552–53; and see Machyn's comments, p. 157, on the 1557 death of 1552–53 sheriff John Maynard (Maynard, a Mercer, seems to have had a particular interest in these kinds of activities).

103 Jor. 16, f. 335r.

104 See William Roper's "The Life of Sir Thomas More," in Richard S. Sylvester and Davis P. Harding, eds., *Two Early Tudor Lives* (New Haven and London: Yale University Press, 1962), pp. 197–198.

105 For More's Mercer status, see Lyell-Watney, p. 320, and also Beaven, I.155, 274.

106 See LB N, f. 317v, and Lyell-Watney, pp. 714, 720. See also Rep. 9, f. 102v. Apparently the same Crane rented lodgings from the Mercers from 1519–20 to mid-1535; see the Mercers' MS Renter Wardens' Accounts 1501–1538, *passim* from 1519–20 (f. 148v) to 1535–36 (ff. 320r and 326v), and Mercers' MS Acts of Court 2 (1527–1560), *passim* from f. 16r (1528) to f. 97r (1536). From 1520 on, Crane was steadily in debt for rent.

107 See the Mercers' MS Acts of Court 2, f. 27r, and Rep. 8, f. 83v, and LB O, f. 206v. Heywood still held the office in 1556, when he is recorded as to receive twenty marks a year from the city in recompense for all the rights

belonging to it; see LB S, f. 107v. For Heywood's involvement in court
entertainments, see, e.g., Streitberger, pp. 149–150.

108 For information on John Rastell, see Axton, *Three Rastell Plays*, pp. 1–10,
and for his son's printing of Heywood's plays, p. 3.

109 See PRO C 239/9/25. I am grateful to Dr. Anne Sutton, Archivist/Historian,
Mercer's Company, for the reference. The inventory also includes garments,
caps, 5 "berdys" and 5 "heres". For the Rastell–Walton law case, see William
Ingram, *The Business of Playing: The Beginnings of the Adult Professional Theater in
Elizabethan London* (Ithaca and London: Cornell University Press, 1992), p. 71.

110 Jean Imray has similarly suggested, about other Mercers of a specific kind
(in the medieval period), men of rank and quality who paid to join the
Mercers and never held company office, that they "performed their serv-
ice to the Company in other ways." See Jean M. Imray, "'Les Bones
Gentes de la Mercerye de Londres': a Study of the Membership of the
Medieval Mercers' Company," in A. E. J. Hollaender and William
Kellaway, eds., *Studies in London History Presented to Philip Edmund Jones*
(London: Hodder and Stoughton, 1969), p. 167.

111 Richard Gibson – producer of royal entertainments under Henry VIII
(see, e.g., Streitberger, pp. 71–74, 140–141) – was a Merchant Taylor (Rep.
8, f. 3r; Streitberger, p. 140 – Gibson bequeathed a silver cup to the company). John Bridges, Yeoman of the Revels under Henry VIII, 1539–1550,
was a Merchant Taylor (Streitberger, p. 154). Two other individuals involved in the 1520s Rastell-Walton lawsuit, as renters of the playing costumes, were a Merchant Taylor and a Stationer (see Ingram, *Business of
Playing*, p. 71).

112 For Brandon's status, see Chambers, *Mediaeval Stage*, II.246, 252–3, and
Mill, *Collections II.3*, p. 286. He was not a member of the king's sponsored
acting troupe (the King's Players).

113 LB N, f. 195r (reproduced in Mill, *Collections II.3*, pp. 286–287); the original
record in Jor. 12, f. 172v, is copied into LB N. (See also Rep. 4, f. 110r, and
also Rep. 5, f. 269r). Neither the king's letter here reproduced, nor the
city's record of the matter, makes any mention of waiving the customary
fee; a marginal note in the Journal specifies "that no mencion ys made in
the king*es* lett*er* / that he shall pay no fyne &c'".

114 LB N, f. 305r (undated), copied from Rep. 7, f. 78v (where it is dated 11 Jan.
1526). The entry does not make clear exactly what kind(s) of entertainment are involved, or whether Brandon is to perform himself or to use his
connections to acquire (an)other performer(s), though it is probable that
Brandon is himself to entertain (through juggling etc.). The mayor's
29 October annual feast was a major civic occasion; the king's trumpeters
were present, e.g., in 1514 (Rep. 2, f. 195r) and perhaps normally; and in
1530 the mayor's guests included the Lord Chancellor, two dukes, nine
earls, and a bishop (Wriothesley, I.16). A city sergeant, John Turnour, in
1527 appears in the civic records (Rep. 7, ff. 205v–206r; see also f. 227r) as
having devised sports, singings, and other pastimes, at Christmas and at

other times, in sheriffs' houses; he is now infirm and is given his lodgings rent-free for the rest of his life.

115 Rep. 2, f. 98v. A similarly reduced rate was charged to five individuals join-ing the Minstrels' Company in 1533 (Rep. 8, f. 281v).

116 Westfall has pointed out, *Patrons and Performance*, pp. 126–127, that some professional players practiced other trades as well as acting; and in 1543, e.g., a minstrel who was apparently also a goldsmith was admitted into the Goldsmiths' Company (Goldsmiths' MS 1524, Book G, p. 61). Interestingly there is a space in the MS where his admission payment should be; but in 1552 (Goldsmiths' MS 1524, Book I, pp. 150 and 152) he is transferred from the Minstrels' Company for four pounds, and pays the Goldsmiths 43s for his admission and oath. It must be kept in mind, however, that an individ-ual's membership in a particular London company (as with Heywood's in the Mercers') did not necessarily mean that an individual practiced that company's trade. Company membership could be acquired in any one of three ways: by apprenticeship, by patrimony (through one's father's mem-bership) or by redemption (i.e., by simply paying a fee).

Other professional entertainers who belonged to London companies in the early sixteenth century included King's Players George Maylor (Merchant Taylor and/or Glazier), George Birche (Currier), and John Young (Mercer); see Chambers, *Mediaeval Stage*, II.187–188, n. 3, and 183–184, n. 2, and E. K. Chambers, *The Elizabethan Stage*, 4 vols. (Oxford: Clarendon Press, 1923), II.81 and 80, n. 5. A lawsuit (*Elizabethan Stage*, II.81) interestingly deals with one Thomas Arthur, tailor, whom Maylor took on as an apprentice in acting. In the late sixteenth and early seventeenth centuries a number of actors and playwrights also belonged to London companies: e.g., Robert Armin and John Lowen to the Goldsmiths, Anthony Munday to the Drapers, John Webster to the Merchant Taylors (see *Collections III*, pp. 141, 167, 165, 139).

117 Rep. 10, f. 116v. In a perhaps similar arrangement at the city (rather than company) level in June 1540, one John Wyllyamson is to become free of the Minstrels' Company "as longe as he well & truely seruyth thys Cytie" (Rep. 10, f. 160*r). In 1547 the Minstrels' Company complains to the Court of Aldermen that the Weavers' Company is admitting both minstrels and apprentices to those minstrels (Rep. 11, f. 368v and ff. 371v–372r). Compa-nies might also acquire musical or theatrical members for other reasons; in 1558 the Bricklayers admit a poor and blind harp player whose father was a company member (Rep. 14, f. 62r). Companies might also have encour-aged some of their existing members to become theatrically expert; or members might have gone into theatrical enterprises on their own and so become useful in theatrical matters to the companies. Playing costumes were rented out, e.g., in the 1530s by one Felsted, a silk dyer (see Muriel St. Clare Byrne, ed., *The Lisle Letters*, vol. 5 [Chicago and London: Univer-sity of Chicago Press, 1981], pp. 237–238; Meg Twycross has drawn together various records of Felsted, in "Felsted of London: Silk-Dyer and Theatrical

Entrepreneur," *Medieval English Theatre* 10.1 [1988], 4–16). Finally we should perhaps remember that individual parish clerks – with their long professional tradition of theatrical involvement – were not only otherwise available to companies (through especially, e.g., the companies' parish churches) but were also sometimes members of companies other than (or as well as) the Parish Clerks' Company. See, e.g., William McMurray's twentieth-century compilation of records of parish clerks, in two small filing cabinets, GL MS 3704, *passim.*

118 In April 1543 a group of twenty London joiners was jailed for performing some sort of disguising on a Sunday morning; rather than being a civic entertainment, however, this sounds like protest or propaganda. See John Roche Dasent, ed., *Acts of the Privy Council of England*, NS I (1542–1547) (London: HMSO, 1890), pp. 109–110 and 122.

6 CIVIC THEATRE AND JOHN LYDGATE

1 For all Lydgate texts discussed and quoted from in this chapter I have used Henry Noble MacCracken's edn., *The Minor Poems of John Lydgate*, 2 vols. (EETS, Extra Series 107, 1911 for 1910, and OS 192, 1934, rpt. 1961). All text titles, including the seven featuring the term "mumming," are MacCracken's.

2 For the court: *A Mumming at Eltham*, *A Mumming at Hertford*, *A Mumming at Windsor* (MacCracken, *Minor Poems of John Lydgate*, II.672–674, 675–682, 691–694); for civic audiences: *The Mumming at Bishopswood*, *A Mumming for the Goldsmiths of London*, *A Mumming for the Mercers of London* (MacCracken, II.668–671, 698–701, 695–698); undetermined: *A Mumming at London* (MacCracken, II.682–691), believed by Derek Pearsall, *John Lydgate (1371–1449): A Bio-bibliography*, English Literary Studies (Victoria, BC: University of Victoria, 1997), pp. 28 and 51, to have been written for performance on an occasion associated with the opening of Parliament in fall 1427, but Glynne Wickham, for example, suggests (*EES*, 1.196) a New Year's Eve occasion of unknown date. Our only knowledge, from a rubric to the MS text of the work, is that it was performed "to fore the gret estates of this lande, thane being at London" (MacCracken, II.682). For greater reading ease (and given that my source is printed), in quoting from Lydgate texts throughout this chapter I have reproduced MacCracken's thorn as th.

3 Wickham discusses Lydgate's mummings in *EES*, 1.191–207, and calls attention (pp. 193–195) to Lydgate's apparent description, in his *Troy Book*, of the performance of this kind of entertainment. He provides (p. 196) a chart comparing the similar and differing features of Lydgate's seven mummings (and of the "poem" *Bycorne and Chychevache* – see below), although the chart involves – as does also his discussion – some textual interpretation rather than being entirely factual.

4 The quotation is from MacCracken, *Minor Poems of John Lydgate*, II.668. For

Bishop's Wood, see *DTR*, An Index of Playing Places, no. 90. The mumming is referred to in Stow's *Survey*, 1.98–99, in relation to mayings.

5 For the 1430 date, see below.

6 For the 1430 date, see below.

7 As Derek Pearsall has noted in *Bio-bibliography*, pp. 17–18, we can expect the information given by Shirley in his rubrics to be largely correct, since he was copying the texts at a time when others also would have known such facts about them as their occasions. He would not have wanted to lose credibility by writing statements about the texts which would have been easily seen as erroneous.

8 For the palatial nature of the houses of early mayors of London, see Betty R. Masters, "The Mayor's Household Before 1600," in A. E. J. Hollaender and William Kellaway, eds., *Studies in London History Presented to Philip Edmund Jones* (London: Hodder and Stoughton, 1969), p. 108.

9 The Goldsmiths had possessed a hall of their own since the fourteenth century (see *Atlas*, Gazetteer, s.v. Goldsmiths' Hall); and the Mercers by at least 1391 were meeting at the hall of St. Thomas of Acre (Jean Imray, *The Mercers' Hall* [London Topographical Society 143, 1991], p. 13).

10 For the new Guildhall facilities at the start of the sixteenth century, see, e.g., Mercers' MS Acts of Court 1, f. 124r, and Stow, *Survey*, 1.272–273.

11 Wickham, *EES*, 1.200, believes that the Bishop's Wood mummers are "emissaries from the Goddesses of Spring and Flowers."

12 Richard Firth Green, *Poets and Princepleasers: Literature and the English Court in the Late Middle Ages* (Toronto: University of Toronto Press, 1980), p. 94, interestingly quotes a French educational tract of *c.* 1409, written for a young French prince, which likens a library carried around with its owner to "a second Ark of the Covenant."

13 Scholars such as Wickham and Marion Jones assume that there were mummers costumed as oriental merchants (Wickham, *EES*, 1.201), bringing silks to the mayor (Jones, "Early Moral Plays and the Earliest Secular Drama," in Lois Potter, gen. ed., *The Revels History of Drama in English*, vol. 1: *Medieval Drama* [London: Methuen, 1983], p. 240; see also Derek Pearsall, *John Lydgate* [London: Routledge and Kegan Paul, 1970], p. 185), although the text does not specify this. The ships are described verbally, and may also have been wheeled spectacles (as Wickham describes, *EES*, 1.201–202). Enid Welsford, *The Court Masque: A Study in the Relationship Between Poetry & the Revels* (Cambridge: Cambridge University Press, 1927; rpt. New York: Russell and Russell, 1962), p. 55, points out that we cannot know.

14 Suzanne R. Westfall, *Patrons and Performance: Early Tudor Household Revels* (Oxford: Clarendon Press, 1990), pp. 32–37, although she wrongly assumes that Lydgate wrote the royal entry pageants she mentions, for which, see below, n. 45. The Mercers' and Goldsmiths' mummings have been most recently analyzed, from an interpretative perspective, by Claire Sponsler, "Alien Nation: London's Aliens and Lydgate's Mummings for the Mercers and Goldsmiths," in Jeffrey Jerome Cohen, ed., *The Postcolonial Middle Ages*

(Houndmills, Basingstoke, Hampshire, and London: MacMillan Press, 2000), pp. 229–242.

15 Shirley's rubric speaks of the Goldsmiths' mumming as for "theyre Mayre Eestfeld" (MacCracken, *Minor Poems of John Lydgate*, II.698), but probably, since Estfeld was a Mercer, he was "theyre Mayre" in the sense that he was so to all Londoners. Some Londoners did, however, in this period have associations with more than one guild; did Estfeld perhaps also have a special connection with the Goldsmiths?

16 Marion Jones, however, suggests ("Early Moral Plays," p. 238) that the variety of terms Shirley uses for Lydgate's texts shows that Shirley did not really know what to call them.

17 As in chapter 3, here too I deliberately avoid the debate on what, if anything, distinguishes a mumming from a disguising, as for my purposes here this is irrelevant; the two are similar kinds of occasional entertainment, performed both at court and elsewhere.

18 For the dates of the civic mummings and of *A Mumming at London*, see below; for the dates of the three court mummings, see Pearsall's *Bio-bibliography*, pp. 28–29 (two of these dates are somewhat extended, below).

19 The slippery nature of early theatrical terms has already been discussed, in chapters 2, 4 and 5; but see also E. K. Chambers, *The Mediaeval Stage*, 2 vols. (Oxford: Oxford University Press, 1903), 1.400 and n. 4 (though above all dealing with the sixteenth century).

20 The quote is from MacCracken, *Minor Poems of John Lydgate*, II.675. A modern performance text of *Hertford*, with discussion of the original, is Derek Forbes's *Lydgate's Disguising at Hertford Castle: the First Secular Comedy in the English Language* (Pulborough, West Sussex: Blot, 1998).

21 Westfall suggests, *Patrons and Performance*, pp. 34–35, that chapel men and children took part in *Hertford*.

22 Pearsall, *Bio-bibliography*, p. 29.

23 LB K, f. 69v. (Oct. 13, the feast of the Translation of St. Edward, was the usual date of a mayor's election at this time, and Oct. 28–29, the feast of Sts. Simon and Jude and the day following it, the usual dates of his swearing-in: at the Guildhall on Oct. 28 and at the king's Exchequer on Oct. 29. Michaelmas [29 Sept.], assigned by Pearsall to the mayor, was the usual date of the swearing-in of the sheriffs [on the eve, 28 Sept.], at the Guildhall.)

24 LB K, f. 171v.

25 Rudolf Brotanek, *Die englischen Maskenspiele* (Wien und Leipzig: Wilhelm Braümuller, 1902; rpt. London: Johnson Reprint, 1964), p. 306. His argument is repeated by Walter F. Schirmer, *John Lydgate: A Study in the Culture of the XVth Century*, trans. Ann E. Keep (London: Methuen, 1961), p. 107, n. 3 (as brought to my attention by Professor Stephen R. Reimer [University of Alberta], of The Canon of John Lydgate Project, e-mail communication of 16 June 2000).

26 Pearsall, *Bio-bibliography*, pp. 28–29, supplies convincing arguments for the

dates of the court mummings, although for two of them the dates should be slightly expanded; see below, n. 31.

27 Green, *Poets and Princepleasers*, pp. 189–190. For court writers of the period, more generally, as government apologists and as royal advisers, see his chapters 6 and 5, *passim*.

28 Pearsall, *Bio-bibliography*, p. 29.

29 F. Maurice Powicke and E. B. Fryde, eds., *Handbook of British Chronology*, 2nd edn. (London: Royal Historical Society, 1961), p. 37: though the date given by them for his English coronation, 5 rather than 6 Nov. 1429, is incorrect – see this book's Appendix A.

30 "Roundel for the Coronation of Henry VI" (MacCracken, *Minor Poems of John Lydgate*, II.622), "The Soteltes at the Coronation Banquet of Henry VI" (MacCracken, II.623–624), "Ballade to King Henry VI upon his Coronation" (MacCracken, II.624–630). Green comments, *Poets and Princepleasers*, p. 189, that there "seems little doubt" that all of these were commissioned.

31 Pearsall, *Bio-bibliography*, p. 29, dates the Windsor mumming as written in 1429 for Christmas; the date span should thus be at least Dec. 1429–Jan. 1430, for Shirley's rubric tells us that the performance was before the king "being in his castell of Wyndesore, the fest of his Crystmasse holding ther" (MacCracken, *Minor Poems of John Lydgate*, II.691), and the Christmas season of entertainments at court ran, at the least, through the twelve days of Christmas, from 26 Dec. to 6 Jan. (Twelfth Night). In civic London (at least in the sixteenth century), as we have seen in chapter 5, it ran from 31 Oct. to 2 Feb.: see above, p. 115. (*Eltham* and *Hertford*, also noted by Shirley as Christmas season productions, should therefore not be dated 25 Dec., as in *Bio-bibliography*, p. 51, but more broadly: though *Hertford* does precede 1 Jan. as it takes place "in the vigyle of this nuwe yeere" [MacCracken, II.675, line 5]. If we take the line literally, it would refer to a 31 Dec. performance.)

32 At May Day 1430 the two London sheriffs were a Goldsmith and a Merchant Taylor, and at May Day 1429, a Mercer and a Fishmonger.

33 McCracken, *Minor Poems of John Lydgate*, II.682. Pearsall in his *Bio-bibliography*, p. 28 and n. 65, in suggesting a 1427 date, notes (n. 65) that a mumming on the occasion of the opening of the 1429 Parliament "could hardly have failed to mention the forthcoming coronation . . . on 6 November 1429" – but the mumming need not have been associated in its performance with Parliament and/or its opening.

34 See BL Cotton MS Nero C.ix, f.173v.

35 MacCracken, *Minor Poems of John Lydgate*, II.433–438 and I.145–154.

36 MacCracken, *Minor Poems of John Lydgate*, II.433.

37 See, e.g., Eleanor Prescott Hammond, "Two Tapestry Poems by Lydgate: The *Life of St. George* and the *Falls of Seven Princes*," *Englische Studien* 43 (1910–11), 21. Sheila Lindenbaum has recently suggested that both "Bycorne and Chychevache" and "The Legend of St. George" were written to be "inscribed on walls" (see her "London Texts and Literate Practice," in David

Wallace, ed., *The Cambridge History of Medieval English Literature* [Cambridge: Cambridge University Press, 1999], p. 297).

38 MacCracken, *Minor Poems of John Lydgate*, II.433. Wickham, *EES*, I.196 and 205, includes "Bycorne and Chychevache" with the seven mummings previously discussed.

39 MacCracken, *Minor Poems of John Lydgate*, I.145.

40 For the latter, see Hammond, "Two Tapestry Poems," pp. 21–22. MS 1522, Book D, of the London Goldsmiths' Company records an excerpt from a will concerning the making of wall hangings, in the early sixteenth century, of the life of St. Dunstan (the company's patron saint): see p. 419 (inner page no.)/420 (outer page no.).

41 Armourers and Brasiers' GL MS 12071/2, p. 483: Armourers' Court Minute Book.

42 See MacCracken, *Minor Poems of John Lydgate*, I.35–43 and II.630–648.

43 MacCracken, *Minor Poems of John Lydgate*, I.35. The procession was a major London religious event: even referred to (as seen in chapter 3, n. 183) in the Skinners' 1392 company charter (see John James Lambert, *Records of The Skinners of London, Edward I. to James I.* [London: The Company, 1933], p. 51), and continuing until the Reformation.

44 MacCracken, *Minor Poems of John Lydgate*, II.648.

45 Kipling, *King*, pp. 142–143, n. 59, discusses the common misperception that Lydgate devised, rather than after the fact described, the pageants. Kipling argues that Lydgate's description was based upon a descriptive letter written by City Clerk John Carpenter; see also his p. 164, n. 108. See also Pearsall, *Bio-bibliography*, pp. 33–34.

46 Lydgate's *Danse Macabre* (not in MacCracken's *Minor Poems of John Lydgate*), a poem-dialogue translated from the French, also has civic associations: contributing, at the request of City Clerk John Carpenter, the verses of the Danse Macabre inscribed on the cloister walls of London's Pardon Churchyard at St. Paul's (see Pearsall, *Bio-bibliography*, pp. 26–27).

47 The work is included in MacCracken, *Minor Poems of John Lydgate*, II.724–738.

48 Pearsall, *John Lydgate*, p. 183.

49 MacCracken, *Minor Poems of John Lydgate*, I.xxiii, no. 90.

50 Professor Stephen R. Reimer, personal e-mail communication, 16 June 2000. Reimer notes that a series of uses of the term "Explicit" divides the whole work into ten sections, or perhaps ten separate works, which appear separately or in groups in other MSS, all together in only one MS.

51 Another possible recitation, with or without visual display, is Lydgate's "Of the Sodein Fal of Princes in Oure Dayes" (MacCracken, *Minor Poems of John Lydgate*, II.660–661), but there is no information about it apart from the opening rubric calling it "seven balades."

52 MacCracken, *Minor Poems of John Lydgate*, II.623–624.

53 Suzanne Westfall has described the prevalence of purpose-written theatrical pieces for private households in this period; see, e.g., her " 'A Commonty

a Christmas gambold or a tumbling trick': Household Theater," p. 52, in
New History.

54 The Goldsmiths' combined accounts and minutes show only minstrels paid
to perform apparently at the company's St. Dunstan's Day celebrations in
1401 (Goldsmiths' MS 1519, p. 33) and in 1402 (Goldsmiths' MS 1518, p. 89),
and a harper, a piper, and morris dancers paid in 1448 (Goldsmiths' MS
1520, p. 18). Minstrel costs are also listed in the 1444–1445 account (MS
1520, p. 11.) (As noted above in chapter 4, Goldsmiths' MSS 1518 through
1523 have been searched by Professor David Parkinson, University of
Saskatchewan, and I am grateful to him for this information.) The Mercers'
MS Wardens' Accounts 1347–1464 show only money collected for a
mumming presented to the king at Eltham in 1400–1401 (f. xxxij v).

55 See above, chapter 4, p. 81 and n. 60.

56 See above, chapter 4, p. 82.

57 Grocers' GL MS 11570, p. 213.

58 For Gloucester's patronage of Lydgate, see, e.g., Pearsall, *Bio-bibliography*,
pp. 23, 32–33.

59 Green, *Poets and Princepleasers*, p. 9.

7 LAND ENTRIES

1 E.g., six pageant stations for the 1501 entry of Katherine of Aragon (see,
e.g., Rep. 1, f. 61v; plus a device running with wine in Paul's churchyard,
Rep. 1, f. 87r), nine stations for the 1522 entry of the Emperor Charles V
(see, e.g., Hall, pp. 638–640), and over nine special locations (not all with
"pageants") for the 1554 entry of Philip of Spain (see: John Elder, *Copie of a
Letter Sent into Scotlande* [1555; rpt. Amsterdam and New York: Da Capo
Press, 1971], sigs. B4r–C5r; *Chronicle of Queen Jane*, pp. 78–81; Holinshed,
IV.62–63; *Grey Friars*, p. 91).

2 Sources for the texts of all six entries are listed in Appendix A. Also extant –
see also Appendix A for sources – are portions of text for the 1554 entry of
Philip of Spain.

3 For Lydgate as describer in 1432, see Kingsford, *Chronicles*, p. ix (Lydgate's
descriptive poem is on pp. 97–116); for Lily in 1522, see Rep. 4, ff. 120r and
134v, Rep. 5, f. 293r, and Rep. 6, f. 4r (*DTR* no. 998 lists text sources); for
Udall and Leland in 1533, see *DTR* no. 1017. The earlier attribution to
Lydgate of the extant verses of the 1445 entry is no longer generally accepted; see Kipling, *King*, p. 191, n. 29, who also states (as noted previously
in chapter 6), pp. 142–143, n. 59, that Lydgate's verse description of the
1432 entry is not an eye-witness account but is based on a prose account by
City Clerk John Carpenter (see LB K, ff. 103v–104v).

4 Rastell devised the pageant set at the conduit by the Stocks (Rep. 4, f. 117v,
and Rep. 5, f. 284r).

5 Heywood in 1553 sat "vnder a vine" in a Paul's churchyard pageant at
Paul's school, and made an oration in both Latin and English (Holinshed,

IV.6). For the 1554 entry of Philip of Spain, Heywood is mentioned in the civic records in June (Rep. 13 (1), f. 166v) as unable to participate in a pageant-devising group to which he had been appointed in January (f. 118r; and see also f. 162v); but the record is unclear as to whether the inability was temporary or involved a permanent withdrawal at this point from all entry preparations.

6 The civic record is of the "scolem*aster*" of Paul's (Rep. 13 (1), f. 191r; also LB R, f. 304v); presumably this was the high master (i.e., head of the school) in 1554, Thomas Freeman, and not his surmaster, James Jacob. For the speech, see Jor. 16, f. 297v.

7 LB Q, f. 183r (and Jor. 15, f. 270r): presumably this is the Palsgrave speech referred to on f. 181r of LB Q. Palsgrave also made other welcoming speeches, e.g., in French to the Great Marshall of France at Durham Place in July 1551 (see Rep. 12 (2), f. 353v), but the texts have not been preserved in the civic records. We also know that the master of St. Paul's school from 1522 to 1532, John Rightwise, wrote the city's formal welcoming speeches on some other (non-royal) entry occasions (see LB O, ff. 61r and 127v); again we have no texts extant.

8 See, e.g., as cited also in chapter 3, Mary-Rose McLaren, "The Aims and Interests of the London Chroniclers of the Fifteenth Century," in Dorothy J. Clayton, Richard G. Davies, and Peter McNiven, eds., *Trade, Devotion and Governance: Papers in Later Medieval History* (Stroud, Gloucestershire, and Dover, NH: Alan Sutton, 1994), pp. 158–176. McLaren has pointed out that the London chroniclers had particular interests to follow in the materials they presented, and notes (p. 171) that they "sought both to record and understand the events *they considered to be important*" (italics mine). Fabyan, e.g., focuses on Henry VI's 1432 reception into London (pp. 603–607) rather than on his 1429 coronation entry; and although the pageant texts of Margaret of Anjou's 1445 coronation entry have survived (see above), and show the elaborateness of the occasion, no chronicler says much about this entry (Fabyan, p. 617, provides the most extensive coverage).

9 BH Annual Accounts and Rentals 3 (1460–84), ff. 94v–95r. The annual accounts for 1404–60 consist of receipts only; and the BH Weekly Payments MS series is missing the records for 1445–1505. Bridge House payments for 1465 entry pageantry appear to have been first noted by Charles Welch in his *History of The Tower Bridge* (London: Smith, Elder, 1894), and were transcribed and published by Glynne Wickham in *EES*, 1.324–331. George Smith's *The Coronation of Elizabeth Wydeville* (London: Ellis, 1935), an edn. of a fifteenth-century MS, deals only with the coronation itself and the following banquet, and not with the civic entry preceding the coronation.

10 Manley, *Culture*, pp. 240, 247. Manley states (p. 247) that the 1533 entry "established what *thereafter* [my italics] became another unbroken custom" – the city's gift-giving at this point in the entry proceedings.

11 In 1432, e.g., the city's gift to Henry VI was presented at Westminster two days after the civic entry (see below, Appendix A); in 1421 Catherine of

Valois received a gift at the Tower (at least Jor. 1, f. 88r, records that plan); in 1498 the prince received a gift at the Bishop of Salisbury's palace in Fleet St. the day following a minor progress through the city (Kingsford, *Chronicles*, pp. 224–225).

12 Gordon Kipling's *King* has impressively countered the trend towards seeing all royal entries on similar occasions as alike; Kipling points out important Christian typological differences, among entries, in the pageants displayed. My focus, complementing his, is on practical differences involving route, timing, and the like, which are also important aspects of overall entry meaning.

13 A few, 1410–1558, are included in *EP*, 1.137–185. Malcolm Smuts counters the contemporary scholarly trend by including, in a discussion of London's royal entries, not simply coronation entries and their equivalents but also the more routine movements of the monarch through the city; see his "Public Ceremony and Royal Charisma: The English Royal Entry in London, 1485–1642," in A. L. Beier, David Cannadine and James M. Rosenheim, eds., *The First Modern Society: Essays in English History in Honour of Lawrence Stone* (Cambridge: Cambridge University Press, 1989), pp. 65–93.

14 In general the Crown required the entry and the city devised and paid for it, but variations could occur within this framework. Wickham in *EES*, 1.284–287, discusses the organizational particulars for the 1501 entry of Katherine of Aragon.

15 For a discussion of research from *c.* 1900 on London royal entries, see this book's Introduction, pp. 9–11. The most recent and extensive historical and interpretative work, for the period pre-1559, has been done by Gordon Kipling and Lawrence Manley, Kipling placing London royal entries within the context of Christian European entry theatre as a whole, and Manley making London street pageantry in general, including royal entries, an important part of his study of the ritualistic, sociopolitical aspects of London culture more generally.

16 For listings of the major historical and contemporary sources for these two entries, see *DTR* nos. 933 (1432) and 963 (1501) and, most recently, Kipling, *King*, p. 143, n. 59, and p. 209, n. 58. Other major royal entries of the period – as defined by their inclusion of pageants and by the extensive amount of information we have about them – are Henry V's in 1415 (Agincourt celebration), Margaret of Anjou's in 1445 (coronation), the Emperor Charles V's in 1522 (welcome), Philip of Spain's in 1554 (welcome), and (all coronation) Anne Boleyn's in 1533, Edward VI's in 1547, and Mary's in 1553.

17 Kipling, *King, passim*. For his interpretation of Henry's entry pageantry as a dramatized "epiphany of Henry's transcendent majesty," and of the sequence of Katherine's pageants as a carefully composed dream-vision, see pp. 142–169 (the quotation is from p. 143) and 209–221. For Sydney Anglo's earlier interpretative work on the 1501 entry, see Anglo, *Spectacle*, pp. 58–97, and "The London Pageants for the Reception of Katharine of Aragon:

November 1501," *Journal of the Warburg and Courtauld Institutes* 26 (1963), 53–89.

18 Lydgate, in Kingsford, *Chronicles*, pp. 97–116; Fabyan, pp. 603–607. Lydgate's poem includes (pp. 114–115) the mayor's prose speech to the king at the gift-giving.

19 Kingsford, *Chronicles*, pp. 234, 246–248; Kipling, *Receyt*, pp. 10–36; and below.

20 Manley, *Culture*, p. 223.

21 There were, e.g., some 20,000 on horseback for the post-Agincourt welcome of Henry V in 1415; see *Gesta Henrici Quinti*, ed. and tr. Frank Taylor and John S. Roskell (Oxford: Clarendon Press, 1975), pp. 102–103.

22 See Appendix A; and for Richard III's entry into London (as opposed to his coronation procession through London from the Tower to Westminster), see below, p. 135 and n. 46. Note that a royal procedural document of the late fifteenth century, "A Ryalle Book" (printed from MS in vol. 1 of Grose), stipulates (1.302) that a queen (consort) coming from abroad must be brought to London to be crowned and must be met by the "cete" five miles outside it.

23 For London as king-maker, see M. McKisack, "London and the Succession to the Crown during the Middle Ages," in R. W. Hunt, W. A. Pantin and R. W. Southern, eds., *Studies in Medieval History Presented to Frederick Maurice Powicke* (Oxford: Clarendon Press, 1948), pp. 76–89.

24 The fifteenth-century coronation procedures documents known today as the "Forma et Modus" and the "Little Device" (the latter prepared originally for Richard III in 1483 and revised for Henry VII in 1485) set down the requirement that the mayor (and other Londoners – "Forma et Modus") process, in the civic coronation entry through the centre of the city, with the king. See Legg, pp. 172, 182, 219, 222–223. See also the "Ryalle Book," in Grose, 1.303, on the mayor and other Londoners as processing with a queen consort, and the account in Legg, pp. 145–146, of the mayor and other Londoners as so processing with Richard II.

25 A coronation entry procession all the way to Westminster (though Henry VI's in 1432 was not for a coronation) is specified in the fourth recension of the *Liber Regalis* (extant from the time of Richard II but probably first used for the coronation of Edward II), as printed in Legg, p. 113 (for the information on the *Liber Regalis* itself, see p. 81); and civic London's part in such an entry is made clear in both the "Forma et Modus" and the "Little Device" (Legg, pp. 182 and 222–223). A civic escort to Westminster for a queen consort about to be crowned is also specified in the "Ryalle Book," in Grose, 1.303.

26 Minor entries did not require the same pattern as did major ones. On 30 October 1498, e.g., Prince Arthur was apparently met by the mayor and aldermen in Cheapside, not outside the city's walls, when he went through London to Westminster; but this was merely a minor journey through the city, although for the occasion the livery companies did line

the streets and a formal speech was made to the prince by the city's Recorder. See Kingsford, *Chronicles*, p. 224.

27 See *L&PH7*, p. 411: though perhaps the Council was focusing on only part of the processional ceremony.

28 See Kipling, *Receyt*, pp. 12–13 and 35, *Great Chronicle*, p. 307, and Kingsford's *Chronicles*, p. 246.

29 See Kipling, *Receyt*, pp. 31 and 35, and Jor. 10, f. 238r.

30 See Hall, p. 507 (and also Holinshed, III.547); BL Cotton MS Tiberius E.viii, f. 101r–v, clarifies the situation (and see also Stow, *Annales*, p. 813).

31 For 1533, see Hall, p. 800 (and *The noble tryumphaunt coronacyon of quene Anne* [*RSTC* 656, 1533], sig. Aiijr); for 1547, see Wriothesley, I.182; for 1553, see Holinshed, IV.6–7 (and Stow, *Annales*, p. 1043); for 1554, see Elder, *Copie of a Letter*, sig. B5r–v. The "Little Device" (see Legg, pp. 222–223) indeed required that the mayor ride with a coronation entrant from the Tower to Westminster. The mayor so riding, and stopping in Cheapside for civic ceremonies there, would explain chroniclers at times seeming to contradict one another on this point: Wriothesley, e.g., I.19, says that the mayor and aldermen stood in Cheapside, the mayor presenting the queen with a gift, in Anne Boleyn's 1533 entry, although Hall, p. 800, indicates that the mayor rode in the entry procession. In the 1547 entry of Edward VI, the mayor as in 1501 was part of the royal procession (see John Gough Nichols, ed., *Literary Remains of King Edward the Sixth*, 2 vols.[Roxburghe Club, 1857; rpt. New York: Burt Franklin(, 1963)], I.cclxxx) but also, with the aldermen, received the king in Cheapside (*Literary Remains*, I.cclxxxviii).

32 In 1533 the mayor escorted Anne Boleyn (by water) from Greenwich to London, for her coronation entry through the city (Hall, pp. 798–799); and he also accompanied to the city (by water) Mary in 1553 for her coronation (Machyn, pp. 44–45). Even in 1540, when Anne of Cleves unusually went from Blackheath to Greenwich rather than to London, to be married to Henry VIII, the mayor met her at Blackheath and rode in the royal procession to Greenwich (see below, chapter 8, p. 150 and n. 49), then subsequently escorted her by water from Greenwich to Westminster (Wriothesley, I.112), though she apparently did not stop in London itself.

33 Kipling, *King*, pp. 115–129, discusses civic gift-giving, generally, in terms of the symbolic significance of the particular gifts a city chooses to present, and comments specifically, pp. 118–120, on gifts and the 1392 entry of Richard II.

34 We have, however, no Bridge coronation-entry pageant information for Joan, queen of Henry IV, in 1403, or for Edward IV in 1461, although both crossed the Bridge; either there were no pageants, or no records of them have survived or yet been found.

35 See, e.g., the "Ryalle Book," in Grose, I.302, on queen consorts going to the Tower after crossing the Bridge; and various coronation descriptive and procedural documents begin with the king or queen *at* the Tower for the procession through the main part of the city (including Cheapside) to

Westminster: see the *Liber Regalis*, p. 113, the "Processus factus" (on Richard II's coronation), in Legg, p. 164, and the "Little Device," in Legg, pp. 222–223. See below, Appendix A. For Henry VI's 1429 coronation we know that the specific route taken to the Tower, after the crossing of the Bridge, was up the lower part of Gracechurch St. and along Fenchurch St. (*Brut*, p. 450).

36 See, e.g., the "Processus factus," in Legg, p. 164, and the "Little Device," in Legg, pp. 222–223.

37 See Appendix A.

38 See the *Brut*, p. 451. Given the normal two-day coronation-entry pattern, however, together with the amounts of time required for the various parts of the ceremonial, probably the events actually of two days have been conflated in the *Brut* into one (as partially with Margaret of Anjou's coronation entry in 1445, as recorded in Gregory; see below, n. 42).

39 See Appendix A.

40 1413 – BH Weekly Payments, Series 1, vol. 2, p. 26; 1421 – BH Weekly Payments, Series 1, vol. 2, pp. 457–468, 478, 480, 488, 496; 1429 – BH Weekly Payments, Series 1, vol. 3, f. 278r; 1445 – see Gordon Kipling, "The London Pageants for Margaret of Anjou: A Medieval Script Restored," *Medieval English Theatre* 4.1 (1982), 5–27; 1465 – BH Annual Accounts and Rentals 3, ff. 94v–95r (printed in *EES*, 1.324–331).

41 In the "Ryalle Book," in Grose, 1.302, Londoners are required to receive a queen consort entering over the Bridge "in the moste honorable wise with a greter yeste for there own worschipe."

42 See, e.g., Gregory, p. 186, on the 1445 coronation entry; it first lists all the pageant stations, which might be taken by the modern reader as involving a single day, but then speaks of the mayor meeting the queen and bringing her to the Tower, and of her procession the next day through the city. The Bridge would have had to be crossed on the way to the Tower. *Brut*, p. 489, is clear and specific about the two-day route. See below, Appendix A.

43 For Catherine of Valois' 1421 entry, we have an account of elaborate civic pageantry – giants, animals, angels singing, apostles, virgins, etc., all set down in the *Vita & Gesta*, pp. 297–298 – apparently accompanying only Catherine's initial city entry to the Tower, with her procession through the city to Westminster being on the following day (see pp. 298–299). But the *Vita & Gesta* apparently conflates two days of pageantry into one, for the *Great Chronicle* refers, p. 115, to pageants on both days (which we would expect from entry norms). For 1421 Bridge pageant records, see below, Appendices A and B.

44 Grafton, II.113; Hall, p. 375.

45 See Appendix A. Elizabeth came the day before her entry through London; Anne and Mary came to the Tower two and three days, respectively, in advance of London land entry. Edward VI in 1547 was at the Tower from his accession until his coronation entry through the city; see LB Q, f. 195v.

46 For the extensive water pageantry in both 1487 and 1533, see below, chapter 8.

For Mary's 1553 civic water escort, see Rep. 13 (1), f. 79v. I have found, to date, no details of Richard III's water journey to the Tower in 1483; Anne F. Sutton and P. W. Hammond, *The Coronation of Richard III: the Extant Documents* (Gloucester/New York: Alan Sutton / St. Martin's Press, 1983/1984), p. 28, speculate that at least a civic water escort might have been provided. For Katherine of Aragon in 1501, with her one-day land entry, a water procession *followed* her marriage, on 16 Nov.: see Appendix A.

47 For Philip's entry, the drawbridge was ordered to be "trymmed" as it had been at the entry of Emperor Charles V (Rep. 13 (1), f. 113r) – the nearest preceding time, 32 years earlier (in 1522), when a royal entry had been made over the Bridge. (Two giants were featured in both entries.) The similarity between Philip's entry and the Emperor's is significant; although Philip became nominally king of England in marrying Mary, Parliament prevented his coronation (see Robert Tittler, *The Reign of Mary I*, 2nd edn., Seminar Studies in History [London and New York: Longman, 1991], pp. 75 and 22).

48 The "Little Device" and the "Ryalle Book" may allow us some assumptions: but they do not necessarily altogether follow previous practice or order later practice. It is also important to note that a focus – as is common for literary scholars – on the chronological "development" of entries may be inappropriate when our specific information for some entries 1400–1558 is extremely slight or seriously incomplete. How can we know, for example, that speeches were first recited in entry pageants in 1445 – as is usually assumed – when (1) pageant texts, and limited ones at that, have survived for only one earlier entry, in 1432, (2) surviving texts are not necessarily wholly informative (the surviving texts for 1445, as we have seen, do not note the two-day format of the entry), and (3) chroniclers were not concerned with providing fully detailed and accurate information about all entries? (And it can also be argued that extant descriptions of the 1432 entry allow for spoken text in at least one pageant.)

49 Kipling, *King*, has also suggested that Henry's age determined this entry's political–religious base: which he finds, p. 143, to be in the Christian liturgical signs of the Epiphany, with Henry as an infant saviour.

50 Rep. 1, f. 61v; individuals are assigned the overall responsibility for six different pageant stations. (Others are appointed, f. 62r, to liaise with the king's commissioners.) The date two years before the 1501 entry caused Withington (*EP*, 1.165) to interpret this record as applying to some unknown different entry, which is then treated as such (no. 962) in *DTR*. Preparation time from accession to coronation entry for the reigning monarch, 1400–1558, seems to have ranged from one week (Richard III) to three weeks (Edward VI) to around three and a half months (Edward IV); but entries resulting from negotiated royal marriages would presumably have had longer preparation times where desired (e.g., seven months for the August 1554 entry of Philip of Spain; see Rep. 13 (1), f. 112r). In Katherine's case, however, the two-year preparation period was a result of unexpected delays: see Gordon Kipling,

The Triumph of Honour: Burgundian Origins of the Elizabethan Renaissance (The Hague: Leiden University Press for the Sir Thomas Browne Institute, 1977), pp. 173–174. Katherine and Arthur had been married by proxy in May 1499 (Anglo, *Spectacle*, p. 57); and Henry VII took a special, active interest in her civic welcome (Kipling, *Triumph of Honour*, pp. 73–74).

51 From a practical perspective, e.g., Edward's age may have determined – as others have suggested – the inclusion of a rope acrobat at St. Paul's in the 1547 coronation entry: a type of display then repeated, however, in the coronation entry of Mary (1553) and in the entry of Philip (1554). Kipling, *King*, p. 168, n. 115, notes that Edward's entry, because of his age, was based on Henry VI's, with the child king as a child saviour; Anglo, *Spectacle*, pp. 284 and 294, had previously pointed out that the use of 1432 materials in 1547 was doubtless because London had less than three weeks to prepare for Edward's entry.

52 Manley, *Culture*, chapter 5: pp. 212–293.

53 See Kipling, *King*, on the entries of 1415 (pp. 201–209), 1432 (pp. 142–169), 1445 (pp. 188–201; see also Kipling, "The London Pageants for Margaret of Anjou," *passim*), and 1501 (pp. 209–221; see also Kipling, *Triumph of Honour*, pp. 72–95, and *Receyt, passim*), 1533 (pp. 330–333; see also Kipling, "'He That Saw It Would Not Believe It': Anne Boleyn's Royal Entry into London," in Alexandra F. Johnston and Wim Hüsken, eds., *Civic Ritual and Drama*, Ludus 2 [Amsterdam and Atlanta, GA: Rodopi, 1997], pp. 39–79), 1553 (pp. 345–347), and 1554 (pp. 347–348).

54 See *DTR* no. 929 (where the entry is misdated, as in Welch's *Tower Bridge* [as there cited], as 1427). The Bridge House MS records are the direct source: Weekly Payments, Series 1, vol. 3, f. 170r–v (week of 26 Jan–1 Feb. 1426) [see below, Appendix B, 5] and f. 171r (week of 3–9 Feb.). I have here included a few points, from these records, not in *DTR* or in Welch. The entry has also been noted in C. Paul Christianson, *Memorials of the Book Trade in Medieval London: The Archives of Old London Bridge*, Manuscript Studies 3 (Cambridge and Wolfeboro, NH: D. S. Brewer, 1987), p. 12.

55 Rep. 11, f. 276v; also LB Q, f. 181r. The Great Admiral landed at Tower Wharf, and so came past the Tower, up Mark Lane, over to Gracechurch St., and up to and along Cheapside to St. Paul's. See Wriothesley, I.172.

56 The term "trimmed" is vague. It may simply mean decorated; on the other hand, see the use of the term in 1554, as noted above, n. 47. For Edward VI's pageant-filled coronation entry in 1547 the conduits were also ordered to be "trym*me*[d]" (Rep. 11, f. 309v). See below, Appendix A, for information sources otherwise on 1547.

57 See Wriothesley, II.28–29, and above all Rep. 12 (1), ff. 154r and 156r–v.

58 Holinshed, IV.156; Rep. 14, f. 90v; Wriothesley, II.142; Machyn, p. 180.

59 See above, chapter 3, p. 46.

60 For all of these entries, see below, Appendix A. The shortness of preparation time for Mary's is specifically commented on in the court minutes of the Armourers and Brasiers' Company, GL MS 12071/1, p. 364.

61 See *Historie of the Arrivall of Edward IV. in England*, ed. John Bruce (Camden Society, OS 1, 1838), pp. 15–16.

62 Wriothesley, I.59–60. The Court of Aldermen on 20 Dec. had inquired as to the king's wishes for his reception (Rep. 9, f. 232v). Compare Henry VI passing through Aldgate to the Bridge and across it to Southwark in 1441 (*Brut*, p. 477) – the mayor and commons welcomed him "in theire best aray" and "made grete Ioye."

63 Kingsford, *Chronicles*, p. 211.

64 For 1498, see Kingsford, *Chronicles*, p. 224; for 1518, see Wriothesley, I.12. There are many other such occasions in the records and chronicles. For the frequency of livery company escorts of the monarch coming and going to and from London, see, e.g., the accounts of the Pewterers (GL MS 7086/1) for 1481–82 (f. 78r), 1482–83 (f. 80v), and 1483–84 (f. 82v), and the Mercers' MS Wardens' Accounts 1347–1464 for 1454–55 (f. 181r), 1459–60 (f. 197r), 1460–61 (f. 200r), 1462–63 (ff. [205r] and [205v]), and 1463–64 (f. [208v]). See also, for examples of chronicle references, Fabyan, *passim*, and Wriothesley, *passim*.

65 See Appendix A: we do not have records of elaborate civic pageants, for a new monarch's coronation, from Edward IV through Henry VIII.

66 In October 1549 musicians are told to be ready for assignments on the morning of the entry (Rep. 12 (1), f. 154r): at which time those assignments are indeed provided (Rep. 12 (1), f. 156r–v).

67 LB N, ff. 119v–120r.

68 See *Gesta*, p. 101, n. 4.

69 Court pageants, e.g., were often constructed in locations in and near the city and then moved to the court: see Streitberger, pp. 46–47, 172–176.

8 WATER SHOWS

1 See above, chapter 1, n. 12.

2 William Fitz Stephen, "Descriptio Londoniae," as translated in Stow's *Survey*, I.92.

3 Stow, *Survey*, I.94.

4 See Machyn, *passim*, from 1559. In 1559, e.g., there were two major water displays for the queen and court – one at London and one at Westminster – within a single week (p. 196), the London one watched by a thousand people.

5 *Collections III*, p. 73.

6 See, e.g.: Merchant Taylors' GL MS 34048/2, f. 18v (1453–54: meeting of queen coming to Greenwich from Westminster); Mercers' MS Wardens' Accounts 1347–1464, f. 181r (1454–55: receiving king leaving Windsor); Merchant Taylors' GL MS 34048/3, f. 140r, Cutlers' GL MS 7146, roll 27, mem. 2 (1480–81: the coming of the Duchess of Burgundy).

7 Mock naval battles such as that performed on the Thames at York Place for the king and queen in 1536 appear normally to have been non-civic in sponsorship. See, for this example, Wriothesley, I.49.

8 See Helen Suggett, "A Letter Describing Richard II's Reconciliation with the City of London, 1392," *English Historical Review* 62 (1947), 209–213.

9 For the wildfire reference, see the Leathersellers' MS Liber Curtes 1, p. 56.

10 The applicable *OED* definition of "wild-fire" is its no. 3 , "A composition of highly inflammable substances, readily ignited and very difficult to extinguish, used in warfare, etc.;" and under "Fire-work," no. 3, the *OED* provides a 1560 military example of the term as synonymous – in military usage – with wildfire, and under no. 4, a 1575 usage of "fire-works" as involving scenic display. In the 1521 London Midsummer Watch, the term "wyldfyre" is used for pyrotechnical entertainment display, in a military/entertainment context (see Drapers' MS +130/1, p. 172). Machyn also uses the term: e.g., p. 261 (1561 – a midsummer mock attack on a castle representation on the Thames). The 1486 wildfire for Henry VII, whatever it involved, was clearly display, although it may have involved only simulated military use.

11 See, e.g., *EP*, I.157–160, and Anglo, *Spectacle*, pp. 21–35.

12 See, e.g., the Merchant Taylors' GL MS 34008/1, f. 5r: the Merchant Taylors pay one Crane (too early for the later master of the Chapel Children, William Crane; perhaps his father or another family member) for his children and organs, i.e., for musical entertainment, on a barge for this entry; and other companies with barge and/or music payments for Henry's entry include the Carpenters, Cutlers, Drapers, Goldsmiths, Ironmongers, and Pewterers. On Crane, see the *Dictionary of National Biography*, ed. Leslie Stephen and Sidney Lee, 22 vols. (Oxford: Oxford University Press, 1921–22; rpt. 1963–64), V.13–14.

13 See above, chapter 7, p. 135. Richard III was certainly the first since before Richard II; I have not checked pre-1377 coronation entrants on this point.

14 *Collectanea*, IV.218.

15 BL Cotton MS Julius B.xii, ff. 34v–35r.

16 For the red dragon, see Frederick W. Fairholt, *Lord Mayors' Pageants*, part 1 (London: Percy Society, 1843), n. on p. 11, and Anglo, *Spectacle*, pp. 44–45. Anglo discusses, p. 44, the vision in Geoffrey of Monmouth's *Historia Regum Britanniae* in which a triumphant red dragon symbolizes the British people, and, pp. 44–45, the dragon's association with Henry and with his coronation celebrations.

17 Henry's entry was of course not for a coronation, so doubtless was much less elaborate than Elizabeth's. As noted above, however, it followed a northern progress during which a number of cities presented elaborate shows to welcome the king. London might well have felt it necessary to offer some kind of elaboration as well.

18 For a discussion of the term "pageant" in this period, see below, chapter 10, p. 177. Another elaborate water show – a mock battle – took place in 1489, when the mayor and other Londoners escorted Prince Arthur from Chelsea to Westminster; but the show itself was presented not by the city but by Spanish ambassadors and merchants (*Collectanea*, IV.250).

19 The terms foist, barge, and shout could be used interchangeably at this time

to indicate a flat-bottomed boat; and a wafter was an armed convoy vessel, so that a foist, barge, etc., accompanying another vessel and with ordinance on board could also be called a wafter. See *OED*, s.v. Barge *sb.*, nos. 2 and 5, Foist *sb.* 1, no. 2, Shout *sb.* 1, Wafter *sb.* 1, no. 1.

20 See Hall, pp. 798–800 (and BL Add. MS 6113, ff. 23r–24v), and (for the Moorish diver) Frederick J. Furnivall, ed., *Ballads from Manuscripts*, 1.i (London: Ballad Society, 1868), pp. 373 and 380 (from BL Royal MS 18 A.lxiv); also Henry Ellis, "Copy of a Letter from Archbishop Cranmer," *Archaeologia* 18 (1817), 77–82 (from BL Harley MS 6148), cited and quoted from in *EP*, 1.181, n. 3. Wriothesley, in commenting on Anne's water entry (1.18), does not mention the dragon, monsters, wildmen, or falcon mount, nor does BL Royal MS 18 A.lxiv mention, e.g., the dragon, falcon, mount, virgins, and bells. As in the 1487 coronation entry of Elizabeth of York, the dragon here is presumably a reference to the badge of the Tudors.

21 Anglo, *Spectacle*, notes, pp. 49–50, that the 1487 pageants were probably similar to the 1533 ones; he does not suggest that such pageants might have been used more widely.

22 For 1533 there are brief references, only, to the water entry in LB P, f. 13v, and Rep. 9, f. 1v, and barge payments in a number of company MSS (e.g., Grocers', GL MS 11571/4, f. 478r). The 1533 water arrangements were left to the mayor's company, the Haberdashers, whose records pre-1559 have largely not survived.

23 LB H, f. 246r. This does not mean, of course, that they had never before journeyed to Westminster by land on foot or by water: only that from 1389 they were to be limited to a water procession or a land procession on foot.

24 In 1439 the mayor and aldermen even decided that the sheriffs themselves should pay for their own barges to Westminster. The sheriffs objected. See Jor. 3, f. 25r.

25 GL MS 5440, f. 70v; printed in R. W. Chambers and Majorie Daunt, eds., *A Book of London English 1384–1425* (Oxford: Clarendon Press, 1931), pp. 142–143.

26 See the MSS records, for the relevant years, especially of the Grocers (GL MS 11570) and Mercers (MS Wardens' Accounts 1347–1464), and also of the Cutlers, Drapers, and Merchant Taylors. The Drapers' MSS also show the sheriffs going by water in 1424 (MS +140, f. C6v), as do the Mercers' (MS Wardens' Accounts 1347–1464, f. 88r); and the Grocers' MSS may show this for 1423 (GL MS 11570, p. 149). (In 1431, 1432, and 1433, and probably also in 1429 and/or 1430, the sheriffs rode on land: see GL MS 11570, pp. 211–212, 227, 230, 205 [in all these years the Grocers pay for a horse for their beadle, specified in all but 1431 as for riding with the mayor and sheriffs].)

27 Sharpe's translation in *Cal. LB L* of two city orders, one in 1481 (pp. 186–187) and one in 1485 (p. 218), for the Westminster presentation journeys of two sheriffs replacing deceased sheriffs for the remainder of their terms of office, uses the phrase "pageant of all the barges;" but the

Latin – and Sharpe's English phrasing – means simply "display of all the barges."

28 See, e.g., GL MS 7146 (Cutlers' Wardens' Accounts), rolls 1–7, for seven of the years from 1442–43 to 1453–54. No Cutler was a sheriff during this period.

29 GL MS 5440, f. 71r. (See below, Appendix B, 4.) In 1415 a different kind of reduced mayoral oath-taking ceremonial had taken place; the mayoral procession had been on foot, rather than on horseback, in thanksgiving for Henry V's victory at Agincourt. It was specified in 1415 that this was not to serve as a precedent for future oath-takings. See LB 1, f. 159r.

30 Records which have previously been interpreted (e.g., by Withington, *EP*, II.6, n. 4) as indicating mayoral oath-taking processions by water to Westminster between 1422 and 1453 should not necessarily be interpreted in that way. The Grocers, e.g., paid for "dyu*ers* Barg*es*" with the mayor and sheriffs to Westminster 1422–24 (GL MS 11570, p. 149): but apart from the 1422 presentation barges for both mayor and sheriffs, the other barges might have been for the sheriffs only, or for other occasions besides the mayor's oath-taking, although the mayor's oath-taking is certainly possible. Barges were used by the city, e.g., to escort royalty and other important personages up and down the Thames; and for other complicating factors, see below.

31 The mayor was certainly riding on land in 1425 (see Kingsford, *Chronicles*, p. 76, and *A Chronicle*, pp. 113–114) and apparently also on land at least in 1431–34, 1436–40, 1442–44, and 1449–52 (see the MSS of the Cutlers [GL MS 7146], Drapers [MS +140], and Grocers [GL MS 11570], which among them include payments for a horse for a company beadle for the mayor's oath-takings in all these years; the mayor apparently does not ride to the river to take his barge, for his oath-taking, until 1501 [see below, n. 40], so presumably a horse for the beadle is required in these years because the mayor's procession is by land). Most significant is the Cutlers' invariable recording of barge hire for the sheriffs' procession, and of horse hire for the beadle for the mayor's riding, in all the years of their extant account rolls between 1442 (the year of the first roll) and 1452; then in 1453 barge hire with the mayor is recorded, and no beadle's horse.

32 Jor. 4, f. 195v.

33 GL MS 11570, pp. 306, 313 and 319.

34 Jor. 5, f. 124v (see below, Appendix B, 7A). An immediate cause might have been the September escorting of the queen by water to Westminster by the mayor and aldermen "in best display" (Jor. 5, f. 120r); a prompt repeating of the barge arrangements might have been financially advantageous. Kingsford has suggested (*Chronicles*, p. 315, n. to p. 164, line 11) that the physical infirmities of 1453 mayor John Norman may have been the cause (a water journey would have been physically easier for him than a land one on horseback). A number of factors – including ongoing cost concerns – may have been involved. Significantly the Crown appears to have opposed (to no

effect) the city's official move to the water (see Jor. 5, f. 126r [see below, Appendix B, 7B]). Was such opposition perhaps responsible for the apparent failure of the attempted change from land to water in 1447? It certainly suggests no regular mayoral presentation journeys by water before 1453.

35 An exception, always, would be the years in which the Exchequer was not in session at Westminster at the time of the mayor's oath-taking, in which years the mayor would make a land journey to the Tower of London to take his oath before the Constable, as the king's representative, there. See chapter 10.

36 See, e.g., GL MS 11570, pp. 303 and 306: the Grocers collect money for a Grocer sheriff's riding, then pay for a barge for the sheriff's procession to Westminster. In 1450 the Mercers pay for trumpets for the sheriffs' "Rydyng" and for a barge to Westminster (MS Wardens' Accounts 1347–1464, f. 170v); and although this barge is not specified by the Mercers as for the sheriffs, it is clustered with other expenses for the "Rydyng", and records of both the Grocers (GL MS 11570, p. 313) and the Cutlers (GL MS 7146, roll 5) show that the sheriffs went to their presentation by barge in 1450.

37 For the requirement, see *Historical Charters*, pp. 34 (1253), 43 (1298). For an example of such a later presentation of the mayor to the king, listed along with the regular oath-taking, see the Mercers' MS Wardens' Accounts 1347–1464, f. 183v (1450s), and also Henry Thomas Riley, ed. and tr., *Chronicles of the Mayors and Sheriffs of London* (London: Trübner, 1863), p. 133 (1270s).

38 See, e.g., the Mercers' MS Wardens' Accounts 1347–1464, ff. 88r (1424–25) and 190v (1457–58); and see also Nightingale, p. 389. The death was commemorated throughout the reign of Henry VI.

39 The companies also rode with the mayor on occasions other than the annual mayor's oath-taking – e.g., to meet important visitors to the city – so unspecified and uncontextualized hirings of horses etc. are also difficult or impossible to identify by occasion, although references to "the" riding are normally to the oath-taking one.

40 In 1409, e.g., the city was intent on cutting the costs of the mayor's Westminster oath-taking (see LB I, f. 87r); but in 1501 the avoidance of the expense of horses for a land procession, by the taking of a water journey, was negated by an order (Rep. 1, f. 88v) that the mayor and aldermen should ride from the Guildhall to the waterside to take their barges to Westminster for both the sheriffs' and the mayor's inauguration journeys, and should likewise ride also from their landing place on their return. In 1521 some cost-cutting took place again (see Jor. 12, f. 127r).

41 GL MS 11570, pp. 353 and 370 (on p. 370, a "gret grefon to stonde be foore the barge", in a list of items belonging to the bachelors). The Grocers' coat of arms includes two griffins.

42 On companies' bachelors' groups see Thrupp, *London*, p. 13, and Steve Rappaport, *Worlds Within Worlds: Structures of Life in Sixteenth-Century London* (Cambridge: Cambridge University Press, 1989), p. 226.

43 Mercers' MS Ordinance Book, ff. 6r–7r. The Mercers' MS Acts of Court 1 record a barge prepared by the bachelors as early as 1465 (see Lyell-Watney, pp. 282–283). In 1507 we find a bachelors' barge as a customary item also in the bylaws of the Merchant Taylors' Company (GL MS 34004, f. 63r).

44 It is unclear as to whether the barge always carried the bachelors themselves. But in 1541, e.g., the Mercer bachelors appear to be on their barge for the mayoral oath-taking journey: see the Mercers' MS Register of Writings, vol. 2, f. 138r (see below, Appendix B, 11B); and the mid-to-late fifteenth century Mercers' bylaws already referred to assume (Mercers' MS Ordinance Book, f. 6r) that the bachelors are on the bachelors' barge for the mayor's oath-taking.

45 Hall, p. 798; see also BL Add. MS 6113, ff. 23r–24r.

46 Withington, *EP*, II.10, assumes that only the barge is being referred to as similar to what is provided in 29 October display. Fairholt, *Lord Mayors' Pageants*, on the other hand, assumes (p. 10) a general similarity between 29 Oct. pageantry and the kinds of display provided on the water for Anne Boleyn's entry. For the general unhelpfulness in this regard of other chronicle accounts of the 1533 entry, see, e.g., *Grey Friars*, p. 36.

47 The records include teasing entries as to what were the normal characteristics of a bachelors' barge, such as the order in LB P, f. 13v (and also Rep. 9, f. iv) that the mayor's company prepare a company barge and a bachelors' barge "with alle other thinges to the same Barge belongynge".

48 See Rep. 10, ff. 152v–154r, and also the Mercers' MS Acts of Court 2, f. 123r, and *Grey Friars*, p. 43; also Hall, p. 836, Grafton, II.471, and Holinshed, III.814. The Grocers (GL MS 11571/5, f. 132v) recorded their barge decoration for the occasion. Wriothesley, I.111, says that two bachelors' barges were provided.

49 *Grey Friars*, p. 43; Wriothesley, I.111; Hall, pp. 833–836; Grafton, II.468–471.

50 See Wriothesley, I.112, Hall, p. 837, Grafton, II.472.

51 On Sat. 19 March 1541 the king went from Westminster to Greenwich by water with the mayor and "crafts masters" (James Gairdner and R. H. Brodie, eds., *Letters and Papers, Foreign and Domestic, of the Reign of Henry VIII*, vol. 16.1, RS 120 [London: HMSO, 1898], no. 650.2, p. 313 – from a letter to Francis I by the French ambassador), "with the solemnity and triumph [customary] at the first passage of new queens," because the present queen [Katherine Howard] had not yet passed under the Bridge.

52 Goldsmiths' MS 1524, Book H, p. 43.

53 Land shows were doubtless also involved in the two-directional influencing process. Court revels in 1494 featured a fire-spitting dragon (Streitberger, pp. 27–28); and one also appeared in, e.g., the London Midsummer Watch in 1521 (a "serpent" spitting fire [see *CSPV*, III.136]), and one in 1541 (Drapers' MS +130/2, p. 650, and MS +143, f. 203r). Animals also spewed fire in, e.g., the 1522 royal entry of the Emperor Charles V and the 1547 coronation entry of Edward VI (Hall, p. 638, and John Gough Nichols, ed., *Literary Remains of King Edward the Sixth*, 2 vols. [Roxburghe Club, 1857; rpt.

New York: Burt Franklin(, 1963)], i.cclxxxvii). Some of these dragons/animals, and other non-London and later ones, are noted by Philip Butterworth, *Theatre of Fire: Special Effects in Early English and Scottish Theatre* (London: Society for Theatre Research, 1998), pp. 9–12. Butterworth's book is focused on how such effects were achieved, and not on their historical chronology; but some of the provincial and continental texts and records he cites show that fire effects generally, and dragon fire specifically, were a special feature of early stagecraft before as well as after 1500: see especially his pp. 25–36 and 79–83.

54 Jor. 7, f. 21v, col. 2. The same stipulation is made in 1501 for the civic escort of the king to Westminster after the marriage of Prince Arthur and Katherine of Aragon: see *The traduction & mariage of the princesse* (*RSTC* 4814, [1500]), f. 7r (pagination of BL copy).

55 See, e.g., the Mercers' MS Acts of Court 2, ff. 217r (1547), 234v (1549), and 299v (1558), and *Collections III* under Lord Mayors' Shows in 1562, 1566, and also 1551, 1556, and 1561. The Grocers' records in 1562 (*Collections III*, p. 45) indicate that the bachelors' barge by then had fallen into disuse in favour of the foist.

56 There were elaborate water shows at Venice in the later fifteenth century: see, e.g., Jacob Burckhardt, *The Civilization Of The Renaissance In Italy*, tr. S. G. C. Middlemore, rev. Irene Gordon (New York: New American Library, 1960), pp. 298–299.

57 Machyn, pp. 47, 73, 96, 117. See also pp. 270 (1561: foist, shooting of guns) and 294 (1562: foist).

58 See Machyn, e.g., pp. 203, 204, and – on the water – 261.

59 Mercers' MS Register of Writings 2, ff. 137v–138r and 148r–149v.

60 Merchant Taylors' GL MS 34105, ff. 2r, 3v, 28v–29v (though on f. 3v it is specified that the foist shall be furnished "with men & other thynges in all thynges as well as hath bene at eny tyme heretofore").

61 See Drapers' MS +130/1, pp. 154 and 336. It is unclear whether the 1521–22 quire also concerned the barge, but this seems very likely. There was also another quire supplied to the bachelors, in both 1520 and 1528, on collecting money to cover costs.

62 See Goldsmiths' MS 1524, Book H, p. 43.

63 Merchant Taylors' GL MS 34105, cited in n. 60, above, deals with some bachelors' arrangements for the Lord Mayor's Shows of 1556, 1561, and 1568.

64 See *Collectanea*, IV.250 (for 1489), and Wriothesley, 1.99–100 (for 1539) and 1.49 (for 1536). In 1554, on the day before their London entry, Mary and Philip were entertained on the Thames by a water hunt/baiting involving a bear and dogs as their boat (from Richmond to London) came down to Paris Garden; see *La Solenne et Felice Intrata delli Serenissimi Re Philippo, et Regina Maria d'Inghliterra, nella Regal città di Londra* (N.p., 1554), sig. Aijr. The sponsors of the water hunt/baiting are not specified. Another such water baiting had taken place in 1539 for Henry VIII: see John Foxe, *The Acts and Monuments of*

John Foxe, ed. George Townsend, vol. 5 (London: Seeley, Burnside, and Seeley, 1846), p. 388. I am grateful, for the 1539 reference, to the REED project and especially to Tanya Hagen.

9 THE MIDSUMMER WATCH

1 Midsummer Watch records are printed on pp. 1–36 of *Collections III*, and a general description of the Watch and its records, on pp. xiv–xxiv. For the 12th Great Company, see below, n. 25.

2 It has been noted, e.g., in *Collections III* (p. xix), as a qualification to Stow's account, that although Stow specifies that the mayor (always, it is implied) had three pageants and the sheriffs two each, the records show a varying number of pageants: by the 1520s to 1530s, usually three to four for the mayor and two to three for each sheriff.

3 Stow, *Survey*, 1.101–103. Most of this account is printed (also from Kingsford's edn.) in *Collections III*, pp. xvi–xvii. Not as well known is a detailed description of the actual 1521 Watch (running from 11 pm to 2 am), by the Secretary of the Venetian ambassador to England, printed in *CSPV*, III.136–137. The description makes clear the visually-interesting mechanical effects within the pageants.

4 Bale, p. 120. (For ease in reading, given the printed source, editor Flenley's reproduced thorn is here printed as "th".) In 1441 Eleanor Cobham was arrested in Cheapside where she had gone to view the Watch (Kingsford, *EHL*, pp. 156 and 340–341); for this reference I am grateful to the REED project and especially to Tanya Hagen.)

5 The Merchant Taylors invited the king and queen that year to their annual St. John's feast (Merchant Taylors' GL MS 34048/2, f. 261r), and one sheriff was a Merchant Taylor.

6 Mercers' MS Acts of Court 1, ff. 32v–33r. The entry refers to St. Peter's night, but the eve (evening to morning, 28–29 June) is clearly meant.

7 Jor. 8, f. 155v; Drapers' MS +403, f. 9r–v It should be noted that the nine worthies in 1557 and 1559 are a part of London May games: see *DTR* nos. 1102 and 1118, and below, p. 168.

8 *A Chronicle*, p. 145.

9 Jor. 10, f. 314r.

10 Drapers' MS +403, f. 77r. Details of pageants are apparently being recorded elsewhere; in 1510, e.g., the records refer (Drapers' MS +143, f. 11r) to separate books of cost details.

11 Four "pagen*tes*" in 1510 cost the Drapers £19 12s 2d (Drapers' MS +143 f. 11r). For a discussion of the meaning of the term "pageant" at this time, see chapter 10, pp. 177–178.

12 Rep. 1, f. 100r.

13 *EP*, II.29.

14 See, e.g., *Collections III*, pp. 12 and 18. Patricia Lusher in her early 1940s two-volume University of London thesis, "Studies in the Guild-Drama in

London in the Records of the Drapers' Company (1515–1553)," argues that the Drapers, between 1521 and 1541, worked variations on only eight basic pageants; see especially her 1.50–58. Entry pageants were of course stationary, and Watch pageants were usually carried by porters; but this would not have prevented the reuse of materials from one type of pageant to another.

15 Drapers' MS +130/1, pp. 172–174 (also partially recorded in *Collections III*, pp. 5–11, which wrongly identifies John Skevington, sheriff, as a Draper; he was a Merchant Taylor).

16 The Mercers, who had a mayor in office at midsummer in both 1536 and 1537, in May 1537 ordered a pageant to be "sett vppe at the greate Cundeth in Chepe Ayenste Mydsomer Nyght", ordered "as it was the yere Laste paste and better yf it maye be" (Mercers' MS Acts of Court 2, f. 102v). For the location of their hall, see fig. 12 on p. 14 of Jean Imray's *The Mercers' Hall* (London Topographical Society 143, 1991). The king and queen were expected to visit the hall on 23 or 28 June 1536 "to se the wache" (Mercers' MS Acts of Court 2, f. 89v). Was the pageant stationary only, or both stationary and portable? In what was probably the 1530 Midsummer Watch (the date is not entirely clear), when also a Mercer was mayor, there were also "two goodly pagenttes in Cheppe-syde at Soper lane ende" (*Grey Friars*, p. 35) – i.e., also at the Great Conduit outside Mercers' Hall.

17 Drapers' MS +130/2, p. 646.

18 Stow, *Survey*, 1.103. Note here (and throughout) that the mayor and sheriffs cited as involved in any one year's Midsummer Watch (in June) are those who were sworn into office in October and September of the previous calendar year.

19 The proposed 1580s revival was indeed in 1585, as Stow says, and not, as *Collections III* says (p. xxiii), in 1584. See John Montgomery's MS proposal for this revival, transcribed in Frederick J. Furnivall, ed., *Harrison's Description of England in Shakspere's Youth*, Part IV, Supplement 2, with additions by C. C. Stopes (London: Chatto and Windus, New Shakespere Society, 1908), pp. 373–410; the date provided internally in the MS (see Furnivall, p. 409) is 1585.

20 Withington, e.g., in *EP*, 1.36–42, does not distinguish between various forms of watches at midsummer (practical or festive, military or pageant-oriented, etc.), and so presents an unclear account of London Midsummer Watch development.

21 See Furnivall, *Harrison's Description*, Part IV, Supplement 2, pp. 373–410.

22 A religious play on the Passion of Christ, however, was performed at the Greyfriars in 1557 (Machyn, p. 138); was there a special connection of the Greyfriars area at this time with theatre?

23 See GL MS 11571/5, f 203r. Another problem, therefore, in relation to this as a Midsummer Watch record, is that the Grocers had no mayor or sheriff in office at midsummer 1543 or 1544, and so would not have been expected to provide a Watch pageant in either of those years.

24 Compare, e.g., with the 1544 Watch entry (*Collections III*, pp. 35–36) the two

short 1537 Watch entries (pp. 30–31 in *Collections III*) from the Mercers' MS Acts of Court 2; the first 1537 entry is as short as the 1544 one, but the second 1537 entry – having to do with an unusual financial problem – shows that the 1537 Watch did indeed include at least one Mercers' pageant. The 1543–44 mayoral year had begun (in October 1543) with a Draper mayor; but on his death in April 1544 he had been replaced by a Mercer mayor, hence the Mercers' responsibility for 1544 Watch pageantry.

25　Jean Robertson, ed., "A Calendar of Dramatic Records in the Books of the London Clothworkers' Company (Addenda to *Collections III*)," in *Collections V* (Malone Society, 1960 for 1959), p. 9.

26　See, e.g., *Collections III*, pp. 32–35.

27　William Herbert, *The History of the Twelve Great Livery Companies of London*, vol. 1 (London: privately printed, 1834; rpt. Newton Abbot: David and Charles, 1968), p. 456, had assumed such a wind-down to have begun in the 1520s; *Collections III* not only proved wrong such an assumption for the 1520s but (p. xxiii) logically argued against it for the 1530s–1541 as well, not only through the surviving records found and printed but also through a specific 1541 reference, in those records (p. 32), to the high costs of Midsummer Watch pageantry in what looks like the immediately preceding years – years involving a number of Mercer mayors and sheriffs.

28　See, e.g., Sheila Williams, "The Lord Mayor's Show in Tudor and Stuart Times," *Guildhall Miscellany* 1.10 (Sept. 1959), 6, though she does not mention the Watch's saints' days performance dates as a potential problem; and also Lusher, " Guild-Drama," 1.179. (Wickham, *EES*, III.56, also very briefly suggests the break with Rome as the cause of the Watch's demise; and see also Manley, *Culture*, pp. 264–265.) Williams, whose article is developed from her unpublished two-vol. 1956 University of London thesis on Lord Mayor's Shows from the late sixteenth to the early eighteenth century, sees religious suppression of the Midsummer Watch as a main cause of the rise of Lord Mayor's Show pageantry.

29　See Michael Berlin, "Civic Ceremony in Early Modern London," *Urban History Yearbook* 1986, pp. 18–19; his work has heavily influenced Manley's *Culture* (in which, see especially pp. 266–267). The editors of *Collections III* in 1954 had suggested (p. xxiii) the death of Watch pageantry because its "principal features had been transferred to the day of the Lord Mayor's inauguration;" they did not suggest, however, why this transfer might have taken place. Sheila Lindenbaum, however, "Ceremony and Oligarchy: The London Midsummer Watch," in Barbara A. Hanawalt and Kathryn L. Reyerson, eds., *City and Spectacle in Medieval Europe*, Medieval Studies at Minnesota 6 (Minneapolis: University of Minnesota Press, 1994), pp. 171–188, argues for the Watch itself as a tool of oligarchic power; and she sees the Watch's ending not as manipulated by the city but as caused by a takeover by Henry VIII in cancelling the Watch in 1539. Older "evolutionary" views of audiences as having become too "sophisticated" for pageants (see, e.g., Lusher, "Guild-Drama," 1.179) are no longer given any credence.

For Ronald Hutton's recent suggestion (*The Rise and Fall of Merry England. The Ritual Year 1400–1700* [Oxford and New York: Oxford University Press, 1994], p. 76) that the Crown opposed the Watch for security reasons, see below.

30 See *Collections III*, p. 37.

31 For the scarcity of pageantry information in Mercers' Company MSS before 1559, see above, pp. 81 and 159.

32 See LB P, f. 119r: though the sheriffs are also ordered to have no giants, bows, guns, or morrispikes, and there is a reduction in the number of musicians and footmen.

33 The sheriffs in 1537 were a Merchant Taylor (accounts but no court minutes extant for this period; Watch records might be found in either type of MS) and a Draper (accounts missing for 1536–37, court minutes incomplete 1536–38). In 1538 they were a Mercer and an Ironmonger: which does present a surprise, since the Ironmongers' accounts are detailed for the 1535 Watch involving an Ironmonger sheriff, but largely silent for the 1538 Watch; see GL MS 16988/1. The Ironmongers do provide their midsummer 1538 sheriff with £6 13s 4d towards his costs (f. 171v).

34 See the Watch records for 1535–45, in *Collections III*, pp. 25–36 (the quotation here is from p. 35).

35 *Collections III*, p. 38; the editors suggest the record concerns the coronation entry of Edward VI in 1547, but since the record comes from the Merchant Taylors' 1548–49 accounts, it likely involves the 1548 Midsummer Watch revival (for which, see above and below).

36 See below, Appendix B, 11.

37 See John Stow, *A Summarye of the Chronicles of Englande* (*RSTC* 23322; 1570), ff. 402r–v (1564), 405v (1565), 411r (1567); see also his *Annales*, pp. 1120 (1564), 1123 (1565), 1127 (1567). In standing watches, watchmen remained within their specific wards (though they could move around within their wards): although to 1558 and on into the 1560s the mayor with an entourage appears to have ridden around the wards, presumably following the traditional Midsummer Watch marching route. In at least 1564 the more elaborate watch referred to by Stow was made " Through the earnest sute of the Armourers" (Stow, *Annales*, p. 1120); the specific dates of this watch were 28–29 June (eve to morning) in 1564 and 1565, and 23–24 June (eve to morning) in 1567. Some sort of further diminishment of the watch at midsummer – seemingly in the riding around of the mayor and in the armourers' contributions – took place from 1569, according to Strype in his 1720 continuation of Stow's *Survey* (see John Strype, *A Survey Of the Cities of London and Westminster*, 6 books in 2 vols. [1720], I.xxix.257); but I have not pursued the Midsummer Watch in any detail past 1558.

38 These financial reasons do not, however, include the complaint, as stated by Berlin ("Civic Ceremony," p. 18), made by a group of citizens about the costs of the shrievalty. This complaint, made in 1535 (a long way from 1539) to the mayor, aldermen, and Common Council (not to the king), argued for reduced expenses within the sheriffs' households but specifically

exempted liveries given to citizens and Midsummer Watch costs. See PRO SP1/89/208.

39 See Christopher Haigh, *English Reformations: Religion, Politics, and Society under the Tudors* (Oxford: Clarendon Press, 1993; rpt. 1995), p. 152.

40 Compare, as noted above, Edward IV's request for an especially elaborate Watch in 1477, because of the presence in London then of ambassadors from France and from Scotland (Mercers' MS Acts of Court 1, f. 32v). King Christian of Denmark was one of those who saw the Watch with Henry VIII earlier in Henry's reign: at midsummer 1523 (see *Collections III*, p. 13, and Hall, p. 658).

41 See Muriel St. Clare Byrne, ed., *The Lisle Letters*, vol. 5 (Chicago and London: University of Chicago Press, 1981), p. 542.

42 Wriothesley, 1.100. Wriothesley also states that the cancellation came only two days before the Watch was to take place: although in fact the king's letter was written almost 10 days before, on 14 June (see LB P, f. 190r–v). For the loss to poor men, see also below, p. 164.

43 In the Goldsmiths' MS 1524, e.g., the accounts running 1542–43 to 1556–57 are dated from after one feast of St. Dunstan (19 May) to the next, until Edward VI comes to the throne, then from after one feast of the Trinity (a movable May/June feast) to the next, until the accession of Mary, and then in 1555–56 from St. Dunstan's feast again.

44 Stow, *Annales*, p. 967; see also Mercers' MS Acts of Court 2, f. 89v. Both Henry and the queen saw the Watch on St. Peter's eve (the *Annales*, like the Mercers' record, says night but presumably means eve), at Mercers' Hall. Henry also was said to have attended the Watch on 23–24 June 1535: see *Calendar of Letters, Despatches, and State Papers, Relating to the Negotiations between England and Spain*, vol. 5.1, ed. Pascual de Gayangos (London: HMSO, 1886; rpt. Nendeln, Liechtenstein: Kraus Reprint, 1969), no. 179, p. 506.

45 See Haigh, *English Reformations*, pp. 152–153. Haigh goes so far as to declare that "On 16 November 1538 Henry VIII stopped the Reformation dead."

46 LB P, f. 190r–v.

47 When in 1585 Elizabeth I thought to revive the Watch (Jor. 21, f. 421v), its muster aspects – men furnished with weapons, ready to fight for England – were also what interested her, and apparently not (from her letter to the city) the Watch's spectacle aspects otherwise.

48 Ronald Hutton, *Rise and Fall*, p. 76, has suggested that Henry's motive for cancelling the 1539 Watch was fear of religious rebellion in relation to it; but, as noted above, by 1539 Henry had become less zealously anti-Roman than previously; and, as also noted above (p. 162 and n. 44), in 1536 he had been so little worried about security at the Watch that he had himself attended it, with his queen Jane Seymour. The Watch, in any case, was in significant part a display of armed civic forces *for* the king; as Hutton notes, p. 122, about watches elsewhere, they in part *kept* the peace. In 1533, however, the Privy Council had indeed been rumoured to have been interested in stopping the Watch, "to guard *against any popular riot or mutiny (mutinacion)*,

of which the King and his Council are mightily afraid just now." In 1533, of course, the Watch followed very shortly after the highly controversial 1 June coronation of Anne Boleyn. A civic revolt might well have been feared. Henry's 1536 Watch attendance with Jane Seymour interestingly followed, by only a few weeks, Anne's execution. (For the quotation, see *Calendar of Letters, Despatches, and State Papers Relating to the Negotiations between England and Spain*, ed. Pascual de Gayangos, vol. 4.2 [London: HMSO, 1882; rpt. Nendeln, Liechtenstein: Kraus Reprint, 1969], no. 1091, p. 721.) All this is not to suggest, of course, that ordinary night-time disorders at the civic level might not in part usually accompany the Watch (midsummer watches indeed, as seen in chapter 3, originated in part because of the potential for celebratory and other disorder at midsummer); see, e.g., the Venetian ambassador's comment in 1521 (see above, n. 3), *CSPV*, III.137, that tumults were always a possibility at Watch times (though the ambassador does not seem to well understand their potential origin).

49 LB P, f. 190v.

50 LB P, f. 194r–v (1 August 1539).

51 John Stow, e.g., in his turn-of-the-century *Survey*, 1.103–104, voices the same concerns as the city's committee in 1539 over the loss, with the Watch, of help for poor men (who were paid as part of the processional bearing of cresset lights). So does John Montgomery in his 1585 proposal for a revival of the traditional Watch (see Furnivall, *Harrison's Description*, Part IV, Supplement 2, p. 374).

52 The 1540 sheriffs were a Haberdasher (no surviving accounts or court minutes for this period) and another Mercer; the 1542 sheriffs were a Mercer and a Merchant Taylor (accounts but no court minutes for this period, and a separate pageantry MS in the 1550s – GL MS 34105 – the existence of which suggests there may have been earlier such MSS now lost); and the 1543 sheriffs were a Merchant Taylor and a Fishmonger (no surviving Fishmonger accounts or court minutes for this period) – although 1543 was also a major plague year in London, from May onward (see Charles Creighton, *A History of Epidemics in Britain*, 2 vols. [Cambridge: Cambridge University Press, 1891–94; rev. edn. London: Frank Cass, 1965], 1.302–303) and the 1528 Watch had been cancelled, in all but its most basic elements, because of plague (see LB O, f. 83v). The Mercers in both 1540 and 1542 thought that the king might attend at their hall for the Watch (Mercers' MS Acts of Court 2, ff. 128r and 151v); and several other companies supplied cressets and/or bowmen in one or both of 1542 and 1543, although this does not prove that any constructed pageants were provided then by the mayor's and sheriffs' companies.

53 Wriothesley, 1.148; also *Grey Friars*, p. 47. The Mercers' 1544 record is simply an agreement as to who will see that the pageants at Leadenhall are in order; the Clothworkers' 1544 record is also about advance preparations.

54 Wriothesley, 1.156. He also notes (pp. 158–59) that London sent 1500 soldiers to the king in July, and that there was also fear of arson in London at the beginning of July, with special watches and searches therefore ordered.

55 See John Roche Dasent, ed., *Acts of the Privy Council of England*, NS I, 1542–1547 (London: HMSO, 1890), p. 447.
56 Wriothesley, 1.163.
57 Wriothesley, 1.163–165.
58 Wriothesley, 1.166. The Grocers' records show 12s 4d paid for cresset light and men's wages on this occasion (GL MS 11571/5, f. 288v); a Grocer sheriff was in office. This kind of more limited Watch appears to have continued in a number of years past 1546 (not including the one year of Watch revival, 1548, for which, see below).
59 LB P, f. 119r.
60 Rep.10, f. 165*r.
61 LB P, ff. 166r and 217r; Rep. 10, f. 259r.
62 Wriothesley, 1.176.
63 Wriothesley, 1.177. For other such cost-cutting see LB Q, f. 191v (Dec. 1546: there will no longer be a mayoral dinner for the aldermen after Epiphany), and also LB S, ff. 28v–29r. In 1545 it had been ruled (LB Q, f. 146r) that because of costs no alderman need be mayor more than once. Midsummer Watch possibilities lingered, however: though perhaps only for the limited, armed, non-pageant watches described above. The Merchant Taylors provided funds to their 1553–54 Merchant Taylor mayor, Thomas Whyte, towards the various charges of his mayoralty, including those of "hauyng a watche at Midsom*er* (if eny suche be" (*sic*; Merchant Taylors' GL MS 34048/4, f. 286v).
64 Presently available evidence points to one pageant only, in later sixteenth-century Lord Mayor's Shows; but my own search of the civic records has not gone past 1558.
65 In 1552 (26 May) there was a maypole, giant, morris dance, and castle (Machyn, p. 20); the mayor ordered the maypole broken.
66 See Machyn, pp. 89, 137, 201 (the quotation is from p. 201); he also mentions (p. 89) a 3 June 1555 May game at Westminster, with (besides guns, drums, and morris dancers) giants, morrispikes, devils, bagpipes, viols, "and many dysgyssyd," and a lord and a lady of the May, with minstrels. *CSPV*, 6.1, no. 154, p. 133, reports to be false a rumour that pageants in London at midsummer 1555 were prohibited.
67 See, e.g., *Collections III*: in 1529 (p. 19) the Drapers hire their giant from Barking, and again (p. 22) in 1534. In 1519 (p. 4) the Skinners work with St. Giles for a pageant of the martyrdom of St. Thomas, and with Barking for one of Our Lady and St. Elizabeth. For parish May games (and plays) in the city generally, see Stow, *Survey*, 1.98, and also 1.99 for comments on civic mayings.
68 Machyn, p. 33. For the custom of the bringing in of the withe, see Stow, *Survey*, 1.98. It was forbidden, for the mayor and sheriffs, by Common Council in 1555 (Jor. 16, f. 335r, and LB S, f. 29v), as a cost-cutting measure.
69 John Stow, *A Summarye*, f. 411r.
70 Machyn's *Diary* unfortunately runs only from 1550 to 1563; there is no comparable earlier or later source to give us extensive information on May

games. May games alone, and/or the merging of May games with a limited watch, around midsummer, would explain George Puttenham's reference in his *Arte of English Poesie* (*RSTC* 20519; 1589), p. 128, to "these midsommer pageants in London, where to make the people wonder are set forth great and vglie Gyunts marching as if they were aliue, and armed at all points, but within they are stuffed full of browne paper and tow . . . ." *Collections III*, with only the traditional civic-pageant Watch in mind, suggests (p. xxiv) that this passage must have been written in the 1540s.

71 BL Add. MS 12,222, f. 5r (p. 9); E. C. Cawte, *Ritual Animal Disguise: A Historical and Geographical Study of Animal Disguise in the British Isles* (Cambridge/Totowa, NJ: D. S. Brewer/Rowman and Littlefield for the Folklore Society, 1978), p. 25. The midsummer expense for St. Giles was £6 9s 9d – about one third of the total payments for the year (£19 13s 7d) recorded in the churchwardens' accounts. There is no other such payment in the extant St. Giles' accounts, 1570–71 to 1579–80 and 1596–97 to 1607–08.

72 See *Collections III*, pp. 27 and 4.

73 My own searches of the civic records currently have not gone past 1558, nor have I explored, further than indicated here, the areas of folk games.

74 See LB Q, f. 244r-v, and Wriothesley, II.3. Hutton, *Rise and Fall*, has suggested, p. 83, that the revival was to compensate Londoners for the loss, because of Protestant reforms, of their annual Corpus Christi processions. Even if so, however, the Watch would clearly not have been considered to be irredeemably Roman, to have been revived at all.

75 Mercers' MS Acts of Court 2, f. 220r.

76 Wriothesley, II.15.

77 Wriothesley, II.35–36.

78 Wriothesley II.41, with "my Lord Mayor and the Sheriffs ryding privilye at midnight with theyr officers to peruse the city and the constables in theyr wardes."

10 THE LORD MAYOR'S SHOW

1 This chapter is a revised version of my "Continuing Civic Ceremonies of 1530s London," in Alexandra F. Johnston and Wim Hüsken, eds., *Civic Ritual and Drama*, Ludus 2 (Amsterdam and Atlanta, GA: Rodopi, 1997), pp. 81–105, and is used here with the kind permission of Editions Rodopi BV.

2 The standard dates for sixteenth-century London mayoral installation ceremonies are those set down in *Liber Albus*, pp. 21–22: Guildhall oath on 28 Oct., and Westminster oath on 29 Oct. except when 29 Oct. fell upon a Sunday, in which case 30 Oct. was supposed to be used instead (as in 1531: see LB O, f. 237r).

3 For details of the typical route, see, e.g., Machyn, pp. 47–48 (on the 1553 Show), and also, for much of the specific 1541 route, the Mercers' MS Register of Writings 2, f. 137v–138r. The Register's record is here included in Appendix B, as II.

4 The Clothworkers' records of drama and pageantry, not included in *Collections III*, were calendared and edited a few years later by Jean Robertson, "A Calendar of Dramatic Records in the Books of the London Clothworkers' Company (Addenda to *Collections III*)," in *Collections V* (Malone Society, 1960 for 1959), pp. 1–16.

5 See, e.g., *EP*, II.11, as noted in *Collections III*, p. 37.

6 Manley, *Culture*, p. 267, citing Berlin (see above, chapter 9, p. 160 and n. 29.

7 Manley, *Culture*, pp. 267–268.

8 Drapers' MS +130/2, p. 617; printed in *Collections III*, p. 37. Transcribed here from the MS.

9 Pp. xxv and 37.

10 Drapers' MS +130/2, p. 646; printed in *Collections III*, p. 32. The record speaks of the "wanton*e* and super*f*luows pr*e*cydence" of Mercer mayors and sheriffs, which has driven up Watch costs by a factor of five.

11 See above, chapter 9.

12 29 Oct. pageant records follow, in *Collections III*, for 1543, 1546, 1551, 1553, 1556, etc.; and the volume's list, pp. xliv–xlvi, of all known years to 1639 with 29 Oct. pageants covers about 50 per cent of the years 1560–1600 and all but six of the years 1601–39. Note also that we cannot assume that in all years not listed there were no pageants; to give only one example, the mayor sworn in 1552 was a Haberdasher, and no Haberdashers' MS records volumes potentially including mayoral installation information (e.g., accounts, minute books) have survived for the mid sixteenth century. Commonly it is assumed today – as, e.g., by Manley, *Culture*, p. 268 – that pageants became a regular feature of 29 Oct. display from 1540 or shortly thereafter.

13 For the Tower-oath alternative, see *Liber Albus*, p. 24.

14 For 1540 as a Tower-oath year, see Rep. 10, f. 178r.

15 For 1535 as a Tower-oath year, see LB P, f. 74r.

16 Drapers' MS +143, f. 200v.

17 The Great Companies with potentially relevant records examined are the Drapers, Fishmongers, Goldsmiths, Grocers, Ironmongers, Mercers, Merchant Taylors, Skinners, and Vintners. No likely-relevant records volumes of the Haberdashers or Salters have survived for this period; and although appropriate Clothworker records volumes are extant from 1528, the Clothworkers had no mayors installed 1528–35. Note, as an example of the unpredictability of MS records in this period, that we know about the Mercers' 29 Oct. 1535 pageant only from the Drapers' records.

The fragmentary MS address (now at Trinity College, Cambridge) to a (Salter?) mayor, noted in 1917 by Elizabeth D. Adams, is not to be connected to a London 29 Oct. mayoral installation and in any case does not mention a pageant. See Adams, "A Fragment of a Lord Mayor's Pageant," *Modern Language Notes* 32 (May 1917), 285–289, and Robert Withington, "A Note on 'A Fragment of a Lord Mayor's Pageant'," *Modern Language Notes* 34 (Dec. 1919), 501–503.

18 See, e.g., for the late fifteenth-century responsibilities of the Mercers'

bachelors, the Mercers' MS Ordinance Book (The Laws and Ancient Ordinances of the Company), ff. 6r–7r.

19 Drapers' MS +130/1, p. 336.

20 Drapers' MS +252, f. 36v; also in MS +130/2, p. 459 (spelling differs, and "for Dyvers consideracions" comes after "yere").

21 See *Collections III*'s records of Midsummer shows for the years 1510, 1512, 1515, 1521, 1522, 1529; for 1525 see Drapers' MS +130/1, p. 265.

22 See *Collections III*'s transcribed records for the three years concerned.

23 See, e.g., William Herbert, *The History of the Twelve Great Livery Companies of London*, 2 vols. (London: privately printed, 1834–37; rpt. Newton Abbot: David and Charles, 1968), 1.389–391 and 441, and A. H. Johnson, *The History of The Worshipful Company of the Drapers of London*, 5 vols. (Oxford: Clarendon Press, 1914–22), 1.111, 151, 283, etc.

24 Drapers' MS +130/1, p. 172.

25 Drapers' MS +130/1, p. 209.

26 For references also to separate bachelors' accounts, monies, pageant costumes, etc., see, e.g., Drapers' MS +130/1, pp. 246 (1523) and 301 (1526).

27 In 1525, when a Draper was mayor at Watch time, the Drapers – main company *and* bachelors – provided armed men instead of pageants for the Watch. See Drapers' MS +130/1, p. 265.

28 This is substantially what Patricia Lusher assumes in her two-vol. 1940 University of London doctoral thesis, "Studies in the Guild-Drama in London in the Records of the Drapers' Company (1515–1553)," 1.59; and she calls the Drapers' 1528 Assumption "the first pageant" carried in a London Lord Mayor's Show (1.144–145).

29 We do not find any reference to a pageant in the Drapers' records for earlier years when a Draper was installed as mayor: e.g., in 1520, 1521, and 1524.

30 LB O, f. 83v.

31 The Drapers, however, would not have put forward a pageant themselves for the 1528 Watch if it had taken place, since they had no mayor or sheriff in office in June 1528.

32 A Mercer mayor was also installed in 1529.

33 Drapers' MS +130/1, p. 173; also printed in *Collections III*, p. 9. Transcribed here from the MS.

34 In 1520, e.g., the company handed over to its bachelors two Assumption banners, along with "all our old store of pagentes"; see Drapers' MS +130/1, p. 154.

35 Drapers' MS +252, f. 33r (and also MSS +130/2, p. 453, and +143, f. 148r). For 29 October 1540 the company also paid for the "new florisshing" of a square (the same?) Assumption banner (MS +143, f. 200v; also MS +130/2, p. 619, without the same detail); the large sum of 10s was involved, though this included as well the renewing of three banner staves.

36 See *OED*, s.v. Pageant *sb.*, no. 3; also 1.d ("A scene represented on tapestry, or the like"), for which one (1557) example is given. A 1450–51 example is found in the Grocers' records, GL MS 11570, p. 315, listing parlour hangings and cushions.

37 See *Collections III*, pp. 13–15, 26–30. These pageants may or may not have been

different from the bachelors' Midsummer Watch Assumption pageant; the records would allow (as Lusher assumes, "Studies in the Guild-Drama," 1.59) for the same pageant, from time to time reworked, to have been used in the Watch by the bachelors in years with a Draper mayor at midsummer and by the company as a whole in years with only a Draper sheriff at midsummer. See the Watch records in *Collections III* for the years 1521, 1522, 1523, 1529, and 1536.

38 Drapers' MS +143, f. 203r.

39 Drapers' MS +130/2, p. 651.

40 See, e.g., *Collections III*, p. 18 (the 1529 Midsummer Watch).

41 See, e.g., F. W. Fairholt, *Lord Mayors' Pageants*, part 1 (London: Percy Society, 1843), p. 14, Sheila Williams, "The Lord Mayor's Show in Tudor and Stuart Times," *Guildhall Miscellany* 1.10 (Sept. 1959), 6, Lusher, "Studies in the Guild-Drama," 1.59, and, recently, Manley, *Culture*, p. 265. (Fairholt, Sheila Williams and Lusher all assume that the Drapers on 29 Oct. 1540 used an actual Midsummer Watch pageant.)

42 *Collections III*, pp. 37–38.

43 LB Q, f. 93v.

44 It consists of a reference to setting up pageants in Merchant Taylors' Hall, and is from the 1548–49 Merchant Taylors' accounts (GL MS 34048/4, f. 129r). As suggested previously (see above, chapter 9, p. 161 and n. 35), it could be related, e.g., to the 1548 Midsummer Watch revival.

45 See *Collections III*, p. 38, and Skinners' GL MS 30708/1, f. 6v.

46 In both 1595 and 1597 the Skinners provided for the Show of a Skinner mayor "a Pageant & a Lusarne" (*Collections III*, p. 56; the quote is from 1595). By that date, at least, was the lynx, then, not a "pageant"?

47 See *Collections III*, pp. 38–40, etc., and also Machyn, pp. 47–48, etc. Withington in *EP*, II.13, has called the year 1553 the year of the first "definite" Lord Mayor's Show.

48 See *Collections III*, p. 38. The company, as noted above (n. 44), does record unspecified pageants being apparently displayed or stored in the hall, at some unspecified time, during 1548–49; and *Collections III* very tentatively links them to 29 Oct. 1546; but, as also noted above, this record is more easily explained in other ways, given its date. (For 1556, 1561, and 1568, a separate [rough] pageants MS has survived: GL MS 34105.)

49 GL MS 11571/5, f 203r. The account is headed 28 May 1543–16 June 1544. *Collections III* lists this record (p. 36) under Midsummer Shows and under the account date 1544–45. See above, chapter 9, p. 159 and n. 23.

50 Goldsmiths' MS 1524, Book H, p. 43. See above, chapter 8, p. 150.

51 Mercers' MS Acts of Court 2, f 234v.

52 Mercers' MS Register of Writings 2, f. 137v. See below, Appendix B, 11A.

53 See *Collections III*, p. xxxi. *Collections III* found the Mercers' earliest record of the maid in 1571, and other such records (before 1642) in 1572, 1603, and 1607, but none mentioning a chariot. The chariot is noted by John Strype, in his revision/continuation (*A Survey Of the Cities of London and Westminster*, 6 books in 2 vols. [London: A. Churchill *et al.*, 1720]) of Stow's *Survey*, II.v.174, as customary, and specifically as used in 1701.

54 Sheila Williams, "The Lord Mayor's Show," p. 6, assumes that the pageant in both 1535 and 1540 was an Assumption pageant (from the Midsummer Watch); but the Drapers' 1540 pageant record does not specify the content of the 1535 precedent-setting Mercers' pageant, and the Mercers would have been unlikely to have displayed a sole pageant relating to the Drapers' major feast and coat of arms.

55 See *Collections III*, p. xviii.

56 GL MS 30727/2, account 1534–35, p. 22.

57 For the specific Skinners' records from both accounts, see *Collections III*, p. 25. Since, however, only one pageant on 29 Oct. appears to have been the norm until the end of the sixteenth century, the two pageants of the Skinners' 1534–35 accounts were probably indeed Midsummer Watch pageants.

58 This decree was not noted in *Collections III*, as the editors handled only company materials, and only from 1485.

59 LB L, f. 169r. See also Jor. 8, ff. 253v, 255r, 257r. Manley, *Culture*, does note this record (p. 264, n. 119) but regards it as unimportant.

60 Drapers' MS +403, f. 9r–v; mentioned in Johnson, *History*, I.158, n.1 (there incorrectly assigned to the 1476 mayoral installation), and transcribed II.273–74 (there correctly assigned to the 1477 Watch). Fourteen porters were required. This Watch, as we have seen in chapter 9, was an especially elaborate one; ambassadors from France and Scotland were in London, and the king wanted to impress them with "the gretter wache" (Mercers' MS Acts of Court 1, f. 32v).

61 See chapter 9; and for the 1541 Watch specifically, see *Collections III*, pp. 32–35.

62 As noted in chapter 9, religious suppression of the Watch in the 1530s and early 1540s, at least in response to pressures from outside the city, would seem unlikely in any case. Christopher Haigh, e.g., in *English Reformations: Religion, Politics, and Society under the Tudors* (Oxford: Clarendon Press, 1993; rpt. 1995) describes Henry VIII's general attitude throughout his reign as comparatively conservative in relation to religious traditions, the major innovations coming with Edward VI. See pp. 121–183; and also Susan Brigden, *London and the Reformation* (Oxford: Clarendon Press, 1989), pp. 302–321 (by 1539 Henry had turned against religious extremism).

63 See LB P, ff. 105v and 115v, for 1536; the other two dates have been previously footnoted.

64 Was there another Tower-oath pageant in 1536, when another Mercer mayor was sworn in as mayor? Perhaps not, since the Drapers in 1540 cited 1535 as their precedent. Might this point to John Aleyn as the specific reason for the 1535 pageant?

65 See below, Appendix B. The 21 April 1544 Westminster oath-taking, however, of Mercer mayor Ralph Warren, elected 17 April to replace the deceased William Bowyer, is recorded in Jor. 15, ff. 86v–87r, and in LB Q, f. 106r. It was supposedly "in all thynges" except those specified in the entry (such as the bachelors' barge) like a 29 Oct. oath-taking. No maid is mentioned: although this does not prove that there was none.

Works cited

MANUSCRIPTS

The manuscripts of most of the London livery companies are on deposit from the companies at the Guildhall Library, Aldermanbury, London. A few companies have retained a few MSS, such as original charters, in their own halls; and a few other companies hold all of their own MSS in their halls. MSS cited are listed here under their locations. Company MSS at the Guildhall Library are largely described here as in the Guildhall Library card catalogue.

British Library (London)

BL Add. MS 6113
BL Add. MS 12,222
BL Add. MS 15,664
BL Cotton MS Julius B.i
BL Cotton MS Julius B.xii
BL Cotton MS Nero C.ix
BL Cotton MS Tiberius E.viii
BL Egerton MS 1142 (Wiresellers/Pinners)
    A photostat copy is also in the Guildhall Library, GL MS 6526
BL Harley MS 5111
BL Royal MS 18 A.lxiv
BL Royal MS Appendix 89 (formerly BL Cotton MS Appendix XXVIII)

Cambridge University Library

Cambridge University Library MS Ee.2.12

Corporation of London Records Office (Guildhall, London)

Bridge House: Annual Accounts and Rentals 3–4
Bridge House: Bridgemasters' account rolls 1381–1405
Bridge House: Weekly Payments, Series 1, vols. 2–3
Letter Books A–S. (Various volumes)

Journals 1–17, 21. (Various volumes)
Repertories 1–14. (Various volumes)

Guildhall Library (Aldermanbury, London; Corporation of London)

GL MS 1574/1 (Bakers). Audit book. (Masters and wardens' accounts)
GL MS 2883/1–2 (Blacksmiths). Wardens' accounts
GL MS 3704 (Parish Clerks). Typescript notes by William McMurray
GL MS 4326/1–2 (Carpenters). Wardens' account books
  These two MSS have been edited by Bower Marsh, *Records of the Worshipful Company of Carpenters*, vol. 2: Warden's Account Book 1438–1516 (Oxford: Oxford University Press for the Company, 1914), and vol. 4: Warden's Account Book 1546–1571 (Oxford: Oxford University Press for the Company, 1916). (The final two years of GL MS 4326/2, 1571–73, are in vol. 5)
GL MS 4646 (Weavers). Account and memorandum book
GL MS 5370 (Scriveners). Common Paper
  This MS has been edited by Francis W. Steer, *Scriveners' Company Common Paper 1357–1628, With a Continuation to 1678* (London Record Society, 1968)
GL MS 5440 (Brewers). Ancient account and memoranda book
GL MS 5442/1–2 (Brewers). Old wardens' account books
GL MS 5535 (Blacksmiths). Memorandum book
GL MS 5606/1 (Coopers). Wardens' account book
GL MS 5614A (Coopers). Quarterage book
GL MS 6152/1 (Tallow Chandlers). Wardens' account book
GL MS 6155/1 (Tallow Chandlers). Yeomanry account book
GL MS 6330/1 (Founders). Wardens' account book
  This MS has been edited by Guy Parsloe, *Wardens' Accounts of the Worshipful Company of Founders of the City of London 1497–1681* (London: University of London, Athlone Press, 1964)
GL MS 6440/1 (Butchers). Wardens' account book
GL MS 6526 (Wiresellers/Pinners). Memorandum and account book
  Photostat copy of BL Egerton MS 1142
GL MS 7086/1–2 (Pewterers). Master and wardens' account books
GL MS 7094 (Pewterers). Yeomanry account book
GL MS 7146 (Cutlers). Wardens' account rolls
GL MS 9481/1 (Wax Chandlers). Renter wardens' account book
GL MS 11570 (Grocers). Memorandum and ordinance book. (The Black Book)
  This MS has been reproduced, transcribed, and translated by John Abernethy Kingdon, ed., *Facsimile of First Volume of MS. Archives of the Worshipful Company of Grocers of the City of London, A.D. 1345–1463*, 2 parts (London: The Company, 1883–86). I have used, for citations, the MS's modern pagination, rather than its older foliation, because Kingdon uses the pagination for his transcription and translation (which is thus continuous pagination through the two printed parts)
GL MS 11571/1–5 (Grocers). Wardens' accounts

GL MS 12065/1 (Armourers and Brasiers). Wardens' account book
GL MS 12071/1–2 (Armourers and Brasiers). Court minute books
GL MS 12073 (Armourers and Brasiers). Yeomanry court minute book
GL MS 14346/1 (Curriers). Master and wardens' accounts
GL MS 15333/1 (Vintners). Wardens' accounts
GL MS 16960 (Ironmongers). Charter, ordinance and memorandum book
GL MS 16988/1 (Ironmongers). Registers. (Wardens' accounts)
GL MS 30727/1–3 (Skinners). Receipts and payments books
GL MS 30708/1 (Skinners). Court book
GL MS 34004 (Merchant Taylors). Ordinance and memorandum book
GL MS 34008/1 (Merchant Taylors). Court minutes
> This MS, along with GL MS 34008/2, has been transcribed and edited by
> Matthew Davies, *The Merchant Taylors' Company of London: Court Minutes
> 1486–1493* (Stamford: Richard III & Yorkist History Trust, in association
> with Paul Watkins, 2000)

GL MS 34048/1–4 (Merchant Taylors). Master and wardens' account books
GL MS 34105 (Merchant Taylors). Memorandum book (concerning the processions and pageants for Lord Mayor's Day)

Livery Company Halls

Drapers' MS +128. Minutes and records
Drapers' MS +130/1–3. Minutes and records
Drapers' MS +140. Wardens' accounts
> Published by the Company as *Drapers' Company: Transcripts of the Earliest
> Records in the Possession of the Company* (London: Chiswick Press, 1910)

Drapers' MS +140a. Minutes and records
Drapers' MS +143. Wardens' accounts
Drapers' MS +252. Minutes and records
Drapers' MS +253. Minutes and records
Drapers' MS +254. Minutes and records
Drapers' MS +255. Minutes and records
Drapers' MS +403. Wardens' accounts
Drapers' MS +795. Ordinance book

Goldsmiths' MS 1518. Wardens' accounts and court minutes
Goldsmiths' MS 1519. Wardens' accounts and court minutes
Goldsmiths' MS 1520. Wardens' accounts and court minutes
Goldsmiths' MS 1522. Wardens' accounts and court minutes
Goldsmiths' MS 1524. Wardens' accounts and court minutes

Leathersellers' MS Liber Curtes 1. Accounts and inventories

Mercers' MS Acts of Court 1 (1453–1527)
> This MS has been transcribed and edited by Laetitia Lyell, assisted by Frank

D. Watney, *Acts of Court of the Mercers' Company 1453–1527* (Cambridge: Cambridge University Press, 1936)

Mercers' MS Acts of Court 2 (1527–1560)

Mercers' MS Ordinance Book

Mercers' MS Register of Writings 2

Mercers' MS Renter Wardens' Accounts 2 (1501–1538)

Mercers' MS Wardens' Accounts 1347–1464

Stationers' MS Wardens' Accounts 1554–1571 (Register A)

Public Record Office

PRO c239/9/25

PRO sp1/89/208

PRINTED WORKS

A Chronicle of London, from 1089 to 1483. See alphabetized under C, below.

Acts of the Privy Council of England. See Dasent, below.

Adams, Elizabeth D. "A Fragment of a Lord Mayor's Pageant," *Modern Language Notes* 32 (May 1917), 285–289.

Adams, Reginald H. *The Parish Clerks of London.* London and Chichester: Phillimore, 1971.

Andreas, Bernardus. *Historia Regis Henrici Septimi, a Bernardo Andrea Tholosate Conscripta,* ed. James Gairdner. RS 10. London: HMSO, 1858; rpt. Lessing-Druckerei, Wiesbaden: Kraus Reprint, 1966.

Anglo-Norman Dictionary, ed. Louise W. Stone and William Rothwell. 7 fascicles. London: Modern Humanities Research Association, 1977–88.

Anglo, Sydney. "The Foundation of the Tudor Dynasty: The Coronation and Marriage of Henry VII," *Guildhall Miscellany* 2.1 (1960), 3–11.

"The Imperial Alliance and the Entry of the Emperor Charles V into London: June 1522," *Guildhall Miscellany* 2.4 (1962), 131–155.

"The London Pageants for the Reception of Katharine of Aragon: November 1501," *Journal of the Warburg and Courtauld Institutes* 26 (1963), 53–89.

Spectacle, Pageantry and Early Tudor Policy. Oxford: Clarendon Press, 1969; 2nd edn. 1997.

Annales Londonienses. In *Chronicles of the Reigns of Edward I. and Edward II.* See Stubbs, below, pp. 1–251.

Annales Paulini. In *Chronicles of the Reigns of Edward I. and Edward II.* See Stubbs, below, pp. 253–370.

The Anonimalle Chronicle 1333 to 1381, ed. V. H. Galbraith. Manchester: Manchester University Press, 1927.

Arber, Edward, ed. *An English Garner,* vol. 2. London: E. Arber, 1879.

ed. *A Transcript of the Registers of the Company of Stationers of London; 1554–1640 A.D.,* vol. 1. London: privately printed, 1875.

Archer, Ian W. *The History of The Haberdashers' Company*. Chichester: Phillimore, 1991.

Arnott, Peter D. *The Ancient Greek and Roman Theatre*. New York: Random House, 1971.

Axton, Richard. *European Drama of the Early Middle Ages*. London: Hutchinson, 1974.

ed. *Three Rastell Plays*. See Rastell, below.

Axton, Richard, and John Stevens, eds. and trs. *Medieval French Plays*. Oxford: Basil Blackwell, 1971.

Bale, Robert. *Chronicle*. In Flenley, see below, pp. 114–153.

Barron, Caroline M. "Centres of Conspicuous Consumption: The Aristocratic Town House in London 1200–1550," *London Journal* 20.1 (1995), 1–16.

"The Later Middle Ages: 1270–1520," in Lobel, *Atlas*, see below, pp. 42–56.

"The Parish Fraternities of Medieval London," in Caroline M. Barron and Christopher Harper-Bill, eds., *The Church in Pre-Reformation Society: Essays in Honour of F. R. H. Du Boulay*. Woodbridge, Suffolk, and Dover, NH: Boydell Press, 1985, pp. 13–37.

"The Quarrel of Richard II with London 1392–7," in F. R. H. Du Boulay and Caroline M. Barron, eds., *The Reign of Richard II: Essays in Honour of May McKisack*. London: University of London, Athlone Press, 1971, pp. 173–201.

Barron, E[dward] Jackson. "Notes on the History of the Armourers' and Brasiers' Company," *Transactions of the London and Middlesex Archaeological Society*, NS 2 (1911–13), 300–319.

Baskervill, C. R. "William Lily's Verse for the Entry of Charles V into London," *Huntington Library Bulletin* 9 (1936), 1–14.

Bate, Keith, ed. *Three Latin Comedies*. Toronto Medieval Latin Texts 6. Toronto: Centre for Medieval Studies and Pontifical Institute of Medieval Studies, 1976.

Bateman, Nick. *Gladiators at the Guildhall: The Story of London's Roman Amphitheatre and Medieval Guildhall*. London: Museum of London Archaeology Service, 2000.

"The London Amphitheatre: Excavations 1987–1996," *Britannia* 28 (1997), 51–85.

"The London Amphitheatre," *Current Archaeology* 137 [12.5] (Feb./Mar. 1994), 164–171.

Bateson, Mary. "A London Municipal Collection of the Reign of John," *English Historical Review* 17 (1902), 480–511 and 707–730.

Beadle, Richard, ed. *The Cambridge Companion to Medieval English Theatre*. Cambridge: Cambridge University Press, 1994; rpt. 1995.

Beaven, Alfred B. *The Aldermen of the City of London*. 2 vols. London: Corporation of London, 1908–13.

Bédoyère, Guy de la. *The Buildings of Roman Britain*. London: B. T. Batsford, 1991.

Roman Towns in Britain. London: B. T. Batsford/English Heritage, 1992.

Bennett, J. A. W., and G. V. Smithers, eds. *Early Middle English Verse and Prose.* Oxford: Clarendon Press, 1966.

Bergeron, David M. *English Civic Pageantry 1558–1642.* Columbia, SC: South Carolina University Press, 1971.

 ed. *Pageantry in the Shakespearean Theater.* Athens, GA: University of Georgia Press, 1985.

 ed. *Pageants and Entertainments of Anthony Munday: A Critical Edition.* New York: Garland, 1985.

 Practicing Renaissance Scholarship. Pittsburgh: Duquesne University Press, 2000.

 ed. *Thomas Heywood's Pageants: A Critical Edition.* New York: Garland, 1986.

Berlin, Michael. "Civic Ceremony in Early Modern London," *Urban History Yearbook* 1986, pp. 15–27.

Bevington, David M. *From 'Mankind' to Marlowe: Growth of Structure in the Popular Drama of Tudor England.* Cambridge, MA: Harvard University Press, 1962.

 ed. and tr. *Medieval Drama.* Boston: Houghton Mifflin, 1975.

 Tudor Drama and Politics: A Critical Approach to Topical Meaning. Cambridge, MA: Harvard University Press, 1968.

Biddle, Martin. "A City in Transition: 400–800," in Lobel, *Atlas,* see below, pp. 20–29.

Bieber, Margarete. *The History of the Greek and Roman Theater.* Princeton: Princeton University Press, 1939; 2nd edn. 1961.

Birch, Walter de Gray, ed. *The Historical Charters and Constitutional Documents of the City of London.* London: Whiting, 1887.

Bird, Ruth. *The Turbulent London of Richard II.* London: Longmans Green, 1949.

Blackmore, Lyn. "From Beach to Burh: New Clues to Entity and Identity in 7th to 9th-century London," in Guy De Boe and Frans Verhaeghe, eds., *Urbanism in Medieval Europe,* Papers of the 'Medieval Europe Brugge 1997' Conference, vol. 1. Zellik: Institute for the Archaeological Heritage, 1997, pp. 123–132.

Blagg, T. F. C. "Monumental Architecture in Roman London," in J. Bird, M. Hassall and H. Sheldon, eds., *Interpreting Roman London: Papers in Memory of Hugh Chapman.* Oxbow Monograph 58. Oxford: Oxbow Books, 1996, pp. 43–47.

The Book of Sir Thomas More, ed. W. W. Greg. Malone Society, 1911.

Boynton, Lindsay. *The Elizabethan Militia 1558–1638.* London/Toronto: Routledge and Kegan Paul/University of Toronto Press, 1967.

Braunmuller, A. R., and Michael Hattaway, eds. *The Cambridge Companion to English Renaissance Drama.* Cambridge: Cambridge University Press, 1990.

Brewer, J. S., ed. *Letters and Papers, Foreign and Domestic, of the Reign of Henry VIII,* vol. 4.1. London: HMSO, 1870.

A Brief Latin Chronicle, in Gairdner, *Three Fifteenth-Century Chronicles,* see below, pp. 164–185.

Brigden, Susan. *London and the Reformation.* Oxford: Clarendon Press, 1989.

Bristol, Michael D. "Theater and Popular Culture," in Cox and Kastan, *New History,* see below, pp. 231–248.

Britnell, R. H. *The Commercialisation of English Society 1000–1500*. Cambridge: Cambridge University Press, 1993.

Brockett, Oscar G. *History of the Theatre*. 7th edn. Needham Heights, MA: Allyn and Bacon, 1995.

Brooke, Christopher. "The Central Middle Ages: 800–1270," in Lobel, *Atlas*, see below, pp. 30–41.

assisted by Gillian Keir. *London 800–1216: The Shaping of a City*. London: Secker and Warburg, 1975.

Brotanek, Rudolf. *Die englischen Maskenspiele*. Wien und Leipzig: Wilhelm Braümuller, 1902; rpt. London: Johnson Reprint, 1964.

Brown, Carleton. "Lydgate's Verses on Queen Margaret's Entry into London," *Modern Language Review* 7 (1912), 225–234.

The Brut, ed. Friedrich W. D. Brie, vol. 2. Early English Text Society, os 136, 1908.

Buck, George. *The History of the Life and Reigne of Richard The Third*, intro. A. R. Myers. Totowa, NJ: Rowman and Littlefield, 1973.

Burckhardt, Jacob. *The Civilization Of The Renaissance In Italy*, tr. S. G. C. Middlemore, rev. Irene Gordon. New York: New American Library, 1960.

Butterworth, Philip. *Theatre of Fire: Special Effects in Early English and Scottish Theatre*. London: Society for Theatre Research, 1998.

Byrne, Muriel St. Clare, ed. *The Lisle Letters*, vols. 3 and 5. Chicago and London: University of Chicago Press, 1981.

Calendar of Letter-Books. See Sharpe, below.

Calendar of Letters, Despatches, and State Papers Relating to the Negotiations between England and Spain, vols. 4.2 and 5.1, ed. Pascual de Gayangos. London: HMSO, 1882 and 1886; rpt. Nendeln, Liechtenstein: Kraus Reprint, 1969.

Calendar of State Papers and Manuscripts . . . Existing in the Archives and Collections of Venice, vols. 3 (1520–1526) and 6.1 (1555–1556), ed. Rawdon Brown. London: HMSO, 1869 and 1877.

Calisto and Melebea, The Interlude of, ed. W. W. Greg. Malone Society, 1908.

Cawte, E. C. *Ritual Animal Disguise: A Historical and Geographical Study of Animal Disguise in the British Isles*. Cambridge/Totowa, NJ: D. S. Brewer/Rowman and Littlefield for the Folklore Society, 1978.

Chambers, E. K. *The Elizabethan Stage*. 4 vols. Oxford: Clarendon Press, 1923. *The Mediaeval Stage*. 2 vols. Oxford: Oxford University Press, 1903.

Chambers, E. K., and W. W. Greg, eds. "Dramatic Records of the City of London. The Remembrancia," in *Collections I.1*. Malone Society, 1907, pp. 43–100.

Chambers, R. W., and Marjorie Daunt, eds. *A Book of London English 1384–1425*. Oxford: Clarendon Press, 1931.

Chaney, David. *Fictions of Collective Life: Public Drama in Late Modern Culture*. London and New York: Routledge, 1993.

Cheney, C. R. *Handbook of Dates for Students of English History*. London: Royal Historical Society, 1945; rpt. 1970.

Chrimes, S. B. *An Introduction to the Administrative History of Mediaeval England*. 3rd edn. Oxford: Basil Blackwell, 1966.

Christianson, C. Paul. *Memorials of the Book Trade in Medieval London. The Archives of Old London Bridge*. Manuscript Studies 3. Cambridge and Wolfeboro, NH: D. S. Brewer, 1987.

Christie, James. *Some Account of Parish Clerks*. London: The Worshipful Company of Parish Clerks, 1893.

Chronica Johannis de Reading et Anonymi Cantuariensis 1346–1367, ed. James Tait. Manchester: Manchester University Press, 1914.

A Chronicle of London, from 1089 to 1483 [, ed. Nicholas Nicolas and Edward Tyrrell]. London: Longman *et al.*, 1827.

The Chronicle of Queen Jane, and of Two Years of Queen Mary, ed. John Gough Nichols. Camden Society, OS 48, 1850.

Chronicle of the Grey Friars of London, ed. John Gough Nichols. Camden Society, OS 53, 1852.

Chronicles of the Mayors and Sheriffs of London. See Riley, below.

The Chronicles of the White Rose of York. London: James Bohn, 1845.

Chronicon Angliae, ed. Edward Maunde Thompson. RS 64. London: HMSO, 1874.

Clode, Charles M. *The Early History of the Guild of Merchant Taylors of the Fraternity of St. John the Baptist, London*. 2 parts. London: privately printed by Harrison and Sons, 1888.

Clopper, Lawrence. "English Drama: From Ungodly *ludi* to Sacred Play," in David Wallace, ed., *The Cambridge History of Medieval English Literature*. Cambridge: Cambridge University Press, 1999, pp. 739–766.

 "London and the Problem of the Clerkenwell Plays," *Comparative Drama* 34 (Fall 2000), 291–303.

Cockburn, J. S., H. P. F. King, and K. G. T. McDonnell, eds. *The Victoria History of the Counties of England. A History of the County of Middlesex*, vol. 1. Oxford: Oxford University Press for the Institute of Historical Research, 1969.

Coldewey, John C. "Some Economic Aspects of the Late Medieval Drama," in Marianne G. Briscoe and John C. Coldewey, eds. *Contexts for Early English Drama*. Bloomington and Indianapolis: Indiana University Press, 1989, pp. 77–101.

Coote, H[enry] C[harles]. "The English Gild of Knights and their Socn," *TLMAS* 5 (1876–80), 477–493.

Coote, Henry Charles, and John Robert Daniel-Tyssen, eds. "The Ordinances of Some Secular Guilds of London, 1354–1496," *TLMAS* 4 (1871), 1–59.

Cox, John D., and David Scott Kastan, eds. *A New History of Early English Drama*. New York: Columbia University Press, 1997.

Craik, T. W. *The Tudor Interlude: Stage, Costume, and Acting*. Leicester: Leicester University Press, 1958.

Creighton, Charles. *A History of Epidemics in Britain*. 2 vols. Cambridge: Cambridge University Press, 1891–94; rev. edn. London: Frank Cass, 1965.

Cromwell, T. *History and Description of the Parish of Clerkenwell*. London: Longman et al., 1828.

Croniques de London, depuis l'An 44 Hen. III. jusqu'à l'An 17 Edw. III., ed. George James Aungier. Camden Society, os 28, 1844.

Daniel, The Play of. See below, Greenberg, Noah.

Dasent, John Roche, ed. *Acts of the Privy Council of England*. NS 1: 1542–1547. London: HMSO, 1890.

Davies, John Silvester, ed. *An English Chronicle of the Reigns of Richard II, Henry IV, Henry V, and Henry VI*. Camden Society, os 64, 1856.

Davies, Matthew, ed. *The Merchant Taylors' Company of London: Court Minutes 1486–1493*. Stamford: Richard III and Yorkist History Trust, in association with Paul Watkins, 2000.

"The Tailors of London: Corporate Charity in the Late Medieval Town," in Rowena E. Archer, ed., *Crown, Government and People in the Fifteenth Century*. The Fifteenth Century Series 2. Stroud/New York: Alan Sutton/St. Martin's Press, 1995, pp. 161–190.

Davis, Norman, ed. *Non-Cycle Plays and Fragments*. EETS, Supplementary Text 1, 1970.

Deadman, Hugo, and Elizabeth Scudder, eds. *An Introductory Guide to the Corporation of London Records Office*. London: Corporation of London, 1994.

Dekker, Thomas. *The Dramatic Works of Thomas Dekker*, ed. Fredson Bowers. 4 vols. Cambridge: Cambridge University Press, 1953–61.

Devizes, Richard of. *The Chronicle of Richard of Devizes of the Time of King Richard the First*, ed. and tr. John T. Appleby. London: Thomas Nelson and Sons, 1963.

Devon, Frederick, ed. *Issues of the Exchequer . . . from King Henry III. to King Henry VI. Inclusive*. London: John Murray, 1837.

Dictionary of National Biography, ed. Leslie Stephen and Sidney Lee. 22 vols. Oxford: Oxford University Press, 1921–22; rpt. 1963–64.

Dillon. See below, [Lee-]Dillon.

Dockray, Keith. *Henry VI, Margaret of Anjou and the Wars of the Roses: A Source Book*. Phoenix Mill, Gloucestershire: Sutton, 2000.

[Dodsley, Robert, ed.] *A Select Collection of Old Plays*, vol. 1. London: R. Dodsley, 1744.

Douglas, David C., and George W. Greenaway, eds. *English Historical Documents*, vol. 2 (1042–1189). London: Eyre and Spottiswoode, 1953.

Drapers' Company: Transcripts of the Earliest Records in the Possession of the Company. London: Chiswick Press, 1910.

Dyson, Tony, and John Schofield. "Saxon London," in Jeremy Haslam, ed., *Anglo-Saxon Towns In Southern England*. Chicester: Phillimore, 1984, pp. 285–313.

Elder, John. *Copie of a Letter Sent into Scotlande*. 1555; rpt. Amsterdam and New York: Da Capo Press, The English Experience 308, 1971.

Ellis, Henry. "Copy of a Letter from Archbishop Cranmer," *Archaeologia* 18 (1817), 77–82.

Erler, Mary C. "Spectacle and Sacrament: A London Parish Play in the 1530s," *Modern Philology* 91 (1993–94), 449–454.

Esdaile, A., ed. "Love Feigned and Unfeigned," in *Collections I.1*. Malone Society, 1907, pp. 17–25.

Fabyan, Robert. *The New Chronicles of England and France*, ed. Henry Ellis. London: F. C. and J. Rivington *et al.*, 1811.

Fairholt, Frederick W. *Lord Mayors' Pageants*. 2 parts. London: Percy Society, 1843–44.

Feuillerat, Albert, ed. *Documents Relating to the Revels at Court in the time of King Edward VI and Queen Mary. (The Loseley Manuscripts)*. Louvain: A. Uystpruyst, 1914.

Fincham, H. W. *The Order of the Hospital of St. John of Jerusalem and its Grand Priory of England*. London: Collingridge, 1915.

Fitz Stephen, William. "Descriptio Londoniae," tr. H. E. Butler ("A Description of London"), in F. M. Stenton, *Norman London: An Essay*, new edn. London: Historical Association Leaflets 93–94, 1934, pp. 25–35.

Flenley, Ralph, ed. *Six Town Chronicles of England*. Oxford: Clarendon Press, 1911.

Flude, Kevin. "The Roman London Amphitheatre" [letter], *London Archaeologist* 7.7 (Summer 1994), 189–190.

Forbes, Derek. *Lydgate's Disguising at Hertford Castle: the First Secular Comedy in the English Language*. Pulborough, West Sussex: Blot, 1998.

Fox, Alistair. *Politics and Literature in the Reigns of Henry VII and Henry VIII*. Oxford and New York: Basil Blackwell, 1989.

Foxe, John. *The Acts and Monuments of John Foxe*, vols. 5 and 6, ed. George Townsend. London: Seeley, Burnside, and Seeley, 1846.

Frank, Grace. *The Medieval French Drama*. Oxford: Clarendon Press, 1954; rpt. 1967.

The French Chronicle of London, in same volume as *Chronicles of the Mayors and Sheriffs of London*, see above, pp. 229–295.

Froissart, John. *Sir John Froissart's Chronicles of England, France, Spain, Portugal, Scotland, Brittany, Flanders, and the Adjoining Countries*, tr. John Bourchier, Lord Berners. 2 vols. London: F. C. and J. Rivington *et al.*, 1812.

Fuentes, Nicholas. "Some Entertainment in Londinium," *London Archaeologist* 5.6 (Spring 1986), 144–147.

Fulford, Michael. *The Silchester Amphitheatre: Excavations of 1979–85*. Britannia Monograph Series 10. London: Society for the Promotion of Roman Studies, 1989.

Furnivall, Frederick J., ed. *Ballads from Manuscripts*, vol. 1.1. London: Ballad Society, 1868.

ed. *Harrison's Description of England in Shakspere's Youth*, Part IV, Supplement 2, with additions by C. C. Stopes. London: Chatto and Windus, New Shakspere Society, 1908.

Gairdner, James, ed. *The Historical Collections of a Citizen of London in the Fifteenth Century*. Camden Society, NS 17, 1876.

ed. *Letters and Papers . . . of Richard III. and Henry VII*. 2 vols. RS 24. London: HMSO, 1861–63.

ed. *Three Fifteenth-Century Chronicles*. Camden Society, NS 28, 1880.

Gairdner, James, and R. H. Brodie, eds. *Letters and Papers, Foreign and Domestic, of the Reign of Henry VIII*, vol. 16. RS 120. London: HMSO, 1898.

Gentleness and Nobility, ed. A. C. Partridge. Malone Society, 1950 for 1949.

Gesta Henrici Quinti, ed. and tr. Frank Taylor and John S. Roskell. Oxford: Clarendon Press, 1975.

Girtin, Tom. *The Mark of the Sword: A Narrative History of the Cutlers' Company 1189–1975*. London: Hutchinson Benham, 1975.

The Triple Crowns: A Narrative History of The Drapers' Company, 1364–1964. London: Hutchinson, 1964.

The Globe and Mail. 17 April 1998. Toronto, Canada.

Grafton, Richard. *Grafton's Chronicle* [, ed. Henry Ellis]. 2 vols. London: J. Johnston *et al.*, 1809.

The Great Chronicle of London, ed. A. H. Thomas and I. D. Thornley. London: Corporation of London, 1938.

Green, Richard Firth. *Poets and Princepleasers: Literature and the English Court in the Late Middle Ages*. Toronto and Buffalo: University of Toronto Press, 1980.

Greenberg, Noah, ed. *The Play of Daniel*. New York: Oxford University Press, 1959.

Greg, W. W., ed. "A Play of Robin Hood for May-Games," in *Collections I.2*. Malone Society, 1908, pp. 125–136.

ed. "The Prodigal Son," in *Collections I.1*. Malone Society, 1907, pp. 27–30.

ed. "Robin Hood and the Sheriff of Nottingham," in *Collections I.2*. Malone Society, 1908, pp. 117–123.

Gregory, William. *Chronicle*. In Gairdner, *Historical Collections*, see above, pp. 55–239.

Grose, Francis, ed. *The Antiquarian Repertory*. 4 vols. London: Edward Jeffery, 1807–09.

Guth, DeLloyd J. "Richard III, Henry VII and the City . . . ," in Ralph A. Griffiths and James Sherborne, eds., *Kings and Nobles in the Later Middle Ages: A Tribute to Charles Ross*. Gloucester/New York: Alan Sutton/St. Martin's Press, 1986, pp. 185–204.

Haigh, Christopher. *English Reformations: Religion, Politics, and Society under the Tudors*. Oxford: Clarendon Press, 1993; rpt. 1995.

Hall, Edward. *Hall's Chronicle* [, ed. Henry Ellis]. London: J. Johnston *et al.*, 1809.

Hammond, Eleanor Prescott. "Two Tapestry Poems by Lydgate: The *Life of St. George* and the *Falls of Seven Princes*," *Englische Studien* 43 (1910–11), 10–26.

Hanson, John Arthur. *Roman Theater-Temples*. Princeton: Princeton University Press, 1959.

Harbage, Alfred, ed. *Annals of English Drama 975–1700*, rev. S. Schoenbaum. Philadelphia: University of Pennsylvania Press, 1964. (The 1989 edn. is unreliable: see review by Anne Lancashire in *Shakespeare Quarterly* 42 [Summer 1991], 225–230.)

Harding, Vanessa, and Laura Wright, eds. *London Bridge: Selected Accounts and Rentals, 1381–1538*. London Record Society, 1995.

Hassall, W. O., ed. *Cartulary of St. Mary Clerkenwell*. Camden Society, Series 3, 71, 1949.

"Plays at Clerkenwell," *Modern Language Review* 33 (1938), 564–567.

Hayward, John. *Annals of the First Four Years of the Reign of Queen Elizabeth*, ed. John Bruce. Camden Society, os 7, 1840.

The First Part of the Life and Raigne of King Henrie the IIII. 1599; rpt. Amsterdam and Norwood, NJ: Theatrum Orbis Terrarum, 1975.

Herbert, William. *The History of the Twelve Great Livery Companies of London.* 2 vols. London: privately printed, 1834–37; rpt. Newton Abbot: David and Charles, 1968.

Heywood, John. *The Dramatic Writings of John Heywood*, ed. John S. Farmer. London: Early English Drama Society, 1905; rpt. New York: Barnes and Noble, 1966.

Higden, Ranulf. *Polychronicon Ranulphi Higden Monachi Cestrensis*, ed. Joseph Rawson Lumby, vol. 9. RS 41. London: HMSO, 1886.

Hilton, R. H. "Towns in English Medieval Society," in Richard Holt and Gervase Rosser, eds., *The Medieval Town: A Reader in English Urban History 1200–1540.* London and New York: Longman, 1990, pp. 19–28.

Historia Vita Et Regni Ricardi Secundi, ed. George B. Stow, Jr. [Philadelphia:] University of Pennsylvania Press, 1977.

Historie of the Arrivall of Edward IV. in England, ed. John Bruce. Camden Society, os 1, 1838.

Hobley, Brian. "Lundenwic and Lundenburh: Two Cities Rediscovered," in Hodges and Hobley, see below, pp. 69–82.

Roman and Saxon London: A Reappraisal. London: Museum of London, 1986.

Hodges, Richard, and Brian Hobley. *The Rebirth of Towns in the West AD 700–1050.* CBA Research Report 68, 1988.

Holinshed, Raphael. *Chronicles of England, Scotland, and Ireland* [, ed. Henry Ellis]. 6 vols. London: J. Johnston *et al.*, 1807–08.

Horace. *Satires I*, ed. and tr. P. Michael Brown. Warminster: Aris and Phillips, 1993.

Humphrey, John H. *Roman Circuses: Arenas for Chariot Racing.* London: B. T. Batsford, 1986.

Hutton, Ronald. *The Rise and Fall of Merry England. The Ritual Year 1400–1700.* Oxford and New York: Oxford University Press, 1994.

Imray, Jean. "'Les Bones Gentes de la Mercerye de Londres': a Study of the Membership of the Medieval Mercers' Company," in A. E. J. Hollaender and William Kellaway, eds., *Studies in London History Presented to Philip Edmund Jones.* London: Hodder and Stoughton, 1969, pp. 153–178.

The Mercers' Hall. London Topographical Society 143, 1991.

Impatient Poverty. Tudor Facsimile Texts, 1907.

Ingram, R. W., ed. *Coventry*, REED. Toronto: University of Toronto Press, 1981.

Ingram, William. *The Business of Playing: The Beginnings of the Adult Professional Theater in Elizabethan London.* Ithaca, NY: Cornell University Press, 1992.

Jack Juggler, ed. B. Ifor Evans. Malone Society, 1937 for 1936.

James, Mervyn. "Ritual, Drama and Social Body in the Late Medieval English Town," *Past and Present* 98 (1983), 3–29.

Society, Politics and Culture: Studies in Early Modern England. Past and Present Publications. Cambridge: Cambridge University Press, 1986.

Johan the Evangelist, The Interlude of, ed. W. W. Greg. Malone Society, 1907.

Johnson, A. H. *The History of The Worshipful Company of the Drapers of London.* 5 vols. Oxford: Clarendon Press, 1914–22.

Johnston, Alexandra F. "'Amys and Amylon' at Bicester Priory," *REED Newsletter* 18.2 (1993), 15–18.

"What if No Texts Survived? External Evidence for Early English Drama," in Marianne G. Briscoe and John C. Coldewey, eds. *Contexts for Early English Drama*. Bloomington and Indianapolis: Indiana University Press, 1989, pp. 1–19.

Johnston, Alexandra F., and Margaret Rogerson, eds. *York*, REED. 2 vols. Toronto: University of Toronto Press, 1979.

Jones, Marion. "Early Moral Plays and the Earliest Secular Drama," in Lois Potter, gen. ed., *The Revels History of Drama in English*, vol. I: *Medieval Drama*. London: Methuen, 1983, pp. 211–291.

Jowett, John. "Henry Chettle and the Original Text," in T. H. Howard-Hill, ed. *Shakespeare and 'Sir Thomas More': Essays on the Play and its Shakespearian Interest*. Cambridge: Cambridge University Press, 1989, pp. 131–149.

Joyce, Sally L., and Evelyn S. Newlyn, eds. *Cornwall*, REED. Toronto/European Union: University of Toronto Press/Brepols, 1999.

Kahrl, Stanley J. *Traditions of Medieval English Drama*. London: Hutchinson, 1974.

Keene, Derek. *Cheapside before the Great Fire*. Economic and Social Research Council, 1985.

"London in the Early Middle Ages 600–1300," *London Journal* 20.2 (1995), 9–21.

Kernodle, George R. *From Art to Theatre: Form and Convention in the Renaissance*. Chicago and London: University of Chicago Press, 1944.

Kingdon, John Abernethy, ed. *Facsimile of First Volume of MS. Archives of the Worshipful Company of Grocers of the City of London, A.D. 1345–1463*. 2 parts (with continuous pagination). London: The Company, 1886.

Kingsford, Charles Lethbridge, ed. *Chronicles of London*. Oxford: Clarendon Press, 1905.

English Historical Literature in the Fifteenth Century. Oxford: Clarendon Press, 1913; rpt. New York: Burt Franklin, Burt Franklin Bibliographical and Reference Series 37, n.d.

ed. "Two London Chronicles from the Collections of John Stow," in *Camden Miscellany* 12. Camden Society, 1910, pp. iii–x, 1–57.

Kinney, Arthur F., ed. *Renaissance Drama: An Anthology of Plays and Entertainments*. Malden, MA, and Oxford: Blackwell, 1999.

Kipling, Gordon. *Enter the King: Theatre, Liturgy, and Ritual in the Medieval Civic Triumph*. Oxford: Clarendon Press, 1998.

"'He That Saw It Would Not Believe It': Anne Boleyn's Royal Entry into

London," in Alexandra F. Johnston and Wim Hüsken, eds., *Civic Ritual and Drama*. Ludus 2. Amsterdam and Atlanta, GA: Rodopi, 1997, pp. 39–79.

"The London Pageants for Margaret of Anjou: A Medieval Script Restored," *Medieval English Theatre* 4.1 (1982), 5–27.

ed. *The Receyt of the Ladie Kateryne*. Early English Text Society, OS 296, 1990.

"Richard II's 'Sumptuous Pageants' and the Idea of the Civic Triumph," in Bergeron, *Pageantry in the Shakespearean Theater*, see above, pp. 83–103.

The Triumph of Honour: Burgundian Origins of the Elizabethan Renaissance. The Hague: Leiden University Press for the Sir Thomas Browne Institute, 1977.

"Wonderfull Spectacles: Theater and Civic Culture," in John D. Cox and David Scott Kastan, eds., *A New History of Early English Drama*. New York: Columbia University Press, 1997, pp. 153–171.

Knighton, Henry. *Chronicon Henrici Knighton, vel Cnitthon, Monachi Leycestrensis*, ed. Joseph Rawson Lumby. 2 vols. RS 92. London: HMSO, 1889–95.

Lambert, John James. *Records of The Skinners of London, Edward I. to James I.* London: The Company, 1933.

Lancashire, Anne. "Chaucer and the Sacrifice of Isaac," *Chaucer Review* 9 (1975), 320–326.

"Continuing Civic Ceremonies of 1530s London," in Alexandra F. Johnston and Wim Hüsken, eds., *Civic Ritual and Drama*. Ludus 2. Amsterdam and Atlanta, GA: Rodopi, 1997, pp. 81–105.

"The Mayors and Sheriffs of London 1190–1558," in Caroline Barron, *The Government of London 1200–1500*. Oxford: Oxford University Press, forthcoming 2002–03.

"Medieval to Renaissance: Plays and the London Drapers' Company to 1558," in Robert A. Taylor, James F. Burke, Patricia J. Eberle, Ian Lancashire, and Brian S. Merrilees, eds., *The Centre and its Compass: Studies in Medieval Literature in Honor of Professor John Leyerle*. Studies in Medieval Culture 33. Kalamazoo, MI: Western Michigan University, Medieval Institute Publications, 1993, pp. 297–313.

"Players for the London Cutlers' Company," *REED Newsletter* 1981:2, pp. 10–11.

"Plays for the London Blacksmiths' Company," *REED Newsletter*, 1981:1, pp. 12–14.

"The Problem of Facts and the London Civic Records," in Alexandra F. Johnston, ed., *Editing London Records* [provisional title]. Toronto: University of Toronto Press, forthcoming 2003.

"St. Paul's Grammar School Before 1580: Theatrical Development Suppressed?" in John H. Astington, ed., *The Development of Shakespeare's Theater*. New York: AMS Press, 1992, pp. 29–56.

Lancashire, Ian, ed. *Dramatic Texts and Records of Britain: A Chronological Topography to 1558*. Studies in Early English Drama 1. Toronto/Cambridge: University of Toronto Press/Cambridge University Press, 1984.

ed. *Two Tudor Interludes: 'The Interlude of Youth', 'Hickscorner'*. Manchester/Baltimore: Manchester University Press/Johns Hopkins University Press, 1980.

Larking, L. B., ed. *Knights Hospitallers in England*. Camden Society, os 65, 1857.

Latham, R. E. *Revised Medieval Latin Word-List*. London: Oxford University Press for The British Academy, 1965; rpt. 1973.

[Lee-]Dillon, Viscount [Harold Arthur]. "The Arms and Armour at Armourers' Hall," *TLMAS*, ns 2 (1911–13), 320–324.

Legg, Leopold G. Wickham. *English Coronation Records*. Westminster: Archibald Constable, 1901.

Legge, M. Dominica. *Anglo-Norman Literature and its Background*. Oxford: Clarendon Press, 1963.

Leland, John, ed. *Antiquarii de Rebus Britannicis Collectanea*, ed. Thomas Hearne. Vol. 4. London: Benjamin White, 1774.

Lerer, Seth. *Courtly Letters in the Age of Henry VIII: Literary Culture and the Arts of Deceit*. Cambridge: Cambridge University Press, 1997.

Liber Albus: The White Book of The City of London, ed. and tr. Henry Thomas Riley. London: Richard Griffin, 1861.

Liber de Antiquis Legibus. See *Chronicles of the Mayors and Sheriffs of London*, above.

Liber Custumarum. In Riley, *Munimenta Gildhallae Londoniensis*, vol. 2, see below.

Liber Regalis. In Legg, see above, pp. 81–130.

Lindenbaum, Sheila. "Ceremony and Oligarchy: The London Midsummer Watch," in Barbara A. Hanawalt and Kathryn L. Reyerson, eds., *City and Spectacle in Medieval Europe*. Medieval Studies at Minnesota 6. Minneapolis and London: University of Minnesota Press, 1994, pp. 171–188.

"London Texts and Literate Practice," in David Wallace, ed., *The Cambridge History of Medieval English Literature*. Cambridge: Cambridge University Press, 1999, pp. 284–309.

"The Smithfield Tournament of 1390," *Journal of Medieval and Renaissance Studies* 20.1 (Spring 1990), 1–20.

"London's Monasteries," *Current Archaeology* 162 [14.6] (April/May 1999), 204–215.

Lobel, Mary D., gen. ed. *The British Atlas of Historic Towns*, vol. 3: *The City of London: From Prehistoric Times to c. 1520*. Oxford: Oxford University Press in conjunction with The Historic Towns Trust, 1989.

Look About You, ed. W. W. Greg. Malone Society, 1913.

Loomis, Roger Sherman. "Edward I, Arthurian Enthusiast," *Speculum* 28 (1953), 114–127.

"Love Feigned and Unfeigned." See Esdaile, above.

Lumiansky, R. M., and David Mills, eds. *The Chester Mystery Cycle*, vol. 1. EETS, Supplementary Series 3, 1974.

Lusher, Patricia. "Studies in the Guild-Drama in London in the Records of the Drapers' Company (1515–1553)." 2 vols. University of London doctoral thesis, 1940.

Lusty Juventus, ed. J. M. Nosworthy. Malone Society, 1971 for 1966.

Lydgate, John. *The Minor Poems of John Lydgate*, ed. Henry Noble MacCracken. 2 vols. EETS, Extra Series 107, 1911 for 1910, and os 192, 1934, rpt. 1961.

Lyell, Laetitia, assisted by Frank D. Watney, eds. *Acts of Court of the Mercers' Company 1453–1527*. Cambridge: Cambridge University Press, 1936.

MacCracken, Henry Noble, ed. See Lydgate, above.

Machyn, Henry. *The Diary of Henry Machyn, Citizen and Merchant-Taylor of London from A.D. 1550 to A.D. 1563*, ed. John Gough Nichols. Camden Society, os 42, 1848.

Maidstone, Richard. "The Reconciliation of Richard II with the City of London," in Thomas Wright, ed., *Political Poems and Songs relating to English History*, vol. I. RS 14. London: HMSO, 1859.

Malfatti, C. V., ed. and tr. *The Accession Coronation and Marriage of Mary Tudor as related in Four Manuscripts of the Escorial*. Barcelona: C. V. Malfatti, 1956.

Malverne, John. Continuation of Higden's *Polychronicon*. See Higden, above, pp. 1–283.

Mancinus [Mancini], Dominicus [Dominic]. *The Usurpation of Richard the Third*, ed. and tr. C. A. J. Armstrong. 2nd edn. Oxford: Clarendon Press, 1969.

Manley, Lawrence. *Literature and Culture in Early Modern London*. Cambridge: Cambridge University Press, 1995.

London in the Age of Shakespeare: An Anthology. London and Sydney: Croom Helm, 1986.

"Of Sites and Rites," in David L. Smith, Richard Strier, and David Bevington, eds., *The Theatrical City: Culture, Theatre and Politics in London, 1576–1649*. Cambridge: Cambridge University Press, 1995, pp. 35–54.

The Marriage between Wit and Wisdom, ed. Trevor N. S. Lennam. Malone Society, 1971 for 1966.

Marsden, Peter. *Roman London*. London: Thames and Hudson, 1980.

Marsh, Bower, ed. *Records of the Worshipful Company of Carpenters*. 4 vols. Oxford and London: The Company, 1913–16.

Marsh, G. D. "Three 'theatre' Masks from London," *Britannia* 10 (1979), 263–265.

Masters, Betty R. "The Mayor's Household Before 1600," in A. E. J. Hollaender and William Kellaway, eds., *Studies in London History Presented to Philip Edmund Jones*. London: Hodder and Stoughton, 1969, pp. 95–114.

McGee, C. E., and John C. Meagher. "Preliminary Checklist of Tudor and Stuart Entertainments: 1485–1558," *Research Opportunities in Renaissance Drama* 25 (1982), 31–114.

McKisack, M. "London and the Succession to the Crown during the Middle Ages," in R. W. Hunt, W. A. Pantin and R. W. Southern, eds., *Studies in Medieval History Presented to Frederick Maurice Powicke*. Oxford: Clarendon Press, 1948, pp. 76–89.

McLaren, Mary-Rose. "The Aims and Interests of the London Chroniclers of the Fifteenth Century," in Dorothy J. Clayton, Richard G. Davies, and Peter McNiven, eds., *Trade, Devotion and Governance: Papers in Later Medieval History*. Stroud, Gloucestershire, and Dover, NH: Alan Sutton, 1994, pp. 158–176.

"The Textual Transmission of the London Chronicles," *English Manuscript Studies 1100–1700*, 3 (1992), 38–72.

McMillin, Scott. "*The Book of Sir Thomas More*: Dates and Acting Companies," in T. H. Howard-Hill, ed., *Shakespeare and 'Sir Thomas More': Essays on the Play and its Shakespearian Interest.* Cambridge: Cambridge University Press, 1989. pp. 57–76.

Medwall, Henry. *The Plays of Henry Medwall,* ed. Alan H. Nelson. Cambridge/Totowa, NJ: D. S. Brewer/Rowman and Littlefield, 1980.

Melchiori, Giorgio, and Vittorio Gabrieli, "A Table of Sources and Close Analogues for the Text of *The Book of Sir Thomas More,*" in T. H. Howard-Hill, ed., *Shakespeare and 'Sir Thomas More': Essays on the Play and its Shakespearian Interest.* Cambridge: Cambridge University Press, 1989, pp. 197–202.

Merrifield, Ralph. *London: City of the Romans.* London: B. T. Batsford, 1983.

"Roman London," in Lobel, *Atlas,* see above, pp. 10–19.

"Roman Metalwork from the Walbrook – Rubbish, Ritual or Redundancy?" *TLMAS* 46 (1995), 27–44.

Metz, G. Harold. "'Voice and credyt': The Scholars and *Sir Thomas More,*" in T. H. Howard-Hill, ed., *Shakespeare and 'Sir Thomas More': Essays on the Play and its Shakespearian Interest.* Cambridge: Cambridge University Press, 1989, pp. 11–44.

Mill, Anna Jean, ed. "Dramatic Records of the City of London: The Repertories, Journals, and Letter Books," in *Collections II.3.* Malone Society, 1931, pp. 285–320.

Millett, Martin. "Evaluating Roman London" [book review], *Archaeological Journal* 151 (1994), 429–430.

Milne, Gustav. *Book of Roman London: Urban Archaeology in the Nation's Capital.* London: B. T. Batsford/English Heritage, 1995.

ed. *From Roman Basilica to Medieval Market: Archaeology in Action in the City of London.* London: HMSO, 1992.

"King Alfred's Plan for London?" *London Archaeologist* 6.8 (Autumn 1990), 206–207.

Morley, Henry. *Memoirs of Bartholomew Fair.* London: George Routledge and Sons, 1892.

Morley, Timothy. *Some Account of The Worshipful Company of Armourers and Brasiers, in the City of London.* London: The Company, 1878.

Morris, John. *Londinium: London in the Roman Empire,* rev. Sarah Macready. London: Weidenfeld and Nicolson, 1982; new edn. 1998.

Mowat, Barbara A. "The Theater and Literary Culture," in Cox and Kastan, see above, pp. 213–230.

Muir, Lynette R. *The Biblical Drama of Medieval Europe.* Cambridge: Cambridge University Press, 1995.

"Medieval English Drama: The French Connection," in Marianne G. Briscoe and John C. Coldewey, eds., *Contexts for Early English Drama.* Bloomington and Indianapolis: Indiana University Press, 1989, pp. 56–76.

Munday, Anthony. *The Death of Robert Earl of Huntingdon*, ed. John C. Meagher. Malone Society, 1967 for 1965.

The Downfall of Robert Earl of Huntingdon, ed. John C. Meagher. Malone Society, 1965 for 1964.

Myers, A. R., ed. *English Historical Documents*, vol. 4 (1327–1485). London: Eyre and Spottiswoode, 1969.

Nelson, Alan H. *The Medieval English Stage: Corpus Christi Pageants and Plays.* Chicago and London: University of Chicago Press, 1974.

Nicholas, David. *The Growth of the Medieval City: From Late Antiquity to the Early Fourteenth Century.* London and New York: Longman, 1997.

Nichols, John Gough, ed. *Literary Remains of King Edward the Sixth.* 2 vols. Roxburghe Club, 1857; rpt. New York: Burt Franklin, Burt Franklin Research and Source Works Series 51[, 1963].

Nicol, Donald M. "A Byzantine Emperor in England: Manuel II's Visit to London in 1400–01," *University of Birmingham Historical Journal* 12.1 (1969), 204–225.

Nicoll, Allardyce. *Masks Mimes and Miracles: Studies in the Popular Theatre.* London: George G. Harrap, 1931.

Nightingale, Pamela. *A Medieval Mercantile Community: The Grocers' Company & the Politics & Trade of London 1000–1485.* New Haven and London: Yale University Press, 1995.

The noble tryumphaunt coronacyon of quene Anne. RSTC 656; [1533].

Norton, George. *Commentaries on the History, Constitution, and Chartered Franchises of The City of London.* London: Henry Butterworth, 1829.

Of the tryumphe/and the verses that Charles themperour/& the most myghty redouted kyng of England/were saluted with/passyng through London. RSTC 15606.7; [1522].

Osberg, Richard H. "The Goldsmiths' 'Chastell' of 1377," *Theatre Survey* 27.1–2 (May and Nov. 1986), 1–15.

Oxford English Dictionary. Compact edn., complete text reproduced micrographically. 2 vols. Oxford: Clarendon Press, 1971.

Page, William, ed. *The Victoria History of the Counties of England. The Victoria History of London.* Vol. 1. London: Constable, 1909.

Paris, Matthew. *Chronica Majora*, ed. Henry Richards Luard, vol. 3. RS 57. London: HMSO, 1876.

Historia Anglorum, ed. Frederic Madden, vol. 2. RS 44. London: HMSO, 1866.

Parsloe, Guy, ed. *Wardens' Accounts of the Worshipful Company of Founders of the City of London 1497–1681.* London: University of London, Athlone Press, 1964.

Pearsall, Derek. *John Lydgate.* London: Routledge and Kegan Paul, 1970.

John Lydgate (1371–1449): A Bio-bibliography. English Literary Studies. Victoria, BC: University of Victoria, 1997.

Perring, Dominic. *Roman London.* The Archaeology of London Series. London: Seaby, 1991.

Pettitt, Tom. "*Mankind*: An English *Fastnachtspiel*?" in Meg Twycross, ed., *Festive Drama.* Cambridge: D. S. Brewer, 1996, pp. 190–202.

Phillpotts, Chris. "The Metropolitan Palaces of Medieval London," *London Archaeologist* 9.2 (Autumn 1999), 47–53.

Pitt, G. Newton. *Notes on the History of the Armourers' & Brasiers' Company*. London: The Company, 1914.

Pitt, Sydney Hewitt. *Some Notes on the History of the Worshipful Company of Armourers and Brasiers*. London: The Company, 1930.

The Play of Daniel. See Greenberg, above.

A Play of Robin Hood. See Greg, above.

Pollard, A. W., and G. R. Redgrave. *A Short-Title Catalogue of Books Printed in England, Scotland & Ireland . . . 1475–1640*, rev. W. A. Jackson, F. S. Ferguson, and Katharine F. Pantzer. 3 vols. London: The Bibliographical Society, 1976–91.

Porter, Gina. "An Early Medieval Settlement at Guildhall, City Of London," in Guy De Boe and Frans Verhaeghe, eds., *Urbanism in Medieval Europe*, Papers of the 'Medieval Europe Brugge 1997' Conference, vol. 1. Zellik: Institute for the Archaeological Heritage, 1997, pp. 147–152.

Potter, Lois, gen. ed. *The Revels History of Drama in English*, vol. 1: *Medieval Drama*. London and New York: Methuen, 1983.

gen. ed. *The Revels History of Drama in English*, vol. 2: *1500–1576*. London and New York: Methuen, 1980.

Powicke, F. Maurice, and E. B. Fryde, eds. *Handbook of British Chronology*. 2nd edn. London: Royal Historical Society, 1961.

Prestwich, Michael. *Edward I*. London: Methuen, 1988.

"The Prodigal Son." See Greg, above.

Puttenham, George. *The Arte of English Poesie*. *RSTC* 20519; 1589.

Pythian-Adams, Charles. "Ceremony and the Citizen: The Communal Year at Coventry, 1450–1550," in Peter Clark and Paul Slack, eds., *Crisis and Order in English Towns 1500–1700*. London: Routledge and Kegan Paul, 1972, pp. 57–85.

Rappaport, Steve. *Worlds Within Worlds: Structures of Life in Sixteenth-Century London*. Cambridge: Cambridge University Press, 1989.

Rastell, John. *Three Rastell Plays*, ed. Richard Axton. Cambridge and Ipswich/ Totowa, NJ: D. S. Brewer/Rowman and Littlefield, 1979.

Reading, John of. See *Chronica Johannis de Reading*, above.

Respublica, ed. W. W. Greg. EETS, os 226, 1952 for 1946; rpt. 1969.

The Resurrection of Our Lord, ed. J. Dover Wilson and Bertram Dobell. Malone Society, 1912.

Reynolds, Susan. *An Introduction to the History of English Medieval Towns*. Oxford: Clarendon Press, 1977.

Rickert, Edith. "Extracts from a Fourteenth-Century Account Book," *Modern Philology* 24 (1926–27), 111–119 and 249–256.

Riley, Henry Thomas, ed. and tr. *Chronicles of the Mayors and Sheriffs of London, A.D. 1188 to A.D. 1274*. London: Trübner, 1863.

ed. and tr. *Memorials of London and London Life in the XIIIth, XIVth, and XVth Centuries*. London: Longmans, Green, 1868.

ed. *Munimenta Gildhallae Londoniensis*. 3 vols. (2nd in 2 parts). RS 12. London: HMSO, 1859–62.

Rimbault, Edward F. Introduction to "Two Sermons Preached by The Boy Bishop," ed. John Gough Nichols. Camden Society, NS 14, 1875, pp. v–xxxii.

Robertson, Jean, ed., "A Calendar of Dramatic Records in the Books of the London Clothworkers' Company (Addenda to *Collections III*)," in *Collections V*. Malone Society, 1960 for 1959, pp. 1–16.

"L'Entrée de Charles Quint à Londres en 1522," in Jean Jacquot, ed., *Fêtes et Cérémonies au Temps de Charles Quint*. Paris: Centre National de la Recherche Scientifique, 1960, pp. 169–181.

Robertson, Jean, and D. J. Gordon, eds. "A Calendar of Dramatic Records in the Books of the Livery Companies of London 1485–1640." *Collections III*. Malone Society, 1954.

"Robin Hood and the Sheriff of Nottingham." See Greg, above.

"Robin Hood for May-Games, A Play of." See Greg, above.

Roper, William. "The Life of Sir Thomas More," in Richard S. Sylvester and Davis P. Harding, eds., *Two Early Tudor Lives*. New Haven and London: Yale University Press, 1962, pp. 195–254.

Rosser, Gervase. *Medieval Westminster 1200–1540*. Oxford: Clarendon Press, 1989.

Rothwell, Harry, ed. *English Historical Documents*, vol. 3 (1189–1327). London: Eyre and Spottiswoode, 1975.

Rymer, Thomas. *Foedera, Conventiones, Literae*, vol. 10. London: A. and J. Churchill, 1710.

Salisbury, John of. *Frivolities of Courtiers and Footprints of Philosophers. Being a Translation of the First, Second, and Third Books and Selections from the Seventh and Eighth Books of the 'Policraticus' of John of Salisbury*, ed. and tr. Joseph B. Pike. Minneapolis/London: University of Minnesota Press/Humphrey Milford, Oxford University Press, 1938.

Policraticus I–IV, ed. K. S. B. Keats-Rohan. Corpus Christianorum, Continuatio Mediaevalis 118. Turnholt: Brepols, 1993.

Salter, Elizabeth. *English and International: Studies in the Literature, Art and Patronage of Medieval England*, ed. Derek Pearsall and Nicolette Zeeman. Cambridge: Cambridge University Press, 1988.

Saul, Nigel. *Richard II*. New Haven and London: Yale University Press, 1997.

Scattergood, John. "Misrepresenting the City: Genre, Intertextuality and William FitzStephen's *Description of London* (c. 1173)," in Julia Boffey and Pamela King, eds., *London and Europe in the Later Middle Ages*. Westfield Publications in Medieval Studies 9. London: Centre for Medieval and Renaissance Studies, Queen Mary and Westfield College, University of London, 1995, pp. 1–34.

Schirmer, Walter F. *John Lydgate: A Study in the Culture of the XVth Century*, tr. Ann E. Keep. London: Methuen, 1961.

Schofield, John. *The Building of London from the Conquest to the Great Fire*. 3rd edn. Phoenix Mill, Gloucestershire: Sutton, 1999.

Medieval London Houses. New Haven and London: Yale University Press for the Paul Mellon Centre for Studies in British Art, 1994.

Schofield, John, and Alan Vince. *Medieval Towns*. Madison, Teaneck: Fairleigh Dickinson University Press, 1994.

Sharpe, Reginald R., ed. *Calendar of Letter-Books Preserved among the Archives of the Corporation of the City of London at the Guildhall*. 11 vols. (A–I, K–L). London: Corporation of London, 1899–1912.

Sheppard, Francis. *London: A History*. Oxford: Oxford University Press, 1998.

Short English Chronicle. In Gairdner, *Three Fifteenth-Century Chronicles*, see above, pp. 1–80.

Sir Thomas More. See *Book of Sir Thomas More*, above.

Skelton, John. *Magnificence*, ed. Paula Neuss. The Revels Plays. Manchester/ Baltimore: Manchester University Press / Johns Hopkins University Press, 1980.

    Magnificence, ed. Robert Lee Ramsay. EETS, Extra Series 98, 1908; rpt. 1958.

Smith, George, ed. *The Coronation of Elizabeth Wydeville*. London: Ellis, 1935.

Smuts, R. Malcolm. "Public Ceremony and Royal Charisma: The English Royal Entry in London, 1485–1642," in A. L. Beier, David Cannadine and James M. Rosenheim, eds., *The First Modern Society: Essays in English History in Honour of Lawrence Stone*. Cambridge: Cambridge University Press, 1989. pp. 65–93.

La Solenne et Felice Intrata delli Serenissimi Re Philippo, et Regina Maria d'Inghliterra, nella Regal città di Londra. 1554.

Somerset, J. Alan B., ed. *Shropshire*, REED. 2 vols. Toronto: University of Toronto Press, 1994.

Southern, Richard. *The Staging of Plays before Shakespeare*. London: Faber and Faber, 1973.

Southworth, John. *The English Medieval Minstrel*. Woodbridge, Suffolk, and Wolfeboro, NH: Boydell Press, 1989.

Sponsler, Claire. "Alien Nation: London's Aliens and Lydgate's Mummings for the Mercers and Goldsmiths," in Jeffrey Jerome Cohen, ed., *The Postcolonial Middle Ages*. Houndmills, Basingstoke, Hampshire, and London: MacMillan Press, 2000, pp. 229–242.

The Statutes at Large, vol. 1, ed. Owen Ruffhead. London: Mark Baskett *et al.*, 1769.

Steel, Anthony. *Richard II*. Cambridge: Cambridge University Press, 1941.

Steer, Francis W., ed. *Scriveners' Company Common Paper 1357–1628, With a Continuation to 1678*. London Record Society, 1968.

Stevenson, Joseph, ed. *Letters and Papers Illustrative of the Wars of the English in France during the Reign of Henry the Sixth, King of England*. 2 vols. (2nd in 2 parts). RS 22. London: HMSO, 1861–64; rpt. Wiesbaden: Kraus Reprint, 1965–68.

Stow, John. *The Annales of England*. RSTC 23334; 1592.

    A Summarye of the Chronicles of Englande. RSTC 23322; 1570.

    A Survey of London, ed. Charles Lethbridge Kingsford. 2 vols. Oxford: Clarendon Press, 1908.

    A Survey of London, continued by John Strype (as *A Survey Of the Cities of London and Westminster*). 6 books in 2 vols. London: A. Churchill *et al.*, 1720.

Streitberger, W. R. *Court Revels, 1485–1559*. Studies in Early English Drama 3. Toronto: University of Toronto Press, 1994.

Strype, John. See Stow, *A Survey of London*, continued by John Strype, above.

Stubbs, William, ed. *Chronicles of the Reigns of Edward I. and Edward II.*, vol. 1. RS 76. London: HMSO, 1882.

ed. *Select Charters and Other Illustrations of English Constitutional History*. 6th edn. Oxford: Clarendon Press, 1888.

Suggett, Helen. "A Letter Describing Richard II's Reconciliation with the City of London, 1392," *English Historical Review* 62 (1947), 209–213.

Sutton, Anne F. "Merchants, Music and Social Harmony: the London Puy and its French and London Contexts, circa 1300," *London Journal* 17.1 (1992), 1–17.

"The *Tumbling Bear* and its Patrons: A Venue for the London Puy and Mercery," in Julia Boffey and Pamela King, eds., *London and Europe in the Later Middle Ages*. Westfield Publications in Medieval Studies 9. London: Centre for Medieval and Renaissance Studies, Queen Mary and Westfield College, University of London, 1995, pp. 85–110.

Sutton, Anne F., and P. W. Hammond. *The Coronation of Richard III: the Extant Documents*. Gloucester/New York: Alan Sutton/St. Martin's Press, 1983/84.

Swanson, R. N. *Church and Society in Late Medieval England*. Oxford: Basil Blackwell, 1989.

Tatton-Brown, Tim. "The Topography of Anglo-Saxon London," *Antiquity* 60 (1986), 21–28.

Thrupp, Sylvia L. *The Merchant Class of Medieval London [1300–1500]*. Chicago: University of Chicago Press, 1948.

Tittler, Robert. *The Reign of Mary I*. 2nd edn. Seminar Studies in History. London and New York: Longman, 1991.

The traduction & mariage of the princesse. RSTC 4814; [1500].

Twycross, Meg. "Felsted of London: Silk-Dyer and Theatrical Entrepreneur," *Medieval English Theatre* 10.1 (1988), 4–16.

Tydeman, William. "An Introduction to Medieval English Theatre," in Richard Beadle, ed., *The Cambridge Companion to Medieval English Theatre*. Cambridge: Cambridge University Press, 1994; rpt. 1995, pp. 1–36.

The Theatre in the Middle Ages: Western European Stage Conditions c. 800–1576. Cambridge: Cambridge University Press, 1978.

Unwin, George. *The Gilds and Companies of London*. London: Methuen, 1908.

Usk, Adam. *Chronicle of Adam Usk*, ed. and tr. C. Given-Wilson. Oxford: Clarendon Press, 1997.

Veyne, Paul. *Bread and Circuses: Historical Sociology and Political Pluralism*, tr. Brian Pearce. Harmondsworth, Middlesex: Penguin, 1992.

Vince, Alan, ed. *Aspects of Saxo-Norman London: II. Finds and Environmental Evidence*. LMAS Special Paper 12, 1989.

Saxon London: An Archaeological Investigation. The Archaeology of London Series. London: Seaby, 1990.

Vita & Gesta Henrici Quinti, ed. Thomas Hearne. Oxford, 1727.

Wacher, John. *Roman Britain*. 2nd edn. Stroud, Gloucestershire: Sutton, 1998.

The Towns of Roman Britain. 2nd edn. London: B. T. Batsford, 1995.

Walker, Greg. *Plays of Persuasion: Drama and Politics at the Court of Henry VIII*. Cambridge: Cambridge University Press, 1991.

The Politics of Performance in Early Renaissance Drama. Cambridge: Cambridge University Press, 1998.

Walsingham, Thomas. *Historia Anglicana*, ed. Henry Thomas Riley, vol. I. RS 28. London: HMSO, 1863.

Wealth and Health, The Interlude of, ed. W. W. Greg. Malone Society, 1907.

Webb, John. "Translation of a French Metrical History of the Deposition of King Richard the Second," *Archaeologia* 20 (1824), 1–423.

Welch, Charles. *History of the Cutlers' Company of London*. 2 vols. London: The Company, 1916–23.

History of The Tower Bridge. London: Smith, Elder, 1894.

Welsford, Enid. *The Court Masque: A Study in the Relationship Between Poetry & the Revels*. Cambridge: Cambridge University Press, 1927; rpt. New York: Russell and Russell, 1962.

Westfall, Suzanne. "'A Commonty, a Christmas gambold or a tumbling trick': Household Theater," in Cox and Kastan, see above. pp, 39–58.

Patrons and Performance: Early Tudor Household Revels. Oxford: Clarendon Press, 1990.

Westlake, Herbert Francis. *Westminster Abbey: The Church, Convent, Cathedral and College of St. Peter, Westminster*. 2 vols. London: Philip Allan, 1923.

The Westminster Chronicle 1381–1394, ed. and tr. L. C. Hector and Barbara F. Harvey. Oxford: Clarendon Press, 1982.

White, Paul Whitfield. *Theatre and Reformation: Protestantism, Patronage, and Playing in Tudor England*. Cambridge: Cambridge University Press, 1993.

Wickham, Glynne. *Early English Stages 1300–1660*. 3 vols. London/New York: Routledge and Kegan Paul/Columbia University Press, 1959–81.

A History of the Theatre. New York: Cambridge University Press, 1985.

The Medieval Theatre. 3rd edn. Cambridge: Cambridge University Press, 1987.

Williams, Gwyn A. *Medieval London: From Commune to Capital*. University of London Historical Studies 11. London: University of London, Athlone Press, 1963.

Williams, Sheila. "The Lord Mayor's Show in Tudor and Stuart Times," *Guildhall Miscellany* 1.10 (Sept. 1959), 3–18.

Williams, Tim. *The Archaeology of Roman London*, vol. 3: *Public Buildings in the South-West Quarter of Roman London*. CBA Research Report 88. London: Museum of London and Council for British Archaeology, 1993.

Wilmott, Tony. *Excavations in the Middle Walbrook Valley. City of London, 1927–1960*. LMAS Special Paper 13, 1991.

Withington, Robert. "The Early 'Royal-Entry'," *PMLA* 32 (1917), 616–623.

English Pageantry: An Historical Outline. 2 vols. Cambridge, MA: Harvard University Press, 1918–26; rpt. New York: Arno Press, 1980.

"A Note on 'A Fragment of a Lord Mayor's Pageant'," *Modern Language Notes* 34 (Dec. 1919), 501–503.

"Queen Margaret's Entry into London, 1445," *Modern Philology* 13.1 (1915–16), 53–57.

Wolffe, Bertram. *Henry VI*. London: Eyre, Methuen, 1981.

Worcester, William of. *Annales*. In Stevenson, *Letters and Papers*, vol. 2.2, see above, pp. 743–793.

Wriothesley, Charles. *A Chronicle of England during the Reigns of the Tudors*, ed. William Douglas Hamilton. 2 vols. Camden Society, NS 11, 1875, and NS 20, 1877.

Wylie, James Hamilton. *History of England under Henry the Fourth*. 4 vols. London: Longmans Green, 1884–98.

The Reign of Henry the Fifth. 3 vols. Cambridge: Cambridge University Press, 1914–29 (vol. 3 with William Templeton Waugh).

Index

Abbreviated printed sources are indexed here under their abbreviations (with their full titles following within square brackets), rather than under their author/editor, unless the author's/editor's name is part of the abbreviation. Contents of footnotes have been indexed (beyond the citations provided) when they go beyond what is included in the text proper. Kings and queens referred to but not named in the text are indexed by name to the relevant pages, with the page numbers placed within square brackets. All references to mayors are indexed under "Mayors, mayoral" unless a specific mayor is named in the text. Non-company MSS used and cited are indexed at the ends of the entries for their specific archives/libraries; company MSS used and cited are indexed at the ends of their companies' entries. MSS only mentioned within the text are included within the index entries for their archives/libraries and companies.

This index does not include the detail of the contents of the transcribed records printed in Appendix B, although it includes their overall subject and the information provided about them in the Appendix's headings.